Indigenous Intellectual Property Rights

CONTEMPORARY NATIVE AMERICAN COMMUNITIES
Stepping Stones to the Seventh Generation

Acknowledging the strength and vibrancy of Native American people and nations today, this series examines life in contemporary Native American communities from the point of view of Native concerns and values. These new publications are intended to be correctives to the misconceptions that still appear in many books and in the American imagination: that Indian people largely disappeared or were assimilated after 1890. Books in the series cover topics that are of cultural and political importance to tribal peoples and that affect their possibilities for survival, in both urban and rural communities.

SERIES EDITORS

Troy Johnson, American Indian Studies, California State University, Long Beach, Long Beach, CA 90840, trj@csulb.edu

Duane Champagne, Native Nations Law and Policy Center, 292 Haines Hall, Box 951551, University of California, Los Angeles, Los Angeles, CA 90095-1551, champagn@ucla.edu

BOOKS IN THE SERIES

1. *Inuit, Whaling, and Sustainability*, Milton M. R. Freeman, Ingmar Egede, Lyudmila Bogoslovskaya, Igor G. Krupnik, Richard A. Caulfield, and Marc G. Stevenson (1999)
2. *Contemporary Native American Political Issues*, edited by Troy Johnson (1999)
3. *Contemporary Native American Cultural Issues*, edited by Duane Champagne (1999)
4. *Modern Tribal Development: Paths to Self Sufficiency and Cultural Integrity in Indian Country*, Dean Howard Smith (2000)
5. *American Indians and the Urban Experience*, edited by Susan Lobo and Kurt Peters (2000)
6. *Medicine Ways: Disease, Health, and Survival among Native Americans*, edited by Clifford Trafzer and Diane Weiner (2000)
7. *Native American Studies in Higher Education: Models for Collaboration between Universities and Indigenous Nations,* edited by Duane Champagne and Jay Stauss (2002)
8. *Spider Woman Walks This Land: Traditional Cultural Properties and the Navajo Nation*, by Kelli Carmean (2002)
9. *Alaska Native Political Leadership and Higher Education: One University, Two Universes,* by Michael Jennings (2004)
10. *Indigenous Intellectual Property Rights: Legal Obstacles and Innovative Solutions,* edited by Mary Riley (2004)

EDITORIAL BOARD

Indigenous Intellectual Property Rights

Legal Obstacles and Innovative Solutions

edited by Mary Riley

ALTAMIRA PRESS

A Division of Rowman & Littlefield Publishers, Inc.

Walnut Creek • Lanham • New York • Toronto • Oxford

This volume is dedicated to the memory of Darrell Posey (1947–2001), eminent anthropologist and indigenous rights advocate, who advanced the notions of indigenous intellectual property rights and traditional resource rights by astonishing leaps and bounds.

AltaMira Press
A division of Rowman & Littlefield Publishers, Inc.
1630 North Main Street, #367
Walnut Creek, California 94596
www.altamirapress.com

Rowman & Littlefield Publishers, Inc.
A Member of The Rowman & Littlefield Publishing Group
4501 Forbes Blvd., Suite 200
Lanham, MD 20706

PO Box 317
Oxford
OX2 9RU, United Kingdom

British Library Cataloguing in Publication Information Available

Library of Congress Cataloging-in-Publication Data Available

ISBN 0-7591-0485-9 (cloth : alk. paper)
ISBN 0-7591-0486-7 (pbk. : alk. paper)

Printed in the United States of America

∞™ The paper used in this publication meets the minimum requirements of American National Standard for Information Sciences—Permanence of Paper for Printed Library Materials, ANSI/NISO Z39.48-1992.

CONTENTS

Acknowledgments vii

Introduction ix

PART I
LEGAL OBSTACLES

CHAPTER 1 "As Long As the Grass Grows": Representing Indigenous Claims 3
Tressa Berman

CHAPTER 2 Digital Vibes and Radio Waves in Indigenous Peru 27
Bartholomew Dean

CHAPTER 3 Intellectual Property Protection and the Market for Alaska Native Arts and Crafts 55
Julie Hollowell

CHAPTER 4 The Amerindian Rights Movement in Guyana and Its Influence 99
Mary Riley

PART II
DEVELOPING INNOVATIVE SOLUTIONS

CHAPTER 5 Land, Tenure Systems, and Indigenous Intellectual Property Rights 127
Catherine M. Tucker

CHAPTER 6 Benefit Sharing Under the Convention on Biological Diversity 153
Katy Moran

CHAPTER 7 Ownership of Indigenous Languages: A Case Study from Guatemala 173
Judith M. Maxwell

PART III
ACCESS AND CONTROL

CHAPTER 8 Intellectual Property Rights and Indigenous Peoples' Rights and Responsibilities 221
Maui Solomon

CHAPTER 9 Biocolonialism and Isolates of Historic Interest 251
Marie Annette Jaimes Guerrero

CHAPTER 10 Indigenous Knowledge and Traditional Plant Resources of the Secwepemc (Shuswap) Nation 279
Kelly P. Bannister

CHAPTER 11 Intellectual Property Rights and Indigenous Cultural Heritage in Archaeology 309
George P. Nicholas and Kelly P. Bannister

CHAPTER 12 Prior Informed Consent and Bioprospecting in Chiapas 341
Elois Ann Berlin and Brent Berlin

Index 373
About the Authors 389

ACKNOWLEDGMENTS

In the organizing and editing of this volume, there are several people along the way who have been extremely helpful and have made the process that much more meaningful (if not any easier!). I am grateful to many people I have met who work at the crossroads of law, anthropology, ethnobiology, and indigenous rights.

I first would like to thank Thomas Greaves, who originally encouraged me to co-organize a session with Katy Moran on indigenous intellectual property rights (IPR) at the American Anthropological Association 98th Annual Meeting in November 1999. A number of the chapters in this book were originally developed from papers presented at that session, although nearly equally as many of the chapters in this volume were solicited at a later point in time, in order to increase the representation of subtopics that now exist within the ever-expanding field of indigenous IPR.

I also would like to thank the following individuals who greatly expanded my ideas about indigenous IPR while I worked on this edited volume and pursued other fieldwork and research related to indigenous IPR over the past few years: Katy Moran, David Stephenson, Kelly Bannister, Maui Solomon, Janette Bulkan Forte, Melinda Janki, Djaja Djendoel Soejarto, Marian Kadushin, Michael Huft, and Charlotte Gyllenhaal.

In addition, I would like to thank the editors at AltaMira Press, Jennifer Collier and Rosalie Robertson, who approached Katy Moran and me with the idea for the edited volume. They have been patient and helpful throughout the entire process of developing, forming, and getting this edited volume to press. I am also grateful to the three anonymous reviewers, who took the time to review the entire manuscript and provided substantially helpful and insightful comments to each contributor's chapter.

Finally, I would like to thank my husband, Sean Labat, for his forbearance during the entire process, but especially during the final stages of production where many hours were spent to complete and finalize this edited volume.

I hope that this work will be seen as both a contribution and an offering to the growing literature on indigenous rights in general, and on intellectual property rights and traditional resource rights for indigenous peoples in particular. The main reason for writing this edited volume, for all of the contributors, is to try to help improve the legal rights of indigenous peoples worldwide. Or at the very least, to explain to others why the struggle for indigenous rights is so important to so many people living in accordance with their traditions, and who want to remain in control of their own destinies.

INTRODUCTION

This edited volume is, in essence, an attempt to report on the current status and issues in the rapidly growing field of indigenous intellectual property rights (IPR) and other closely related legal systems that directly impact upon the legal rights of indigenous groups.

Since the early 1990s, there has been nothing less than an explosion of activity and publications from all corners of the indigenous rights movement: Especially striking is the new-found ability of indigenous groups themselves to organize and communicate on a global scale—something that would have been unheard of a generation ago. News of tribal protests, as well as indigenous conferences, is now broadcast worldwide because of the capabilities of the Internet. Increasingly and especially after the sudden "discovery" of and interest in global biodiversity and its importance to humankind, new attention has focused on indigenous peoples, as they are viewed as the keepers of all varieties of traditional knowledge, including knowledge of medicinal plants, unique arts and expressive traditions, natural resources (including land and mineral and the landscape), and traditional concepts of worldview that often have no counterpart in the language of the dominant societies to which indigenous groups belong.

While some view traditional knowledge with the "salvager mentality," as something that is in grave danger of being lost if it is not recorded, preserved, valuated, and encouraged within indigenous groups to pass on to the next generation, the questions of how indigenous groups can prevent their knowledge from being exploited, misappropriated, and commodified for profit by nonindigenous persons for commercial interests (e.g., a pharmaceutical corporation exploring the market potential of traditional medicinal plants) are tricky indeed. Many people acknowledge the contributions of indigenous knowledge to agricultural technologies, medicine, land, and resource development, but the dominant system currently in place—the Western legal system of defining and protecting intellectual property—is not adequate as a system toward the protection of collectively held, community-based knowledge, which has been passed down through the generations, as is the case with indigenous knowledge.

Limits of Intellectual Property Systems in Protecting Indigenous Peoples' Rights

During the 1990s, the argument shifted from how traditional knowledge is defined to how traditional knowledge should be protected. The crux of the problem of attempting to use the Western legalistic intellectual property framework to protect indigenous knowledge has to do with fundamental differences in definitions and orientations of persons and property within Westernized countries vis-à-vis indigenous communities.

While Western intellectual property systems focus upon the needs and rights of the individual person (or the fictive corporate individual, such as the corporate entity) and the rights and relationship of this individual to any new creation or invention in which rights are vested, indigenous communities tend to place individuals within a larger web of relationships and memberships, whose interests overtake the interests of the individual person. In the case of indigenous knowledge, this represents knowledge that is not invented or owned by any one individual within an indigenous group—traditional knowledge is communally held and activated through the actions and practices of the entire community.

Likewise, while individuals may come up with new ways of doing things, new herbal medicines and new artistic and expressive designs, it is only if and when these indigenous individuals are commodifying their culture and thus acting in a way that would be consistent with the Western IP framework (i.e., selling their art in a gallery, applying for patent protections for an invention, etc.) that Western intellectual property law can adequately protect the products of their cultural tradition.

However, there are several kinds of artistic expressions, innovations, or domains of traditional knowledge that are not defined by indigenous groups as constituting a form of property to which any individual has the sole right of ownership. This is not to say that the notion of intellectual property per se is an entirely Western phenomenon. In cases where this does occur, rules governing property rights and relationships are recognized and worked out within the indigenous group in order to fairly compensate any entitled individual when others use traditional knowledge, perform a song or dance, and the like created by the individual person within that society. These indigenous IP systems follow the logic and tradition of the indigenous culture itself—these hidden legal, customary systems of compensation and licensure are often not recognized by Western legal frameworks (which tend to assume that oral legal traditions are not "real" legal traditions).

Additionally, these indigenous systems governing intellectual property concerns—consisting of indigenous definitions, relationships, and protections for specific kinds of traditional knowledge, artistic expressions, and/or usage of objects—are nearly universally not recognized under Western law because national laws take precedence over those of communities (or customary law), and especially those of indigenous communities, whom governments have traditionally viewed as "problem peoples" in sore need of management and assimilation rather than peoples deserving autonomy and possessing the right to self-determination.

The unique problems inherent in protecting indigenous knowledge and traditions have been discussed in continuing international fora such as United Nations Economic, Scientific, and Cultural Organization (UNESCO's 1989 Recommendation on the Protection and Safeguarding of Folklore and Traditional Knowledge), the World Intellectual Property Organization (WIPO), and the Convention on Biological Diversity (CBD, first convening date 1992). While many sets of guidelines for protecting indigenous intellectual property have come out of these ongoing meetings, the biggest problem remaining in this regard is that although any number of guidelines can be set out from the top (at the international level), all nations are recognized as being sovereign entities, and they can choose whether they will prioritize the protection of indigenous knowledge, the valuation of traditional knowledge and life-ways, and the diversity of languages within their citizenry.

Moreover, each nation has to figure out for itself as to how it will handle (or ignore) these issues, with or without the funding necessary to tackle these issues. For many nations, the issue of indigenous intellectual property rights may only be part of a longer positive or negative relationship a national government has with its indigenous population. In addition, the devaluation of indigenous knowledge systems has occurred for so long in some countries that the notion of indigenous traditional knowledge as being something valuable and worth making a priority may seem laughable, an oxymoron, or as the foolish musings of First World countries who have long since decimated their native populations.

Other developing nations may be very keen on the idea of protecting and valuing indigenous knowledge, especially with regard to traditional medicinal knowledge, which often comprises the primary health care system for the majority of their citizens. However, these countries are equally likely to not have the funds or resources to realize these goals. It is unreasonable to expect a cash-poor but biodiversity-rich developing country to protect its forests, lands, and indigenous groups—as though all were museum pieces—to the detriment of the nation's ability to develop, without any outside assistance. Further, when a multinational corporation begins to court the cash-strapped government and suggest that, in exchange for access to lands, plants, and genetic resources, the government could hope to receive a (small) percentage of the profits, negotiating for more may be a laughable and moot alternative. The amount a desperate government hopes to see in return for such concessions may seem minuscule (and unjust) to us, but to a country that has no other offers and is desperate for money to take care of the basics, it is in no real position to bargain otherwise (see Greaves 1994 for examples).

What This Edited Volume Hopes to Contribute

This edited volume, in its own small way, hopes to contribute to the larger issues and problems in indigenous legal protections by shedding light on the legal obstacles that befall some indigenous groups worldwide in this regard. Additionally, the edited volume also includes cases where innovative solutions have been developed, and the issue of who controls the process of indigenous self-determination is discussed (to varying degrees) by each of the contributors. In looking at all of these levels of the issue, this volume touches upon the interrelationships present between legal policies and statutes, enforcement of existing legal protections, how to devise new legal protections, as well as looking "on the ground" to see what legal instruments have actually worked over time. There are now several fora to showcase "best practices" toward traditional resource rights and intellectual property protections. This edited volume was written in a similar vein, by bringing together a number of case studies highlighting the problems and successes in implementing legal (as well as nonlegal) protocols and protections to safeguard indigenous knowledge and practices pertaining to medicine, agriculture, land and resource management, and all other spheres of traditional life that are now in danger of being misappropriated and commodified by outsiders, with neither the knowledge nor consent of indigenous peoples until "after the fact."

The Organization of This Edited Volume

Deciding how to organize the contents of this edited volume was by no means an easy task. Virtually all of the chapters touch upon, to varying degrees, the same topics that are all inextricably bundled together under the rubric of indigenous IPR: (1) problems and obstacles present in legal policy frameworks, no matter how well-meaning, designed to protect indigenous groups; (2) indigenous activism; (3) IPR bound up with land and land-use rights, resource rights, development, and the right to collective self-determination; (4) legal and nonlegal solutions to protecting indigenous IPR; and (5) the issue of who grants control and access to indigenous resources, especially in the context of scientist/researcher and indigenous tribe or village. All of these issues are embedded, to varying degrees, in most (if not all) of the chapters included in this edited volume. In addition, there are several others working in this field who, for various reasons, could not contribute to the current edited volume, so this volume is by no means (and could never hope to be!) an exhaustive listing of the current work being done in the arena of indigenous intellectual property rights. The amount of research and literature generated in even the past five years on indigenous IPR and related subjects is absolutely bewildering.

The chapters to this edited volume are presented in the following order:

Part I: Legal Obstacles. This section provides a sampling of some of the obstacles indigenous groups may encounter from the policy-making and legal systems within their own countries. If there are few to no protections for indigenous groups existing under national law, then this lack of protection is the first problem that needs to be addressed, before anything else "on the ground" can be followed. While there may be very practical, admirable nonlegal solutions in place at the regional or village level, an analysis of what degree of protection indigenous peoples have, under national law, is still required. Even though it is more than ten years after the CBD first convened, there are still many member signatory countries that have not yet created or revised their national laws in order to comply with current international legal protections for indigenous peoples.

In chapter 1, Tressa Berman examines how Aboriginality and native art forms are legally constructed and viewed, in both Australia and America, and she argues that rights to art, expressive designs, and identity, are inextricably linked to land rights. Berman also reviews several court cases involving the misappropriation of Aboriginal art forms, analyzing the pitfalls of the public domain and of applying IPR law to collectively produced artistic works. Ultimately, Berman asserts that only innovative, sui generis systems of law will be able to provide the flexibility required for the protection of indigenous intellectual property in all of its various forms.

The danger inherent in the commodification of traditional expressive forms, such as musical performances, is the subject of chapter 2, written by Bartholomew Dean. Dean reviews recent trends and consequences of commodification of traditional music and artistic expressions in Peru. The problem of the inadequacy of Western IPR to accommodate non-Western systems of artistic expressions, music, and the like, and Western legal definitions of the public sphere are examined head-on in this chapter, and its implications for the formulations of legal policies in Peru to protect indigenous expressive forms are reviewed. As in Berman's chapter, the issue of how indigenous groups can exert collective control over their expressive and performative arts to protect communally held songs and art forms from misappropriation is at the forefront of the discussion.

The subject of using trademarks to protect art produced by Alaskan Natives is the subject of chapter 3, written by Julie Hollowell. What is fascinating about Hollowell's study of the use of the Silver Hand as both a trademark and as a marker of "native authenticity" in artwork is how the Silver Hand itself has been misappropriated and distorted by non–Alaskan Natives in order to blur the distinction between authentic indigenous and commercial non-native arts and crafts. The strategies employed by shopowners, artisans, and companies involved in the mass production of native-looking curios and souvenirs, whose wares directly compete in the shops where Alaskan Native art is sold, seem to tell us that just because trademarks and copyrights can be applied to some forms of indigenous intellectual property, it does not mean that the protection is guaranteed. In this vein, Hollowell in chapter 3 continues Dean's thread of how artistic expressions and IPR legal systems are not designed to deal with violations of traditional artistic design, and are not adequate to protect indigenous cultural heritage because indigenous notions of cultural property are collective in nature. She also skillfully contextualizes the *how* and the *where* intellectual property protections take place, the passing of laws and statutes toward this end, and the linkages (or overlaps) of new laws with others in existence.

In chapter 4, Mary Riley reviews the Amerindian rights movement in Guyana since 1990. In this case, the largest legal obstacle is the problematic definition of "Amerindian" under the law and the archaic legislation that was originally designed to "protect" Amerindians, the Amerindian Act. This chapter shows in stark terms how legal tools once designed to protect indigenous groups can in effect act as a legal straightjacket, rendering indigenous peoples nearly powerless to change or control their own destinies, trapped by laws not of their own creation.

Part II: Developing Innovative Solutions. This section outlines solutions that have been formulated to address indigenous intellectual property rights concerns in specific contexts and are presented here as potential models for establishing protections for communally held resources, land, and traditional knowledge. Approaches to community collaboration with researchers to provide equitable access and benefit sharing has also been discussed at length in other works (e.g., Brush and Stablinsky 1996; Greaves 1994; Posey and Dutfield 1996; Warren, Slikkerveer, and Brokensha 1995).

In chapter 5, Catherine Tucker examines the linkages between traditional resource rights (TRR) and IPR, which are inseparably linked among the Lenca in Honduras. Tucker presents the historical evolution of land tenure, land use, and resource use rights among the Lenca, in particular highlighting the changes in land-tenure rights and their effects on traditional resource rights and indigenous intellectual property rights. Her contribution is valuable, because it shows how changing notions of ownership, propriety, control, and access affect land-tenure systems—none are static entities, and that includes "tradition" within the Lenca communities themselves. Tucker's discussion of the embedded nature of indigenous intellectual property rights, closely tied together with land and resource rights, echoes points made in the chapters by Berman, Riley, and Solomon (chapter 8)—that in many non-Western cultures, all sets of communally held rights are inextricably linked together. Attempts to examine and improve one set of "rights" in isolation of the others can lead to disastrous, unintended consequences.

In chapter 6, Katy Moran reviews bioprospecting ventures in three very different settings: India, Nigeria, and Suriname. What is clear in her analysis is that several factors must be taken into account at the beginning of any joint collaborative effort between researchers, governments or companies, and the villagers or indigenous groups working together. The issues of access and benefit sharing—who will receive royalties, under what circumstances, and how will they be transmitted to the intended beneficiaries?—must be addressed before any other work is commenced. As Moran demonstrates, the ability for indigenous groups to negotiate for more favorable terms of benefit sharing may be linked to the relative amounts of power these same groups hold (or do not hold) within national society. The interests of indigenous groups in this context require special advocacy and communication measures, so that the voice of a dubious "one" does not become the sole representative voice of an entire group.

Finally, in chapter 7, Judith Maxwell reviews how the Maya have been able to reclaim their language as an expression of cultural heritage, and as a kind of intellectual property, in which indigenous knowledge, worldview, and culture is embedded. Many indigenous languages are endangered globally. While indigenous groups are aggressively working to prevent them from dying out, the status of indigenous spoken languages is far from stable. By examining the Maya in Guatemala, Maxwell's chapter provides insights as to how to encourage and promote language preservation among other marginalized communities worldwide, especially those in polylingual countries.

Part III: Access and Control. This section is by far the most volatile, with a variety of opinions. The other chapters discussed earlier indirectly touch upon issues of access and control of indigenous practices and knowledge—indeed, the issue of control is the subtext of the entire topic of indigenous rights—but the following chapters discuss access and control head-on.

Chapter 8, written by Maui Solomon, a barrister and a member of the Maori tribe in New Zealand, provides the dual perspective of someone versed both in Western (British) legal systems as well as Maori perspectives. What Solomon demonstrates in this chapter is how the Maori worldview sees physical and spiritual realities as inseparable. This basic fact, then, underlies Maori objections to any scientific processes that tamper with the physical integrity of life forms, because of the inevitable damage to the spiritual integrity as a result. In other words, to reexploit or reengineer some life forms (e.g., the creation of life patents or the harvesting of a plant species for the sole purpose of extracting a chemical compound) without paying attention to the natural order of things is just plain wrong. The government's past record of inaction in supporting Maori culture and cultural values, and the concomitant fear of losing traditional plant, animal, and Maori traditional heritage (which is tied to sacred places, plants, and animals), Solomon explains, is the reason why the Maori have formulated a claim to the Waitangi Tribunal. Solomon goes on to explain how, by respecting and upholding Maori values in contemporary New Zealand society, both traditional peoples and whites can benefit.

In chapter 9, Marie Annette Jaimes Guerrero provides a Native American perspective on the Human Genome Diversity Project, which she argues is, in essence, a form of biocolonialism against indigenous peoples worldwide. Her perspective is not the only Native American perspective on the subject; her analysis of the Human Genome Diversity Project is echoed elsewhere by other Native American rights activists (e.g., see the Declaration of Indigenous Peoples of the Western Hemisphere, located at Indigenous Peoples Council on Biocolonialism at www.ipcb.org/resolutions.html). Jaimes Guerrero also disagrees with some of the other contributors in this volume over the merits of bioprospecting, which she discounts as being a way to legitimize biopiracy, since the goals of bioprospecting, in her view, are ultimately set by the monied interests approaching the indigenous groups to conduct research and not the other way around. And in many places in the world, of course, Jaimes Guerrero is absolutely correct!

In chapter 10, Kelly Bannister explores the ethics of publishing traditional knowledge uses and practices, including the plant and animal species employed, in an era of misappropriation and commodification of indigenous knowledges and practices. As Bannister rightly points out, the act of publishing research findings on, for example, the medicinal plant species of a remote tribe widely disseminates that information, placing it within the public domain where anyone can then use that knowledge as he or she sees fit. Once traditional knowledge is published in academic journals and monographs, there is little to prevent a pharmaceutical corporation from reading this information and then following up these "leads" in the laboratory, without having to provide any credit or recompense to the indigenous group that originally provided the information that subsequently showed up in print. Her recommendations for how to balance ethical and research obligations ring controversial to some academicians, but her insights demonstrate that scientific and social scientific researchers working with indigenous groups today have many more sets of interests to consider than just their own interests as academic researchers.

George Nicholas and Kelly Bannister continue this same theme in chapter 11, but apply the notion of intellectual property rights for indigenous peoples and the right to ownership and control over archaeological remains. What is key to their exploration of archaeological remains and intellectual property rights is an examination of access and control. That is, if indigenous groups are routinely allowed to have control over the *products* of archaeology—not just the artifacts, but also the intellectual products of archaeological research, such as the right to allow or refuse publication of research results, the right to restrict further archaeological operations on an indigenous site (i.e., a sacred site, burial ground, etc.), the right to set agendas and goals of an archaeological project, and so on—it will inevitably change the status quo for archaeological research, including the career prospects and funding opportunities for archaeologists and departments at universities. The implications of these questions extend well beyond the field archaeology, since issues of control—both in terms of rights and responsibilities—are always at the heart of any collaborative research effort.

Finally, Elois and Brent Berlin discuss the issue of prior informed consent (PIC) in chapter 12. PIC is a research protocol that has become familiar to nearly all researchers working with people (or, in the language of the medical and health sciences, with "human subjects"), whether working with specific individuals or in entire groups. Chapter 12 outlines both the evolution of PIC protocols over time as well as the changing nature of bioprospecting, and the role of PIC in a bioprospecting project headed by the Berlins, the Maya Inernational Cooperative Biodiversity Group (ICBG). The Berlins outline the factors that led to the demise of the Maya ICBG and discuss the implications of that episode for bioprospecting in the future.

In conclusion, this book hardly expects to be—or wants to be, for that matter—the last word on indigenous IPR. There is a vast amount of excellent material published since the 1990s up to the present time on IPR issues, with the concomitant issues of access, control, and benefit sharing. These issues continue to receive attention at all levels of society—at the international level, and increasingly, at national, regional, and local levels; they are in no danger of disappearing any time soon. Furthermore, the issue of indigenous IPR is dovetailing with larger discussions of North-South relations and anxieties about the dynamic and direction of forces of globalization, which is viewed as a largely (though not entirely) North to South process.

While these discussions may evolve and overlap with other closely related issues in the future, it is our hope that this edited volume will be used as an introductory text for students, providing a survey of at least some of the concerns encompassed by the field of indigenous intellectual property rights. We also hope to demonstrate, through the chapters presented in this volume, that answers to the difficult questions raised by an exploration of indigenous intellectual property rights, and questions concerning indigenous rights in general, can only come about by and through the full participation of the indigenous peoples themselves in the process—which is what so many indigenous groups worldwide are asking for right now.

References

Brush, Stephen B., and Doreen Stablinsky (eds.)
Valuing Local Knowledge: Indigenous People and Intellectual Property Rights. Washington, D.C.: Island Press, 1996.

Greaves, Thomas
Indigenous Intellectual Property Rights: A Sourcebook. Oklahoma City: Society for Applied Anthropology, 1994.

Posey, D. A., and G. Dutfield
Beyond Intellectual Property: Toward Traditional Resource Rights for Indigenous Communities and Local Communities. Ottawa: International Development Research Centre, 1996.

Warren, D. M., L. J. Slikkerveer, and D. Brokensha (eds.)
The Cultural Dimension of Development: Indigenous Knowledge Systems. London: Intermediate Technology Publications, 1995.

Part One

LEGAL OBSTACLES

CHAPTER ONE
"AS LONG AS THE GRASS GROWS": REPRESENTING INDIGENOUS CLAIMS

Tressa Berman

Representing (Ab)originality

February 2003: I am sitting in a pub in central London with Wallace Coffey, master of ceremonies, sometime comedian, and former Chairman of the Comanche Nation. He is accompanied by his son, a young man from Oklahoma who will some day inherit all the rights and responsibilities of his father's social and ceremonial positions. We are in London for the occasion of a conference organized by the British Museum called *Powwow: Performance and Nationhood in Native North America.* In the back of this Bloomsbury gathering place, where we sit at a worn mahogany table among the ghosts of English letters, I reflect on the strange (dis)placements of American Indian images I have seen here—an Indian head advertising tobacco, the beaded bags on Oxford Street, and now behind us, on the wall below the dart board, a scoreboard to tally the points of the "Six Nations." Of course our reading of this "sign" moves us instantly to our own points of indigenous reference, not once considering who or what the Six Nations might signify in England, other than the Iroquois Confederacy itself, once the grand diplomats of treaty negotiations with Europe.

The Huadenosaunee still hold many international treaties with the colonizing countries of Europe, including the Netherlands, France, and Great Britain. The title of this chapter derives from among these first treaties with England in 1692, whereby the Covenant Chain of peace and friendship was extended for "as long as the sun shines upon the earth; as long as the waters flow; as long as the grass grows green."[1] According to Huadenosaunee tribal history, the treaty was renewed in 1755 by Sir William Johnson and proclaimed that the British and Iroquois meet every year to strengthen the terms of the Covenant. Now, sitting in a London pub on the occasion of a powwow conference at the British Museum, while honoring the very constructions of Native nationhood in that context, it takes on greater significance to reassert the first terms of international agreements between Native Nations and Great Britain, and, by extension, all of her settler continents.

This binding spirit of agreement was reiterated in 1829 by President Andrew Jackson at the launch of his American Indian removal policies. Even as the most heinous form of dislocation and dispossession, they still guaranteed certain reserved rights to American Indians in perpetuity or "as long as the grass shall grow." (See Ojibwe artist Anthony White's visual statement in figure 1.1.) Despite removal of thousands of Native peoples west of the Mississippi, basic principles of treaty agreement were upheld in the 1830s in a series of landmark court

Figure 1.1. "As Long as the Grass Shall Grow," by Anthony White. Anthony White is a member of the Redlake band of Ojibwe.

decisions, known as the Marshall Trilogy, that underpin federal Indian law. One of the most cited of these cases is Justice John Marshall's summary ruling in *Worcester v. Georgia*, which denied state jurisdiction into Aboriginal territories (thus upholding federal jurisdiction and tribal rights to self-governance). Taken together, these sets of rights held in part that

- discovery gave title, against all other European governments, to the government by whose subjects discovery was made;
- the rights of the original inhabitants were not entirely disregarded, but were considerably impaired;
- they remained the rightful occupants and possessors of the land but their sovereignty was diminished.[2]

While laying the foundations for indigenous claims to title in Canada and Australia, U.S. doctrine reveals two main differences between itself and Australia:

- In the United States, limited sovereignty is recognized, whereas in Australia, indigenous sovereignty is extinguished;
- Indian title (in the United States) can only be extinguished by Congress, whereas in Australia, both the states and Commonwealth can extinguish title, or allow its acquisition by a third party (Dorsett and Godden 1998: 50–55).

Although these legal points may make for interesting fine-tuning of legislative outcomes and activist strategies, their points of agreement and departure have ongoing implications for sovereignty and, in particular, key issues of land rights and expressive culture.

At center stage to expressive movements are issues of representation—whether that representation is legal (as in sovereign jurisdiction), artistic (as in the rights to control production and public display of art forms), individual, or collective. In this chapter, I examine these various sites as opportunities for self-representation and reappropriation of indigenous control over cultural resources, motifs, and art forms.

Several cases spring to mind—most notably recent engagements with issues of cultural appropriations and the investigations into the elastic meanings of the term. Indigenous artists directly confront representations of the *ideas* of "sovereignty" on the one hand and actual "appropriations" on the other. The thematic of dispossession runs the gamut of cultural appropriation, where it sits at the extreme end as theft. In fact, First Nations Cree artist Joane Cardinal-Schubert has remarked plainly that "appropriation is stealing" (Cardinal-Schubert 1997).

In a legal context, artworks not only *represent* identity and indigenous claims to sovereignty, but they also provide *evidence* for indigenous assertions. These assertions can serve as precedent, as in the case of depictions of Aboriginal territories in Aboriginal paintings that uphold claims to title, and they can spring up as new inventions of tradition in ceremony and public performance. For instance, repatriation ceremonies at the end of the twentieth century posed a new challenge to Native Americans in designing never-before performed rites, necessitated by successful decolonizing legislation. Proliferation of art forms through indigenous movements and currents presents other opportunities for invention and appropriation. What I am concerned with here are what anthropologist Nicholas Thomas refers to as "paradigms of authorship" (1995: 98) in the performance and display of identity. These converging points were brought together at the British Powwow conference, most notably in anthropologist Bea Medicine's award-winning film *Seeking the Spirit: Plains Indians in Russia.* This documentary shows the earnest attempts of Russian powwow enthusiasts to re-create the Plains powwow on the remote outskirts of Moscow, and the reaction to the footage by the Lakota community at Standing Rock reservation. Taken together, this kind of appropriation signals a new form of cultural "exchange." On one side, appropriation erupts without actual contact or immersion. To the skilled eye and ear, this hurts. Yet with characteristic generosity, one tribal member remarked to the effect, "If they're going to do that [singing and dancing], they should have someone teach them to do it right."

Playback to Australia 2000: Is It Live or Is It Memorex™?

The year 2000 was a remarkable one for Australia's public image. Australia played host to the International Olympics and the world's attention was focused for a few intense weeks on the expected and unexpected stream of images transported via telecast to private monitors worldwide. The year also marked the one-year anniversary of Aboriginal Reconciliation, a federally sponsored initiative to mollify more than one hundred years of settler colonialism through platforms and partnerships, but none that would grant title, treaties, or a public apology for historical atrocities committed against the first occupants of the land.

The games began with the grand entry of scores of Aboriginal dancers, painted in chalk-white body paint and dancing in staged ceremony around a fire. We hear the authoritative, gently booming voice of African American actor James Earl Jones as he narrates the performance sequence. We are told that "huge fires are not uncommon" in Australia—the image juxtaposed against the choreographed rites evoked one of distant tribes dancing in random ritual throughout the vast continent. When we are told that 80 percent of Australia's population lives along its coastlines, the idea of inland desert peoples stretches even more remotely. One would not consider, for instance, the homelands of northeast coast peoples of Queensland up into the shrouded rainforests north of Cairns and the Great Barrier Reef, nor the southlands of Adelaide and into the capital district of Canberra, which has one of the longest urban political occupations across from the federal Parliament building—the Aboriginal Embassy. Nor would the unsuspecting tourist expect to encounter Aborigines in the bustling cities of Melbourne, Darwin, Perth, or Sydney, unless they were clad in body paint and playing the didgeridoo.

The narrative counterpart to this lead-in in the pregames extravaganza introduces a little white girl named Niki, who falls asleep and dreams her Australia into being (an oblique reference to Aboriginal Dreamtime here?). She is a little mermaid among the fish, floating through the stage-set of the Great Barrier Reef. Following from her encounter with the natural world, she is surrounded by benevolent Aborigines, led by the popular celebrity Jakapura. In this sequence, the sportscasters—one male, one female—banter about the "longest culture of any people on earth," and remark at the spectacle of more than fifteen hundred Aborigines brought to the center of the games, "many of them riding a bus or riding on the escalator for the very first time." While noting that there were groups of indigenous protestors outside the games who were attempting to call attention to land rights, no one wondered how they transported themselves there. Following the amazing spectacle in a kind of Darwinian procession—from fish to Aborigines to the rugged individualist Ned Kelly, from prison settlements to the parade of "new arrivals" of immigrants in diasporic display—Niki and Jakapura are lifted high above the scene, joining hands in the grand finale of what could possibly be read as a symbolic gesture toward Reconciliation.

The perception of Aboriginality in the white imagination is a critical underpinning to the reading of colonial law and state-sanctioned policies—both in Australia and in the United States. While reflecting on federal Indian policy in the United States, I have attempted to make some comparisons with Australia, despite the fact that serious differences mark the two histories from the first exercise of British Common Law. Where the United States granted treaty rights as early as the 1700s, British colonizers in Australia viewed the continent as a terra nullius, an uninhabited space with no prior claim than by the Crown. While U.S. treaties with American Indian Tribes were systematically abrogated through time, they nonetheless provide an important launch for sovereignty movements of the last several decades. As Australia grapples with the question of treaties (as the popular Indigenous rock band Yothu Yindi proclaim in their 1980s hit song "Treaty Now"), legally speaking, the question of treaties raises renewed concerns about the extinguishments of *title*—a question that builds on national momentum in Australia since 1992, when the first Indigenous land rights case was won.[3]

In this chapter, I link land rights to art rights and identity by suggesting the collective representation of claims (viz. Berman 1997), and the recognition of group rights that inhere in "tribal" identities. Ultimately, I see these sets of "rights" as threaded through the discourse on sovereignty and suggest their inextricable linkages. While we can reflect on the popular media constructions of Aboriginality and Indianness both abroad and at home, I invoke an underlying question: How does the law construct Aboriginality? By extension, how does the law govern indigenous art forms?

I come at these questions from several vantage points. First, I suggest that the rights over art (and how rights shape art) are constructed out of the rights to land and resources (collectively held). These rights in turn emanate from the rights to property. If understood as flowing from land rights, then indigenous claims to appropriation of artistic designs, for example, would insist on a need for *title* (Davies 1997). In this way, I suggest that laws that govern cultural and intellectual property (including art) consider laws over Native land and (real) property. Such an approach attempts to extend Native title to cultural property and art forms that are inextricable from land-based claims to political sovereignty and self-determination.

Indigenous Arts (Un)Titled

The origins of property loss must be understood to flow from the dispossession of Native title itself, that is *land.* In today's (post)colonial practices, cultural rights to production and responsibilities to safeguard artistic motifs and techniques have recently come under scrutiny as the last harbors of indigenous knowledge, where cultural codes of meaning embedded in art forms and processes of *making* art seek new forms of protection.

In redressing Aboriginal en[title]ment, some extensions of property law can be read as attempts at decolonization, such as repatriation legislation in the United States. However, Aboriginal notions of rights—to production, to use, and as caretakers of cultural "property"—are written out of the law, except as "facts" that inform the law, but do not compete with it (Berman 1997; Davies 1997). In this way, the law retains its narrative authority over indigenous claims to appropriation of indigenous knowledge (cf. Woodmansee and Jaszi 1994).

In attempts to formulate indigenous theories of property, Native scholars (Tsosie 1997; Worl forthcoming) and artists have insisted on the cultural aspects of cultural property that legitimize Native claims—as in oral histories (stories) (Keeshig-Tobias 1997), collective assertions of identity (cf. Riley 2000), and the point taken up here: that Native title to cultural property and art forms is not only inextricable from land-based claims to sovereignty, but its legal reach grasps the embedded relationships of land, art, and indigenous knowledge systems more firmly than copyright protections over creative works.

In copyright claims, Australian Aboriginal artists have won ground in legal cases involving the appropriation and mass reproduction of Aboriginal images on tourist items, such as T-shirts, sarongs, and an array of other items (Johnson 1996). Rights to production in these and other cases are linked to clan stories of the Dreaming and are held with particular keepers of the stories in relation to specific sites (Sutton 1988). Many of these designs are collectively owned by men and women who have the rights to particular Dreamings and cannot be replicated without their permission or certain harm will result. Aboriginal law recognizes these linkages as customary rights that carry penalties for infractions. In the now famous "Carpets case," Aboriginal plaintiffs cited "cultural harm" as an effect on the violation of copyright.[4] The case cited the Vietnamese manufacturers of woolen carpets with copyright infringement under the Australian 1968 Copyright Act for their flagrant appropriation of Aboriginal art and artists' designs taken from published works by the National Gallery of Australia. The decision in the Carpets case has been compared to the precedent-setting Mabo land claims case, in which title was restored to Torres Strait Islanders off the coast of Australia (viz. Attwood 1996). While the Carpets case may have been a landmark case in terms of reparations to Aboriginal artists, significant differences accrue between "copyright" and "title" as legal defense more widely applied.

Anglo-Australian law remains premised on nonrecognition of *Aboriginal law* (i.e., as governed by the Dreaming). A restoration of sovereign rights through title—rather than copyright—might have invoked a more broad ruling by which rights to a particular site entitle artists to the rights over images that flow from that site. From this perspective, a central issue of sovereignty gets raised: Native title [to land] cannot be alienated. The same can be said, and U.S. law now accepts,[5] that certain cultural objects cannot be alienated from their caretakers and their places of origin. In such cases, cultural appropriation, seen at the extreme end in the confiscation of cultural property, "*merges with the wider process of colonization*" (Davies 1997: 24; italics mine) and thus signals how Euro-American and Euro-Australian law are premised on the abrogation of indigenous sovereignty—as in the freedom to practice Native religions, which requires exclusive use rights to certain artifacts, images, and sites.

By extension, appropriation of indigenous iconography into state and national symbols signifies assimilative practices whereby Native art stands in for Native. Examples range from the Australian boomerang as a marker of Australian national identity to the appropriation of the Zia sun sign as a symbol for the state of New Mexico (Pino 1995) and the Australian Aboriginal flag as a symbol of Aboriginality. In legal practice, the only way to protect indigenous objects and motifs at points of market intersection is to treat them like (private) property. Otherwise free-floating images can be appropriated when they are released into the market, where they are sometimes mistaken for public domain.

Public Domain

In a seminal article in *Current Anthropology*, "Can Culture be Copyrighted?" anthropologist Michael Brown raised a cautionary flag in the movement to protect indigenous knowledge through legal mechanisms of copyright and intellectual property (1998). The author's concerns for what he construes as "special rights" to "*collective* privacy" warrant attention—if only to allay the fears that intellectual property rights (IPR) "run amok" would result in a cultural apartheid of creative ideas and their execution. The concern for the regulation of *information* and *knowledge* (note the distinction I make) is reminiscent of the retentionist arguments put forth in the early 1990s in the United States around repatriation of cultural property, when, it was feared, historic and cultural information that had long been in the public trust would be restricted and "lost" to the greater good of public knowledge. In a larger argument that situates notions of the public trust within liberal democratic ideals, a critical view insists on interrogating the assumptions of "public domain" by asking "whose public" and by what standards of "trust"?

What Brown and others argue in a move *away* from extending IPR to Native ideas and knowledge is a rightful concern that sees the commodification of knowledge as counter to cultural preservation. These arguments, while instructive, are based on a limited view of property rights as economic rights, which become privileged in the discourse around IPR. As Tsosie (1997) has pointed out, what is missing from an economic rights position is attention to the moral rights that Western property regimes also embody. Furthermore, *access* to the law extends beyond the "bundle of rights" inherent in property law to what some theorists have proposed as "bundles of power" (Ribot 1998; Ribot and Peluso 2003).

Access to the law then becomes not only a question of application, but also one of authorship—again, invoking the question, whose "public"? At the extreme end of unequal access to the law, it could be argued that Western law itself does not extend to the variety of public constituents (e.g., Indigenous peoples) evenly or equitably. For instance, for American Indians in the United States, the notion of a *public* trust resides with a *federal* trust that serves as an overarching regulator and legal artifact of U.S./Indian relations, and one that carries juridical and fiduciary responsibilities.

Some scholars (Echo Hawk 1986; Riley 2000) have suggested that the federal trust relationship that grants federal oversight to tribal land-holdings has already put a legal doctrine of collective rights in place. Elsewhere (Berman 1997), I have suggested that collective rights to "property" inhere in use rights, a legal acknowledgment first laid down by reserved rights doctrines in the nineteenth century (cf. Wilkins 1997; Deloria and Wilkins 1999).[6] These connections point to the possibility of invoking existing structures within federal Indian law for IPR protections in collective claims to creative works—especially if those "works" emanate from, and "belong" to, a collectivity of family, clan, or tribe (as with songs, images, and names). Clearly, the 1990 Native American Graves Protection and Repatriation Act has recognized the right of the collectivity to file claims for objects held in museums when such objects are "needed" by the group and for its social and ceremonial continuity.

So, how do Tribes reclaim those objects, images, songs, and stories that have fallen into unprotected territories of public domain? In Australia, manufacturers of Flash T-shirt designs claimed that the Aboriginal designs they appropriated were in the public domain because they had taken them from books (viz. Johnson 1996). Following from the Flash T-shirt case, which resulted in an out-of-court settlement for Aboriginal artists, subsequent legal decisions have ruled in favor of Aboriginal plaintiffs claiming violation of copyright, as in the Carpets case cited earlier. But the uneven application of IPR protections cannot stop the churning proliferation of unprotected images into the commercial sphere. Just as ubiquitous boomerangs stand in for Aboriginality in Australia, in Arizona, Hopi *katsinas* signify "Indianness" from dry cleaners to travel agencies (viz. Pearlstone 2002). Almost anywhere where indigenism has been replaced with commercialism (a new brand of colonialism), examples abound. In Bismarck, North Dakota, Native street names now replace the peoples who once lived there. By extension, indigenous arts are often exalted at the expense of Indigenous peoples.

In Aboriginal customary practices, the complicated proprietary rights bestowed by the Dreaming are further fragmented by collectively sanctioned *use rights*. Australian museums have responded to the need for "privacy rights" by creating men's rooms and women's rooms in storage facilities that house culturally sensitive objects assigned by gender. The argument for a generalized collective privacy becomes a problematic that must then consider rights to production, use rights, and proprietary rights (see Berman 1997).

Representation becomes a critical issue in asserting a collective identity, especially in the case of "use rights," by which tribal sovereignty at the level of government-to-government relations sometimes conflicts with the use rights of objects entrusted to medicine people. In other words, by serving the interests of tribal governments that represent a collective identity ("the Sioux"), community-level sanctions can sometimes be overlooked or overruled. Extensions of collective privacy rights run counter to U.S. property regimes that are based on notions of possessive individualism and force a unitary voice in tribal claims—such as the singular representation, "the Sioux," "the Navajo," "the Cheyenne"—without accounting for segmentary political organization (Northern Cheyenne/Southern Cheyenne), jurisdictional divides (one reservation straddling two states), or intracultural and linguistic variation (Lakota, Dakota, Nakota). These are but a few examples that lend support to a sui generis approach to tackling IPR on a case-by-case basis (Berman, Seitel, and McCann 2001).

Case law can set precedents for testing the efficacy of intellectual property rights and cultural property laws; however, indigenous rules governing the production and "ownership" of indigenous cultural objects often do not follow legal principles. Instead, as in the Australian Carpets case, expressions and objects are subject to community-based sanctions. In local community contexts, indigenous knowledge bears upon cultural property claims by conferring collectively recognized forms of "precedents" and "evidence"—enabling a form of "cultural copyright" (Pinel and Evans 1994) as a collective right.

Secrecy

The flip side of public domain is privacy. For instance, property law recognizes privacy rights as flowing from rights to exclusion. In cultural property cases, customary practices govern rules for production, display, and (re)distribution. Cultural patrimony—that is, the return of cultural objects to their originating communities—relies on evidence based on the kinds of criteria mentioned above (namely, a recognition of collective rights). In distinguishing *information* from *knowledge* it becomes quite clear that indigenous knowledge cannot be extracted as an isolate, like a gene cell (viz. Coombe 1998a; 1998b). Rather, it is embedded within shifting matrices of cultural systems that include rights vested through kinship and upheld by community sanction. Extreme forms of privacy lie with "hidden knowledge"—often the very customary practices that sanctify public representatives (such as Aboriginal lawyers or Native American spokespeople) to act on behalf of cultural groups seeking just compensation under IPR in international settings and forums (see Posey 1998; UNESCO 2000). Forms of cultural knowledge solicited as evidence in cultural property claims may be better preserved *off the record*, as Indigenous peoples increasingly evoke their "right to remain silent," especially in matters of ceremonial disclosure. For instance, as Philip Minthorn, a Cayuse artist and cultural historian, says in relation to Native claims to museum objects of cultural patrimony: "Native communities are now required to divulge sacred and esoteric forms of knowledge in order to substantiate their claim or to insure the appropriate disposition of such objects . . . without the guarantee of the protection of that knowledge" (1995: 11).

IPR in such cases offers no protections at the level of community-based group rights. But just as land becomes property, cultural knowledge becomes information when it is taken out of its social and ceremonial contexts, where it is then subject to misappropriation and legal protections. Furthermore, intellectual and property rights law requires that indigenous knowledge stand as a kind of "evidence" (Torres and Milun 1990/1994), subject to the scrutiny of the public record. Repatriation serves as a case in point in the United States, where tribal elders may be asked to testify about the sacred nature of objects in cultural patrimony cases. While the Native American Graves Protection and Repatriation Act (NAGPRA) states that oral histories and cultural codes of meaning can be used to determine cultural claims to objects, the fact is that ethnohistorical, archaeological, and legal records are privileged in documenting museum collections, and in some cases, American Indian spokespeople report that Native testimony has been expunged from the historical record (Yellow Bird and Milun 1994). In short, it's about whose story gets told, and who has the right to tell it (Cook-Lynn 1996).

The issue of secrecy is related to silence as a way to control the flow of cultural knowledge, and in recent years, as a way to ensure that indigenous knowledge does not become a matter of public record (such as in repatriation cases). On the other hand, silence can be the result of totalizing claims to intellectual property rights and cultural property in the legal debates of who speaks for whom. For example, ways in which some customary practices are silenced lie in the erasure of women's knowledge from museum and legal records—even where women serve as keepers of rights to indigenous designs and redistributors of cultural objects (Berman 2000; Yellowman 1994). However, the positioning of objects within social and ceremonial life, and the position of specific individuals to objects themselves, would be impossible to untangle without considering "women's ways of knowing"—from customary rights that govern artistic production to social divisions that allocate the distribution of goods and labor among women who stand at the center of their kin-based networks (e.g., viz. Berman 2003).

Decision making in repatriation claims takes place at deep community levels, where kinship and ceremonial knowledge of Native American women figures highly. By turning attention to women's contributions, we see that it is not just in the rhetoric of repatriation that women sometimes stand as spokespeople, but repatriated objects are frequently *family* objects, associated with family histories, clans, and places of origin, where people and objects converge to create a *context* for cultural meanings and uses. By comparison, Queensland Murri artists, in referencing artworks that signify their "country," make such claims in relation to homeland as a point of origin and return. As Daisy Manybunharrawuy, an Aboriginal bark painter describes: "I still kept going at bark painting after I married. . . . My father used to tell me a story from the painting. . . . I use white clay from the beach; black from the tree from the bush . . . at Milingimbi. Milingimbi is like home—Milingimbi is like *momu* [grandmother]" (cited in Caruana and Lendon 1997: 156). In a similar sentiment, Nora Noranjo-Morse reflects upon returning to Santa Clara Pueblo after her years away at urban art centers: "Holding that clay was the first time I ever felt a connection with something greater than myself . . . I had come home" (in Abbott 1994: 197).

When we consider Aboriginal and Native American women's knowledge in the context of homelands and cultural continuity, women's "property" takes on new significance and allows us to consider aspects of property law in more culturally relevant terms. While many of the cultural codes that inform the production and circulation of indigenous art objects fall outside of the regime of U.S. property law, some aspects of common law allow us to shift the discourse of repatriation away from totalizing accounts. An example of indigenous women's redistributive role is highlighted in the documentary film *Potlatch*, which shows how the return of repatriated objects symbolizes the redistribution of power relations *through the transfer of title.*

In these ways, the redistribution of property rights through repatriation has the potential for redistributing knowledge and power in ways that are symbolized by the act of return itself. For example, the film shows the Kramner family's stake in the "continuity and legitimacy of the Kwakiutl potlatch in general and the Kramner family's claim to returned potlatch items from the 1922 confiscation" (Jacknis 1996: 274). The image of the reapportionment of repatriated objects reveals several things: First, the centrality of women is marked by the amassing and redistribution of goods and objects. Second, the social purpose of objects preserved through customary rights becomes reempowered by a collectively sanctioned locality, in this case the Kwakiutl potlatch at Alert Bay (Harding 1997: 757).

Here we see how cultural appropriation, shown at the extreme end in the confiscation of cultural property, signals how Western law is premised on the abrogation of Native sovereignty. Sovereignty, as both a political and philosophical dimension of cultural rights, is tied to claims of Native title, whether that title is to land, cultural property, or art forms.

Restoration of Sovereign Rights through Title

The earlier discussion—by exploring some of the dimensions and limitations of IPR for indigenous knowledge systems—suggests that where copyright infringement and IPR can uphold cultural rights to production, distribution, and use, it may also serve to reinforce Native title. Conversely, where IPR and copyright result in the commodified transformation of cultural knowledge to information bytes for public consumption, then new approaches need to be explored.

If we were to take the view that Native title to cultural and intellectual property and their expressions, such as art forms, are inextricable aspects of sovereignty, then a cultural rights argument begins to sound less like "special rights" and more like "human rights" (i.e., toward self-determination). A restoration of sovereign rights through title, rather than copyright, might have invoked a broader ruling in the Carpets case, by which rights to a particular site entitle artists to the rights over images that flow from that site. From this perspective, a central issue of sovereignty gets raised: Native title (to land) cannot be alienated. The same can be said, and U.S. law now accepts (again, as in the NAGPRA), that certain cultural objects cannot be alienated from their caretakers and their places of origin.

While alienation generally implies privatization, especially of land, inalienability does not conversely (or so it would seem logically) lend itself to the public domain. In the United States, the use of images, generally conceptualized as publicity rights, has been a source of contention between Native communities and commercial exploiters. In the well-documented case of the *Estate of Tasunke Witko a/k/a Crazy Horse v. Vultaggio and Sons, Inc.*, the descendants of Sioux Chief Crazy Horse asserted "defamation, violation of the Estate's right of publicity, and negligent and intentional infliction of emotional distress (in addition to violations of the Lanham Act and American Indian Arts and Crafts Board Act)" (Newton 1997; Gough 1995 and forthcoming). Of relevance here is that the defendants argued that the rights of publicity were in the public domain and did not constitute a violation of privacy.[7] In 2001, after an eight-year legal battle, the defendants (Stroh Brewing Company) settled with the Estate of Crazy Horse and the Rosebud Sioux tribe. The settlement agreement provides for a public apology and acknowledgment of the Estate's right to protect the name of Crazy Horse and for delivery of culturally appropriate damages—seven race horses and thirty-two Pendleton blankets, braids of tobacco, and sweet grass, in compensation for defamation of character to the spirit of Crazy Horse.[8]

The case lingered in the halls of justice where it volleyed between the Rosebud Sioux tribal court and federal district courts until jurisdiction and legal standing could be determined. Given the jurisdictional problem in the Crazy Horse case, and the general trust relationship between the federal government and Indian tribes in the United States, it would seem that the "special rights" argument could be newly considered in light of the unique legal status ascribed to Indigenous peoples, especially in North America and increasingly in Australia. This was the point I raised earlier when I invoked extant doctrines of federal trust and reserved rights, especially to water and other natural resources.

In hammering out legal solutions to the global concern over *appropriation without compensation*, it would seem that the only way to protect indigenous creations at the points of their intersection with the market is to treat them like property. The questions unleashed by such an approach demand careful attention to power relations, local knowledge, collective and individual rights, jurisdiction, authorship, and access to the law.

In Australia, I have so far observed that the possibilities to amend copyright laws to better address Aboriginal concerns about appropriation of creative works are moving at a steady, if not snowballing rate, despite recent setbacks in land title victories.[9] Indigenous organizations are at the forefront of these movements—especially as they link land rights to rights over art. While the tome of legal briefs in Australia has nowhere reached U.S. proportions with respect to a body of case law analogous to federal Indian law, I think that the opportunities for including intellectual and cultural property protections into a revised "bundle of rights" in property law may be better positioned in Australia at this time when land rights have merged with cultural rights. In this light, the rethinking of "property" will force new sets of questions to the fore: Not rhetorically "can culture be copyrighted?" but more practically "How will Indigenous peoples write themselves into the law?" Questions of privacy and secrecy as matters of indigenous knowledge may yet find protections, if the public domain is not just a playing field for commodifying Indigenous knowledge, and the rule of law is not just a matter of public opinion.

Conclusion

This chapter has considered several interrelated and complicated themes. First, the question of representation is raised in the context of public display, thus signaling the trope through which "Indianness" and "Aboriginality" are captured and highlighted in the global imagination. Not only can indigenous display—through art and public ceremony—"stand in" for indigenous cultures, but the whole scale treatment of "Indigenism" serves as a gloss for economic and cultural marginality. Reconstructing Aboriginality or "American Indian-ism" in the context of the colonial rule of law is one of the tasks we set ourselves when looking for legal ways to protect Indigenous intellectual and cultural property.

While it is clear that there are areas of social life where the law has no reach, customary practices and sanctions do prevail. The 1999 UNESCO Global Assessment on the Safeguarding of Traditional Culture, for which I was legal rapporteur, recommended a sui generis approach to international issues of IPR protections extended to indigenous knowledge and cultural "property." The problematic of what is suggested by Western property regimes and their inadequacies for addressing such collective aspects of use rights, authorship, and ownership has now been well realized and supported by advances and extensions of the law (back) into group rights. In these ways, indigenous claims to indigenous knowledge and motifs meet at the intersection of more ethereal and rapidly transforming aspects of IPR in cyberspace and biotechnology. The irony of this juxtaposition is that it is forcing a reconfiguration of notions of copyright, patent, and royalties. Taken as a whole, this movement can only lend veracity to other, nonindigenous claims for justice in recompensation.

While the extension of copyright protections to Native ideas was a logical extension of IPR into indigenous realms of "ownership," the philosophical underpinnings related to individual authorship, and a "realized" or fixed work of art, run counter to dynamic and collective modes of indigenous artistic production—what I call "the community as worksite" (Berman 1998; 2003). This is evident not only in Native American contexts where it has been applied, but also a high-profile case in point can be found in the work of (deceased) Anmatyerre artist Emily Kngwarreye, whose genius can only be explained—and remunerated—through group context and consensus in her own central desert community of Alhalkere, Utopia, Australia (Neale 1998, forthcoming).

The intimate relationship of land to other aspects of Native creativity and invention lend support to an argument for extending title into rights that emanate from the land base. Likewise, the reserved rights granted to American Indians in water and subsistence needs for "as long as the grass shall grow" (in perpetuity) are a set of rights that can be reasserted in new contexts, such as rights to cultural property. As pointed out, the 1990 Native American Graves Protection and Repatriation Act is a step in this direction of (re)asserting collective rights. International law presents another potential mechanism for extending IPR. Moreover, the awareness raised and the relationships forged—both contentious and cooperative—have given rise to new extra-legal methods of collaboration, negotiation, permissions, and respect.

Finally, innovation, both as a creative act to be protected and as a means for reconfiguring the law, will ultimately yield the most pliable strategy for effecting legal and social changes at the sites of indigenous production (i.e., communities) and protection against the unsanctioned proliferation and appropriations of images and creative works.

Notes

1. See citations available at the Huadenosaunee website: www.sixnations.org/Lessons_from_History.
2. For full discussion of the Marshall Trilogy, see Deloria and Lytle 1984.
3. *Mabo v. State of Queensland*, 1992, was the landmark title case for recognizing indigenous rights of Torres Strait Islanders based on the claim filed and won by Torres Strait Islander (TSI) Eddie Mabo.
4. *Mulpurrurru et al. v. Indofurn Pty. Ltd. et al.*
5. One of the better-known cases is of the repatriation of the Zuni War gods (Ahayu:da) to the Pueblo of Zuni (see Ferguson, Anyon, and Ladd 1996).
6. Reserved rights include hunting and fishing and water rights that refer in the spirit of the law to rights that extend "as long as the grass grows."
7. The Rosebud Sioux Tribe has argued that the Rosebud Sioux tribal court has inherent and exclusive jurisdiction over *personal property rights* vested in the case [U.S. Court of Appeals for the Eighth Circuit, 1998 U.S. App.].
8. From the September 20, 2001, Press Release from the Estate of Tasunke Witko as put forth by Seth Big Crow, descendant and administrator for the Estate, and Robert P. W. Gough, attorney for the Estate.
9. See the 1998 *Wik* Title ruling in Australia for details.

References

Abbott, Lawrence
I Stand at the Center of Good: Interviews with Contemporary Native American Artists. Lincoln: University of Nebraska Press, 1994.

Attwood, Bain (ed.)
In the Age of Mabo: History, Aborigines and Australia. St. Leonards, N.S.W.: Allen and Unwin, 1996.

Berman, Tressa
Beyond the Museum: The Politics of Representation in Asserting Rights to Cultural Property. *Museum Anthropology*, vol. 21, no. 3 (1997): 19–27.

The Community as Worksite: American Indian Women's Artistic Production. In *More Than Class: Studying Power in U.S. Workplaces,* edited by Ann Kingslover, 73–93. Albany: State University of New York Press, 1998.

Native Women's Knowledge in Cultural Property Claims. Invited Lecture. Department of Anthropology, University of Oslo, Norway, 2000.

Circle of Goods: Women, Work and Welfare in a Reservation Community. Albany: SUNY Press, 2003.

Berman, Tressa, Peter Seitel, and Anthony McCann
Local Empowerment and International Cooperation: A Report on a Working Conference. *Cultural Survival Quarterly,* vol. 24, no. 4 (Winter 2001): 28–33.

Brown, Michael F.
Can Culture Be Copyrighted? *Current Anthropology,* vol. 39, no. 2 (1998): 193–222.

Cardinal-Schubert, Joane
Seeing Red. *Borrowed Power: Essays on Cultural Appropriation.* New Brunswick, New Jersey: Rutgers University Press, 1997.

Caruana, Wally, and Nigel Lendon
The Painters of the Wagilag Sisters Story, 1937–1997. Canberra, ACT: National Gallery of Australia, 1997.

Cook-Lynn, Elizabeth
The Relationship of a Writer to the Past: Art, a Literary Principle, and the Need to Narrate. In *Why I Can't Read Wallace Stegner and Other Essays: A Tribal Voice,* edited by Elizabeth Cook-Lynn, 63–77. Madison: University of Wisconsin Press, 1996.

Coombe, Rosemary
Comment. In "Can Culture Be Copyrighted?" Michael F. Brown. *Current Anthropology,* vol. 39, no. 2 (April 1998a): 207–208.

The Cultural Life of Intellectual Properties; Authorship, Appropriation and the Law. Durham: Duke University Press, 1998b.

Davies, Tony
Aboriginal Cultural Property? *Law in Context,* vol. 14, no. 1 (1997): 1–28.

Deloria, Vine, Jr., and Clifford Lytle
The Nations Within. Austin: University of Texas, 1998. (Originally published New York: Pantheon Books, 1984.)

Deloria, Vine, Jr., and David E. Wilkins
Tribes, Treaties and Constitutional Tribulations. Austin: University of Texas Press, 1999.

Dorsett, Shaunnagh, and Lee Godden, Faculty of Law, Griffith University, Australian Institute of Aboriginal and Torres Strait Islander Studies
A Guide to Overseas Precedents of Relevance to Native Title. Prepared for the Native Title Research Unit. Canberra, ACT: Panther Publishing, 1998.

Echo Hawk, Walter R.
Museum Rights vs. Indian Rights: Guidelines for Assessing Competing Legal Interests in Native Cultural Resources. *NYU Review of Law and Social Change*, vol. 14 (1986): 437–453.

Feld, Steven, and Keith Basso
Senses of Place. School of American Research. Santa Fe: New Mexico, 1996.

Ferguson, T. J., Roger Anyon, and Edmund J. Ladd
Repatriation at the Pueblo of Zuni: Diverse Solutions to Complex Problems. *American Indian Quarterly,* vol. 20, no. 2 (Spring 1996): 274–286.

Gough, Robert
Malt Liquor Mythos, or "Will the Original Crazy Horse Please Rise?" Cultural Facts and Legal Fictions in the Settlement of Competing Property Claims. Paper presented at the American Anthropological Association meetings, San Francisco, California, November 15–19, 1995.

The Application of Lakota Tribal Customary Law in the Protection of Culturally-Based Property Rights: The Case of Crazy Horse Malt Liquor. In *No Deal! Indigenous Arts and the Politics of Possession*, edited by Tressa Berman. Forthcoming, in preparation for University of Washington Press.

Harding, Sara
Justifying Repatriation of Native American Cultural Property. *Indiana Law Journal,* vol. 72 (1997): 722.

Jacknis, Ira
Repatriation as Social Drama: The Kwakuitl Indians of British Columbia, 1922–1980. *American Indian Quarterly,* vol. 20, no. 2 (1996): 274–286.

Johnson, Vivien
Copyrites: Aboriginal Art in the Age of Reproductive Technologies. Sydney: National Indigenous Arts Advocacy Association and Macquarie University, 1996.

Keeshig-Tobias, Lenore

Stop Stealing Native Stories! In *Borrowed Power: Essays on Cultural Appropriation,* edited by Bruce Ziff and Pratima V. Rao, 71–73. New Brunswick: Rutgers University Press, 1997.

McMaster, Gerald

Borderzones: The "Injun-uity" of Aesthetic Tricks. *Cultural Studies,* vol. 9, no. 1 (1995): 74–90.

Minthorn, Philip

Medicine Bundles as Aboriginal Curation. Paper presented at AAA 93rd annual meeting, Atlanta, Georgia, 1995.

Neale, Margo

Emily Kame Kngwarreye: Paintings from Utopia. Brisbane: Macmillan Press, Queensland Art Gallery. 1998.

Two Worlds, One Vision. The Emily Kngwarreye Retrospective. In *No Deal! Indigenous Arts and the Politics of Possession*, edited by Tressa Berman. Forthcoming, in preparation for University of Washington Press.

Newton, Nell

Memory and Misrepresentation: Representing Crazy Horse in Tribal Court. In *Borrowed Power: Essays on Cultural Appropriation,* edited by Bruce Ziff and Pratima V. Rao. New Brunswick: Rutgers University Press, 1997.

Pearlstone, Zena

Katsina: Commodified and Appropriated Images of Hopi Supernaturals. Tucson: University of Arizona Press, 2002.

Pinel, Sandra Lee, and Michael J. Evans

Tribal Sovereignty and the Control of Knowledge. In *Intellectual Property Rights and Indigenous Peoples: A Source Book,* edited by Tom Greaves, 41–55. Oklahoma City: Society for Applied Anthropology, 1994.

Pino, Manny

Panelist. Invited Roundtable on Intellectual Property Rights and Indigenous Peoples. Society for Applied Anthropology meetings, Albuquerque, New Mexico, 1995.

Posey, Darryl

Effecting International Change. *Cultural Survival Quarterly* (Summer 1998): 29–35.

Ribot, Jesse
Theorizing Access: Forest Profits Along Senegal's Charcoal Commodity Chain. *Development and Change*, vol. 29, no. 2 (April 1998): 307–341.

Ribot, Jesse, and Nance Lee Peluso
A Theory of Access: Putting Property and Tenure in Place. *Rural Sociology*, vol. 68, no. 2 (2003): 153–181.

Riley, Angela R.
Recovering Collectivity: Group Rights to Intellectual Property in Indigenous Communities. *Cardoza Arts and Entertainment*, vol. 18, no. 125 (2000): 175–225.

Rosaldo, Renato
Culture and Truth. Stanford: Stanford University Press, 1987.

Sutton, Peter (ed.)
Dreamings: The Art of Aboriginal Australia. New York: George Braziller Publishers and the Asia Society Galleries, 1988.

Thomas, Nicholas
Kiss the Baby Good-bye: *Kowhaiwhai* and Aesthetics in Aotearoa, New Zealand. *Critical Inquiry*, vol. 22 (Autumn 1995): 90–121.

Torres, Gerald, and Kathryn Milun
Translating Yonnondio by Precedent and Evidence: The Mashpee Indian Case. In *Critical Race Theory: The Cutting Edge,* edited by Richard Delgado, 48–55. Philadelphia: Temple University Press, 1994. (Originally published in *Duke University Law Journal,* vol. 1990, no. 4 [September]: 625–659.)

Tsosie, Rebecca
Indigenous Peoples' Claims to Cultural Property: A Legal Perspective. *Museum Anthropology*, vol. 21, no. 3 (1997): 5–11.

UNESCO Report
Safeguarding Traditional Culture. UNESCO Conference Proceedings. Center for the Study of Folklife, Smithsonian Institution, 2000.

Wilkins, David
American Indian Sovereignty and the U.S. Supreme Court: The Making of Justice. Austin: University of Texas Press, 1997.

Woodmansee, Martha, and Peter Jaszi (eds.)
The Construction of Authorship: Textual Appropriation in Law and Literature. Chapel Hill: Duke University Press. 1994.

Worl, Rosita
Tlingit *At.oow* as Art and Artifacts. In *No Deal! Indigenous Arts and the Politics of Possession,* edited by Tressa Berman. Forthcoming, in preparation for University of Washington Press.

Yellow Bird, Pemina, and Kathryn Milun
Interrupted Journeys: The Cultural Politics of Indian Reburial. In *Displacements: Cultural Identities in Question*, edited by A. Manner, 3–24. Bloomington: Indiana University Press, 1994.

Yellowman, Connie Hart
"Naevahoo'ohtseme"—We Are Going Back Home: The Cheyenne Repatriation of Human Remains—A Woman's Perspective. *St. Thomas Law Review*, vol. 9 (1994): 103.

CHAPTER 2
DIGITAL VIBES AND RADIO WAVES IN INDIGENOUS PERU

Bartholomew Dean

Over the past generation, the international community has witnessed a change in the political climate such that many states have become increasingly more tolerant of cultural difference. Indigenous peoples have used this political climate to advance rights-based claims for self-determination, political participation, and cultural autonomy. But to avail themselves of these new political apertures, Indigenous peoples face a double bind—they must become activists to protect their rights, yet by becoming cultural activists they may jeopardize their special status as "Indigenous." Without electoral clout, economic prowess, or military might, the symbolic capital accompanying authentically performed cultural identities represents one of the most influential political resources available to Indigenous peoples (Dean and Levi 2003).[1]

Consumerism, the ineluctable allure of the foreign, and mass telecommunications have made the ostensibly "traditional"[2] cultural products of Indigenous peoples available to a much wider global audience. Paradoxically, this affords Indigenous peoples (and ethnic minorities) with both opportunities and great risks. Articulation of rights-based claims provides Indigenous peoples with the promise of becoming real stakeholders in decision-making processes, especially those involving cultural expertise. New technologies like the Internet and the digitization of information (i.e., translation of data—sound, text, image—into digital form or binary coded files for use in computers) provide Indigenous peoples and those living at the margins of state power with an opportunity to advance public acknowledgment of distinctive worldviews and alternative cultural practices. This can legitimize Indigenous peoples' struggles for cultural autonomy by providing the subaltern with a forum for mobilizing much-needed public support.

While not without peril and compromise, when given the opportunity Indigenous peoples often choose to support cultural revalorization projects through the revenue generated from marketing their resources. Nevertheless, experience has shown that when Indigenous peoples share information or genetic materials extracted from their ancestral lands, they usually lose control over such resources, regardless of whether they are compensated in an equitable fashion. Increased global access to the cultural products of Indigenous peoples also poses risks to the continued cultural survival of local systems of knowledge, including what is often described as "traditional" or "local" music.

Reproducing Music: Globalization and the Commodification of Culture

Music is deeply ambiguous: It conveys community, articulates collective memory, expresses personal identities, and induces a wide range of emotional states. As a symbolically dense cultural field, music provides people with a way to articulate community and personal concerns and serves as a means for challenging dominant hegemonies. It is a creative space for novel cultural forms, and a vehicle for remembering local histories. While deeply personal, music is also instrumental in framing broader regional, national, or even transnational imaginaries. Given its centrality to social life, study of the reproduction and intercultural use of music alerts us to the challenges globalization and the commodification of culture pose for Indigenous peoples, regardless of how we define their intellectual property.[3]

Long before the establishment of a global network of electronic media, intellectuals have been grappling with the moral and political implications of mechanically reproducing artistic creativity. In his 1935 essay on the ethics of reproducing art, Walter Benjamin asserts that even the most perfect reproduction lacks an *aura*—"its presence in time and space, its unique existence at the place where it happens to be" (1968; see also Taussig 1992: 9). Few, I think, would argue that recorded music is superior to live musical performances—no matter what Memorex declares in its seductive advertisements.[4] In spite of this romantic appeal to authenticity (often tied to the patina of nostalgia or figurations of exotica), the world has seen a massive increase in access to and distribution of digitally recorded information.

The global music industry has experienced enormous changes over the past generation. Most notably, this has included the concentration of ownership and market share for a relatively small number of multinational corporations and technological innovations that have radically transformed the ways music is performed, distributed, and consumed (Burnett 1996). Music is now more commonly experienced as a recording than as a live performance (Seeger 1997b). Recorded music is enjoyed every day by billions of people, and as a result, cultural practices predicated on localized systems of knowledge are being undermined by the pervasive and homogenizing corporate culture business (Maybury-Lewis 1997; Novick 1997). While numerous theorists of globalization have emphasized increasing cultural homogenization accompanying Euro-American socioeconomic and political ascendancy (Wallerstein 1976, 1984; Wolf 1982; Mattelart 2000), it would be misleading to deny the proliferation of cultural difference stemming from "a world fundamentally characterized by objects in motion" (Appadurai 2002: 274).[5] Diversity and contradiction remain integral aspects of human experience—even in what some have fittingly branded our "postmodern predicament" (Weiner 1995:18). Globalization has given rise to rebellions, "against the forces of cultural uniformity and against the appropriation of Indigenous peoples' sovereignty by states" (Niezen 2003: 2). Indeed, just as the various forms of life around the planet seem to be becoming homogenous, peoples everywhere are asserting their cultural distinctiveness in response to global capitalism (Sahlins 1999: 410; Meisch 2002).[6]

While commodification promotes the mass consumption of diverse musical types, it leaves the vital, participatory aspects of cultural performances in the hands of specialists and the corporate arbiters of fashion. What Steven Leuthold (1998: 176) calls music's "local immediacy" is invariably forfeited to commerce. To increase profit margins, the corporate culture industry restricts copying and other uses of music, which ostensibly abridges creativity. Similarly, the commodification of Indigenous ceremonial objects and cultural products and appropriation of ritual practices through the language of possessive individualism pose the danger of cultural dissolution

(Coombe 1998). The digital revolution has led to the cultural appropriation of local, collectively held knowledge, which now has the potential to be electronically recorded, decontextualized, marketed, or accessed in ways that may undermine the creative integrity or cultural dignity of the producers.

The recording, distribution, and popular consumption of Indigenous music raise serious questions about copyright and intellectual property regimes (Graham 2003: 220n.36; Seeger 1997c). Anthony Seeger's (1997c) framing of the thorny issue of music ownership is instructive, particularly because intellectual property rights regimes are predicated on individual, rather than collective rights. Yet ethnography has demonstrated that we do not need to invoke Western copyright law to reveal the intricate network of rights and obligations associated with Indigenous music (Seeger 1997c: 58). Like many native Amazonian peoples, the Suyá of Brazil have two primary types of songs—collective (*ngere*) and individual (*akia*). While individuals control *akia* songs, Suyá groups are the considered the owners of *ngere* collective songs (Seeger 1997c).[7] Shaped by Occidental cultural presuppositions, copyright law often fails to secure the rights and obligations of collectivities. Ownership of the Suyá's "Big Turtle" song appearing on the recording *A Arte Vocal dos Suyá* defies the individualist spirit of U.S. copyright law. Composed more than eighty years ago, the "Big Turtle" song is owned by the community who attribute its authorship to a particular variety of honeybee (Seeger 1997c: 60–61).

As an overtly public yet deeply personal medium, traditional music is dependent on collective memory for its continued performance. In this regard, music represents a special case of the threat to Indigenous peoples as its fate is intimately tied to the broader challenge facing linguistic diversity. In light of the prospects of worldwide "language death" (Crystal 2000) support for and understanding of Indigenous peoples' expressive genres have become important to their cultural survival (Watahomigie, McCarty, and Yamamoto 1999; Dean 1999). The threat is both to linguistic diversity and to local cultural traditions and industries, which have become increasingly difficult to sustain in the face of cultural imperialism—the growing hegemony of the English language (Crystal 1998) and the U.S.-based entertainment business, which, along with weapons and food, represents one of our most profitable "national" exports (Jameson 2000; Jameson and Miyoshi 1998).

Commenting on how the popular culture industry incorporates musics from across the globe into market-oriented top 40 hits, Steve Feld writes, "appropriation means that the issue of 'whose music' is submerged, supplanted, and subverted by assertion of 'our music'" (1988: 31; see also 1995). While traditional music has become a coveted resource for reproducing the hegemonic, popular appreciation of local musical styles has seen an increased marginalization by commercial radio and television, often in favor of Western pop and rock styles with their infectiously melodic electric instrumentation, appeals to modern "life styles," and heavy reliance on marketing (among others, see Wallis and Malm 1984; Regis 1990).

The growing significance of intellectual property rights debates has accompanied the increasing commoditization of knowledge, which is all too often now conceptualized first and foremost in proprietary terms. No wonder then that throughout much of the postindustrial West the neoliberal privatization of schooling, research endeavors, and the expressive arts have concurrently led to a decline in the appreciation of knowledge as a public, collective good. Protecting Indigenous knowledge through legal channels remains an elusive goal. Intellectual property rights law emerged from "a Western view of knowledge as a commodity owned by an individual, not a community" (Riley and Moran 2001: 6).[8] The issue of Indigenous rights to digital cultural property, especially with the spread of reproductive electronic technologies, has yet to be fully understood, let alone adequately resolved. There are scores of examples where Indigenous music and imagery continue to appear without permission in movies and on websites, CDs, and the airwaves. The recording of local music for supralocal distribution involves, among other impulses, contractual business models that intersect local models of moral intentionality and authority. For Indigenous peoples the outcome of these encounters often results in a series of unanticipated consequences and vexing misunderstandings over their cultural property.

Melodic Fusion in Indigenous Peru

No single style of music expresses Indigenousness in Peru, a pluriethnic nation-state that boasts prodigiously diverse Indigenous and transcultural musical and creative arts heritages (among others, see Holzmann and

Arguedas 1965; Arguedas 1977; Bolaños et al. 1985; Roel Mendizabal 2000; Cánepa Koch 2001). Numerous Indigenous cultural traditions flourished millennia before the arrival of the Spanish and the emergence and zenith of the Incan empire (Olsen 2002). The colonial encounter signaled a fundamental realignment in daily life, including the way music was created, performed, and appreciated. Starting in the sixteenth century, the Spanish tried to suppress Indigenous expressive forms, including music, song, and dance.[9] Their efforts at cosmological extirpation were unsuccessful. The Spanish did, however, manage to introduce their own cultural practices, including the use of musical instruments, such as mandolins, harps, and violins. African slaves brought their percussive traditions and rich verbal cultures. Under the sway of nineteenth-century liberals looking to modernize the country, brass instruments associated with Western military bands became part of the Peruvian musical inventory. The wealth of transformations and incorporation of non-Andean aspects includes the famous scissor-dancers—reflecting medieval Spanish imagery—of Ayacucho and Huancavelica, and the pervasive use of saxophones in the Mantaro valley,[10] a by-product of local participation in military bands (Rowe and Schelling 1991; Romero 1993, 2001).

Local communities throughout rural and urban Peru continue to celebrate religious festivals, recognize ritual occasions, and mark significant life-stage transitions by performing music, and through dancing and holding communal festivals where songs are sacred. At the vaulted rim of the high Andes, mountains are worshipped, marriages celebrated, and holidays observed with a creative fusion of pre-Columbian, colonial, and more recent postcolonial melodies. In contemporary Andean communities, a song style with pre-Columbian roots, called *qarawi*, can still be heard at collective gatherings. Performed in a doleful style by pairs of elderly women, the *qarawi* often herald celebratory events (Cavero 1985). In the highlands, lilting flute and rhythmic drum ensembles (*conjuntos*), along with *charangos* (small ten-string lutes customarily fashioned from an armadillo shell) and violins, share the town plaza, country lanes, and family courtyards with accordions and brass bands (Romero 2002). Similarly, in Amazonian communities, traditional music is produced with bamboo end flutes, wooden drums, rattles, whistles, and panpipes[11] (Tschopik 1954; Isuiza Trigoso n.d.; Pinilla 1988).

Throughout Peruvian Amazonia, musical forms are deeply inflected by Andean cultural sensibilities, as demonstrated by the regional popularity of musical rhythms known as *chimaychi*, which are similar to Andean *huayno* music.[12] In a related way, an entire musical genre comprised of songs called *Los Cunchos* ("The Savages," Quechua *ch'unchu*) is reflective of Andean peoples' ethnocentric attitudes toward the inhabitants of the Amazonian lowlands. Indigenous peoples in Amazonia have used their mythical and musical expressions of life to accommodate their experiences of colonial domination (Hill 1990). Among many native Amazonian societies, such as the Warao of the rain forests of the Orinoco, music is constitutive of existence, offering entertainment, social solidarity, security, and ritual efficacy (Olsen 1996). Often linked to shamanism, music in Indigenous Amazonia is a way of inscribing the world with meaning: common throughout the region is the belief the world is ritually chanted into being (Hill 1992, 1993; Bellier 1986).

After centuries of transcultural blending, Peru has a very diverse repertoire of musical styles and performative genres employing many types of musical instruments. In Loreto, this includes musical hybrids, such as *bombo baile* ("drum dance"), a melodic fusion of *tanguiño* music from Brazil, and *cumbia* from Colombia. Similarly, significant musical variation characterizes urban Peru. *Huaynos*, *chicha*, *mulizas*, and Afro-Peruvian *cajón* (drum) music—to name but a few popular styles—intermingle in the fertile audioscapes of urban, coastal Peru, in the nightclubs, *peñas* (folkloric saloons), provincial association gatherings, and family events, like weddings or a young girl's *quinceñera* ("sweet fifteenth" birthday party).

Radio and Recorded Music

Throughout the latter half of the twentieth century, the primary means of mass communication in rural Peru was the radio. Broadcasting sounds without wires was a major technological achievement, yet one dwarfed by comparison to the social and cultural implications of coming to terms with the novel electromagnetic environment. When it first appeared on the social horizon, radio immediately became a significant site of cultural production and contestation. Rather than a *type* of cultural phenomenon, radio waves continue to function as a "*zone* of cultural debate" (Appadurai 1996: 5). Pace Adorno and the Frankfurt School's view of radio as isolating people by encouraging atomized listening, radio in rural Peru sustains imagined—albeit fractal, if not fragmented—communities. The Cocama-Cocamilla peoples—the so-called invisible natives (Stocks 1981,

1983; cf. Espinosa 1935)—provide but one of the more well-documented examples of the contested and fluid nature of collective identities in Peruvian Amazonia (Regan 1983; Agüero 1994; McKinley 2003).

When commercial radio began in Peru in the 1920s and 1930s, there were only a few stations operating in urban, coastal centers, mainly Lima. The lower powered AM transmitters available then prevented radio broadcasters from reaching anything approaching a national audience. It was not until the introduction of relatively inexpensive shortwave technology that radio became available to much wider regional, and ultimately national audiences. Most shortwave radio stations were located in Lima. This trend began to change when several dozen shortwave stations were established in the 1950s and 1960s in provincial capitals, especially in the principal market towns of the Andes. Not surprisingly, listeners preferred tuning in to these regional ("local") radio broadcasts, rather than those relayed from the coast. Because of large-scale urbanward migration, many of the prominent radio stations eventually suspended their shortwave broadcasts. This trend corresponded with the decentralization of shortwave broadcasting over the past thirty years. Throughout the 1970s and early 1980s, radio stations began to appear in the smaller provincial towns, chiefly in the northern Andean and Amazonian regions of the country.

The commercial recording industry in Peru dates to the middle of the twentieth century when Andean "folkloric" music became a staple theme of the emergent national consumer market in mass popular culture. At this time, the country's recording industry was responsible for catapulting *huayno* and *huaylas* performers to the status of "rock stars" (Otter 1985). Previously, urban elites and the nascent middle class had access to 78 rpm records, which helped popularize foreign music and dance styles, such as the *tango*, Mexican *ranchera*, and North American fox-trot, to name but a few of the novel styles introduced into the country. Following three decades of growth, the late 1980s marked the death of the LP format in favor of cheaper cassette recordings that became widely available through piracy (Romero 2001: 109–112). Today, CDs are increasingly replacing cassette recordings, though this trend is considerably less apparent in rural areas, particularly Amazonia.

The social life of radio and recorded music is a significant part of what Benedict Anderson aptly calls the "circulating sap" of the imagined community of the nation (2000: 353).[13] As a supplier of "serialized information" and a conduit of the entertainment industry, radio simultaneously produces national and regional *publics* on the one hand, and modes of local disengagement and fragmentary personal connection on the other hand. In this world-in-motion, "the various flows—of objects, persons, images, and discourses—are not coeval, convergent, isomorphic, or spatially consistent" (Appadurai 2002: 274). In this globalized world of "disjunctive flows," problems that manifest themselves in intensely local forms are often framed by contexts that are anything but locally determined (Appadurai 1990, 1996, 2002: 274). This paradox of connection and disconnection is readily apparent in radio broadcasts emanating from Lima that engage listeners in rural Peru with messages of modernity, while also accentuating people's acute disconnections from its conventional promises.

Over the past quarter of a century, the widespread introduction of portable radios and cassette players has led to the rapid diffusion of regional, national, and international musical styles throughout rural Peru. Internet cafés, televisions, CD players, and VCRs all serve to connect periurban and urban Peru with the rest of the world. Longing for the promises of modernity, younger people across the country are now vigorously embracing new musical rhythms—such as glossy techno-pop, modern Latin American dance music or *salsa*, rock, and rap—instead of the traditional musical forms that have sustained the cultural vitality and distinctiveness of their parents and grandparents' communities for generations. Aspects of Peruvian music are also making their way to a wider world audience, thanks in part to migration,[14] cultural tourism, the popular music industry, and the growing appeal of Worldbeat music.

Media Technologies and Cultural Activists

While the economic viability of the corporate music industry is reliant on encryption technologies and intellectual property regimes celebrating individual authorship, Indigenous peoples are obliged to rely on alternative strategies for cultural survival, including collaborative partnerships with cultural activists. Intellectual property debates in Peru highlight rights to biogenetic resources (see, for instance, Greene 1998; Indecopi, 2000), though there are many efforts under way to conserve and revalorize local, expressive traditions of Indigenous societies. Embracing both old and new communications technologies, many of these efforts are a special type of cultural activism: They self-consciously use the production of media and other expressive forms as means not only for nurturing local and Indigenous communities, but also for transforming them through a sort of "strategic cultural conservatism" (Ginsburg 2000).

While new technologies underpinning global interconnectedness encourage social and cultural transformations that can lead to the fragmentation of community,[15] they can also strengthen collective memory, promote social awareness, and help cultural preservation efforts. Older technologies like print media are usually not suitable for the curation of oral-based performative genres. In contrast, newer technologies—including online databases, CDs, MP3 recorded files, and digital audio players—provide promising curatorial alternatives, particularly for cultural activists interested in celebrating oral expressive forms such as music, stories, and ritual chants. CDs can combine high-fidelity audio recordings with multimedia to provide audiences with "accurate, contextualized presentations of linguistic and cultural knowledge" (Zimmerman, Zimmerman, and Bruguier 2000). For cultural activists, novel technologies like digital recorders and cameras, CD burners, and the Internet can be an important means to revalorize local, customary systems of knowledge much in the same way that older communicative technologies, such as radio broadcasting, continue to be fundamental to articulating local community identities, concerns, and aspirations.

Two particular initiatives in Peru are noteworthy examples of what I have in mind by cultural activists: the Lima-based Center for Andean Ethnomusicology (CAE), and the Iquitos-based radio project founded by the human rights nongovernmental organization (NGO) partnership, Amazonian Peoples' Resources Initiative (APRI) and Minga-Perú, a community-based women's health and development organization (Dean, Elías, McKinley, and Saul 2000). The work at the CAE is important because of its leadership role in the systematic documentation of the expressive cultures of Peru's contemporary Indigenous peoples, while Minga-Perú's innovative radio project provides culturally sensitive, locally based programming to rural Amazonian communities.

Curating Cultures: The Center for Andean Ethnomusicology

With support from the Ford Foundation, the Center for Andean Ethnomusicology (Centro de Etnomusicología Andina, formerly the Archivo de

Música Tradicional Andina) was established in 1985 at the Riva-Agüero Institute of Peru's Catholic University. Its primary mission is to document, conserve, and promote research on Andean musical traditions. Through intensive ethnographic research, members of the Lima-based CAE have audiovisually documented Andean and coastal Peruvian music through its main cultural contexts—festivals, rituals, and dances.

The CAE has long-term research experience in many regions of Andean and Coastal Peru, including the Mantaro Valley (Junin), Cajamarca, the Colca Valley, Cusco, Lambayeque, Puno, Callejón de Huayalas, Canta, Huarochiri, Piura, Ayachucho, Apurimac, and Huancavelica. Representing Peru's diverse musical expressions, the Center's holdings are extensive.[16] The Center for Andean Ethnomusicology has hundreds of hours of primary video recordings and an ample slide collection, and thousands of audiotapes, including important recordings made by José María Arguedas,[17] one of Peru's most important *indigenista* intellectuals, are represented. In addition to publishing four books, CAE staff members have produced nine albums in Spanish, nine bilingual video documentaries, one multimedia CD-ROM, and a comprehensive series of music CDs in collaboration with the Smithsonian Institution's Folkways Recordings.

The CAE is a major repository of field recordings of the music and performative dimensions of social life. Its unrivaled collections include important recordings of diverse life cycle rites, house buildings, brandings, saints' festivals, communal agrarian work sessions, and times of enjoyment, herding, carnival, and documentation of elaborate dances, like the *Danza de los Turcos* (Dance of the Turks), as well as the costumed theatrical performances accompanying the celebration of the Virgin of Carmen.

The CAE is taking the lead in developing a network of sound archives (*Red de Archivos Sonoros Andinos*). Future Center plans include expansion into Amazonia and the other Andean Republics, particularly Ecuador and Bolivia. To this end, the Center recently entered into collaborative partnership with the Institute for Otavaleno Anthropology (IOA) in Ecuador and with the Center for the Documentation of Bolivian Music (Centro Patiño) in Cochabanmba, Bolivia. Archival collections of this nature are important, given how sound recordings have contributed to the survival, revitalization, and defense of local cultural traditions elsewhere, such as in the United States and Australia (Seeger, 1997a).

Broadcasting [C]ulture: Amazonian Peoples' Resources Initiative Radio Education Project

Cultural activism is also apparent in regional media projects, such as the radio education project launched by APRI in partnership with Minga-Perú. Established in 1995, APRI is a human rights organization working with Indigenous and rural communities in the Peruvian Amazon (Dean and McKinley 1995, 1997). In collaboration with Minga-Perú, APRI helped create a radio program that disseminates culturally appropriate reproductive health education through radio broadcasts aired throughout Loreto, Peru's largest Amazonian department. Given its size, geographical isolation, poverty, and lack of transport infrastructure, Loreto is the least integrated region of the nation-state.[18] Radio plays a vital role in relaying information and entertainment and in facilitating interriverine communication in Loreto, an area whose vast proportions (134,000 square miles) and widely dispersed settlement patterns make translocal communication difficult. In Peruvian Amazonia, shortwave radio programs are important in building a sense of regional and national consciousness. They connect isolated villages with larger entities beyond their physical borders. Although regional radio stations like the Iquitos-based *La Voz de la Selva* ("The Voice of the Jungle") now compete with national and international commercial programming, the regional/local stations nonetheless retain a loyal following in riverine communities because of their attention to matters of more localized interest. The radio stations to which people listen are intimately connected to their sense of identity and place in the world.

While radio sound is often grouped into the same mass-media category as television in the decidedly televisualist-dominated field of mass-media studies, radio as a medium does have distinctive characteristics. Radio listening is often referred to as a unisensory experience in which only the audience's sense of hearing is engaged, whereas both hearing and vision is engaged in television watching. Radio sounds do, however, assume a three-dimensional *presence*. This follows from Walter Ong's (1982) seminal description of radio listening as an *enveloping experience*, or what J. E. Hayes refers to as the "felt 'presence' of radio's voices" (2000: 21).[19] Radio provokes various kinds of intense bodily responses, not to mention activating numerous social networks, cultural practices, and imagined communities.

The urban and periurban Iquiteña population receives a multitude of radio station broadcasts (shortwave, AM, and FM), but communities situated farther upriver receive only two or three different signals. These include the state radio station, several slick commercial stations broadcasting Lima-based programming, and a community-based radio station run by the Catholic Church. Outside the larger towns of Loreto (such as Nauta and Requena), *ribereño* or peasant communities typically have no amenities (electricity and running water), making the mass medium of choice the battery-powered shortwave radio. Shortwave radio is a principal method of communication between Amazonian settlements. Radio listeners contact distant relatives through paid personal messages—called *comunicados* or *servicios sociales*—which are broadcast from Iquitos to reach distant areas.

With the technical and financial support of APRI, Minga-Perú began in 1998 to broadcast a radio program, *¡Bienvenida Salud! (Welcome to Health!)*, three evenings a week for twenty-five minutes to an audience of more than 800,000. Through a lively mix of "sociodramas" (minisoap operas), testimonials, interviews, and local music, *¡Bienvenida Salud!* engages the audience with health themes, human rights matters, and cultural revalorization issues. Minga-Perú's radio project reflects a practical and culturally responsive participatory approach to revivifying culture, community well-being, and individual self-esteem through its treatment of issues of consequence.

In response to low levels of literacy, a network of community-based correspondents was created to record testimonials, stories, and music[20] and to report on local news and events of importance. Minga-Perú's Iquitos office receives dozens of letters each week from radio program listeners, and tapes many interviews and musical performances during regular visits to rural communities throughout the province of Loreto. Letters are sent to Minga-Perú from communities located as much as two weeks away from Iquitos by river travel. The production staff at *¡Bienvenida Salud!* uses the letters, taped testimonials, interviews, and music as a basis for selecting program themes (Dean et al. 2000; Davenport, Mckinley, Ventsam, and Elías 2002; McKinley and Jensen 2003). In this way, Minga-Perú's radio program plays a critical role in spreading culturally sensitive health information in an entertaining format, using dramatic and vernacular musical forms to encourage involvement in community welfare. Moreover, by inserting their own stories and expressive forms into the national and regional "mediascapes" (Appadurai 1990), local Amazonian communities have begun to see radio broadcasts as a means for furthering social and political transformation.

Unlike commercial radio, which undermines local cultural traditions by stressing the products of the corporate culture industry, Minga-Perú's broadcasts have from their inception self-consciously used media to help members of widely scattered communities to uphold local knowledge and strengthen distinctive cultural identities. The potential for cultural revitalization is significant among the numerically dominant Cocama-Cocamilla peoples of Loreto, who have historically been encouraged to deny their cultural heritage (Faust 1963; Stocks 1981). A combination of local programming, an extensive grassroots network of correspondents, and a production staff responsive to community issues has facilitated educating the public on matters of health and human rights through radio broadcasts of narratives and tape-recorded music that stresses local cultural themes, traditions, and interpretations of history. Radio broadcasting that embraces programming emphasizing vernacular modes of speech[21] as well as regional and local expressive traditions holds the promise of cultural revalorization for Indigenous peoples like the Cocama as they struggle to imagine their place in the Peruvian nation.

Reconceptualizing the Public Sphere: Indigenous Peoples and the Global Cultural Economy

Controversy over ownership of Indigenous music encourages us to pay much closer attention to the broader framework of human rights. In assessing the anthropological nature of intellectual property rights and Indigenous peoples, we must attend to a number of the political possibilities and moral dilemmas such legal mechanisms pose for the vitality of local systems of knowledge. Given that rights are radically contingent on the culturally constructed worlds in which they are embedded, common recourse to legal frameworks for achieving instrumental aims does not imply the existence of a shared moral order. Conflict over the ownership of local or traditional music highlights the extent to which we must consider both the possibilities and limitations implicit in translating essentially European ideas about rights into non-Western cultural contexts.

Calling into question the efficacy of overarching international instruments rather than locally inspired initiatives, observers have noted the tensions between protection of intellectual property and the maintenance of a rich and vital public domain. (See Cultural Survival 1991; Riley and Moran 2001; Jerome and Laveaga 2001.) The pragmatic efficacy and moral rightness of legislation intended to safeguard the intellectual property rights of marginalized groups should always be queried. The difficulty of achieving "informed consent" in transcultural interactions accentuates this point. While intellectual property protection mechanisms have been designed with an eye to defending Indigenous peoples from misappropriation of their knowledge, these mechanisms will not in and of themselves shield traditional knowledge, nor protect the languages that encode such knowledge from the radically transformative pressures of global capitalism. What this calls for is cultural activism employing novel technologies in such ways that secure the universal human right to be *different*.

In light of the digital revolution and the global cultural economy that now threatens to make the romantic notion of authorship redundant, is it naïve to believe that Indigenous peoples' intellectual rights can be respected, let alone adequately defined (Boyle 1997)? However one responds to these questions, what is clear about globalization is that cultural and political claims for sovereignty are integral to Indigenous peoples' struggles for autonomy (Dean 2002a, 2002b). Invariably, access to digital information transforms customary systems of knowledge and intergenerational systems of authority and power. How then can Indigenous peoples respond to those forms of cultural appropriation that seriously compromise their ability to decide their own futures? How should digital information be curated, not to mention accessed? And how do we develop culturally appropriate mechanisms for equitable sharing of local systems of knowledge in ways that ensure intergenerational, cultural continuity? The issues involved are complex, and the repercussions profound, for what is at stake is the cultural survival of Indigenous peoples. Nowhere is this more apparent than for the spoken and sung word.

From musical performance to mythical utterances, the cultural vitality of Indigenous peoples' expressive traditions depends on a radical reconceptualization of the public sphere in such a manner that considers collective interests, rather than mere commercial gain (García Canclini 2001: 133). In engaging a pluralistic, collective public sphere the mass media and networks of information must go beyond what García Canclini calls a "Gutenbergian conception of culture" (2001: 155; cf. Tyler 1992). Expanding alternative media—particularly local, regional, and minority controlled radio, television, film, and recording industries—is clearly central to establishing democratic, pluricultural institutions that can resist the violent and dehumanizing tendencies of global capitalism.

Acknowledgments

I would like to acknowledge the contributions that my colleagues at the University of Kansas and the Universidad Nacional Mayor de San Marcos, as well as Cultural Survival have made to this chapter. I have also benefited from the keen insight of Michelle McKinley, Mary Riley, Santiago Rivas, Raul Romero, and the anonymous reviewers of this text.

Notes

An abbreviated version of this chapter appeared in *Cultural Survival Quarterly* under the title "Digitizing Indigenous Sounds," vol. 24, no. 4 (2001): 41–45.

1. This is not to imply that Indigenous peoples necessarily agree on what is the "authentic tradition," particularly when the process of cultural revalorization is itself animated by nationalist aspirations of political liberation (Hanson 1997).

2. By "traditional" I do not mean to imply that cultural practices are static. As many commentators have noted, traditions are "invented" (Hobsbawm and Ranger 1983).

3. For a recent discussion of the economic aspects of intellectual property rights law, biotechnology, and sustainable development, see Cottier and Mavroidis (2002).

4. Associated with high fidelity and a slogan made famous when Ella Fitzgerald first shattered glass with her voice recorded on audiotape, Memorex is one of the most recognized names in consumer goods. With its corporate slogan "is it live . . . or is it . . . ?" Memorex skillfully markets the ambiguities of reproducing authenticity.

5. In our "world of flows" (Appadurai 1996), "objects include ideas and ideologies, people and goods, images and messages, technologies and techniques" (Appadurai 2002: 274).

6. In the words of Sahlins, "localization develops apace with globalization" (1999: 410; among others, see also Strathern 1995; Appadurai 1996, 2002).

7. In a somewhat similar fashion, David Guss's masterful ethnography of the Yekuana of Venezuela highlights the fundamental distinction between collective chants (*ademi*) and individual chants (*aichudi*) (1989: 65–68, 146–147).

8. Riley and Moran note that the nearest approximation to collective ownership is corporate ownership of patents (2001: 7, fn. 1).

9. According to Arguedas (1977), colonial Spanish overlords prohibited Indigenous musicians from playing guitars but encouraged them to play the harp and violin.

10. A wonderful example of music featuring saxophones, clarinets, violins, harps, and drums from this region is the CD *Traditional Music of Peru, Vol. 2: The Mantaro Valley* (1995). Smithsonian Folkways Recordings #40467.

11. For a relatively early example of recorded Indigenous music from Peruvian Amazonia, consult *Indian Music of the Upper Amazon* (1954, Ethnic Folkways Library).

12. An insightful analysis of *huaynos* as Quechua oral poetry is given in Escobar (1985).

13. In the age of globalization, cultural production has challenged the way national culture has been conceived as a bounded entity (Buell 1994). For a cogent examination of the dynamics of cultural survival and contemporary nationalism, see Anderson's recent contribution (2003).

14. The role of migration is addressed in Turino's study (1993) of the social forces shaping contemporary Peruvian musical life. The multicultural and transnational experiences of Andean immigrants living in the United States are provided in the ethnographic documentary *Transnational Fiesta: 1992*. Produced by Wilton Martinez and Paul Gelles, this critically acclaimed video chronicles the lives of the Quispes, a family of Peruvian immigrants living in Washington, D.C., who return to their Andean hometown, Cabanaconde, to sponsor the annual patron saint celebration (Virgin of Carmen). *Transnational Fiesta* illustrates how the migrants' identities are shaped both by their ongoing participation in the ceremonial life of their natal community and by their lived experiences in the United States. In so doing, the video reveals the nuances of cultural production, the importance of religious syncretism and transnational migration, as well as the enduring legacy of racism.

15. A dramatic example of this communal fragmentation was brought home to me a few years ago while I was visiting an Alamas-Quichua community in the Peruvian Amazon. Thanks to their collaboration with the illicit drug economy, the community had just been introduced to satellite TV broadcasts when I arrived on the scene. While quizzing me on how it was possible to shrink people so that they could perform inside the small television set, elders bitterly complained about the socially atomizing impact of TV. Rather than socializing collectively, members of

the community spent their evenings viewing their own personal or family TV. This pattern of audience participation differs dramatically from the social consumption of radio in rural Amazonia, a topic that has received limited scholarly attention.

16. The Center for Andean Ethnomusicology currently has over 600 videos, 900 audio recordings, and at least 18,000 photographic slides.

17. José María Arguedas (1911–1969) made a series of music recordings during the 1960s while he was associated with the Casa de Cultura and the Museo Nacional de Cultura (Romero 2002: 157). A number of these recordings, including an example of the "Los Chunchos" songs, appear on CD 2 of *Sonidos Andinos: una antología de la música campesina del Perú* (Centro de Etnomusicología Andina, IRA-PUCP).

18. Loreto occupies roughly one third of Peruvian national territory and is among the least-populated regions of the country. In terms of cultural, linguistic, and biological diversity, it is Peru's richest department (Dean et al. 2000). However, judged in terms of traditional indicators of poverty, Loreto is the most impoverished region of Peru.

19. Hayes argues persuasively that even though the scholarly community has often described "radio sound as 'disembodied' and 'ethereal,' many listeners report being bodily 'moved' and 'touched' by the intimate, emotional resonances of radio voices" (2000: 22).

20. To date, no music has been marketed by Minga-Perú. Instead, the recordings have been used as primary content for the radio broadcast *¡Bienvenida Salud!*

21. Speaking the Loretano dialect of Spanish is referred to as *charapeando*, a term derived from the word *charapa* (tortoise), a euphemism for residents of Loreto. On the Loretano dialect of spoken Spanish, see Castonguay (1990); Alvarez Vita (1990), and Tovar (1996).

References

Agüero, O. A.
El milenio en la Amazonía: mito-utopía tupi-cocama o la subversión del orden simbólico. Quito: Abya-Yala, 1994.

Alvarez Vita, Juan
Diccionario de Peruanismos. Lima: Librería Studium Ediciones, 1990.

Anderson, Benedict
"El Malhadado País." In *The Spectre of Comparisons: Nationalism, Southeast Asia & the World*, 333–359. London: Verso, 2000.

"Nationalism & Cultural Survival in Our Time." In *At the Risk of Being Heard: Identity, Indigenous Rights, and Postcolonial States*, edited by Bartholomew Dean and Jerome Levi, foreword by Winona LaDuke, 165–190. Ann Arbor: University of Michigan Press, 2003.

Appadurai, Arjun

"Disjuncture and Difference in the Global Cultural Economy." *Public Culture,* vol. 2, no. 2 (1990): 1–24.

Modernity at Large: Cultural Dimensions of Globalization. Minneapolis: University of Minnesota Press, 1996.

"Grassroots Globalization and the Research Imagination." In *The Anthropology of Politics: A Reader in Ethnography, Theory, and Critique*, edited by Joan Vincent, 270–284. Oxford: Blackwell Publishers, 2002.

Arguedas, José María

Nuestra Musica Popular y sus Intérpretes. Lima: Mosca Azul y Horionte Editores, 1977.

Bellier, Irene

"Los cantos Mai Huna del yaje (Amazonia Peruana)." *América Indígena*, vol. 44, no. 1 (1986): 128–145.

Benjamin, Walter

"The Work of Art in the Age of Mechanical Reproduction." In *Illuminations—Walter Benjamin*, edited by H. Arendt, 217–252. New York: Schocken, 1968.

Bolaños, César, et al.

La música en el Perú. Prólogo de Edgar Valcárcel. Presentación de Alvaro Llona Bernal. Lima: Patronato Popular y Porvenir Pro-Música Clásica, 1985.

Boyle, J.

Shamans, Software, and Spleens: Law and the Construction of the Information Society. Cambridge: Harvard University Press, 1997.

Buell, Frederick

National Culture and the New Global System. Baltimore: Johns Hopkins University Press, 1994.

Burnett, Robert

The Global Jukebox: The International Music Industry. New York: Routledge, 1996.

Cánepa Koch, Gisela (ed.)
Identidades Representadas: Performance, experiencia y memoria en los Andes. Lima: Pontifica Universidad Católica del Perú, 2001.

Castonguay, Luis
Vocabulario Regional del Oriente Peruano. Iquitos: Centro de Estudios Teologicos de la Amazonía, 1990.

Cavero, Jesús
"El qarawi y su función social." *Allpanchis*, vol. 15, no. 25 (1985): 233–270.

Coombe, R. J.
The Cultural Life of Intellectual Properties: Authorship, Appropriation, and the Law. Durham: Duke University Press, 1998.

Cottier, Thomas, and Petros C. Mavroidis (eds.)
Intellectual Property: Trade, Competition, and Sustainable Development. Ann Arbor: University of Michigan Press, 2002.

Crystal, David
English as a Global Language. Cambridge: Cambridge University Press, 1998.

Language Death. Cambridge: Cambridge University Press, 2000.

Cultural Survival
"Intellectual Property Rights: The Politics of Ownership." *Cultural Survival Quarterly*, vol. 15, no. 1 (1991).

Davenport, B., and M. Mckinley, S. Ventsam, and E. Elías
"Fostering Reproductive Health through Entertainment-education in the Peruvian Amazon: The Radio Broadcast '*Bienvenida Salud!*'" *Communication Theory*, vol.12, no. 2 (2002): 192–205.

Dean, Bartholomew
"Language, Culture & Power: Intercultural Bilingual Education among the Urarina of Peruvian Amazonia." *Practicing Anthropology.* (Special Issue: Reversing Language Shift in Indigenous America., L. Watahomigie, T. McCarty, and A. Yamamoto eds., vol. 20, no. 2 [1999]: 39–43.)

"State Power & Indigenous Peoples in Peruvian Amazonia: A Lost Decade 1990–2000." In *The Politics of Ethnicity: Indigenous Peoples in Latin American States*, edited by David Maybury-Lewis, 199–238. Cambridge: Harvard University Press, 2002a.

"Critical Re-vision: Clastres' Chronicle and the Optic of Primitivism." In *Best of Anthropology Today, 1974–2000*, edited by Jonathan Benthall, 66–71. London: Routledge, 2002b.

Dean, B., E. Elías, M. McKinley, and R. Saul
The Amazonian Peoples' Resources Initiative: Promoting Reproductive Rights and Community Development in the Peruvian Amazon. *Health and Human Rights: An International Journal*, vol. 4, no. 2 (2000): 219–226.

Dean, Bartholomew, and Jerome M. Levi (eds.)
At the Risk of Being Heard: Identity, Indigenous Rights, and Postcolonial States. Foreword by Winona LaDuke. Ann Arbor: University of Michigan Press, 2003.

Dean, Bartholomew, and Michelle McKinley
The Project: Amazonian Peoples Resources Initiative (APRI). *Indigenous Knowledge and Development Monitor*, vol. 3, no. 3 (1995).

Building Partnerships in Health, Education and Social Justice. *Cultural Survival Quarterly*, vol. 21, no. 3 (1997): 14–15.

Escobar M., Gabriel
The Words of the Quecha Waynos of Cuzco. *Latin American Indian Literatures Journal*, vol. 8, no. 1 (1985): 1–12.

Espinosa, Lucas
Los tupí del oriente peruano, estudio lingüistico y etnográfico. Madrid: Publicaciones de la Expedición Lingüistico, 1935.

Ethnic Folkways Library
Indian Music of the Upper Amazon. Sung by Ucayali Indians (Shipibo, Conibo, Campa, and Cocama) with percussion. Program notes by H. Tschopik and W. Rhodes. Folkways Records FE 4458. Ethnic Folkways Library Album No. P 458. New York: Folkways Records & Service Corp,. 1954.

Faust, Norma
El lenguaje de los hombres y mujeres en cocama. *Perú Indígena*, vol. 10, nos. 22–23 (1963): 115–17.

Feld, Steven
Notes on the World Beat. *Public Culture Bulletin*, vol. 1, no. 1 (1988).

From Schizophonia to Schismogenesis: The Discourses and Practices of World Music and World Beat In *The Traffic in Culture: Refiguring Art and Anthropology*, edited by George Marcus and Fred R. Myers, 96–126. Berkeley: University of California Press, 1995.

García Canclini, Néstor
Consumers and Citizens: Globalization and Multicultural Conflicts. Trans. and intro. by G. Yúdice. Minneapolis: University of Minnesota, 2001.

Ginsburg, Faye
Resources of Hope: Learning from the Local in a Transnational Era. In *Indigenous Cultures in an Interconnected World*, edited by C. Smith and G. K. Ward, 27–47. Vancouver: University of British Columbia Press, 2000.

Graham, Laura
How Should an Indian Speak? Amazonian Indians and the Symbolic Politics of Language in the Global Public Sphere. In *Indigenous Movements, Self-Representation, and the State in Latin America*, edited by Kay Warren and Jean Jackson, 181–228. Austin: University of Texas Press, 2003.

Greene, Shane
The Shaman's Needle: Development, Shamanic Agency, and Intermedicality in Aguaruna Lands, Peru. *American Ethnologist*, vol. 25, no. 4 (1998): 634–658.

Guss, David
To Weave and Sing: Art, Symbol, and Narrative in the South American Rain Forest. Berkeley: University of California Press, 1989.

Hanson, F. Allan
Empirical Anthropology, Postmodernism, and the Invention of Tradition. In *Present Is Past: Some Uses of Tradition in Native Societies*, edited by M. Mauzé, 195–214. New York: University Press of America, Inc., 1997.

Hayes, J. E.
Radio Nation: Communication, Popular Culture, and Nationalism in Mexico 1920–1950. Austin: University of Texas Press, 2000.

Hill, Jonathan
Myth, Music, and History: Poetic Transformations of Narrative Discourse in an Amazonian Society. *Journal of Folklore Research*, vol. 27, nos. 1/2 (1990): 115–132.

A Musical Aesthetic of Ritual Curing in the Northwest Amazon. *Portals of Power: Shamanism in South America*, edited by E. Jean Matteson Langdon and Gerhard Baer, 175–210. Albuquerque: University of New Mexico Press, 1992.

Keepers of the Scared Chants: The Poetics of Ritual in an Amazonian Society. Tucson: University of Arizona Press, 1993.

Hobsbawm, Eric, and Terence Ranger (ed.)
The Invention of Tradition. Cambridge: Cambridge University Press, 1983.

Holzmann, Rodolfo, and José María Arguedas
Panorama de la música tradicional del Perú. Lima: Escuela Nacional de Música y Danzas Folklóricas, 1965.

Indecopi
Propuesta de regimen de protección de los concomientos colectivos de los pueblos indígenas. *Documento de Trabajo* N° 010-2000, Área de Estudios Económicos del Indecopi: Lima, 2000.

Isuiza Trigoso, Javier
La Amazonía y sus Canciones. Iquitos. (n.d.)

Jameson, Frederic
Globalization and Strategy. *New Left Review*, vol. 4, second series (2000): 49–68.

Jameson, Frederic, and Masao Miyoshi (eds.)
The Cultures of Globalization. Durham: Duke University Press, 1998.

Jerome, Jessica, and Gabriela Laveaga
Intellectual Property Rights & Indigenous People: The Making and Unmaking of an Anthropological Object of Study. Panel presented at the 100th annual meeting, American Anthropological Association, Washington, D.C., Nov. 29, 2001.

Leuthold, Steven
Indigenous Aesthetics: Native Art, Media, and Identity. Austin: University of Texas Press, 1998.

Martinez, Wilton, and Paul Gelles
Transnational Fiesta. Berkeley: University of California Extension, Center for Media and Independent Learning, 1992.

Mattelart, Armand
Networking the World, 1794–2000. Trans. by Liz Carey-Libbrecht and James A. Cohen. Minneapolis: University of Minnesota Press, 2000.

Maybury-Lewis, David
Traditional Music in Community Life. *Cultural Survival Quarterly*, vol. 20, no. 4 (1997): 3.

McKinley, Michelle
Planning Other Families: Negotiating Population and Identity Politics in the Peruvian Amazon. *Identities: Global Studies in Culture and Power*, vol. 10, no. 1 (2003): 30–58.

McKinley, Michelle, and Lene Jensen
In Our Own Voices: Women's Radio Programming in the Amazonian Mediascape. *Critical Studies in Media Communication*, vol. 20, no. 2 (2003): 10–31.

Meisch, Lynn
Andean Entrepreneurs: Otavalo Merchants and Musicians in the Global Arena. Austin: University of Texas Press, 2002.

Niezen, Ronald
The Origins of Indigenism: Human Rights and Politics of Identity. Berkeley: University of California Press, 2003.

Novick, A.
Drumming in the Shadow of a Satellite Dish. *Cultural Survival Quarterly*, vol. 20, no. 4 (1997): 33–37.

Olsen, Dale
Music of the Warao of Venezuela: Song People of the Rain Forest. Gainesville: University Press of Florida, 1996.

Music of El Dorado: The Ethnomusicology of Ancient South American Cultures. Gainesville: University Press of Florida, 2002.

Ong, Walter
Orality and Literacy: The Technologizing of the World. London: Routledge, 1982.

Otter, Elisabeth den
Music and Dance of Indians and Mestizos in an Andean Valley of Peru. Delft, The Netherlands: Eburon, 1985.

Pinilla, Enrique
La música de la selva peruana. *Shupihui*, vol. 13, nos. 45/46 (1988): 9–35.

Regan, Jaime
Hacia la tierra sin mal. Estudio de la religion del pueblo en la Amazonía. Iquitos: CAAAP-IIAP, 1983.

Regis, Humphrey
American Appropriation of Reggae. *Caribbean Review*, vol. 16 (1990): 7.

Riley, Mary, and Katy Moran
Protecting Indigenous Intellectual Property Rights: Tools That Work. *Cultural Survival Quarterly*, vol. 24, no. 4 (2201): 6–7.

Roel Mendizabal, Pedro
De Folklore a Cultura Híbridas: rescatando raíces, redefiniendo fronteras entre nos/otros. In *No hay país más diverso: Compendio de antropología peruana*, edited by Carlos Iván Degregori, 74–122. Lima: Red para el Desarrollo de las Ciencias Sociales en el Perú, 2000.

Romero, Raúl
Cambio musical y resistencia cultural en los Andes centrales del Perú. In *Musica, Danzas y Mascaras en los Andes,* 21–60. Lima: Pontifica Universidad Católica del Perú, 1993.

Debating the Past: Music, Memory, and Identity in the Andes. New York: Oxford University Press, 2001.

(ed.) *Sonidos Andinos: una antología de la música campesina del Perú.* Lima: Centro de Etnomusicología Andina, Pontifica Universidad Católica del Perú, 2002.

Rowe, William, and Vivian Schelling
Memory and Modernity: Popular Culture in Latin America. London: Verso Books, 1991.

Sahlins, Marshall
Two or Three Things That I Know about Culture. *Journal of the Royal Anthropological Institute*, no. 5 (1999): 399–421.

Seeger, Anthony
Traditional Music in Community Life: Aspects of Performance, Recordings, and Preservation. *Cultural Survival Quarterly,* vol. 20, no. 4 (1997a): 20–22.

The Sound of Music: Suyá Song Structure and Experience. *Cultural Survival Quarterly*, vol. 20, no. 4 (1997b): 23–28.

Ethnomusicology and Music Law. In *Borrowed Power: Essays on Cultural Appropriation*, edited by Bruce Ziff and Pratima V. Rao, 52–67. New Brunswick: Rutgers University Press, 1997c.

Stocks, Anthony
Los natives invisibles. Notas sobre la historia y realidad actual de los cocamilla del Río Huallaga. Lima: CAAAP, 1981.

Native Enclaves in the Upper Amazon: A Case of Regional Non-Integration. *Ethnohistory*, vol. 30, no. 2 (1983): 77–92.

Strathern, Marilyn
The Nice Thing about Culture Is That Everyone Has It. In *Shifting Contexts*, edited by M. Strathern, 153–176. London: Routledge, 1995.

Taussig, Michael
Tactility and Distraction. In *Rereading Cultural Anthropology*, edited by George Marcus, 8–14. Durham: Duke University Press, 1992.

Tovar, Enrique D.
Vocabulario del Oriente Peruano. Lima: Universidad Nacional Mayor de San Marocs, 1996.

Tschopik, Harry
The Setting. *Indian Music of the Upper Amazon*. Ethnic Folkways Library Album No. P 458. New York: Folkways Records & Service Corp, 1954.

Turino, Thomas
Moving Away from Silence: Music of the Peruvian Altiplano and the Experience of Urban Migration. Chicago: University of Chicago Press, 1993.

Tyler, Stephen
On Being Out of Words. In *Rereading Cultural Anthropology*, edited by George Marcus, 1–7. Durham: Duke University Press, 1992.

Wallerstein, Immanuel
The Modern World-System: Capitalist Agriculture and the Origins of the European World-Economy in the Sixteenth Century. New York: Academic Press, 1976.

The Politics of the World-Economy: The States, the Movements, and the Civilizations. New York: Cambridge University Press, 1984.

Wallis, Roger, and Krister Malm
Big Sounds from Small Peoples: The Music Industry in Small Countries. New York: Pendragon Press, 1984.

Watahomigie, Lucille, Teresa McCarty, and Akira Yamamoto (eds.)
Reversing Language Shift in Indigenous America: Collaborations and Views from the Field. *Practicing Anthropology*, vol. 21, Theme Issue (1999): 2.

Weiner, Annette
Culture and Our Discontents. *American Anthropologist*, vol. 97, no. 1 (1995): 14–40.

Wolf, Eric

Europe and the People without History. Berkeley: University of California Press, 1982.

Zimmerman, L., K. Zimmerman, and L. Bruguier

Cyberspace Smoke Signals: New Technologies and Native American Ethnicity. In *Indigenous Cultures in an Interconnected World*, edited by C. Smith and G. K. Ward, 69–86. Vancouver: University of British Columbia Press, 2000.

CHAPTER 3
INTELLECTUAL PROPERTY PROTECTION AND THE MARKET FOR ALASKA NATIVE ARTS AND CRAFTS

Julie Hollowell

> My people will sleep for one hundred years. When they awake, it will be the artists that give them back their spirit.
>
> —Louis Riel in Cardinal-Shubert 1989: 20

In many indigenous communities, commercial art production, stimulated in part by global tourism and consumption, is one form of livelihood people pursue to cope with the economic pressures of a cash economy and the disruption of subsistence lifestyles. (For further reading on the contemporary market in indigenous arts, see Belk and Groves 1999; Blundell 1993; Dubin 2001; Graburn 1976; Marcus and Myers 1995; Mullin 2001; F. Myers 2001; Nash 1993; Phillips and Steiner 1999; Steiner 1994; Tice 1995.) This worldwide expansion of the market for indigenous arts has come with a parallel escalation in the commercial exploitation of indigenous designs, stories, performance, and other art forms. The proliferation of products on the market that imitate, misrepresent, and profit from alleged associations with indigenous culture has compelled indigenous peoples to turn to the domain of intellectual property law to find ways to clarify and protect their rights.

The inability of current intellectual property law, grounded in Western concepts of individualism and innovation, to protect collective or perpetual interests in indigenous forms of cultural expression is well documented. (For examples, see Brown 1998; Coombe 1995, 1997; Janke 1998; Golvan 1992; Hoban 2002; Pask 1993; Posey 1996; Ziff and Rao

1997.) Works of art and craft, as tangible objects that enter a commercial market, tend to be more compatible with prevailing legal interpretations of intellectual property—copyright, trademarks, rights to designs, and protection against misrepresentation and unfair competition—than many other forms of indigenous knowledge. While efforts are underway to draft new national and international guidelines and frameworks for indigenous intellectual property protection (Daes 1993, 1998; Janke 1998; López 2002; WIPO 2001), indigenous artists and organizations have become ever more vocal and persistent about pursuing remedies by whatever means are available, including mobilizing intellectual property laws to meet their needs (Pask 1993: 80–82).

This chapter looks at the Silver Hand, a trademark used since 1972 to identify work produced by indigenous peoples of Alaska, and evaluates its ability to protect intellectual property rights of Alaska Native artisans.[1] After describing some of the problems faced by indigenous arts that enter

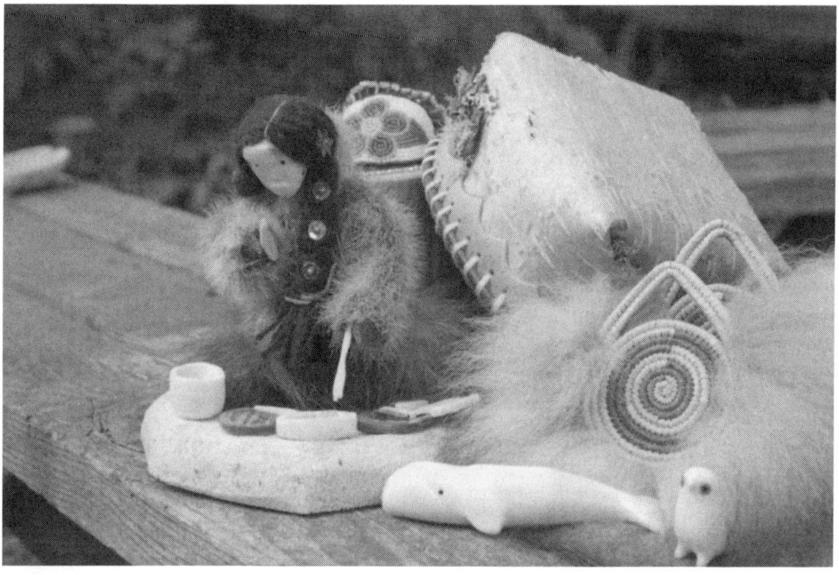

Figure 3.1. Work by Alaska Native artisans. Clockwise, from left: Yup'ik dance fans by Florence Nanuk of Hooper Bay (grass and fox fur); basket by Verda Paul of Northway (birchbark, willow); hairpiece by Laura Kaningok of Gambell (beads, seal hide); doll (woman cooking) by Kimberly Iyakitan of Gambell (old and new ivory, baleen, beaver fur, sealskin, cloth, yarn, sequins on whalebone base); walrus by Mark Nupowhotuk of Gambell (walrus ivory and baleen); owl by Maxine Ungott of Gambell (old and new walrus ivory, baleen, india ink).

the marketplace in Alaska today, I explain the Silver Hand program and summarize responses to its use. A brief history of trademarks issued for Native-made arts in Alaska outlines the role taken by federal and state agencies in the development of the Native arts market. Finally, I consider additional ways to strengthen intellectual property protection for Alaska Native arts and artists and return to the overarching need to support indigenous initiatives to define, protect, and manage intellectual and cultural property rights.

The Importance of Native Art Production

According to the Indian Arts and Crafts Board, by 1997, sales of Native arts and crafts in the United States generated well over a billion dollars in gross revenues annually (Abeita n.d.: 3). In some areas of the country, particularly those with large Native populations, arts and crafts are a primary source of income for a majority of Native families.[2] In Alaska, home to over 98,000 indigenous peoples who comprise 15.6 percent of the state's population (U.S. Census Bureau 2000), the economic importance of Native art production can hardly be overestimated, though few statewide statistics exist to gauge its actual significance.[3] Over half of all Alaska Natives live in mixed cash and subsistence economies, and, for many of them, locally produced arts and crafts act as vital supplements to income and one of the only sources of cash not dependent on government programs. Taking artwork to town is almost like having money in your pocket. But arts and crafts are more than just a safety net; they are, as one carver described, a cultural gift and a source of self-esteem and identity within the Native community (Alaska *News Nightly*, 2 September 1999, heard on KNBA radio station, frequency 90.3, Anchorage, Alaska).

On the other hand, government agencies have, since the 1930s, heavily promoted the commercialization of Native arts in Alaska for their economic development potential, not so much as a way to improve the economic situation of Native artisans as for the benefit of the state's fastest growing industry—tourism. Since 1990, the number of tourists coming to Alaska has grown by over 60 percent, and in 2001, 1.2 million summer "visitors" spent over 1.5 billion dollars in the state (Northern Economics, Inc. 2002a, b). At the same time, more and more tourists are choosing to spend their money on Native cultural experiences and attractions (Alaska

DCED 1994: 4).[4] This makes the sale of Native arts big business in Alaska, important not only to Native producers but to a host of other commercial interests.

Problems with Misrepresentation

Each year about half of the 80 million dollars tourists spend on retail purchases in Alaska goes to purchase goods marketed as Native arts and crafts (Haines 1996). But what are people really buying? The Alaska Department of Commerce and Economic Development estimates that 75–80 percent of what gets displayed and sold as Native work is not actually made by Alaska Natives at all (CSANAC 1994: 18; MacPherson 1994a). Shops are filled with imitation and imported Native-style art with labels that skirt legal definitions of misrepresentation and consumer fraud.

Consider the following scenario:

> You're on an Alaskan cruise, and your ship, a huge moving hotel, has docked at the foot of the mountains in Juneau for thirty-six hours. The narrow streets are crammed with tourists and gift shops, and you find yourself in a store called Native Arts, browsing for something that truly reflects Alaska, maybe something made in a Native village, to take home. Animal figurines, miniature totem poles, dolls, mugs, and T-shirts fill the shelves, and displays of jewelry, baskets, and carvings line the walls. You pick up a small totem pole, but put it down after noticing a tiny label, "Made in China." Another totem pole, about eight inches tall, has a tag that reads "Authentic Reproductions, Inc. Designed by an Alaska Native artist."[5] The back of the tag tells a story about the pole, but dozens of these stare from the shelf, all alike and, on a closer look, all made of a wood-like resin. Your eye catches a slightly larger totem pole of real wood, the only one of its kind. It has a black and silver "Authentic Alaska Native Art" sticker on the bottom and the signature of someone from the Native village of Saxman, but the price is ten times higher than you had planned to spend.
>
> In the corner stand some knee-high, brightly painted totem poles labeled "Hand-painted Native Alaskan cedar. Made in

Alaska." The price seems reasonable, and the clerk tells you they represent an original Haida design. She doesn't mention that the poles came from a dealer who sent Alaskan cedar to workshops in Bali for carving, or that the right to use the Haida artist's design had resulted from a messy legal settlement.[6]

You move to a case near the front of the store to look at carvings of bears, seals, walruses, and birds made from walrus ivory. Some of the whiter ivory carvings have price tags of up to $100 an inch, while other pieces, less expensive and made from a darker-colored ivory, sit next to a handwritten sign that says "Native style." You ask the clerk why the whiter ivory pieces are more expensive. She explains that white ivory is "new" ivory. Only Alaska Natives can legally kill walrus and use the new, white ivory, so the price of these "Native-made" pieces is higher. If I'm concerned about people killing walrus, she adds, perhaps I should choose the older "fossil" ivory, since "no animals were killed to make the piece." She neglects to say that Native carvers depend on the sale of carvings of new ivory almost as much as their families depend on walrus meat for subsistence and survival, or that non-Natives have produced the Native-style ivory carvings, using pieces of old ivory mined from archaeological sites.

You inquire about Chupak, the name on most of the bone sculptures of Inuit hunters filling a table. The clerk hands you a card about a Cambodian carver, now living in Alaska, named Chivly Chup. "Inspired by the indigenous cultures of the great state of Alaska," Chup uses Native themes in his work and has added "-ak" for "Alaska" to his signature. The card doesn't mention that in 1994, Chup's agent, a major wholesaler of Native-style art, used state economic development funds to set up an ivory carving workshop in a Native village. He sent Chup there to carve and marketed his carvings as "Made in a Native Alaskan Village." Today Chup works out of Chupak Carving Arts, a large workshop in Juneau that produces thousands of "Native-style" bone and soapstone sculptures for the tourist market.

Next you inquire about the black label with a silver hand. The clerk informs you that some Native artists like to put the "Silver Hand" on their work to show that an Alaska Native made it, but

> by no means do all Natives use the stickers. "Then how can I tell if something was made by an Alaska Native or not?" you wonder out loud. "Well, if there's a Silver Hand sticker you know for sure. Otherwise, you might be able to tell by the sound of the name."

In 1996, violations of the intellectual property rights of Alaska Native artists prompted the Federal Trade Commission (FTC) to take its most aggressive action against counterfeit Native art in decades. After years of investigation, the agency accused Ngoc Ly and his backer, Native art dealer Kurt Tripp, of misrepresenting work as that of Alaska Native carvers. Tripp had provided Ly, a Vietnamese carver also known as Eddie Lynd or Eddie Lee, with a workshop in Seattle where Ly carved old ivory, bone, and soapstone under the name "Lyngoc." Tripp and Ly also paid Ron Komok, a Nome Native living on the streets of Seattle, to use his name (MacPherson 1994a). The FTC probably would not have bothered to pursue a smaller operation, but Ly was making half a million dollars a year selling Native-themed sculptures. Both men received fines of $20,000—a sum Tripp called "miniscule"—and had to clearly label pieces as *Native made* or *Native style* and stop using Native-sounding names (Melzer 1996). A year after the settlement, pieces by "Lyngoc" still sat on the shelves of shops throughout Alaska, sometimes next to work signed by "Eddie Lee."

Problems with misrepresentation of indigenous art like those described above are certainly not new, nor are they specific to Alaska. Studies estimate that around 50 percent of all Native or Indian arts and crafts sold in the United States have not been made by American Indian people (Abeita n.d.: 4), and in places with higher indigenous populations, like Alaska or the American Southwest, the situation is more severe.[7] Given a choice between two similar items, most buyers prefer to purchase Native-made goods—according to the FTC, people will pay up to 30–40 percent more for work made by Native artists (Haines 1996)—but price is still the bottom line (McDowell 1991: 24). Retailers earn higher profits by selling cheaper mass-produced imitation Native goods, and any claim of Native affiliation they can make about a piece works to their advantage. Some Native-style art even wears a "price disguise" to mimic not just the style but the value of Native-made work (Haines 1996). By all means, not all Native-style art involves misrepresentation. Many non-Native Alaskan

Figure 3.2. The FTC required this shop to label native-style carvings to distinguish them from the few native-made products on its shelves.

artists create unique work inspired by Native forms and respectfully ask permission to depict certain images from clans or elders.

In Alaska, dealers and retailers have two major complaints about Native arts that, they claim, force them to turn to Native-style sources of goods. First, Native artists have priced themselves out of the market, demanding values for their work that can't withstand the standard 100 percent mark-ups imposed by a wholesaler and again by the retail shop owner. Second, they don't produce enough work on a consistent basis or of consistent quality to supply the growing tourist demand. Perhaps the real problem is that everyone (including Native artists themselves) expects work produced by Native artisans to compete with imitations on the souvenir market.

Policy Regimes and Global Markets

Many locally available and traditionally used materials find themselves heavily enmeshed in policy regimes that restrict their use, access, and commercial potential. (See "A Customs Guide to Alaska Native Arts" developed by the Alaska Department of Community and Economic Development and posted on their website at www.dced.state.ak.us/cbd/nag/nativearts.htm, last accessed December 31, 2003.) Another threat to indigenous art production involves the ability to use indigenous materials. Many locally available and traditionally used materials find themselves heavily enmeshed in policy regimes that restrict their use, access, and commercial potential. Artwork exported to markets in other countries must comply with the Convention on International Trade in Endangered Species (CITES), which requires permits for goods that contain many materials used in indigenous arts and crafts, including walrus ivory. Whale parts (bone or baleen) are illegal to export under any circumstance. U.S. federal laws prohibit buying, selling, or trading in objects containing feathers, fur, or any part of animals listed as protected or endangered (Berlo 1994; McCoy 1991). The Migratory Bird Treaty Act covers all but a few species, so that feathers from most birds are illegal to possess or incorporate in a work of art.[8] One Inupiat artist placed raven feathers on a mask he made in protest of these laws and had it confiscated by federal authorities. He eventually obtained a waiver so the mask could appear in an exhibit at the Anchorage Museum of History and Art on the impact of regulation on Native art (Berlo 1994).

Sometimes even laws like these have creative applications that meet indigenous objectives. Recent indictments under the "feather law" have put a damper on the collectors' market for twentieth-century American Indian and Alaska Native art that contains feathers (McCoy 2001). In December 1998, endangered species regulations were invoked to force the removal of several Pomo Indian baskets from a Sotheby's auction in New York City after the consignors refused requests to take them out of the sale.

The U.S. Marine Mammal Protection Act (MMPA) has had a significant impact on the market for Native art in Alaska. Passed in 1972, the MMPA included an exemption for Alaska Natives allowing them to harvest marine mammals for their own subsistence use and utilize the by-products (furs, bones, walrus tusks, baleen) to create arts and crafts. This provision acknowledged the importance of the relationship between subsistence and artistic production for Alaska's indigenous peoples, but it still allowed non-Natives to purchase and create marketable products from any marine mammal parts harvested *before* the 1972 passage of the act. Today non-Native carvers pay up to $200 a pound for old ivory and $10 a pound for old whalebone, most of it mined by Native villagers from archaeological sites along the Bering Sea and sold through wholesale dealers. As the scenario earlier pointed out, one of the marketing ploys used to sell articles made predominantly by non-Natives from old or "fossil" ivory and whalebone touts these pieces as the only politically and morally correct choice for consumers concerned with animal rights. Other Alaskan manufacturers avoid MMPA restrictions altogether by employing Alaska Natives as pieceworkers to carve small parts for jewelry made from new, white ivory.

On the global market, wholesale dealers export raw materials—wood, ivory, and bone—purchased in Alaska Native villages to carving workshops in Indonesia. Here skilled artisans, many of them carvers displaced by the global ban on elephant ivory, make $5 a day copying "traditional" and "authentic" Native designs.[9] Most of these goods return to the United States via the same exporters and make their way back to the retail tourist market in Alaska. Practices like this are unlikely to stop as long as a dealer can have a carving made in Bali for $3 similar to one a Native carver insists on selling for $75 (Melzer 1995). After passing through U.S. Customs, dealers can legally remove the required "country of origin" labeling.

In many cases, unless a customer asks, there is no way to know if a Native-style carving was produced overseas or by an Alaska Native. It particularly distresses Alaska Natives to see their indigenous materials and designs used to make Native-style imitations and fraudulent art, often sold using appeals to Native culture.

The Silver Hand

In the midst of all the confusion that surrounds the market for Native art in Alaska, there is a symbol that assures the buyer that an article was made by an Alaska Native. I first encountered the Silver Hand in 1988, hanging from a pair of ivory earrings sent to me by a friend from Alaska. I saved the tag because I wanted to remember the name of the artist, who had printed his name inside, along with his Yup'ik heritage and hometown of Hooper Bay. I had seen something similar on Inuit carvings made in Canada, but knew nothing more about the symbol, or whether I would see it again when I traveled to Alaska the following year.

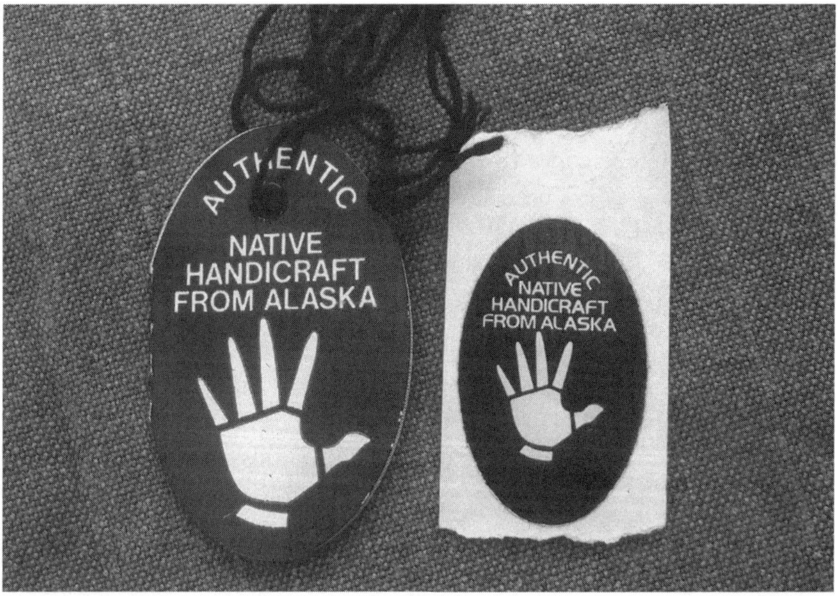

Figure 3.3. The Silver Hand emblem. Published with permission of the Alaska State Council on the Arts, Native Arts Program.

The Silver Hand is a state-sponsored registry program, available without charge to any Native person residing in Alaska who can prove him- or herself to be one-quarter or greater Alaska Native ancestry. A Silver Hand tag or sticker provides consumers with a "guarantee of authenticity" for Native handicrafts, meaning that the article (to quote from inside the tag) was "made in Alaska, handcrafted and finished by an Alaska Native artist or craftsman." The state statute authorizing the Silver Hand (AS 45.65.010–070) defines an "Authentic Native Handicraft" as "an article made in the state which is composed wholly, or in some significant respect, of natural materials, and which is produced, decorated, or fashioned by an Alaska Native." Abuse of the trademark constitutes a Class B misdemeanor. The Silver Hand emblem has nothing to do with quality or with the authenticity of Native designs or art forms. What it actually marks as "authentic" is the ethnicity of the maker, defined by the state in terms of blood quantum. The same blood quantum standard determines access to other government-controlled rights and privileges accorded to indigenous Alaskans, including membership in a Native corporation, health care, and education.

Perceptions of the Silver Hand

Over the course of four seasons of fieldwork from 1995 to 1999 on the walrus ivory trade in Alaska, I gathered comments about the Silver Hand's use and lack of use from a variety of sources including retail shop owners, wholesale dealers, Native artists, consumers, and arts administrators. Information from studies done by government agencies and the reports of committees dealing with Native arts in Alaska supplement and verify some of these remarks.

A Visible Blur

Tourists coming to Alaska find themselves bombarded with information about Native arts and crafts, including ads and brochures telling them to "Look for the Silver Hand." The actual appearance of the trademark on goods sold in shops remains inconsistent and uneven, though its use and visibility have increased over the past decade, along with the numbers of artisans participating in the program. In 1994, only about half of the retailers responding to a survey conducted by the Institute of Alaska Native

Arts sold any items at all with Silver Hand labels (IANA 1994: 7). A 2001 survey of several dozen Alaskan gift shops reported that over a third of the owners required or preferred handmade Native items to have a Silver Hand (Buy Alaska Program 2001). Since retail shops control so much of the interface between Native art and consumers, their support for the Silver Hand is critical.

Reluctance to use the Silver Hand on the part of many retailers does not stem from ignorance about the program. On the contrary, many retailers don't want to use a symbol that appears to mark anything in the store without it as not authentic. Several sources told me of shop owners who illegally removed Silver Hand stickers so that non-Native items in their stores would not suffer from this "implication of inauthenticity." On the other hand, retailers know that having at least *some* Native-made work in a shop helps to sell other items, particularly goods that resemble but cost less than their Native-made counterparts (Wolff 1971: 26–29). From this perspective, it becomes desirable to blur the distinction between Native and non-Native work. Since the Silver Hand sharpens this distinction, it comes as no surprise that many retailers seek ways to reduce the mark's visibility.

Many people considered the Silver Hand virtually meaningless without adequate enforcement and public education for tourists and shop owners. Several retailers told me tales of unethical dealers who put Silver Hand tags on non–Native-made objects. I never witnessed this myself, but in the tourist-heavy towns of Juneau and Skagway, I found tags on merchandise that so closely mimicked the Silver Hand, they border on copyright infringement (figure 3.4). These facsimiles don't just emulate the trademark, they intentionally reduce its ability to distinguish Native-made goods.

Use of the Silver Hand by Native Artists

The number of Native artists using the Silver Hand has risen dramatically in recent years. In 1995, the Silver Hand Directory listed only 334 Native artists as registered users. By 1997, this number had risen to 643, and in 1999, to 925 (Make It Alaskan, Incorporated [MIAI] 1995, 1997, 1999). By 2001, approximately 1,500 Alaska Natives had registered for the program (Northern Economics, Inc. 2002b). Funding for the program has not kept up with this rate of expansion, and Natives and non-

Figure 3.4. On the left, this tag mimicking the Silver Hand, found in tourist-heavy regions of Alaska, borders on copyright infringement.

Natives alike view the insufficient budget as symptomatic of the state's lack of commitment to Native arts.

Native artists, especially those living in more remote areas, have problems with access to the program and its materials. They offered comments like, "I would use it if I knew where to get it" and "It's too hard to get tags." Others found the paperwork required to register for the program a hassle, particularly the need to prove one-quarter Native blood (Alaska DCED 1994: 8). The geographic distribution of artists registered in the program has been very uneven. For example, only six people out of over a hundred artisans living in the Native village of Gambell had registered as Silver Hand artisans in 1999, three of them members of the same family. By comparison, 133 people had registered from Shismaref, a village of comparable size in the same region (MIAI 1999).

One of the biggest concerns of Native artists was that tourists might assume anything sold without a Silver Hand is not Native made, and this would be unfair to artists who hadn't registered for the program or had run out of tags. Some Native artists worry that participation in the program will identify them as a business or force them to start paying taxes on income from sale of their work. In families with more than one artist (a common situation), each person is supposed to register separately, but sometimes artists share tags with unregistered family members or in a few cases, with a non-Native spouse. Indigenous artisans around the world use similar strategies to gain access to materials and markets, especially since art and craft production so often involves multiple family members and reflects communal notions of authorship.[10]

Some Native artists, generally the more successful ones who market their work as fine art, chose not to use the Silver Hand at all. One artist pointed out that the definitions of "authentic" associated with the Silver Hand discourage artists who use nontraditional materials and contemporary designs. Others preferred not to have their artwork labeled as "Native" at all. They wanted their work recognized not for their ethnicity but for the artwork's character within the wider art community.[11]

Multiple Meanings of Symbols and "Authenticity"

Perceptions about the Silver Hand show that the emblem, like most symbols, signifies different things to different people. Some people even perceive its ability to identify indigenous-made Alaskan art as a negative quality. Not surprisingly, the strongest support for the Silver Hand program has come from dealers of exclusively Native products, and their biggest criticism has been its lack of enforcement.

A word of caution is in order. Appeals to "authenticity" like the one that accompanies the Silver Hand can mask essentialized attitudes based on racial or cultural purity that serve to maintain social, political, and economic boundaries or perpetuate exploitation. (For additional sources on the implications of authenticity in indigenous arts see Cohodas, Hickox, and Basketry 1999; Coombe 1995, 1997; Hoban 2002; Marcus and Myers 1995; Myers 2001; Phillips and Steiner 1999; Spooner 1986; Steiner 1994; Ziff and Rao 1997.) Some of the loudest voices advocating authenticity today tend to come from people who want to promote and profit from some version of authentic Native art and culture. Defining authenticity in terms of cultural purity or natural materials is especially problematic for Native artists who want to push beyond traditional boundaries. In a very real sense, the use of blood quantum to establish authenticity amounts to little more than a subtle form of institutionalized racism. Needless to say, most consumers don't realize that the state-issued trademark is based on blood quantum.

Historical Trajectory of the Silver Hand

Coombe (1995: 266–267) emphasizes the importance of looking at the specific social, political, and historical contexts and bureaucratic structures that support the marking and marketing of indigenous authenticity, whether merchants, governments, or artists, to see how this slippery concept gets defined, by whom, and for what purpose. A brief look at the bureaucratic history of the Silver Hand and its forerunners sheds some light on the role of government involvement in the promotion and production of Native arts and authenticity and helps explain some of the attitudes that Native artists and retail shop owners have toward the symbol today.

Channeling Native Production

At least three government-issued trademarks guaranteeing the authenticity of Alaska Native work preceded the Silver Hand. The first was a trademark to guarantee the genuineness of handmade "Eskimo" products, issued in 1939 by the Department of the Interior's Indian Arts and Crafts Board (Collier 1939). The trademark was used by Alaska Native Arts and Crafts (ANAC), a clearinghouse set up in 1937 by the Alaska Native Service, a branch of the Bureau of Indian Affairs (BIA), to act as a wholesaler of Native arts and crafts. Programs like this were spin-offs of the 1935 Indian Arts and Crafts Act (IACA) (49 Stat. 891; USC 25, § 305) and other New Deal legislation meant to help Native people find ways to make the presumably inevitable adjustment to a cash economy. The BIA required its teachers stationed in Native villages in Alaska to act as agents for the ANAC clearinghouse. They directed the output of Native artists into products like moccasins, dolls, buttons, ivory animal figurines (priced by the inch), napkin rings, salt and pepper sets, cigarette holders, paperweights, and other novelties. In ANAC's first year, over 14,000 items received the official government trademark,[12] but its use quickly waned after the onset of World War II when Native artisans found they could get higher prices for their work by selling directly to military personnel stationed across the state.

Protection against Imports and Imitations

After the war, Native-style crafts mass produced overseas and in Seattle and Portland factories inundated the Alaskan market as the tourism industry started its steady climb. As Steiner (1999) notes, the tourist art market measures authenticity in terms of redundancy, not originality, because tourists look for familiar or preimagined forms that validate their experience. ANAC continued to pay Native artisans to produce quantities of goods and responded to the competition from imports by registering a trademark in 1949 for its own merchandise, all exclusively made by Alaska Native artisans. The emblem was an obvious forerunner of the Silver Hand—silver and black with the name of the artist's village (but not the artist) on the back. This trademark stayed with ANAC after it became a private cooperative in 1956 and remained in use until the business closed in 1998.

By the 1960s, most states in the United States with large Native populations found it necessary to pass legislation modeled after the 1935 federal Indian Arts and Crafts Act, which had made it a criminal act to "offer or display for sale any good . . . in a manner that falsely suggests" that it was produced by an American Indian or Alaska Native (49 Stat. 891; USC 25, § 305). New Mexico even passed a law in 1953 that required disclosure of all imitation Indian arts and crafts (U.S. Department of the Interior 1965; NMSA 1953 Comp. § 40.21.27.7). In 1961, Alaskan legislators, in an effort to impact the burgeoning market in Native-style products made outside of the state, introduced the Native Arts and Crafts Sales Act (HB 4), which would require every article not qualified as a genuine Alaskan Native product to be labeled "imitation" ("Negative Approach," Editorial, *Fairbanks Daily News-Miner*, 10 February 1961, p. 4). Dealers and retailers vociferously opposed this disclosure clause, and the bill passed in a much weaker form, authorizing the Alaska Department of Commerce to issue tags to identify "authentic" Native-made arts and crafts. The act also changed the definition of authentic to include arts and crafts made with the use of sewing machines and power tools.

Government "Rehabilitation" of Native Arts

The total number of Native artisans actually dropped in the 1960s as many Alaska Natives found more profitable employment in the state's construction boom or industrial development. In 1965, official studies estimated the value of Native-type handicrafts on the Alaskan market at over $1.4 million, with only 31 percent of these products actually made by Alaska Natives; by 1971, this had declined to 25 percent (Wolff 1971: 21, 25). It became evident that Native artisans could not compete with imports or meet the demands of Alaska's growing tourist market, so state and federal officials began to change their strategy about how to best develop the economic potential of Native art (Frederick 1972; Rogers 1964; Wolff 1971).

In the 1950s and 1960s, government agencies had assumed that, once the acculturation of Alaska's Native population was complete, Native arts and crafts would die out as other "more viable" economic pursuits took their place (Rogers 1964: 28). State and federal agencies, with the help of corporations who had taken an interest in Alaska's oil resources (Rosenthal 1972), began to fund "rehabilitation" projects that focused on training a few promising artists in new techniques, moving away from the "souvenir-type items . . . relentlessly produced for the less discriminating consumer" to which Native arts had "degenerated" (U.S. Department of the Interior, Indian Arts and Crafts Board 1966: 5). Whether the Indian Arts and Crafts Board realized its own role in this "degeneration" after channeling indigenous production into the souvenir market remains questionable.

These new approaches were in part modeled after the success of Inuit art cooperatives in Canada. Beginning in the 1950s, the Canadian government had supported the development of new art forms and marketing strategies by producer-owned cooperatives in Inuit communities. The Inuit coops attempted to combine Inuit values and local decision making with capitalist enterprise and international marketing (Berlo 1999; Goetz 1993; Myers 1984; Rogers 1964: 83–115). In 1964, sales from these cooperatives amounted to $730,000, and 80 percent of this came from objects sold as fine arts. In contrast, Alaskan Inuit art sales in the same year came to around $220,000, with 60 percent of this from the sale of ivory souvenirs (Hoag 1981: 61–63). By the 1970s, Canadian Inuit art had achieved recognition in the international art world. Some of the "rehabilitation programs" in Alaska even hired Canadian advisers in hopes of generating similar results (Rosenthal 1972: 26; Frederick 1972: 40).[13]

ANCSA

More assimilationist policy was embodied in the 1971 settlement of indigenous land claims in Alaska, catalyzed by the desire to explore for oil on the North Slope. The Alaska Native Claims Settlement Act (ANCSA) "entitled" all Alaskans with one-quarter or more Native blood—the same criterion used by the Silver Hand to define an Alaska Native—to become stockholders in regional and village corporations that received land (40 million acres) and money ($962.5 million) in return for extinguishing *all* further claims to Aboriginal title (Arnold 1978). Until its amendment in 1989, ANCSA stipulated that after 1991, stockholders could begin to sell their stock on the open market (to non-Natives), and that no more stock would be issued to Alaska Natives born after this date, measures that could easily be interpreted as institutionalized cultural genocide.

Making the Silver Hand Work—But for Whom?

In 1972, the Alaska Department of Economic Development began to distribute the Silver Hand emblem. Prior to this, the department had sent tags with a smiling Eskimo face to a handful of distributors who requested a label for authentic Native work (Wolff 1971: 52–53). At first, only agents authorized by the state could distribute Silver Hand tags and affix them to Native goods. The original purpose of the trademark was to protect consumers and the state's economic base and actually had little to do with Native artists. The Institute of Alaska Native Arts (IANA) had formed to serve the needs of Native artists in 1976, after the federal Indian Arts and Crafts Board closed its Alaska office. IANA realized that getting tags and stickers into the hands of Native artists was one way the artists themselves could have an impact on the flood of "fake art," and the organization began outreach efforts to help this happen (IANA 1994: 7).

Ironically, in 1976, the FTC used the existence of the Silver Hand as one of the reasons to dismiss a suit brought by the State of Alaska against six Seattle and Portland manufacturers for consumer fraud and misrepresentation. The FTC reasoned that because of the Silver Hand, consumers in Alaska had less chance of being deceived by imitation Native products than in comparable tourist regions (UPI 1976).

State support of the Silver Hand program was inconsistent over the following years. For periods of time, the program didn't even receive enough funding to operate (McDowell Group 1991: 31). But in the early 1990s, after Alaska Natives had been declared a "People in Peril" (*Anchorage Daily News*, 11 September 1988, p. D2), their arts and crafts "A Threatened Market" (Alaska Division of Economic Development 1994), and with cultural tourism on the rise, funds were reinstated. Several federal and state committees received mandates to evaluate how to strengthen support for the Silver Hand and improve the overall visibility and marketability of Native arts. The Alaska Department of Commerce organized a task force with members from the public and private sectors. Since the department was responsible for the Silver Hand program, why it "wasn't working" became a major agenda item. The group proposed legislation requiring mandatory posters in retail outlets to explain the Silver Hand and certificates of origin to accompany all items selling above $100. A bill with these measures entered the 1996 and 1997 legislatures sponsored by Senator Georgianna Lincoln, a Native Athabascan, but failed to pass even though it had the support of state officials, Native artists, and the few dealers who handle only Native work.

The task force also concluded that the newly amended 1990 Indian Arts and Crafts Act did not meet Alaska's needs since the state had no jurisdiction over federal acts or federally issued trademarks, and no one wanted to depend solely upon federal agencies to enforce a problem that had so great an impact at the state level. The group recommended that the State fund an analysis of the current Native arts and crafts industry to assess the monetary loss to Native artisans from sales of fraudulent or counterfeit material. (To my knowledge, this never occurred.) Finally, the task force concluded that without support from the Institute of Alaska Native Arts and the Native community, any recommendations they made to the governor were unlikely to work (Alaska DCED 1994).

In some ways, there was never a chance for them to work. In 1995, when the governor's "Marketing Alaska" initiative reorganized the State Divisions of Tourism, Trade, and Economic Development, the Native Arts and Crafts Task Force became the "Marketing Alaska Cultural Resources Sector Group" and lost its focus and its steam. The Institute of Alaska Native Arts folded in 1997, after its director became immersed in fund-raising $15 million dollars for the new Alaska Native Heritage Center that opened in Anchorage in time for the 1999 tourist season. The new center showcases Native artists making traditional crafts, but its gift shop is still loaded with mass-produced Native-style products.

In 1995, the administrator of the Silver Hand expressed some of his frustrations to me about dealing with Native corporations and artists to promote what he perceived as the Native arts and crafts industry. "Why don't Native artists seem to want to organize and make group decisions about their role in the community? Is it because artists have such little status in a Native community?" As we talked, the notion emerged that perhaps Native artists see their arts as something other than an industry that needs promoting. When indigenous people have relinquished so much already, why allow the state to promote their art for them as a profit-making venture?

Native Artists Inherit the Silver Hand

Similar feelings probably led the governor to sign Executive Order No. 100 in March 1998, transferring the Silver Hand program from the Division of Commerce and Economic Development to the Alaska State Council on the Arts (AKSCA). The director of the Council's Native Arts Program immediately put together an advisory committee of enthusiastic Native artists, but when I spoke with several of them in the fall 1999, a sense of discouragement had settled in. The director had taken a position with the new Native Heritage Center, funding to run the program was virtually nonexistent, and people felt the state had essentially abandoned the Silver Hand.

Over the following year a virtual outpouring of news releases, legal cases, and conference reports from across the continent and beyond drew significant attention to issues of misrepresentation and protection of indigenous arts. With a new Native Arts Program director, the Arts Council renewed its efforts, and in May 2001 facilitated a conference on ways to improve the Silver Hand with participation from indigenous artists, the Indian Arts and Crafts Board (IACB), the Council for Indigenous Arts and Crafts, the State of New Mexico, and the FTC.

Just before the 2002 tourist season, the FTC, in collaboration with the Alaska Attorney General's Office, the State Council on the Arts, and the federal Indian Arts and Craft Board, unveiled a new public awareness campaign to help consumers identify arts and crafts made by Alaska Natives and bring attention to the Silver Hand. That season, almost a million educational brochures and postcards describing how to distinguish Native-made work from imitations joined the slew of pamphlets that confront tourists coming to the state. Most importantly, by the end of the summer, several consumers and a few gift shop employees had filed complaints about deceptive marketing practices, generating more hard evidence than the FTC had come up with in years of their own investigations (AP 2002; Schell 2002).

Potential of the Silver Hand

Can the Silver Hand really help protect indigenous intellectual property rights? The original stated intent of the 1961 statute authorizing a trademark for Native arts was *consumer* protection; there was no claim to protect Alaska Native art or Native artists, only to *identify* "authentic" Native work.[14] Today, the intent of the program has expanded, at least in official discourse, so that now "the Silver Hand program . . . authenticates Alaska Native art while protecting consumers *and Alaska Native artists*" (emphasis added, Alaska State Council on the Arts 1999). Some think it's unrealistic to believe that use of the Silver Hand could have an impact on the market in cheaper, mass-produced items, but others claim that it's precisely in this murky environment that the trademark can have the greatest effect on consumer choices (see McDowell Group 1991: 32). As long as a consumer is aware of the symbol's meaning, the Silver Hand does protect both the buyer and the artist by differentiating Alaska Native work from goods of other or unknown origins (though many of these might also be Native made).[15] In general, the wider the use of the Silver Hand by artisans and retailers, the more protection it provides to both consumers and Native artists.

In spite of all its problems, the Silver Hand is considered one of the best Native arts authentication programs in the United States. The geometric growth in artisans who have registered to use the emblem over the past five years attests that Native artists value its use, whether for material or symbolic reasons.

Strengthening Protection of Intellectual Property Rights for Alaska Native Arts

Several other avenues exist for increasing the protection of intellectual property rights of Alaska Native and other indigenous artists. Some of these involve mobilizing existing intellectual property laws, or "mechanisms of dominance," as sites of indigenous resistance (Pask 1993: 80–81). The very legal structures developed by a colonialist bureaucracy can sometimes be used to challenge an institution from within and force the recognition of alternative claims not adequately addressed by the dominant system.

Strengthening or Expanding Existing Fair Trade Legislation

One route to strengthening intellectual property rights for indigenous artists involves making better use of existing labeling, copyright, and trademark laws and developing new, more specific state legislation on unfair trade practices. An Anchorage lawyer I spoke with stressed that without more severe penalties, distributors and retailers would simply continue to sell fraudulent goods. He advocated a new state law, modeled after the Indian Arts and Crafts Act and similar to legislation passed in several other states,[16] that would allow Native groups and artists to sue retailers for misrepresentations of Native work. But, based on the failure of recent legislative initiatives to strengthen the Silver Hand, an act like this would likely face major opposition from retailers. Other states, like New Mexico and Arizona, that already have comprehensive laws to protect Native arts from imitations, have generally had trouble trying to prosecute alleged violations and find it more effective to use existing fair trade laws and consumer fraud legislation (Kaufmann 2001).

Meanwhile, increased attention to problems that affect the livelihoods of Native artisans across the country and around the world has had some initial results. In the fall of 2000, legislation finally passed to fund enforcement of the federal IACA and make prosecution easier and more effective, extending the right to sue to individual Native artists and Native organizations (Associated Press, "House Passes Bill to Protect Integrity of Indian Arts," *Albuquerque Tribune*, 24 October 2000). The recent efforts in Alaska by the FTC to collaborate with the IACB, the state attorney general's office, and, most importantly, Alaska Native artists to define what constitutes misrepresentation and unmask its occurrence and effects count as positive steps in a long road to better protection for intellectual property rights.

Invoking Copyright Law

Both copyright and trademark law are tools used most often by large corporations, but nothing precludes their use by individual artists or their organizations to protect intellectual property. In spite of the inadequacy of copyright in covering perpetual or collective ownership, the law does protect an artist's original designs. Artists need to know that they have the right to demand that any reproductions they do allow others to make of their work stay within agreed-upon parameters of form and quality. A workshop on intellectual property rights, held in Ottawa in April 1999, attended by seventy indigenous craftswomen from across the Americas, developed a sample contract for artisans to use to protect the copyright to their designs.[17] Simple measures like these have proved very effective in strengthening indigenous control over traditional arts and designs.

Pursuing copyright infringements is both costly and time consuming, but individual artists can address this by forming copyright collectives to promote their concerns as a group. In the Bulun-Bulun case in Australia, an Aboriginal artist whose designs were wrongfully used on T-shirts joined with over a dozen other Aboriginal artists and several advocacy groups to successfully pursue a settlement. The positive results of this and other recent prosecutions for copyright violation indicate that even one successful settlement sends a potent message to people who allow illegal reproductions to enter the commercial market (Gibson 2000; Golvan 1992).[18]

Most older ethnographic objects and designs created by unnamed artists, including many held by museums or illustrated in books, exist in the public domain, unprotected by copyright.[19] In Alaska, blatant appropriations of older indigenous art forms, some mass produced overseas and others replicas, have invaded the market. To give just one example, the national success of an exhibit featuring Yup'ik masks from Alaska (Fienup-Riordan 1996) spawned numerous commercial variations on these ceremonial objects. One antique shop in Anchorage sold life-sized reproductions of some of the masks, made by a non-Native and painted to look old. At an Anchorage art fair, I met an elderly couple selling Fimo™ brooches of miniature Yup'ik masks with tags that cited the page in the exhibit catalog illustrating the original. In Seattle, another artist created expensive metallic jewelry replicating specific Yup'ik masks (Starbuck 1998). Many of these artists claim their work pays homage to the indigenous art forms that inspire them, but others view these incidents as ripping off the intellectual property of people who have already lost so much. But what about the Athabascan artist I met in a gift shop in Haines, Alaska, who was carving small replicas of well-known Yup'ik masks from an indigenous culture other than his own? Shouldn't he also request permission to use these designs, and if so, from whom? Indigenous peoples will have to decide where to draw the lines of intellectual property ownership, and who has the power to make these decisions.

UNESCO and the World Intellectual Property Organization (WIPO) have worked (albeit for many years with few results) to develop models for protecting expressive arts and folklore that extend concepts of copyright to unpublished works with unknown authorship (Berryman 1994: 325–333; Blundell 1993: 76–77; WIPO 2001). The most promising legal model comes from a landmark law passed by Panama in June 2000 that grants collective and perpetual copyright over indigenous artistic creations—including art, design, music, performance, and dress—that authorized indigenous councils or congresses register as their intellectual property (López 2002).[20] Others who want to use a registered form of intellectual or cultural property must seek permission from the indigenous entity that controls the copyright. Article 10 of the legislation authorizes use of a certification emblem, much like the Silver Hand. In spite of the fact that implementation of the Panama law has hardly begun, it has already inspired an organization of Inuit women in Canada to develop similar legislation to protect the design of the amauti, a woman's parka (Blackduck 2001).

In Australia, studies have investigated how to best incorporate new standards for copyright into the legal system to protect Aboriginal art and designs (Janke 1998), but indigenous groups have not waited for these slow-moving structural changes. Many Australians have begun to acknowledge an extralegal form of "indigenous copyright" and to understand some of the cultural and ethical implications of the use and ownership of Aboriginal designs. This comes in the wake of several scandals surrounding Aboriginal art and through constant efforts of the Aboriginal and Torres Strait Islander Society and other advocacy groups, including dealers of Aboriginal art, to educate the public. (For more information about recent controversies, intellectual property protection, and ethical trade for Aboriginal art and artists in Australia, see Kavanagh 1999; Donnan 2000; Hoban 2002; Myers 2001 and websites of the National Indigenous Arts Advocacy Association [NIAAA], http://www.niaaa.com.au, and the Australian Indigenous Art Trade Association, http://www.arttrade.asn.au, both last accessed March 21, 2003.)

Creating Collective Trademarks

Unlike copyright, trademarks don't protect designs; they indicate the origin or source of goods or services. Their purpose is to protect corporations from having their products imitated or wrongfully appropriated by others. Unlike copyright, trademarks remain valid as long as they are in use (Brown 1998: 197). On the other hand, trademarks only cover materials used in commercial trade and have no ability to protect noncommercial forms of cultural or intellectual property.

Artists' organizations like the West Virginia Guild of Artists and Craftsmen have long used trademarks to identify work created by their members (Wolff 1971: 53–58). In 1958, Canada's Department of Indian and Northern Affairs registered the "igloo trademark" certifying the authenticity of Inuit-made art.[21] Many Inuit artists also add the trademark of their local cooperatives to their work. The Inuit art trademark has encountered problems similar to the Silver Hand. Not all Inuit artists use igloo tags, nor do all shops or galleries. Studies describe the Canadian government's monitoring of the tag as far from satisfactory, and close copies of the symbol sometimes appear on non-Native products (Scott 1997). The igloo trademark doesn't prevent imitations from entering the market, but it has become widely recognized as a symbol of authentic Inuit work, and nonindigenous look-alikes command only a fraction of the value of trademarked pieces (St. Fleur 1999).

Trademarks issued by the state like the Silver Hand and the Inuit art emblem originally had less to do with protecting indigenous artists than

Figure 3.5. Canada's Inuit art trademark. Published with permission of the Inuit Art Centre, Indian and Northern Affairs Canada.

with protecting consumers, but things have changed. Over the last few years more and more tribal governments and indigenous arts organizations have initiated the use of trademarks to guard against rip-offs of indigenous arts in the marketplace. The Council for Indigenous Arts and Culture has worked with the Zuni Cultural Arts Council and other tribal groups on developing trademarks (Gibson 2000: 17; Kaufmann 2001).[22] In January 2000, just in time for the onslaught of tourists for the Olympics, Australia's National Indigenous Arts Advocacy Association, with support from the Aboriginal and Torres Strait Islander Commission, unveiled a "label of authenticity" for Aboriginal products. Like the Silver Hand, "indigenous creators" register to use the trademark and receive free labels. Firms that reproduce Aboriginal designs under equitable reproduction agreements can obtain a version of the label called a "collaboration mark." The Australian Mark of Authenticity received official approval, but its future is uncertain, as NIAAA offices closed in late 2002 due to lack of funding (Janke 2003). Meanwhile, many regional Aboriginal arts and crafts centers have developed their own labeling systems. In New Zealand, the Maori Arts Board registered a trademark in 2002, the Toi Iho™, which is awarded to indigenous artists based on the quality of their work (Janke 2003: 16).

According to intellectual property rights expert Darrell Posey (1996), certificates of origin or trademarks may well be the *most* useful mechanisms currently available to protect products coming from indigenous lands or produced by indigenous peoples. One reason trademarks work so well is that, as symbols, they have the power to mark identity and denote authenticity (Coombe 1996; Ziff and Rao 1997: 14–15). As corporations, the regional and village Native corporations of Alaska and their nonprofit subsidiaries have the capability to register their own trademarks to certify products made by their shareholders or coming from their lands.[23]

Alternative Trade Organizations

Indigenous-owned and -managed arts and crafts cooperatives all over the world now offer positive examples of alternative production and marketing strategies that return greater benefits to artists.[24] When indigenous art producers become involved with more direct marketing of their work, they have more control over how it's represented in the marketplace and gain valuable information about the global art world system and their position in it. With fewer middlemen, they realize higher profits and also attract buyers who, particularly with indigenous art, like to purchase as directly from the source as possible. Another positive direction for alternative trade networks involves the growing number of indigenous-to-indigenous joint ventures that cut across political borders to share knowledge, experience, and products. One example is the collaboration between the Inuit Circumpolar Conference and the Belize Indigenous Training Institute that provides training in developing and marketing local arts and crafts.[25]

A handful of successful indigenous-owned arts and crafts cooperatives have existed in Alaska for some time.[26] But the recent explosion of e-commerce on the Internet tremendously expands possibilities for direct marketing of Native arts. Several Native corporations have gone online with arts and crafts made by their shareholders, and entrepreneurs in Native villages have developed websites to market local products. At a conference held in Nome in February 2001 entitled "Launching E-Business Into Our Traditional Economies," George Olanna, coordinator of the carving workshop in Shismaref, described how he can triple the money carvers earn for their artwork by developing a website and using e-mail. Another example comes from the Chukchi Sea Trading Company, which does business on the Internet from the Native village of Point Hope, Alaska. The website, which heartily endorses the Silver Hand, sells arts and crafts, shares stories and photos of the village, and earmarks a percentage of its profits for local scholarships. Internet sales solve many of the problems of marketing from a remote location and allow greater flexibility in supply and demand, since even one-of-a-kind pieces can be placed on a website as they become available.

Both buyer and maker should be wary however, since global marketing channels can be exploited by anyone with a computer and a phone line. Wholesalers and retailers of Alaska Native art from coast to coast also peddle their wares on the Internet. Global marketers who specialize in "visible commerce" and "community sourcing" of indigenous arts and crafts have found a lucrative niche in the marketing of indigenous arts. One recently formed business uses websites to illustrate indigenous artisans talking about their art while they work in a village setting. Images like these create a strong "virtual link" between buyers and artisan, a powerful marketing device when combined with the claim that your purchase helps preserve sustainable cultural practices (Friedman 2001).

The potential for indigenous-operated alternative trade organizations to play an important role in promoting the intellectual property rights and economic position of indigenous artists has barely been tapped. Local firms and indigenous products, as Ger (1999) has pointed out, have an intrinsic advantage when it comes to operating in global markets. They can use cultural capital and distinctiveness as resources to enhance the perceived value of products. Works of art and craft are ideally positioned to accomplish this, and symbols of authenticity can play an important role by visibly accrediting the owners of intellectual and cultural capital to distinguish them from others who may try to appropriate it.

Regulating Imports

Regulating the import or sale of imitation products constitutes another way to protect indigenous arts. Panama took this approach as early as 1967, when legislation made it illegal to import items that competed with locally produced handicrafts. This approach has been taken in Panama where the Kuna produce *molas*, a unique indigenous form of textile art that has become a global commodity (Tice 1995). In 1984, the Panamanian legislature, which by now included Kuna representatives, passed additional laws to specifically prohibit the import of designs or articles that copied or competed with indigenous crafts. Like so many cultural property laws, these have suffered from lack of enforcement (Tice 1995: 87), but the recent developments in intellectual property law in Panama could increase the effectiveness of this approach. Because of the primacy of free trade in the United States, state or federal laws restricting the import of indigenous-style arts are an unlikely prospect. But on a microlevel, socially responsible businesses and alternative trade organizations can practice similar measures within their own organizations. For example, several retailers in Alaska have chosen to restrict their inventory to merchandise made by Native artisans or to items that carry the Silver Hand and even use this exclusivity as a successful marketing strategy.

Advocacy and Activism

Public advocacy and activism also help increase awareness of the intellectual property rights of indigenous artists everywhere. A few Alaska Native artists sustain an activist role by writing articles and editorials to keep indigenous concerns in the public conscience.[27] Other overt forms of public activism, whether picketing a shop in downtown Anchorage in the height of the tourist season, handing out literature listing shops that abuse the Silver Hand, or filing complaints about specific incidents of fraud and misrepresentation all count as effective ways to raise awareness about the misrepresentation of Native arts. All over the world, organizations like the National Indigenous Arts Advocacy Association in Australia and the Council for Indigenous Arts and Culture in New Mexico provide encouraging examples of groups formed to protect and advance the intellectual property rights of indigenous artists.

Conclusion: Revisiting Indigenous Intellectual Property Rights

Issues that affect the intellectual property rights of Alaska Native arts and artists are entwined with ongoing struggles by Alaska's Native peoples for sovereignty, self-determination, subsistence rights, social and economic stability, and cultural integrity. At the state level, intense political debates impact how Alaska Natives can even define their subsistence needs and practices, as respect for indigenous life-ways erodes before the demands of sport hunters, regulatory agencies, and developers. Alaska Natives readily realize the relationship between art and other social issues in their communities, and at least one successful village-based arts workshop started with funds for suicide prevention and substance abuse (Olanna and Fosdick 1988).

Concerns about the intellectual property rights of indigenous artists link Alaska Native artists and their communities to economic and political struggles shared with indigenous peoples all over the world. Alaskans have taken an active part in international indigenous organizations, like the Inuit Circumpolar Conference, that champion indigenous rights on many fronts. But until discussions about how to best define and protect intellectual property rights appear on the agendas of local and regional Native organizations, external laws and policies will likely continue to define or disregard them. As it is, Native councils and corporations all over Alaska increasingly face decisions related to cultural and intellectual property in contexts like the ownership of the results of research, repatriation, and control over the use of traditional knowledge.

Attempts to revise existing intellectual property law and the emergence of comprehensive concepts like traditional resource rights (Posey 1996) are part of the search for more integrated and useful approaches to indigenous rights. Some argue that indigenous intellectual and cultural property should not be treated separately (Daes 1993), but others contend that more generalized or international approaches, though important in pushing the overall agenda, may have less ability to protect indigenous rights than locally developed policies that articulate with existing legal or institutional structures. The World Customs Organization, for example, advises that international policies for the protection of indigenous handicrafts are unlikely to coalesce until precedents exist at local and national levels (Abeita n.d.: 6–7). In Australia, legislative initiatives have gathered input on how to best revise the bundle of laws that constitutes intellectual and cultural property rights (Janke 1998). Panama's new law protecting the collective intellectual property rights of indigenous peoples over their creations breaks ground for similar initiatives in other countries. In the midst of these discussions, indigenous voices adamantly agree that decisions about the ownership and management of intellectual property need to be worked out by indigenous communities themselves (Fourmile in Janke 1998: part 3, p. 5; Posey 1996).

Instead of waiting for new forms of intellectual property law to emerge, indigenous communities and artists have started utilizing available legal mechanisms, developing new ones, negotiating agreements, building alternative trade networks, and taking other creative approaches to strengthen intellectual property protection for their arts. The use of a tag to certify the origin of indigenous art forms is one small aspect of a host of intellectual property concerns, but trademarks like the Silver Hand, especially if they are endorsed, managed, and used widely, can play an important role in protecting indigenous intellectual property rights of goods on the commercial market. Indigenous organizations like the Native corporations of Alaska may well decide to add their own certification tags alongside ones issued by the state as visible symbols of collective rights of indigenous artisans from their regions.

Acknowledgments

I wish to thank the following for contributions to funding related to this research: the Office of Polar Programs, Arctic Social Sciences of the National Science Foundation (OPP-9633760); the David C. Skomp Fund of Indiana University's Department of Anthropology; the Phillips Fund of the American Philosophical Society; the Jacob's Research Fund of the Whatcom Museum in Bellingham, Washington; the Arctic Institute of North America; and the University Graduate School of Indiana University. Thanks also go to the village of Gambell, Alaska State Historical Library, Molly Lee, Steve Henrikson, Rachel Epstein, and the many people—particularly the artists, shop owners, dealers, and curators—who shared their thoughts and concerns.

My experience with Alaska Native arts is informed primarily by multisited fieldwork on the market in walrus ivory carvings from northwestern Alaska, ongoing since 1995, which has exposed me to Alaska Native arts in its many forms.

Notes

1. I use the term *Alaska Native* as it is the term most commonly used at present for self-reference by indigenous peoples of Alaska. I am partial to the definition of "Native" as a person "originating from a particular place" as distinguished from "visitors or invaders" (*American Heritage Dictionary* 1981). And although *Eskimo* is still an accepted term in Alaska, I refer to these peoples as "Inuit" or by their more specific identity (i.e., Yup'ik or Inupiat) unless using terminology used in the source material.

2. A 1980 survey found that arts and crafts were the primary or secondary source of income for about 85 percent of all families in southwestern tribes (Abeita n.d.: 3).

3. This lack of statistics exists partly because so much of the art people produce is marketed through informal distribution channels. Studies and reports conducted by various Alaska Native corporations often include some information on the economic role of Native arts on a regional basis (Bering Straits Regional Plan [Draft] 1986; Calista Native Corporation 1985; McDowell 1991), but statewide statistics on the importance of art production to Alaska Natives are lacking.

4. In 1997, as defined by the Alaska Department of Commerce, "Native cultural attractions" do not necessarily involve any *living* Native people (Alaska DCED 1994: 4).

5. In this context, "authentic" can mean any of the following: something executed in a Native style, but not necessarily Native made; a replica of an object from a past or present culture; or, as in this case, a reproduction of a design whose

copyright has been purchased from a Native artist for commercial use on mass-produced goods like T-shirts, mugs, or greeting cards. Blundell (1993) documents a similar situation in Canada.

6. In 1993, wholesale dealer Kurt Tripp was awarded a contract to supply reproductions of a Haida totem pole for the Friends of the Alaska State Museum. Profits from sales of the pole were earmarked for Native groups and museum exhibits, and a Native artist had designed a prototype. When it became known that Tripp's plan was to ship Alaskan cedar to Bali for carving, then back to Alaska to be painted, the museum group pulled out of the contract. Tripp threatened to sue, and in the settlement received rights to the prototype design. He had the poles carved in Bali and marketed them as "Hand-painted Native Alaskan cedar, Made in Alaska." The poles barely met the requirements for the amount of value added in state to legally sell as "Made in Alaska." When questioned about the misleading advertising, one retailer (a friend of Tripp's) responded, "I don't see how anybody in their right mind could say it was Native carved. . . . If it was being carved by a Native, we would state that it was being carved by a Native" (MacPherson 1994b).

7. In the Southwestern United States in the 1980s, about 75 percent of turquoise on the market was neither indigenous to the Southwest nor worked on by Native people indigenous to the Southwest (Toelken 1982: 11). In 1991, New Mexico passed specific labeling requirements, aimed at the problems with turquoise.

8. Card-carrying Native Americans can possess (not sell) eagle feathers if they obtain a federal permit, but not other restricted species except for limited educational uses.

9. The U.S. Fish and Wildlife Service began tracking the legal export of walrus ivory in 1990. In 1994, 1,300 pounds of old walrus ivory were declared leaving the United States, with 90 percent going to Indonesia. Ivory exports have dropped since 1998, but wood and bone have taken their place. Balinese carvers are well known for their ability to replicate intricate designs and apparently have very loose concepts of design ownership, though they often want to know if the creator of a design is still living (Melzer 1995).

10. Tice (1995) reports that among the Kuna women of Panama who produce *molas* and other indigenous products for the market, sometimes one woman in the household joins the *mola* cooperative and shares her membership benefits with other female householders. In Native households throughout Alaska, ivory carving, doll making, and other arts and crafts typically involve family members of all ages in various stages of the production process. In Australia, the execution of a painting, though the Aboriginal artist owns the design, can reflect the work of more than one person. Controversy over concepts of authenticity and intellectual property rights erupted in 1996 when an Aboriginal artist won a prize for a painting produced at least in part by her non-Aboriginal spouse. An official board

eventually ruled that the artist could keep her prize since the painting was produced according to legitimate cultural standards (Hoban 2002: 184–186).

11. Morphy noted similar attitudes among some Aboriginal artists in Australia (1995: 232).

12. This statistic comes from the correspondence of H. W. Starling, Director of Alaska Native Service; 1943 Report of Native Arts and Crafts; Box 16, File 904, Native Arts and Crafts; Bureau of Indian Affairs, Juneau Area Office; General Subject Correspondence, 1933–1954; Record Group 75; National Archives, Anchorage, Alaska.

13. Peter Hoag (1981) compared success rates of government-sponsored art programs in Inuit communities of Alaska and Canada from 1945 to 1975. During this period, less than 10 percent of the projects launched in Alaskan Inuit communities succeeded, whereas government initiatives in Canada were generally successful. Hoag attributes this both to the different development styles of the two governments and to a general lack of social or economic interest in a government-directed arts and crafts industry by rural Alaskans (1981: 233). Others have blamed the inadequacy of government programs in Alaska. In my view, the Canadian development style, with its worker-owned cooperatives, shared profits, and government advisers who were long-term residents invested in the community, encouraged more equitable and rewarding participation by indigenous art producers. In contrast, many Alaskan Inuit involved with government-sponsored art projects didn't realize the projects met social or economic needs of their communities.

14. Behind the apparent motive of consumer protection was the state of Alaska's desire to minimize the economic impact of products made elsewhere that were flooding the tourist market. This differs from the objectives of the federal trademarks that preceded the Silver Hand. These earlier trademarks were for the most part attempts to involve members of the Native community (as many as possible) in activities that would help their transition to a cash economy. This backfired in the sense that for several generations it channeled production into supplying a souvenir market where before long Native-made goods competed with cheaper mass-produced imitations.

15. This dependency on consumer awareness is made clear from the language accompanying most of the promotional literature: "Look for the Silver Hand!" "Buy Smart." Or, from an ad in the Anchorage Visitors' Guide: "If you don't see it, ask for it."

16. New Mexico, Arizona, Texas, and Colorado all have laws that deal specifically with misrepresentations of American Indian art in the marketplace. Oklahoma and South Dakota have similar but less comprehensive statutes. In addition to Alaska, California, Montana, and Nevada have laws authorizing an emblem or registered trademark to certify Native-made work (Kaufmann 2001).

17. Documents from the Inter-American Workshop on Intellectual Property Rights held in Ottawa in April 1999 on the topic of indigenous women's art designs, including the sample contract, can be found by searching the website of the International Centre for Human Rights and Democratic Development at: www.ichrdd.ca, last accessed March 21, 2003.

18. In another landmark case in late 1994, a federal court in Australia awarded more than $145,000 in copyright infringement to Aboriginal artists whose designs were made into carpets in Vietnam and sold in Australia for $3,000 apiece (Associated Press 1994; Janke 2002).

19. After the thunderbird design on Cowichan sweaters was mass produced at profits of millions of dollars, the Canadian First Nation whose name and design were being used by the manufacturer filed suit. The settlement required removal of the name "Cowichan" from products, but since the design had been in the public domain, it was ruled that the tribe did not have standing to receive compensation for use of the design (Chartrand 1996).

20. Act No. 20 of the Republic of Panama, published in *Gaceta Oficial* No. 24,083 of June 27, 2000.

21. Years ago, red maple leaf tags were used to identify Indian-made goods in Canada (Rogers 1964: 112). These tags are still around, but they no longer mark Indian-made items; now they simply mark goods "Made in Canada" to distinguish them from imports.

22. Though individual Native artists can also register their own trademarks, lawyers say greater protection results when a trademark is used collectively (Gibson 2000: 17).

23. Many Native corporations and organizations have logos for business use, and T-shirts and jackets printed with logos act as salient markers of indigenous identities in Alaska.

24. The International Federation of Alternative Trade helps coordinate many of these grassroots organizations and activities. Visit the website at: www.ifat.org, last accessed March 21, 2003.

25. Information about this alternative trade venture can be found on the website of Canada's Inuit Circumpolar Conference at: www.inuitcircumpolar.com, last accessed March 13, 2003. Go to "Activities," "International Trade and Development," then to "Belize Indigenous Training Institute."

26. Arts and crafts–related businesses include the Shismaref Tannery, the St. Lawrence Island ivory carving cooperative, and the Oomingmak cooperative that deals in musk-ox yarn and products. Several Native corporations, like Sitnasuak in Nome and the Northwest Alaska Native Association in Kotzebue, operate gift shops featuring work created by their shareholders.

27. Examples of this refreshing commentary include Tlingit weaver Helen McNeil's editorial "Alaska Squanders Native Art Riches" about the impact of cheap imported Native-style art on the state's reputation and economy; Inupiat artist Joe Senungetuk's "Beyond the Veneer of Civic Beauty" in which he questions how much of the $90 million donated by a philanthropist to the Anchorage Museum of History and Art will benefit indigenous arts; and St. Lawrence Island Yupik carver Susie Silook's "Adaptation is Traditional; Get Used to It," asking why Native lifestyles and arts seem to require justification unless they come packaged as tourist attractions.

References

Abeita, A. P.
American Indian Arts and Crafts: A Study on Handcrafts and the Industry. Peralta, New Mexico : Council for Indigenous Arts and Culture, n.d.

Alaska DCED (Alaska Department of Commerce and Economic Development)
Alaska Native Arts and Crafts Task Force, minutes of the meeting. Anchorage, Alaska, October 26, 1994.

Alaska Department of Community and Regional Affairs, Division of Municipal and Regional Assistance and Divisions of Community Development; and the Alaska Power Authority
Bering Strait Regional Plan (Draft). Volume II: Component Strategies; Component B: Economic Strategy (September). Nome, Alaska: n.p., 1986.

Bering Straits Regional Plan (Draft). Volume IIL Nome, Alaska: n.p., 1986.

The Alaska Cultural Resources Marketing Handbook. Juneau, Alaska: Division of Trade and Development and Division of Tourism, 1997.

Alaska Division of Economic Development
Alaska Native Arts and Crafts: A Threatened Market. Report to the Assistant Secretary for Indian Affairs, U.S. Department of the Interior (November 1994). Appendix D. Anchorage, Alaska: n.p., 1994.

Alaska State Council on the Arts
Communique, vol. 6, no. 11 (May 1999): 1.

The American Heritage Dictionary, edited by W. Morris. Boston: Houghton Mifflin, 1981

Anchorage Daily News
"People in Peril." *Anchorage Daily News*, 11 September 1988, p. D2.

Arnold, R. D.
Alaska Native Land Claims. Anchorage, Alaska: Alaska Federation of Natives, 1978.

Associated Press (AP)
FTC Probes Counterfeiting of Native Art. *Anchorage Daily News,* 4 November 2002, B9.

Associated Press (AP)
House Passes Bill to Protect Integrity of Indian Arts. *Albuquerque Tribune,* 24 October 2000.

Associated Press (AP)
"Aborigines Pleased with Big Art Award for Copying Their Art" (International News, P.M. cycle). Darwin, Australia (December 14, 1994).

Belk, R. W. and R. Groves
Marketing and the Multiple Meanings of Australian Aboriginal Art. *Journal of Macromarketing,* vol. 19, no. 1 (1999): 20–34.

Berlo, J.
Material Issues: The Impact of Regulation on Inuit Art (Exhibition). *Inuit Art,* vol. 9, no. 4 (1994): 36–40.

Drawing (upon) the Past: Negotiating Identities in Inuit Graphic Arts Production. In *Unpacking Culture: Art and Commodity in Colonial and Postcolonial Worlds,* edited by R. Phillips and C. Steiner, 178–193. Berkeley: University of California, 1999.

Bering Straits Regional Plan (Draft)
Volume II: Component Strategies; Component B: Economic Strategy (September). Nome, Alaska: n.p., 1986.

Berryman, C. A.
Toward More Universal Protection of Intangible Cultural Property. *Journal of Intellectual Property Law,* vol. 1 (1994): 293–333.

Blackduck, A.
Protecting Inuit Clothing Designs: Pauktuutit Looks to Panama for Legal Model. *Nunatsiaq News,* 25 May 2001.

Blundell, V.
Aboriginal Empowerment and Souvenir Trade in Canada. *Annals of Tourism Research,* vol. 20 (1993): 64–87.

Brown, M. F.
Can Culture Be Copyrighted? *Current Anthropology*, vol. 39, no. 2 (1998): 193–222.

Buy Alaska Program
"Alaskan Gift Shop Questionnaire" (results of a survey performed by the Buy Alaska Program, University of Alaska Small Business Development Center, Anchorage, Alaska), dated October 25, 2001.

Calista Native Corporation
Yukon-Kuskokwim Region Arts and Crafts Opportunities Study. Anchorage, Alaska: Calista Native Corporation, 1985.

Cardinal-Shubert, J.
In the Red: Money, Appropriation and Native Imagery. *Fuse Magazine*, vol. 13 (1989): 20.

Chartrand, H. H.
Intellectual Property Rights in the Postmodern World. *Journal of Arts Management*, vol. 25, no. 4 (1996): 306–320.

Cohodas, M., Elizabeth Hickox, and Karuk Basketry
A Case Study in Debates on Innovation and Paradigms of Authenticity. In *Unpacking Culture: Art and Commodity in Colonial and Postcolonial Worlds,* edited by R. Phillips and C. Steiner, 143–161. Berkeley: University of California, 1999.

Collier, J.
Regulations for Use of Government Marks of Genuineness for Alaska Eskimo Hand-Made Products (23 January 1939). Washington, D.C.: Indian Arts and Craft Board, U.S. Department of the Interior, 1939.

Coombe, R. J.
The Properties of Culture and the Politics of Dispossessing Identity: Claims in the Cultural Appropriation Controversy. In *After Identity*, edited by D. Danielsen and K. Engle, 251–272. New York: Routledge, 1995.

Marking Difference in American Commerce: Trademarks and Alterity at Century's End. *Political and Legal Anthropology Review*, vol. 19, no. 1 (1996): 105–115.

The Properties of Culture and the Possession of Identity: Postcolonial Struggle and the Legal Imagination. In *Borrowed Power: Essays on Cultural Appropriation*, edited by B. Ziff and P. Rao, 74–96. New Brunswick : Rutgers University, 1997.

CSANAC (Committee in Support of Alaska Native Arts and Crafts)
Report to the Assistant Secretary for Indian Affairs, U.S. Department of the Interior (November 1994). Anchorage, Alaska: United States Department of the Interior, 1994.

Daes, E. I.
A Study on the Protection of Cultural and Intellectual Property of Indigenous Peoples. United Nations' Economic and Social Council, Sub-Commission on Prevention of Discrimination of Minorities. 28 July 1993. Doc. No. E/CN.4/SUB.2/1993/28.

Some Observations and Current Developments on the Protection of the Intellectual Property of Indigenous Peoples. WIPO Roundtable on Intellectual Property and Indigenous Peoples, 23–24 July 1998, Geneva, Switzerland. www.wipo.int/eng/meetings/1998/indip/daes.htm; last accessed March 19, 2003.

Dawes, K.
Re-appropriating Cultural Appropriation. In *Borrowed Power: Essays on Cultural Appropriation,* edited by B. Ziff and P. Rao, 109–121. New Brunswick: Rutgers University, 1997.

Donnan, S.
Aboriginal Art Industry Grows Up—and Faces Fraud. *Christian Science Monitor*, vol. 92, no. 63 (2000): 7.

Dubin, M.
Native America Collected: The Culture of an Art World. Albuquerque: University of New Mexico, 2001.

Ernst & Ernst Management Services Division. Alaska Native Arts and Crafts Cooperative Association, Inc.: A Recommended Program for Alaska Native Handicraft Development. Seattle: The Division, 1967.

Federal Trade Commission (FTC), Office of Information
Federal Trade Commission Announces Enforcement Policy with Respect to Misrepresentation of Certain Articles as Genuine and Authentic Products of American Indian Craftsmanship. News Release. 18 April 1968. Washington, D.C.: FTC, 1968.

Fienup-Riordan, A.
The Living Tradition of Yup'ik Masks: Agayuliyararput *(Our Way of Making Prayer)*. Seattle: University of Washington, 1996.

Friedman, T.
Torn by a Need to Scale the Digital Divide. *Indianapolis Star*, 19 March 2001.

Frederick, S. A.
Alaskan Eskimo Art Today. *The Alaska Journal*, vol. 2, no. 4 (1972): 30–41.

Ger, G.
Localizing in the Global Village: Local Firms Competing in Global Markets. *California Management Review*, vol. 41, no. 4 (1999): 64–83.

Gibson, D.
Copycats Try to Corner Native Arts and Crafts. *Native Peoples*, vol. 13, no. 5 (2000): 16–17.

Goetz, H.
Inuit Art: A History of Government Involvement. In *In the Shadow of the Sun: Perspectives on Contemporary Native Art*, edited by Canadian Museum of Civilization, 357–381. (Mercury Series, Canadian Ethnology Service, No. 24). Hull, Quebec: Canadian Museum of Civilization, 1993.

Golvan, C.
Aboriginal Art and the Protection of Indigenous Cultural Rights. *European Intellectual Property Review*, vol. 14 (1992): 227–232.

Graburn, N. H. H. (ed.)
Ethnic and Tourist Arts: Cultural Expressions from the Fourth World. Berkeley: University of California, 1976.

Haines, T.
Counterfeited "Native" Art Objects Subjects of New Federal Crackdown. *Indianapolis Star*, 19 June 1996, G8.

Hoag, P. L.
Acculturating Eskimo Arts: The Diffusion of Government Sponsored Production Facilities in Alaska and Canada. Ph.D. Diss., Ann Arbor, University of Michigan, 1981. (Available through UMI, publication number AAT 8116254.)

Hoban, C. H.
The Field of Art Production and Western Desert Acrylics. *The Australian Journal of Anthropology*, vol. 13, no. 2 (2002): 178–190.

IANA (Institute of Alaska Native Arts)
Supporting Authenticity in Alaska Native Art: Silver Hand Program. *Journal of Alaska Native Arts* (winter 1994): 7.

Janke, T.

"The Carpets Case: M*, Payunka, Marika and Others v. Indofurn." Case Study One of *Minding Culture: Case Studies on Intellectual Property and Traditional Cultural Expressions.* Commissioned 2000–2001 by the World Intellectual Property Organization (WIPO), Geneva, Switzerland, 2002. Available at: http://www.wipo.int/tk/en/studies/cultural/minding-culture/index.html; last accessed on December 31, 2003.

"Indigenous Arts Certification Mark." Case Study Eight of *Minding Culture: Case Studies on Intellectual Property and Traditional Cultural Expressions.* Commissioned 2000–2001 by the World Intellectual Property Organization (WIPO), Geneva, Switzerland, 2000, revised 2003. Available at: http://www.wipo.int/tk/en/studies/cultural/minding-culture/index.html; last accessed on December 31, 2003.

Our Culture, Our Future: Indigenous Cultural and Intellectual Property Rights. For M. Frankel and Associates, 1997. Available at: http://www.icip.lawnet.com.au; Last accessed March 13, 2002. Also republished in 1998, Australian Institute of Aboriginal and Torres Strait Islander Commission, and Michael Frankel & Company, Surrey Hills, NSW, 1998.

Kaufmann, L. J.

Indian Art: Fakes and Frauds. *State Legislatures*, vol. 27, no. 10 (2001): 28+.

Kavanagh, J.

Art: Indigenous Art Survives Scandals. *Business Review Weekly*, vol. 21, no. 27 (1999): 35.

López, A. V.

Experience with Act 20, June 26, Year 2000: Panama's Indigenous Intellectual Property Law. Ottawa: International Centre for Human Rights and Democratic Development, 2002.

McCoy, R.

Legal Briefs: Feathers. *American Indian Art Magazine*, vol. 16, no. 3 (1991): 20.

Legal Briefs: United States v. Kornwolf: Has the Ideal Feather Law Case Emerged? *American Indian Art Magazine*, vol. 26, no. 2 (2001): 38+.

McDowell Group

Southeast Alaska Native Artists Cooperative Marketing Study. Report to Sealaska Heritage Foundation (May 1991). Juneau, Alaska: n.p., 1991.

McNeil, Helen

Alaska Squanders Native Art Riches. *Anchorage Daily News*, 17 September 2000, H4.

MacPherson, J.

"Genuine" Native Art Often Fake. *Juneau Empire*, 23 October 1994a.

Totem Tale is One of Dissension. *Juneau Empire*, 24 October 1994b.

Make It Alaskan, Incorporated (MIAI)

Alaskan Products Directory 1995–96. Anchorage, Alaska: Make It Alaskan, Inc., 1995.

Alaskan Products Directory, 1997–98. Anchorage, Alaska: Make It Alaskan, Inc., 1997.

Alaskan Products Directory, 10th Edition, 1999–2000. Anchorage, Alaska: Make It Alaskan, Inc., 1999.

Marcus, G. E., and F. R. Myers (eds.)

The Traffic in Culture: Reconfiguring Art and Anthropology. Berkeley: University of California, 1995.

Melzer, B. Bali, Alaska

Anchorage Daily News, 10 December 1995, C1+.

Art Native to Seattle Loses Alaska Label. *Anchorage Daily News*, 13 April 1996, A-1+.

Morphy, H.

Aboriginal Art in a Global Context. In *Worlds Apart: Modernity through the Prism of the Local*, edited by D. Miller, 211–239. London: Routledge, 1995.

Mullin, M.

Culture in the Marketplace: Gender, Art, and Value in the American Southwest. Durham: Duke University, 2001.

Myers, F.

The Wizards of Oz: Nation, State, and the Production of Aboriginal Fine Art. In *The Empire of Things: Regimes of Value and Material Culture*, edited by F. Myers, 165–204. Santa Fe, N.M.: School of American Research, 2001.

Myers, M.

Inuit Arts and Crafts Cooperatives in the Canadian Arctic. *Canadian Journal of Ethnic Studies*, vol. 16, no. 3 (1984): 132–153.

Nash, J. (ed.)
Crafts in the World Market. Albany: State University of New York, 1993.

Negative Approach
Editorial. *Fairbanks Daily News-Miner*, 10 February 1961, p. 4.

Nisga'a Final Agreement 1998
www.gov.bc.ca/tno//negotiation/nisgaa/default.htm; last accessed March 19, 2003.

Northern Economics, Inc.
Alaska Visitor Arrivals and Profile, vol. 2, Summer 2001. Prepared for State of Alaska Department of Community and Economic Development in association with Nustats International Inc. and Klugherz and Associates. Anchorage, Alaska: Northern Economics, Inc., 2002a.

Alaska Visitor Expenditures and Opinions, vol. 2, Summer 2001. Prepared for State of Alaska Department of Community and Economic Development in association with Nustats International Inc., Klugherz and Associates. Anchorage, Alaska: Northern Economics, Inc., 2002b.

Olanna, M., and R. A. Fosdick
Interview: Melvin Olanna. *Journal of Alaska Native Arts* (September–October 1988).

Pask, A.
Cultural Appropriation and the Law: An Analysis of Legal Regimes Concerning Culture. *Intellectual Property Journal*, vol. 8 (1993): 57–86.

Phillips, R. B., and C. B. Steiner (eds.)
Unpacking Culture: Art and Commodity in Colonial and Postcolonial Worlds. Berkeley: University of California, 1999.

Posey, D. A.
Protecting Indigenous Peoples' Rights to Biodiversity. *Environment*, vol. 38, no. 8 (1996): 6–17.

Rogers, G. W.
Alaska Native Arts and Crafts: Potential for Expansion. Report to Bureau of Indian Affairs, U. S. Department of the Interior (Contract No. 14-20-06050-1053), Alaska Institute of Business, Economic and Government Research No. 2 (July 1964). College, Alaska: University of Alaska, 1964.

Rosenthal, H.
New Skills for Nanook. *The Alaska Journal*, vol. 2, no. 4 (1972): 25–29.

St. Fleur, L.
Trademarks on Canadian Inuit Carvings. Case study on Indigenous Women's Art Designs presented at the Inter-American Workshop on Intellectual Property Rights, April 21–24, 1999, Ottawa.

Schell, S.
Native Art 101: Campaign to Teach Public What's Authentic, What's Not. *Anchorage Daily News* 15 May 2002: E1.

Scott, M.
Faking It: The Appropriation of a Culture. *Inuit Art Quarterly*, vol. 12, no. 2 (1997): 18–22.

Senungetuk, Joe
Beyond the Veneer of Civic Beauty. *Anchorage Daily News*, Special Section: Arts for the New Millennium, 5 September 1999, 14–15.

Silook, Susie
Adaptation is Traditional; Get Used to It. *Anchorage Daily News*, 15 October 2000.

Spooner, B.
Weavers and Dealers: The Authenticity of an Oriental Carpet. In *The Social Life of Things: Commodities in Cultural Perspective,* edited by A. Appadurai, 195–235. Cambridge: Cambridge University, 1986.

Starbuck, J.
Jewelry Arts: Joan Tenebaum *Ornament*, vol. 22, no. 2 (1998): 58–59.

Steinbright, J.
Tribal House Arts: An Organizational Plan for an Alaska Native Artists Organization. Report for Sealaska Heritage Foundation with Support from Community Enterprise Development Corporation of Alaska (March 1992). Juneau, Alaska: Sealaska Heritage Foundation, 1992.

Steiner, C. B.
African Art in Transit. Cambridge: Cambridge University, 1994.

Authenticity, Repetition, and the Aesthetics of Seriality: The Work of Tourist Art in the Age of Mechanical Reproduction. In *Unpacking Culture: Art and Commodity in Colonial and Postcolonial Worlds*, edited by

R. Phillips and C. Steiner, 87–103. Berkeley: University of California, 1999.

Tice, K.
Kuna Crafts, Gender, and the Global Economy. Austin: University of Texas, 1995.

Toelken, B.
Seeing with Both Eyes. In *Native Arts Issues 81/82*, edited by S. Jones, 8–13. Anchorage: Alaska State Council on the Arts, 1982.

UPI (United Press International)
FTC Puts Seal of Approval on Fake Alaska Souvenirs. Unknown source. Found in Alaska Native Arts and Crafts Clearinghouse Files, Ethel Montgomery Papers, Historical Collections, Alaska State Library, Juneau, 1976.

United States Census Bureau
Census 2000, Redistricting Data Summary File, Matrices PL1, PL2, PL3, PL4. Washington, D.C., 2000.

United States Department of the Interior
Protection for Consumers and Producers of Indian and Eskimo Arts and Crafts. Fact Sheet. No. 3/10-65 (70822). Washington, D.C., 1965.

United States Department of the Interior, Indian Arts and Crafts Board
Alaska: Design for Today. *Smoke Signals*, vol. 50–51 (fall/winter 1966): 5–6.

Wolff, H.
Native Handicraft Identification. Report to Alaska Department of Economic Development, July 15, 1971. Anchorage, Alaska.

World Intellectual Property Organization (WIPO)
Statement Made by the World Intellectual Property Organization on Intellectual Property, Biodiversity and Traditional Knowledge at the meeting of the Committee on Trade and Environment, Council for Trade-Related Aspects of Intellectual Property Rights, October 24–25, 2000. Document WT/CTE/1821P/C/W/2426, February 2001 (01-0574).

Ziff, B., and P. Rao (eds.)
Borrowed Power: Essays on Cultural Appropriation. New Brunswick, N.J.: Rutgers University, 1997.

CHAPTER 4

THE AMERINDIAN RIGHTS MOVEMENT IN GUYANA AND ITS INFLUENCE

Mary Riley

> The Chief Officer may, where he thinks it desirable so to do, grant a certificate to any Amerindian exempting such Amerindian from the provisions of this Act, and thereupon such Amerindian shall, while such certificate remains in force, for the purposes of any of the provisions of any Act or regulations relating to Amerindians, be deemed not to be an Amerindian.
>
> Section 42 of the Amerindian Act, last revised in 1976

The most pressing issue for Amerindians[1] in Guyana today is for the legal recognition and enforcement of their basic human rights, as outlined in international law for indigenous peoples.[2] These rights include the right to self-determination, self-governance, occupation and ownership of land and use of its resources, and the ability to have a say in land, timber, mineral, and bioprospecting concessions that are granted by the government to non-Amerindian individuals and companies that are situated on or near Amerindian lands and are often disruptive to Amerindian ways of life.

It is generally agreed by proponents of Amerindian rights that the legal standing of Amerindians, as codified in the Amerindian Act, is in need of serious legal reform. However, exactly how this will be done and what mechanisms will be needed to put these resultant reforms into practice is unclear. Equally important is how Amerindian voices and perspectives will be incorporated into the process of creating this new legislation, especially given that Amerindians in Guyana are physically, socially, and economically marginalized within Guyanese mainstream society, and their voices are usually ignored.

The Amerindian rights movement in Guyana gained momentum since the early 1990s in large part because a series of events occurred that brought international attention to Guyana and its interior-dwelling Amerindian groups. Each of these events, in its own way, highlighted the lack of control Guyanese Amerindians presently have over their own lands, resources on or beneath those lands, and even their traditional knowledge. These events and their aftermath make it abundantly clear that, as already pointed out in Tressa Berman's chapter (chapter 1), Catherine Tucker's chapter (chapter 5), and Maui Solomon's chapter (chapter 8), intellectual property rights for indigenous peoples are in interrelationship with other systems of rights, such as rights to land use and ownership, resource rights, and the right to control the transmission of collectively held indigenous knowledge.

Amerindians in Guyana are currently demanding these rights in order to safeguard their own way of life and future for their children. Far from the policies of assimilation, the full legal recognition (and reform) of Amerindian legal rights would further underscore the real differences in how Amerindians live in contrast to most non-Amerindian Guyanese. This, however, threatens assimilationist Guyanese ideologies that attempt to minimize differences between ethnic and racial groups. The motto "We are all Guyanese" hopes to thwart ongoing racial and ethnic strife in the country, and fuels accusations of Amerindians holding "special" rights apart from all other groups in Guyana. These accusations conveniently ignore the fact that the Amerindian experience of Guyanese society *is* qualitatively different from that of non-Amerindians. Guyanese Amerindians, as a group, are economically the worst off in the country, and the least likely to have access to adequate employment opportunities, education, housing, and health care. Guyanese Amerindians, especially those living in the interior, often must go to Brazil or Venezuela in order to find wage-earning employment, and their coastal counterparts (Carib and Arawak) living in urban areas are frequently the victims of discrimination because of their Amerindian status.

This chapter is divided into three parts. In the first section, I review the policies created to govern Amerindians under Dutch and British colonial rule and the concomitant formulation of Amerindian land and resource rights leading up to the legislation of the Aboriginal Indians Protection Ordinance (the precursor to the present Amerindian Act) in 1902. In the second section, I demonstrate how the Amerindian Act in fact restricts Amerindians in their efforts for self-governance and self-determination, to have control over their own lives and destinies as Amerindians and as Guyanese citizens. In the third section, I outline the sequence of events that occurred in the 1990s that disproportionately impacted Amerindians and, ironically, strengthened the Amerindian rights movement in Guyana. I then conclude with a discussion of the implications of these events for the future of Amerindian legal rights reform in Guyana.

The above analysis is also supplemented with attitudes and sentiments expressed by Amerindians concerning their legal rights that were recorded during my anthropological fieldwork carried out in 1993–1994.[3] I also had the privilege to attend the National Conference for Amerindian Representatives, or AMIRANG, as an observer in April 1994. I have followed later developments in the Amerindian rights movement and news concerning Amerindians by consulting Guyanese newspapers online (such as *Stabroek News* and the *Guyana Chronicle*) and reports from several other online websites of organizations concerned with environmental and legal rights for indigenous peoples. This historical approach to and analysis of present events in Guyana should provide a clearer understanding of the processes involved that, over the past decade, contributed to the present "Amerindian condition" in Guyana.

Colonial History and Tribal Groups in Guyana

In the interest of brevity and owing to the limited scope of this chapter, I do not give a detailed overview of the colonial history of Guyana here. (There are several sources that provide complete and excellent accounts of the colonial history and Amerindians in Guyana, notably Whitehead 1988, 1990a, 1990b, 1992, 1996, 1998.) What I do examine, however, is the treatment of tribal groups by their colonial rulers, first the Dutch and later the British, in colonial *Guiana*.[4] While the Dutch and British did not differ in claiming all territory within the boundaries of Guiana as their own, changes to the trade and export economies of the colony over time, and a shift in attitudes toward "Aboriginal" populations within British colonies worldwide during the nineteenth century, caused significant changes to British policies governing the tribal groups—later referred to as "Aboriginals" and "Amerindians"—in Guiana.

The Dutch were primarily interested in trade with the tribal populations, establishing their coastal forts and plantations only some time after an alliance with the powerful Carib tribe and their allies was established (Edmundson 1906: 40; Riley 2000: 66; Whitehead 1988: 94). The Dutch-Carib trade networks ran all the way along the Essequibo River, going well beyond the plantation holdings on the coast. This economic alliance ensured that the Dutch could harvest resources from deep within the interior of Guiana—timber and valued hardwoods, gold, annatto dye, red slaves—without molestation by tribal groups residing there, due to the lure of trade goods and the protection that the much-feared Caribs provided. The Dutch also employed tribesmen as "bush police" (to capture runaway African slaves), boat drivers, guides, and trackers and to help defend the coastal plantations against slave insurrections (La Rose and MacKay 1999: 30).

In return for the services provided to the colony by the tribal population, the Dutch government established a regular practice of giving substantial presents to tribal settlements. These gifts included trade items such as woven cloth and clothing, metal tools, glass beads, metal and ceramic wares, and other items that became essentials to Amerindian life over time. Although all of the lands were Crown lands, in practice, tribal groups in the interior were for the most part left alone, except when recruited to help defend against Spanish attacks in the interior or slave uprisings on the coastal plantations (Menezes 1977: 47–48; Menezes 1979: xviii; Whitehead 1988: 156–161, 163–166).

When Guiana was ceded to the British by the Dutch in 1814, policies concerning indigenous groups changed drastically. The red slave trade was banned by the new British government. In addition, with the abolition of African slavery in the years 1833–1838, the traditional role that tribesmen played in recapturing runaway slaves ended. Consequently, the tradition of giving substantial presents to Amerindian groups in exchange for their services declined and ceased. The Amerindian was no longer useful to the colony under British rule, and thus many drifted back into the more remote regions of the colony to make a living.

Land Rights, Timber and Resource Rights, and Tribal Groups

The British had an eye for harvesting the interior's resources to a greater extent than the Dutch had done. Thus, new legislation regulating the harvest and commerce in forest products, timber, and other products from the interior was established. As early as 1815, the British government began granting land, timber, and mineral concessions to newly arrived European settlers, with subsequent protests and complaints of Amerindians upon whose lands these concessions encroached (Menezes 1977: 206).

It was recognized that tribal groups still had rights to occupation of their lands, at least in theory, while all lands in Guiana were simultaneously declared as belonging to the state. However, as Menezes (1977: chapter 7) points out in her analysis of British policy in the nineteenth century toward Amerindians that while the colonial government felt that it was, through its actions, being more than charitable toward its Amerindian subjects, the reality was that the government could concession all Amerindian lands away by way of offering timber concessions to settlers who applied for licenses to cut wood in the interior.

Another contentious issue was the amount of wood that could be cut down by either tribespersons or settlers. There were regulations in place that stated that only Amerindian subjects could freely cut timber wherever they wanted, while anyone else had to obtain a license in order to do so and could only cut a limited amount for sale. However, to get around these limits, unscrupulous white settlers employed Amerindians to cut wood for them, since there was no limit to the amount of wood a tribesperson could harvest. The white settlers typically paid the Amerindian woodcutters only a fraction of what the wood was worth on the coast; often these payments were either in rum or in the form of credit that made them deeply indebted to traders and local shopkeepers. The wood would then be sold at much higher prices for export in Georgetown, with white traders and merchants receiving the bulk of the profits (Menezes 1977: 123–125, 149; Menezes 1979: 203–205, 210–211).

Because tribespersons traded wood to shopkeepers and unlicensed woodcutters for quick cash or liquor instead of selling it legally to government posts for sale to the state, this led to increasing regulation on timber cutting by Amerindians. Arguments over whether Amerindians should be prohibited from cutting as much timber as they pleased, since they were being taken advantage of by unlicensed white settlers, went back and forth in Georgetown (Menezes 1979: 199–205). As Attorney General J. Lucei Smith stated in 1861, "No doubt the rights and interests of the Indians ought to be regarded, but on the other hand the Revenue must be protected, and it is necessary to guard against dishonest traders carrying on an illicit traffic under color of the aboriginal owners of the soil" (C.O. 111/331, in Menezes 1977: 203).

Additionally, the negative aspects of European civilization, alcoholism, and materialism, were seen by some white colonists as debauching traditional tribal life and values. Explorer Robert Schomburgk, witnessing the demise of the Amerindian under alcohol and materialistic greed, described the worst elements of European civilization:

> The Indian alone, the owner of the soil which Europeans have usurped, and peopled with the descendants of Africa, he alone is completely neglected, and but little care has been evinced to impart to him Christian knowledge, and the adoption of the habits of civilized life. . . . It is to be hoped that the spiritual and temporal destitution of the aborigines in British Guiana may obtain the consideration of this government . . . would it not be worthy of an enlightened government, not only on religious, but likewise on political grounds, to advise some plan for the amelioration of their forlorn situation? Like the African, they are the descendants of our common parent, and *have the same claim upon our pity and protection.* (1840: 55–57; italics mine)

These same sentiments, providing Christianity, evangelization, and the "civilization" of the Indians in exchange for the loss of their lands, were echoed by several other voices in the colony, including Dr. John Hancock (1840: 47–48, cited in Menezes 1977: 207). Within thirty years, tribal groups in colonial Guiana went from being viewed as powerful, autonomous savages—whose alliance was propitiated with presents—to helpless, feckless, ignorant children in need of instruction, guidance, and protection by the colonial masters, with the assistance of Christian missionaries (Menezes 1977: 257, chapter 8).

The increasing paternalistic and protectionist stance of the British government toward its Aboriginal subjects continued, up until the legislation of the Aboriginal Indians Protection Ordinance, which regulated nearly all aspects of tribal life.

The Amerindian Act[5]

The Aboriginal Indians Protection Ordinance was created in 1902, in part to create Amerindian land reserves and to regulate the amount of contact Amerindians had with non-Amerindian Guyanese and with foreigners (Sanders 1987: 31). This was widely regarded as a positive step, in an effort to curtail Amerindian sociocultural disintegration and alcoholism. Non-Amerindians were required to obtain official written permission to even enter these areas. Furthermore, Amerindian villages could refuse, theoretically, to allow an individual entry into their villages even if the proper written permission was obtained in Georgetown. The ordinance also prohibited the sale or furnishing of "intoxicating alcohol" to Amerindians, except for medical or religious purposes (i.e., the Christian sacraments).[6]

The Amerindian Act gave an extraordinary amount of power to the government to control nearly all aspects of the lives of Amerindians including the regulation of: (1) land and land use; (2) property acquisition and disposal; (3) the welfare and education of Amerindian children; (4) traditional livelihood making; (5) work opportunities and conditions for employment of Amerindians, including child labor; (6) determining who can or cannot live on Amerindian reserve lands; (7) determining the status of Amerindian land and villages as either titled or not titled; and even (8) the power to define who is and who is not an Amerindian.[7]

The ministers or chief interior development officer also had the power to appoint or remove village captains and village council members as they saw fit.[8] In a society that was divided into ethnic and racial blocs—East Indian, African, Madeiran Portuguese, Chinese—and now "Amerindian"—Amerindians alone were governed and regulated in a manner that was unique to any of the ethnic groups in the colony. All other ethnic and racial groups in British Guiana were neither defined nor restricted in this way, nor were any of the latter ever in danger of losing their ethnic or racial identities based on how they decided to live—which was certainly possible for Amerindians who lived in urban areas, not on the reserves, and not in traditional Amerindian ways (Sanders 1987: 31).

With each successive expansion, revision, and amendment to the Aboriginal Indians Protection Ordinance, which later became the Amerindian Act in 1951, its main tenet never changed: the Amerindian population was always subject to government control, including its relationship to the non-Amerindian British Guianese populace. The overall message of the Amerindian Act, the only legislation of its kind in multiracial, multiethnic British Guiana, was clear: Amerindians need someone to represent and speak for their interests; they are incapable of determining their needs for their best interests themselves (APA Executive Committee and MacKay 1998: 1).

Since 1951, the Amerindian Act has been amended or revised only six times, without any input from Amerindians themselves (Forte/ARU 1994; APA Executive Committee and MacKay 1998; APA Executive Committee 2000). In a recent analysis of the Amerindian Act jointly undertaken by the Amerindian Peoples Association (APA) and human rights attorney Fergus MacKay, it is pointed out that much of the language of the Act is obviously and completely outdated. All references to the minister (it does not specify which one) and the chief officer, for example, are thoroughly outdated; Guyana does not, at present date, have a chief officer. Exactly what role and powers are given to the minister of the more recently created Ministry for Amerindian Affairs, with regard to the rights and responsibilities of the "minister" described in the Amerindian Act, is not clearly discernable by strict application of black-letter law standards to the Act (APA Executive Committee and MacKay 1998: 3).

The sections of the Amerindian Act pertaining to land rights and land titles for Amerindians are even more dismal and disempowering. While the revisions added in 1976 allowed for the recognition of communal title for Amerindian lands, very few villages have in fact received such land titles. Many other Amerindian villages are not titled because they are not villages that are formally recognized by the government as being "Amerindian." In addition, section 20A(2)(b) of the Act prohibits Amerindians from claiming subsurface mineral rights on lands occupied by Amerindians, even on titled land (Amerindian Act 1976: 11).

The current structure and wording of the Amerindian Act makes it next to impossible for individual Amerindians or entire Amerindian villages to stop the government from repossessing Amerindian lands on behalf of the public interest, however the term *public interest* may circumstantially be defined. In essence, APA and MacKay (1998: 6) state that:

> in almost every part of Section 20A, the Minister can interfere with Amerindian land rights without having to show a good reason why he is doing so. 20A(6), for instance, allows the Minister to suspend or change Amerindian land titles for an indefinite period of time without having to say why, by issuing a simple order. These restrictions upon Amerindian land titles do not apply to other Guyanese and are discriminatory and in violation of Guyana's Constitution and international human rights laws. Also, many of the decisions taken by the Minister cannot be challenged in court.

Amerindian groups such as the Amerindian Peoples Association and others (i.e., the Guyanese Organization for Indigenous Peoples [GOIP]) have called upon the government to appoint a committee to review and revise the Amerindian Act and to include Amerindian input at every phase of the review process. The United Nations Committee on Economic, Social and Cultural Rights (UNCESCR) singled out the Amerindian Act as "overrestrictive and disturbing" at its 1997 meeting (*Stabroek News,* May 20, 2001). In 1993, the Guyana Parliament did move to revise the Amerindian Act. However, this was then shelved for the next several years and seems to have only begun in earnest in 2002 (*Guyana Chronicle,* June 23, 2002; *Stabroek News,* September 6, 2002, and November 6, 2002).

Little has been reported, at the time of this writing, as to any progress or results of the review of the Act. However, one recent news report states that the Ministry for Amerindian Affairs, headed by Minister Carolyn Rodrigues, has employed a technical team to gather recommendations from Amerindian villages (M. La Rose 2003; *Guyana Chronicle,* February 22, 2003). Exactly how the results of the technical team will be incorporated into the process of review and reform has yet to be seen.

The Amerindian Rights Movement: 1990 to the Present

In the late 1980s, the deforestation of the Amazon rain forest became international news. The killing of indigenous activists like rubber-tapper Chico Mendez in Acre, Brazil, made international headlines. Likewise, the protests by the Kayapó Indians of Brazil against hydroelectric dam projects, certain to flood out traditional Brazilian Indian lands, also made international news. The Kayapó, in part to gain publicity, appeared at protests in their most traditional finery, demonstrating to viewers their authenticity as *indios* and as stewards of the Brazilian rain forest (Ramos 1998: 215–218).

News of these events, and many others like these across the Amazon, made their way to other indigenous groups in North America and the Caribbean as well as to Amerindians living in the Guyanese interior. Makushi and Wapishana Amerindians, in particular, knew of or had at least heard of the brutality that their Brazilian counterparts suffered at the hands of landowners, gold and diamond miners, and ranchers. Accounts of Brazilian Makushis and Wapishanas killed by Brazilians living in the frontier state of Roraima were easily broadcast back to Guyana—in some cases, the Makushi or Wapishana victims were relatives or friends of Makushi and Wapishana Amerindians living in Guyana (Amnesty International Index 1988; Human Rights Watch 1994; Ramos 1998; Rabben 2000). During my own fieldwork in the Rupununi, one Makushi woman recounted to me how her son was killed by a Brazilian rancher for unknowingly "trespassing" on the rancher's lands.

In Guyana, violence of this nature against Amerindians by non-Amerindian Guyanese was extremely rare to nonexistent: I heard of no cases of such violence, either in the present, recent past, or long past. Altercations may occur between Amerindian and non-Amerindian Guyanese, and while ethnic conflict may play a role, these are treated as isolated events, not as part of some larger, systemic agenda of genocide. While Amerindians in Guyana have been aware of and influenced by indigenous rights movements in Amazonian South America and in North America, the indigenous rights movement in Guyana could be best described as "in its infancy" by long-time advocates of Amerindian rights in Guyana (J. La Rose 1997: viii; La Rose and MacKay 1999).

Nevertheless, the events that unfolded during the 1990s, affecting primarily Amerindian areas, illustrated to the international community the powerlessness of Guyanese Amerindians under the Amerindian Act, and under a government that did not appear to listen to their pleas or concerns. Sadly, these recent events have only added to the Amerindian perception that the current elected government has broken the promises it made to Amerindian groups in 1992, in terms of respecting their way of life and their right to use their own land as they see fit, and in preventing outsiders from taking advantage of or misusing Amerindians for their own profit.

Environmental Destruction and the Indigenous Rights Movement[9]

Over the past fifteen years, concerns over conservation of biodiversity and sustainable development increased in Guyana. Guyana, as a country, is quite aware that, with nearly 80 percent of its land mass comprising untouched tropical forest, it possesses substantial economic assets in the form of timber and hardwoods, wildlife and exotic animal species, rare plant species, and potentially vast mineral wealth in gold and diamonds (Colchester 1997; Forte 1996b: 16).

At the same time, the pressure on Guyana to increase its mining and timber extraction is substantial because of the country's extremely depressed national economy and crushing foreign debt load. Since 1992 the Guyanese government, in a desperate effort to attract foreign investment and to gain revenue, dramatically boosted the attractiveness of its land and mining concessions to multinational corporations. A 1995 World Bank study showed that Guyana's royalties, taxes, and forest fees are among the lowest in the tropics, less than a tenth of those paid in African and Asian countries (Rainforest Action Network 1996). Unfortunately, this has done little to boost the domestic economy of Guyana since very little is given back to the government in royalties, and in many cases the multinational corporations pay no taxes, tariffs, or fees for their operations in the interior.[10] And of course, these land, timber, and mining concessions are on or near Amerindian lands and communities, so it is the Amerindians who have learned firsthand, unfortunately, the impact of environmental disasters.

The Omai Cyanide Spill

Since the early 1990s, many Amerindians and environmental groups in Guyana have become increasingly vocal in their protests over the signing away of massive land concessions to mining and timber companies. With the election of Cheddi Jagan as president in November 1992, Jagan began to do all that he could to attract new business to Guyana after decades of postcolonial economic decline. The Jagan administration employed the strategy of attracting foreign investment by liberally awarding generous land, timber, and mining concessions, with the government demanding little in royalties, taxes, or fees.

But no one was prepared for the environmental disaster that lay ahead, which was produced by the multinational mining company Omai Gold Mines Limited. Omai originally received the appropriate permits from the Guyanese government to open and operate an open-pit gold mine in January 1993. Facing increasing pressure from environmentalists in North America, Omai decided to locate a new operation in the Guiana Shield precisely because of the relaxed environmental regulations and standards in Guyana (Colchester 1997: 80–81).

The Omai mine operated for the next sixteen months without much fanfare, except for additional requests from the government for environmental impact assessments to ensure that the sluice ponds used for storing processed waste water (containing cyanide) were in fact safe and not leaking out into local water resources. On May 15, 1995, Omai discharged the contents of one of its sluice ponds into the Omai River, killing several hundred fish. The incident was not reported by Omai to the government until six days later, most likely in hopes that the evidence of any resulting environmental damage would have dissipated by then. However, on August 18, 1995, another sluice pond broke, and over the next five days three-fourths of the contents of this pond ran into the Essequibo River, Guyana's principal waterway stretching from the coast through the deep interior of the country. All in all, three million cubic meters of cyanide-laced waste water were released into the Essequibo, killing fish and livestock and contaminating a water source that many interior-dwelling Guyanese, both Amerindians and non-Amerindians, use for drinking, cooking, cleaning, and bathing (Colchester 1997: 80–81).

Environmental groups worldwide were outraged by the disaster. Assignations of blame (and denials of blame) were thrown around abundantly. However, behind the headlines and protests, it was found that Amerindian groups living along the Essequibo and its tributaries were adversely affected by the tainted water. Many Amerindians experienced skin irritations from handling contaminated water; vomiting, diarrhea, and fever from ingesting contaminated water; and problems with the supply of fish, depended upon for food, problems with livestock, and crop failure were also reported, on top of the general problem of a shortage of potable water for cooking, cleaning, and drinking (Colchester 1997: 83). Approximately 186 individual claims were filed against Omai, but the outcome of these claims is still pending at the time of this writing.

Some of the reports in the national newspaper *Stabroek News* since the time of the Omai disaster have been encouraging, albeit in a disturbing way. In a news article dated May 20, 2001, quoting David Singh, Institute of Applied Science and Technology, University of Guyana: "The Omai spill was a good thing, in that it was a watershed for us. We were made aware of what we can do to the environment" (*Stabroek News,* May 25, 2001). This may be so, but environmental groups in Guyana, as well as the Amerindian Peoples Association, had been warning about the degradation of the environment for years—but it took a national disaster to make people sit up and listen. Amerindians living in the interior had also been warning about this sort of danger for years, because they already knew too well the consequences of rivers damaged by the waste waters from gold mining by Brazilian miners, who illegally crossed the border to pan for gold in Guyana. The government expelled an influx of Brazilian miners in the mid-1990s only after repeated complaints by Amerindians of the problem. In the estimation of many Amerindians, far too much time passed before anything was done, which only confirmed prevailing beliefs that the current government was no more interested in helping Amerindians than were any of the previous administrations.

The Expansion of Mining Concessions

The mining sector likewise saw an explosive expansion in the 1990s, resulting in concomitant environmental destruction, including polluted water, fish with high concentrations of mercury, a rise in cases of malaria, and general disruption of social life in the interior (Forte 1996a: 70–71). Because the government controls the granting of mining concessions, Amerindians have felt like they have control over neither the scope nor the intensity of mining activities that are occurring near, or in some cases, on Amerindian lands (GLA et al. 2000). Even the mining operations that are near, but not technically on, titled Amerindian lands still have an adverse effect on subsistence activities since the polluted water flows downstream to Amerindian villages, further damaging aquatic life, and the noise created by dredge mining operations scares off wild game from the gallery forests. By 2000, no fewer than thirty-six multinational mining companies held mining concessions in Guyana; the vast majority of these companies were (and still are) Canadian-owned (GLA et al. 2000: 67).

While the 1989 Mining Act contends that the state owns all mineral resources, including minerals located below the surface on Amerindian lands, the Guyana Geology and Mines Commission is supposed to notify Amerindian communities of any mineral prospecting or mining activities that are to commence on or near Amerindian lands (GLA et al. 2000: 48). However, Amerindian communities throughout Guyana have emphatically stated time and again that they were never consulted, nor was their permission obtained, for several recent exploratory leases granted by the Guyanese government to multinational mining companies for initial mineral prospecting. For instance, exploratory leases granted to Migrate Mining, Ltd., a South African multinational mining company, and Vannessa Ventures, a Canadian multinational mining company, jointly comprise about 20,000 square miles—all located on Amerindian lands in the Rupununi savannas, home to Makushi, Wapishana, and Wai Wai villages (Cultural Survival 1998; GLA et al. 2000: 89–90). Amerindian groups that only found out about the leases "after the fact" were upset that they were not consulted in the first place.

The Upper Mazaruni Mining Case

In the case of the Upper Mazaruni, which has long had land concessions granted to individual miners and mining companies throughout the twentieth century, large-scale mining activities intensified during the 1990s, also resulting in the massive pollution of rivers, forests, aquatic life (upon which Amerindian villages depend for food), and hostile, sometimes violent encounters between Amerindians and arrogant miners who disdained the presence of Amerindians on "their" mining lands. The captains, or *toshaos*, of several of the Amerindian villages in the Upper Mazaruni repeatedly petitioned the Guyanese government, over a period of several years, in an attempt to halt the widespread environmental degradation. Their repeated complaints were ignored and the destruction by mining operations continued (GLA et al. 2000: 63–66; see also Roopnarine 1996).

Finally, out of sheer frustration, the *toshaos* jointly filed a lawsuit against the government of Guyana in 1998 (Forest Peoples Programme 1998). This lawsuit was the first of its kind in the colonial and postcolonial history of Guyana. Only after this action were some of the mining activities closed down in the Upper Mazaruni. But since then, it was reported that the Guyanese Environmental Protection Agency (EPA) intends to allow mining operations to resume in a more controlled way (*Stabroek News,* May 20, 2001).

Bioprospecting and Biopiracy

Another concern in recent years for Amerindians in Guyana is the possibility of biopiracy, that is, the misappropriation of traditional medicinal or agricultural knowledge by drug companies and research scientists, who then develop new drugs and agricultural products that could potentially be worth millions—without any compensation returned to the indigenous groups that provided the "leads" to the actual discovery. At the AMIRANG conference in April 1994, the message was clear: Amerindians were angry that ethnobotanists were allowed to collect plants anywhere they wanted in the interior so long as they possessed a government permit to do so, without Amerindians themselves having a say in the issuance of the permit itself.

It was in this context that the Wapishana Amerindians agreed to allow a scientist into one of their villages. In 1997, biochemist and ethnobiologist Conrad Gorinsky approached the Wapishana Amerindians of the village of Sand Creek and requested permission to conduct research on traditional medicinal plants. As an interesting aside, although Dr. Gorinsky was educated as a biochemist in England, some accounts state that he lived in either Roraima or Guyana during his childhood.[11] In any case, he claimed to be of Amerindian descent: He was born of a Polish father and an Atorad Amerindian mother. The Atorads and Wapishanas, as tribal groups, were closely related in the past. The few full-blooded Atorads that remain have been, by and large, absorbed by the Wapishana tribe. Dr. Gorinsky worked for several months with the Wapishana Amerindians in the South Rupununi savannas, recording the uses of and collecting traditional medicinal plants, and using his Amerindian background to gain the trust of the Wapishana villagers.

Back in the laboratory, Dr. Gorinsky isolated some entirely new compounds. One of the isolated compounds was an antipyretic compound from the greenheart tree (*Ocotea rodiaei*), a well-known medicinal plant among Amerindians with multiple uses. Dr. Gorinsky named this new compound rupununine. He also isolated a new polyactelyne, which he named cunaniol, from a plant commonly used as a fish poison by the

Wapishana, the cunani bush (*Clibadium sylvestre*). He patented both of these under his own name. In the text of the patent applications, he named the Wapishanas of Sand Creek and Roraima as providers of the information, but the patents themselves belong to Dr. Gorinsky alone (Villamea and Caminoto 2000).

Upon hearing the news of Dr. Gorinsky's actions, the Wapishanas of Sand Creek were outraged and immediately prepared to file a lawsuit in the European court system against Dr. Gorinsky on the grounds of biopiracy. Brazilian Wapishanas in Roraima were also notified and joined in the suit (Villamea and Caminoto 2000; Vidal 2000). But Dr. Gorinsky defended his actions, stating: "We can't talk about how to share the pie if there's no pie," referring to royalties that can only be made by filing patents in the first place.[12]

But for the Wapishanas, this seemed to be beside the point: Their anger lies in the fact that Dr. Gorinsky went ahead and patented compounds without their consent. With other reports of U.S. patents on *ayahuasca* being fought by Amazonian Indians in Peru (Dutfield 2000: 62), the Wapishanas of Sand Creek decided on their own to ban any researchers from entering the village. This is a reversal of traditional Amerindian hospitality, due to sentiments that Amerindian traditional medicinal plant knowledge, and traditional knowledge in general, cannot be protected from misappropriation by outsiders, given the current absence of legal mechanisms in place to protect traditional knowledge in Guyana.

Discussion

The Amerindian response to all of these events has been increased distrust and suspicion toward both outsiders as well as the Guyanese government. Another response, spearheaded by the Amerindian Research Unit at the University of Guyana, is the establishment of new research protocols for all outsiders conducting research among Amerindian groups. Outsiders must enter into memoranda of understanding (MOUs) that outline specifically what can and cannot be taken out of Amerindian communities, and what uses to which traditional knowledge can be put (World Intellectual Property Organization [WIPO] 2001: 200). Measures such as these can easily be taken to protect traditional knowledge; they can also be used to outline the terms of access and benefit sharing among researchers, companies, investors, and indigenous communities (Moran, King, and Carlson 2001). However, none of these measures, without true legal reform, will affect the lack of control Amerindians have over their own land and their powerlessness in stopping the timber, mining, and land concessions operating on or near their lands.

This is not to say that there are no positive developments occurring in Guyana. In addition to the access and benefit-sharing mechanisms, the Iwokrama Rain Forest Programme has been working with nearby Amerindian villages (primarily Makushi) in recording and protecting indigenous knowledge, they also employ memoranda of understanding to formalize these research agreements. In addition, the Makushi Research Unit was formed in 1996 to record and promote the value of Makushi traditional knowledge. The Makushi Research Unit produced a number of publications that received wide acclaim in Guyana, including *Makusepe Komanto Iseru* (1996).

However, the overall findings of WIPO noted that, for Guyana, no laws for the protection of folklore and traditional knowledge existed, and the need to develop modern intellectual property legislation was obvious (2001: 197). WIPO outlined several steps that would have to be taken in order to get basic intellectual property protection legislation drafted, including how to set up a sui generis system for Amerindian rights and protection of traditional knowledge, which was suggested as a possibility (2001: 198). The summary list of steps to draft, implement, and enforce modern intellectual property and traditional knowledge legislation is admittedly daunting (2001: 204).

Conclusion

The events reviewed earlier, when taken together, reveal a chilling message. In the absence of legal protections of traditional knowledge, and in the absence of land rights, resource rights, and rights to self-government, Guyanese Amerindians will be forced to see their way of life disappear without being able to legally do anything about it. It is hoped that the increasing visibility of the Amerindian rights movement in Guyana, aided by international support, will continue to pressure the government until some real positive legal reforms are implemented for Guyanese Amerindians. On a closing note, in March 2000, the Centre for Amerindian Rights and Environmental Law was established in Georgetown, to provide assistance and advice to Amerindians on legal matters of all kinds. It is telling, however, that the Centre for Amerindian Rights was created through the collaborative efforts of the APA, the Rainforest Foundation, and Guyanese lawyer Melinda Janki. The funding for the Centre—like the funding for the highly respected Iwokrama Rain Forest Programme—came from *international* sources, not from sources within Guyana.

Editor's Note

At the time this chapter went to press, it was reported in *Stabroek News* on February 14, 2004, that a modernized, revised Amerindian Act is scheduled to go before the National Assembly later this year and, hopefully, will be passed. Guyanese President Bharrat Jagdeo noted that, since a technical team was initially set up in 2002 to work on revising the Amerindian Act, 30 locations and 111 communities were consulted in the process of reforming the language of the Amerindian Act to more adequately reflect present-day legal realities of Guyanese Amerindians. While the final outcome in the National Assembly will not be known until later in 2004, it is hoped that certain language from the current Amerindian Act, in particular the excerpt that begins this chapter, will be excised from it.

To search for articles on Amerindians and the Amerindian Act, go to http://www.landofsixpeoples.com and select the link "Popular Pages" to search for newspaper articles in the site archives.

Acknowledgments

I would like to thank Katy Moran for her unfailing support in my learning more and more about the issues related to indigenous peoples and intellectual property rights. I also want to thank Melinda Janki for her comments on an earlier draft of this chapter. Any errors, of course, are my own.

Notes

1. In Guyana, there are ten Amerindian groups: Warao, Carib, Arawak, Kalina, Akawaio, Arecuna, Patamona, Makushi, Wapishana, and Wai Wai. The

Karinya is by far the smallest group, numbering fewer than 100 individuals, a seminomadic/trekking group that has been only recently studied by the premier Guyanese anthropologist Janette Forte. The population of all Guyanese Amerindians is estimated to be about 60,000 persons, or about 8 percent of a national population of 750,000 (1996 Census).

2. Guyana is a signatory member of the following international intellectual property treaties: the Paris Convention (1994); the Berne Convention (1994); and the TRIPS Agreement (2000). Guyana is also a signatory member of the following traditional knowledge-related treaties and processes: UNESCO Heritage Convention (1977); the Convention on Biological Diversity (CBD, 1994); and the United Nations Convention to Combat Desertification in Those Countries Experiencing Serious Drought and/or Desertification, "Traditional Knowledge." Human rights lawyer Fergus MacKay also lists several older international treaties and legal instruments that were ratified by Guyana that have relevance to indigenous peoples' rights (MacKay 1997: 1).

3. I held a Fulbright IIe Grant that provided the bulk of financial support for my dissertation fieldwork. Earlier feasibility studies were supported by a Tinker Travel Grant and from fellowship grant monies received from Tulane University.

4. Here I use the term *Guiana,* but the colonial holdings of the Dutch were historically referred to by their plantations established on the coast—of which Pomeroon, Essequibo, Demerara, and Berbice were later ceded to the British to become British Guiana.

5. This section primarily draws upon the recent, well-done joint analysis of the Amerindian Act by the APA Executive Committee and indigenous rights lawyer Fergus MacKay.

6. The minister himself had the power to override that rule, as well as any other regulation listed in the Amerindian Act, as he saw fit under the circumstances.

7. As Sanders (1987) points out, the Amerindian reserve lands are not the only places where Amerindians reside and, more importantly, the reserves represent only a fraction—about 7 percent—of all lands that are occupied by Amerindians and are said, according to Amerindians, to be the ancestral homelands (Melinda Janki, personal communication, 2000). Also, according to Sanders (1987) and APA Executive Committee and MacKay (1998), the list of Amerindian Communities listed in the Amerindian Act does not include all Amerindian settlements and villages—it only includes those villages that have titles issued by the government. Nevertheless, all Amerindian villages, whether they possess titles or not, are still governed by the rules of the Amerindian Act.

8. The village captain and village council are a layer of Amerindian village governance that was formalized by the legislation of the Amerindian Act.

9. This section is by no means an exhaustive list of environmentally and ecologically disastrous events in Guyana. Due to space considerations, I have chosen to focus on only a few of the incidents that have affected Amerindians in the 1990s. See especially Colchester (1997) and Global Law Association (GLA) et al. (2000) for a more in-depth treatment of environmental degradation in Guyana, and Forte (1997) for an overview on the timber industry and deforestation.

10. Colchester (1997: 103) outlines this process, using the multinational timber company, Barama-Simling, as an example.

11. See Vomero (2001). Given the fact that, for many Guyanese Amerindians, family and relatives have always lived on both sides of the border; *both* accounts of where Gorinsky spent his childhood could be true.

12. Dr. Gorinsky did attend and present at the First International Congress of Ethnobiology in 1988 (see Gorinsky 1988). While his subsequent work in ethnobiology seems to suggest that he believes wholeheartedly in collaborating with indigenous peoples fairly, he also seems to also have an uncritical view of the patent system's ability to safeguard and protect traditional knowledge that has been commodified. Whether a *written* agreement of any kind was drawn up between the Wapishanas and Dr. Gorinsky prior to his patenting the compounds is not mentioned in any of the reports detailing the incident. I find it surprising that Dr. Gorinsky, given his subsequent involvement with the International Society of Ethnobiology, did not seem aware of the issues and (apparently) did not think to enter into a written agreement with the Wapishana to clarify the benefit-sharing issues rather than relying upon verbal assurances.

References

Amerindian Act

Chapter 29:01, Laws of Guyana. Act 22 of 1951; Amended by 6 of 1961, 6 of 1976. Authorized by L.R.O. 1/1977, pp. 1–35.

Amerindian Peoples Association (APA) Executive Committee and Fergus MacKay

A Plain English Guide to the Amerindian Act. June 1998. Available at: www.sdnp.org.gy/apa/topic7.htm; last accessed on July 13, 2001.

Amerindian Peoples Association (APA) Executive Committee

APA Elects New Executive Committee and Calls for Land Claims Settlement Procedure and Urgent Review of the Amerindian Act. Press Release, May 4, 2000. Available at: www.sdnp.org.gy/apa/5th_ga_pr_2.htm; last accessed on July 13, 2001.

Amnesty International Index

Brazil: Cases of Killings and Ill-Treatment of Indigenous People. *AI Index: AMR 19/12/88* (November). New York: AI National Office, 1988.

Colchester, Marcus

Guyana, Fragile Frontier: Loggers, Miners and Forest Peoples. Kingston: Ian Randle Publishers, 1997.

Cultural Survival

Guyana Government Grants 5.1 Million Acre Mining Concession on Indigenous Lands. Available at: http://www.centrelink.org/Guyana.html and at http://web.archive.org/web/20010222221235/ and http:/cs.org/publications/featuredarticles/1998/guyana2.htm; last accessed January 1, 2004.

Dutfield, Graham

Intellectual Property Rights, Trade and Biodiversity. London: Earthscan Publications, 2000.

Edmundson, Rev. George

Early Relations of the Manoas with the Dutch, 1606–1732. Part I. *English Historical Review,* vol. 21 (1906): 229–253.

Forest Peoples Programme

Indigenous Peoples in Guyana Seek Recognition and Enforcement of their Land Right in an Historic Lawsuit. News Release, November 10, 1998. Available online at: www.cs.org/publications/featuredarticles/1998/guyana1.htm; last accessed on 01/09/02. Also archived at: www.forests.org.

Forte, Janette, and Amerindian Research Unit (eds.)

Amerindian Concerns: A Compilation from the Written Submissions Received by the Amerindian Research Unit from Amerindian Village Councils in Preparation for the National Conference of Amerindian Representatives. Document published and circulated at the AMIRANG conference, April 1994. Georgetown, Guyana: Janette Forte, 1994.

Forte, Janette

About Guyanese Amerindians. Georgetown, Guyana: Janette Forte, 1996a.

Thinking about Amerindians. Georgetown, Guyana: Janette Forte, 1996b.

Land-Use Planning and Social Aspects of Sustainable Forest Management. In *Seminar Proceedings: Research in Tropical Rain Forests: Its Challenges for the Future, 25–26 November 1997,* 139–148. Wageningen, the Netherlands: The

Tropenbos Foundation, 1997. Available at: www.tropenbos.nl/files/proc1997.htm; last accessed on January 1, 2004.

Global Law Association, Forest Peoples Programme, Amerindian Peoples Association of Guyana, and Upper Mazaruni Amerindian District Council (GLA/FPP/APA/Upper Mazaruni Amerindian District Council)
Indigenous Peoples, Land Rights and Mining in the Upper Mazaruni. Nijmegan (Netherlands): Global Law Association, 2000.

Gorinsky, Conrad
Ethnobiology and Medicine. In *Ethnobiology: Implications and Applications. Proceedings of the First International Congress of Ethnobiology (Belém, 1988),* edited by Darrell Posey, 2 vols., 119–123. Belém, Brazil: Emílio Goeldi, 1990.

Guyana Chronicle
APA Wants Equal, Full, Participation in Amerindian Act Review. June 23, 2002. Available at: www.landofsixpeoples.com/gynewsjs.htm; last accessed on April 15, 2003.

Team Gathering Recommendations for New Amerindian Act. February 22, 2003. Available at: www.landofsixpeoples.com/gynewsjs.htm; last accessed on April 15, 2003.

Human Rights Watch
Brazil: Violence Against the Macuxi and Wapixana Indians in Raposa Serra do Sol and Northern Roraima from 1988 to 1994. *A Human Rights Watch Report*, vol. 6, no. 7 (June 1994).

La Rose, Jean
Foreword. In *Guyana's Fragile Frontier: Loggers, Miners and Forest Peoples*, edited by Marcus Colchester, vii–viii. Kingston: Ian Randle Publishers, 1997.

La Rose, Jean, and Fergus MacKay
Our Land, Our Life, Our Culture: The Indigenous Movement in Guyana. *Cultural Survival Quarterly,* vol. 23, no. 4 (Winter 1999): 29–34.

La Rose, Miranda
New Law Should Empower the Amerindian—Consultation on New Act Told. Many Views on Land, Elected Chiefs and Alcohol. *Stabroek News*, May 13, 2003. Available at: www.landofsixpeoples.com/gynewsjs.htm; Last accessed on January 1, 2004.Laurenzo, Neely. New Amerindian Rights Center Advocates for Indigenous Peoples of Guyana. *Cultural Survival Quarterly,* vol. 24, no. 3 (fall 2000): 4.

MacKay, Fergus
Briefing Paper on the Rights of Indigenous Peoples in International Law. 1997. Available at: www.sdnp.org.gy/apa/topic3.htm; last accessed on July 13, 2001.

Makushi Research Unit
Makusipe Komanto Iseru: Sustaining Makushi Way of Life. Compiled by the Makushi Research Unit, edited by Janette Forte, as a project commissioned for the Iwokrama International Rain Forest Programme. Georgetown: BusinessPrint, 1996.

Menezes, Mary Noël
British Policy Towards Amerindians in British Guiana 1803–1873. Oxford: Clarendon Press, 1977.

(ed.). *The Amerindians in Guyana 1803–1873: A Documentary History.* Totowa, New Jersey: Frank Cass, 1979.

Moran, Katy, Steven King, and Thomas Carlson
Biodiversity Prospecting: Lessons and Prospects. *Annual Review of Anthropology,* vol. 30 (2001): 505–526.

Rabben, Linda
Hostages to Fortune: Macuxi, Wapixana, Ingarikó and Taurepang of Raposa-Serra do Sol. Active Voices: Cultural Survival's Online Activist Forum and Information Center. Available at: www.cs.org/AVoices/articles/Rabben.html; last accessed on June 5, 2000.

Rainforest Action Network
Timber Feeding Frenzy in Guyana. May–June Action Alert, dated May 21, 1996. Archived at: www.forests.org; last accessed on April 15, 1999.

Ramos, Alcida Rita
Indigenism: Ethnic Politics in Brazil. Madison: University of Wisconsin, 1998.

Riley, Mary
Measuring the Biomedical Efficacy of Traditional Remedies among the Makushi Amerindians of Southwestern Guyana. Ph.D. diss., Ann Arbor: UMI Dissertation Services, 2000.

Roopnarine, Terence
Freighted Fortunes: Gold and diamond mining in the Pakaraima Mountains, Guyana. Ph.D. diss., Department of Anthropology, University of Cambridge, 1996.

Sanders, Andrew

The Powerless People: An Analysis of the Amerindians of the Corentyne River. Warwick University Caribbean Studies No. X. London: MacMillan Publishers Ltd., (Caribbean), 1987.

Schomburgk, Robert H.

A Description of British Guiana, Geographical and Statistical: Exhibiting Its Resources and Capabilities, Together with the Present and Future Tradition and Prospects of the Colony. London: Simpkin, Marshall, and Company, 1840.

Stabroek News

Guyana Not Living Up to Amerindian Rights Obligations. April 15, 2000. Available at: www.landofsixpeoples.com/gynewsjs.htm; last accessed on April 15, 2003.

Mining: The Environmental Dimension. May 20, 2001. Available at: www.landofsixpeoples.com/gynewsjs.htm; last accessed on April 15, 2003.

The Amerindian Act. Editorial. September 6, 2002. Available at: www.landofsixpeoples.com/gynewsjs.htm; last accessed on April 15, 2003.

Revision of Amerindian Act—No Request Received for Extension of Consultations—Ministry. November 6, 2002. Available at: www.landofsixpeoples.com/gynewsjs.htm; last accessed on April 15, 2003.

Vidal, John

Biopirates Who Seek the Greatest Prizes. *The Guardian* (U.K.), November 15, 2000. Available at: www.guardian.co.uk/Print/0,3858,4090906,00.html; last accessed on March 15, 2003.

Villamea, Luiza , and João Fabio Caminoto

Indians Want Patent: Chiefs Prepare International Law Suit Against Scientist Who Registered Indigenous Knowledge. *ISTOE Magazine*, no. 1581 (January 19, 2000). Available at: www.zaz.com.br/istoe/brasileiros/2000/01/13/000.htm. English translation by David Hathaway. Accessed from Protecting Knowledge Listserv, January 17, 2000.

Vomero, Maria Fernanda

Piratas da floresta. *Superinteressante*, novembro 2001. Available at: super.abril.com.br/revista/reportag/1101/1702.html; last accessed on March 15, 2003.

Whitehead, Neil L.

Lords of the Tiger Spirit: A History of the Caribs in Colonial Venezuela and Guyana, 1498–1820. Koninklijk Instituut Voor Taal-, Land- en Volkenkunde, Caribbean Series 10. Providence: Foris Publications, 1988.

Carib Ethnic Soldiering in Venezuela, the Guianas, and Antilles: 1492–1820. *Ethnohistory*, vol. 37, no. 4 (1990a): 357–385.

The Snake Warriors—Sons of the Tiger's Teeth: A Descriptive Analysis of Carib Warfare: 1500–1820. In *The Anthropology of War*, edited by Jonathan Haas, 146–171. Cambridge: Cambridge University Press, 1990b.

Tribes Make States and States Make Tribes: Warfare and the Creation of Colonial Tribe and State in North-eastern South America, 1492–1820. In *War in the Tribal Zone*, pp. 127–150, edited by R. Brian Ferguson and Neil Whitehead. Santa Fe: SAR Press, 1992.

The Mazaruni Dragon: Golden Metals and Elite Exchanges in the Caribbean, Orinoco and the Amazon. In *Chieftains, Power, and Trade: Regional Interaction in the Intermediate Area of the Americas*, edited by C. H. Langebaek and F. Cardenas-Arroyo, pp. 107–132. Bogotá, Colombia: Departamento de Antropología, Universidad de los Andes, 1996.

Colonial Chieftains of the Lower Orinoco and Guayana Coast. In *Chiefdoms and Chieftaincy in the Americas*, edited by E. Redmond, pp. 150–163. Gainesville: University of Florida Press, 1998.

World Intellectual Property Organization (WIPO)

Intellectual Property Needs and Expectations of Traditional Knowledge Holders. WIPO Report on Fact-finding Missions on Intellectual Property and Traditional Knowledge (1998–1999). WIPO Publication No. 768E. Geneva, Switzerland: WIPO, April 2001.

Part Two

DEVELOPING INNOVATIVE SOLUTIONS

CHAPTER 5

LAND, TENURE SYSTEMS, AND INDIGENOUS INTELLECTUAL PROPERTY RIGHTS

Catherine M. Tucker

Major issues for Honduras's indigenous populations include legal recognition of land rights and the freedom to manage their natural and cultural resources as they see fit. Exercise of these rights is frequently associated with traditional systems of land-tenure and joint-use rights that differ from the national emphasis on private property. Traditional land use and tenure systems can be fundamental to indigenous peoples' natural resource management practices; moreover, these systems comprise a form of indigenous knowledge that is integral for traditional resource rights (TRR) and indigenous intellectual property rights (IIPR).

The linkages between land-tenure systems, land rights, and IIPR/TRR merit greater attention. From the perspective of many indigenous peoples, IIPR/TRR are part of the complex whole of their cultural heritage, collective knowledge, and territorial rights (Suagee 1994: 205; Posey and Dutfield 1996: 1–3) that may include traditional land-tenure systems. As understood in this chapter, land-tenure systems are definitions about rights to land and resources; they encompass concepts and rules (formal or informal) about rights and duties related to land use and access. Given that land-tenure systems depend upon ideas that are held and practiced jointly, and because such ideas can be integrally valuable and uniquely meaningful to a people, they constitute a form of indigenous knowledge. Indigenous knowledge often includes intimate understanding of natural resources; therefore it has great relevance for global issues such as environmental conservation, preservation of biodiversity, and discovery of pharmaceuticals (Brush 1996; Cox 2000; Greaves 1994; Nazarea 1999;

Ostergard, Tubin, and Altman 2001; cf. Ten Kate and Laird 2000). Recognizing the role of land-tenure systems for protecting and producing this knowledge comprises a necessary dimension of IIPR/TRR and for addressing the future of indigenous cultures and their alternative forms of resource management.

The following discussion explores the relationships between indigenous land-tenure systems and IIPR/TRR with respect to international accords, Honduran policies, and the illustrative experiences of a Lenca indigenous community in western Honduras. The case study considers the historical contexts of land tenure with respect to IIPR/TRR. It reviews the changes that have been occurring in the region as they affect IIPR/TRR and the land-tenure system, particularly the processes of market integration, adoption of modern agricultural technology, and the imposition of a land-titling program. While arguing that land-tenure systems represent a fundamental component of IIPR/TRR, it also shows that multiple challenges to indigenous knowledge and IIPR/TRR exist from within as well as from outside the group. The discussion provides a perspective of the peoples' approaches to integrate processes of change with traditional values, knowledge, and practices.

Indigenous Land-Tenure Systems and IIPR/TRR

Indigenous means of holding land and managing resources often encompass alternative land-tenure systems that do not conform well to international norms based upon private and government-owned property. Indeed, many traditional indigenous societies do not conceive of land and resources as "property" in the western sense (Posey and Dutfield 1996: 3). Whereas Western notions of intellectual property rights and land rights emphasize the individual, indigenous traditions generally recognize collective rights, shared knowledge, and common lands (Brush 1996; Johns 1999; Lagrotteria and Affolter 1999; Nazarea 1999).

In Honduras, as in other parts of the world, traditional land-tenure systems have been pressured to transform into arrangements more amenable to the national government's bureaucratic structures and economic development goals. Typically, this takes the form of privatization programs. Legislation and initiatives to transform communal lands into private property have historically constituted a means to expropriate lands for the state and the elite (e.g., Behar 1986: 190; Fernández 1987: 269–270; cf. Shiva 1997). Privatization processes in Central America have typically impinged upon indigenous land rights (Lapper and Painter 1985: 19), with a concomitant displacement of traditional land tenure systems and loss of IIPR/TRR.

The problem is not simply one of land ownership, but of the types of ownership and property rights that are legally recognized. At issue for indigenous peoples are the rights to define property and manage land and its resources in ways congruent with indigenous knowledge, cultural heritage, and livelihood needs. These rights underlie intellectual property rights, because many forms of indigenous knowledge that are relevant for IIPR/TRR (e.g., ethnobotanical knowledge, art, crafts, music, dance, cultural symbols) relate intimately to specific natural resources and land areas (Lagrotteria and Affolter 1999; Ford 1999). The propagation and protection of intellectual property can depend upon certain relationships to the land and natural resources as provided in an indigenous land-tenure system. Changes in land-tenure systems, such as the imposition of private ownership without consultation with the affected groups, can endanger IIPR/TRR by changing access to resources that are integral to the peoples' knowledge base, compelling transformations in traditional uses of natural resources and undermining cultural patterns. Therefore, perpetuation of indigenous land-tenure systems represents a fundamental component for peoples who seek legal recognition of land rights and resource management strategies. Such rights must provide protection from incursions, external intervention, and expropriation. Achieving these goals poses legal hurdles and practical challenges for indigenous peoples as well as national governments.

Many indigenous peoples' land-tenure systems have experienced change as they have struggled in the face of conquest, colonization, and subjugation to maintain traditional territories and assert land rights. As a result, indigenous concepts of property and land-tenure systems represent centuries of adaptation, accommodation, and resistance, rather than pristine survivals of a pre-Colombian era. This is no less true for other forms of indigenous knowledge more widely recognized as intellectual property. Indigenous music, dance, artwork, and religious rituals also express the experiences of colonization, imperialism, and cross-cultural interactions (Urban and Sherzer 1991; Adams 1991).

Perspectives from International Accords

A number of international declarations acknowledge that for indigenous peoples, IIPR/TRR cannot exist apart from the intimate relationships they have with their territories and the systems of land use and resource management that they have developed. Accords drawn up by indigenous peoples in particular make clear that rights to land, traditional institutions (such as land-tenure systems), cultural practices, and intellectual property rights are inseparable and interrelated dimensions of indigenous rights.

The Charter of the Indigenous-Tribal Peoples of the Tropical Forests explicitly calls for "the recognition, definition, and demarcation of our territories in accordance with our local and customary systems of ownership and use" (Article 14, reproduced in Posey and Dutfield 1996, Appendix 6). Moreover, "the form of land tenure will be decided by the people themselves, and the territory should be held communally, unless the people decide otherwise" (Article 15). Addressing biodiversity and conservation, the charter states in Article 40 that "programs related to biodiversity must respect the collective rights of our peoples to cultural and intellectual property." Article 42 links the protection of biodiversity to land management and tenure rights: "The best guarantee of the conservation of biodiversity is that those who promote it should uphold our rights to the use, administration, management and control of our territories" (www.mtnforum.org/resources/library/citpt92a.htm).

The Indigenous Peoples' Earth Charter (cited in Posey and Dutfield 1996: 190–198) states in Article 10, "Indigenous peoples' distinct and separate rights within their own territories must be recognized." Article 32 expands, "Our territories are living totalities in permanent vital relation between human beings and nature. Their possession produces the development of our culture. Our territorial property should be inalienable, unceasable, and not denied title. Legal, economic, and technical back-up are needed to guarantee this." Article 97 notes that "traditions cannot be separated from land, territory or science," and Article 104 observes, "The protection, norms, and mechanisms of artistic and artisanal creation of our peoples must be established and implemented in order to avoid plunder, plagiarism, undue exposure and use."

The Declaration of Principles of the World Council of Indigenous Peoples states in Article 3, "Every nation-state within which Indigenous

Peoples live shall recognize the population, territory, and institutions belonging to said peoples." Article 7 adds, "Indigenous Peoples have the right to determine the form, structure and jurisdiction of their own institutions." Traditional resource rights and intellectual property rights are encompassed in Articles 10, 11, 12, 13, and 18; these elements build on the prerequisites of rights to land and institutions (www.ces.iisc.ernet.in/hpg/envis/doc33.html).

The United Nations also has made notable contributions to recognizing the links between indigenous rights to land, traditional land-tenure systems, resource management practices, and IIPR/TRR through the UN Draft Declaration on the Rights of Indigenous Peoples, the COICA-UNDP Regional Meeting on Intellectual Property Rights and Biodiversity, and the UNDP Consultation on the Protection and Conservation of Indigenous Knowledge. Even when international accords and declarations on indigenous rights and intellectual property rights do not explicitly mention traditional land-tenure systems, they generally call for self-determination and resource rights. The right to control the access to and use of resources is a component of self-determination, which is fundamental for all dimensions of indigenous peoples' rights. This implies support for indigenous land-tenure systems and traditional resource rights, even when the relationships between them are understated or left implicit. An example occurs with the International Labor Organization's Convention 169 on Indigenous and Tribal Peoples.

Ratified by the Honduran legislature in 1994, Convention 169 (Organización Internacional del Trabajo [International Labor Organization, ILO] 1994) asserts in Article 4, Section 1, "Special measures shall be adopted as appropriate for safeguarding the persons, institutions, property, labour, cultures and environment of the peoples concerned." Article 5, parts (a) and (b), notes that "the social, cultural, religious and spiritual values and practices of these peoples shall be recognized and protected, and due account shall be taken of the nature of the problems which face them both as groups and as individuals." Moreover "the integrity of the values, practices and institutions of these peoples shall be respected." Article 13 directly addresses land rights: "Governments shall respect the special importance for the cultures and spiritual values of the peoples concerned of their relationship with the lands or territories, which they occupy or otherwise use, especially the collective aspects of this relationship." Although indigenous tenure systems are not specifically mentioned, they often involve a collective relationship with the land and are a form of institution that encompasses both values and practices. The ILO convention provides limited protection for indigenous knowledge, but with the recognition of collective rights it offers fundamental support for IIPR/TRR (Posey and Dutfield 1996: 117).

Honduran Land Titling Programs and Indigenous Property Rights

Recent land-titling programs of the Honduran government have tended to promote privatization as a uniform policy, while ignoring the variety of land-tenure systems and resource rights that exist among not only indigenous groups but also poor ladino farmers. Many indigenous groups traditionally manage their land through hybrid property systems that include private and communal dimensions (Dodds 1998; Rivas 1993; Tucker 1999). The hybrid aspect of these property systems appears to be poorly appreciated by external agents, and policy implementation has been slow to recognize that a uniform land-tenure system, however practical for administrative and bureaucratic purposes, may not be equally suitable or beneficial for all locales. Even less concern has existed for the potential ramifications of private titling programs for indigenous groups and their TRR/IIPR, although pressure from indigenous groups has attempted to win greater respect from the government for their cultural traditions and land rights.

The national emphasis on private property reflects the perspective of neoclassical economics theory and many donor agencies. This perspective perceives private and government-owned property as the best contexts for economically efficient land management. It argues that private property results in optimal tenure security, improves access to credit, and allows owners to capture benefits from land improvements, thus encouraging more profitable and sustainable land uses. In many parts of the world, this perspective has contradicted local realities. The assumptions favoring private property do not apply well to poor farmers who face constraints related to the size and quality of their land. They often encounter problems with the availability and affordability of inputs, which can limit their profitability and competitiveness and place them at risk of defaulting on loans and losing their lands (Fandino 1993).

Private property proponents have also erred in believing that common property necessarily results in resource degradation (i.e., Hardin

1968). Many studies have shown that people can work together to manage common-property resources sustainably (i.e., Berkes 1987; Bromley 1992; McCay and Acheson 1987; McKean 1992, 1982; McKean and Ostrom 1995; Netting 1976; Ostrom 1990; Stanley 1991; Stevenson 1991; White and Runge 1994). Moreover, common-property arrangements in marginal areas can provide important resources and benefits for poor, rural populations. For example, shared rights can lead to a more equitable distribution of scarce or dispersed resources and reduce risk in the face of environmental uncertainty (Berkes, Feeny, McCay, and Acheson 1989; Maybury-Lewis 1996; McCay and Acheson 1987; Runge 1986; Wilson and Thompson 1993). The imposition of private property in the place of common-property arrangements can destroy traditional access and uses, counteract long-established group practices of resource management, and result in exacerbated poverty and dislocation of those who lose access rights or fail to obtain sufficient land to meet subsistence needs (Johns 1999; McCay and Acheson 1987: 8; Utting 1993). When men are the main recipients of private land titles, women can lose resource rights with deleterious consequences for their economic options and nutritional status as well as their children's health. These outcomes affect traditional rural populations as well as indigenous peoples (Agarwal 1997; Jodha 1992). These circumstances raise questions as to the efficacy of private titles as an economic development tool in developing countries (Fandino 1993).

Honduras has implemented a series of programs to provide land titles. Agrarian reform laws (1962–1992) attempted to mitigate inequitable land distribution by allowing small and landless farmers to obtain titles to unused or illegally claimed lands. The laws achieved only limited success against opposition by powerful landholding interests and inconstant support from successive government administrations (Kincaid 1985; Thorpe et al. 1995). The focus on agrarian reform was replaced in the 1980s with an emphasis on rationalizing land markets. Through the Honduran Land Titling Project for Smallholders (*Proyecto de Titulación de Tierras para los Pequeños Productores*, PTT), the government intended to title lands to de facto landholders, in order to encourage producers to take advantage of market incentives, increase production, and improve agricultural techniques. The project failed to achieve its objectives, even increasing land insecurity in certain cases (Jansen and Roquas 1998).

Land-titling programs have tended to overlook indigenous peoples' demands for land rights, and indigenous groups have struggled to gain government respect for their territorial claims. With the passage of Convention 169, Honduras's indigenous peoples found legislative grounds for recognition of their land rights. In 1994, indigenous groups marched on the capital to present a list of demands consistent with Convention 169, in which recognition of land rights and TRR figured strongly. Government officials agreed to many of the demands, but fulfillment has been sketchy. Many indigenous peoples have yet to gain legal titles to their territories, and even fewer have regained expropriated lands. Miskito and Garífuna groups have had to fight revisions to Article 107 of the constitution, which would have allowed foreign buyers to purchase land within forty kilometers of the coast where many indigenous communities are located (*La Prensa,* August 18, 1999; *La Prensa,* August 24, 1999). Negotiation between indigenous groups and government officials led to a tabling of the constitutional change, but many Garífuna communities have still lost land to Honduran interests (Morgan 1999; *La Prensa*, October 13, 1999).

Data Collection and Fieldwork Methods

The information presented here is based upon a total of sixteen months of fieldwork in Honduras distributed over an eight-year period (1992–2000). The researcher conducted interviews, surveys, archival research, and field observations addressing land use, property arrangements, and processes of change with a focus on the *municipio* (county) of La Campa, in western Honduras. The work has included data collection from government offices, national archives, and libraries (Tucker 1996). Extended ethnographic fieldwork (August 1993–July 1994) included a land-use survey of 103 households, a demographic census, and interviews with residents and representatives of nongovernment organizations (NGOs), indigenous groups, and governmental organizations. Fieldwork periods in 1995, 1997, 1998, and 2000 involved a follow-up household survey (1997) and additional interviews and field observations conducted with the assistance of fieldwork teams. The 1998 research provided initial data on the land-titling program that was being implemented at that time. The 2000 fieldwork included exploration of the early outcomes of the new property system and peoples' perceptions of its effectiveness.

The Case Study: An Overview of the Site

The *municipio* ("county") of La Campa is located in the mountains of western Honduras. The people ("Lacamperos") are descendants of the Lenca civilization that once occupied the majority of western Honduras and parts of El Salvador (Newson 1992). Five hundred years after the Spanish conquest, the Lenca culture and social organization have been profoundly transformed. The present-day Lenca have been described as "peasants of Lenca descent," due to the loss of their language and their accommodations to ladino society (Chapman 1985; Hamp 1976). Yet they continue to recognize their indigenous heritage, and many communities practice rituals, customary dances, and cultural traditions that distinguish them from the dominant culture (Castegnaro de Foletti 1989: 261; Chapman 1985). Aspects of IIPR/TRR of particular significance for La Campa relate to the production of traditional Lenca pottery, the rituals and dances surrounding its patron saint's day, and forest use.

Western Honduras is known for its mountainous topography and a historically marginal position in the national economy. Less than 10 percent of the land in the region is considered suitable for permanent agriculture (Pineda Portillo 1984). Pine-oak forests represent the most important natural resource, but agriculture and logging have led to notable clearing. La Campa is typical of the region, but it has preserved nearly 60 percent of its land as forest. The people depend primarily upon subsistence production of maize and beans; small gardens produce bananas, herbs, seasonal fruits, and coffee. Communal forests provide medicinal plants, firewood, timber, grazing areas, and various nontimber forest products for household use (Tucker 1999).

The Traditional Land-Tenure System in La Campa

La Campa has managed its lands under a tenure system that has combined several forms of de facto property rights: permanent usufruct, temporary usufruct, and communal. Until 1998, with the advent of the new land-titling program (discussed later), all lands belonged jointly to the residents under ejidal and communal land titles; thus by legal (de jure) definition it was all common property. A council of locally elected officials and representatives served to oversee land use, enforce local rules, mediate conflicts, and conduct bureaucratic functions with regional and national governments. The system reflected the Castilian model mandated under Spanish rule, but some symbols and rituals integral to municipal government related to pre-Hispanic traditions and more recent adaptations (Tucker 1996). Colonial, precolonial, and modern elements thus contributed to the land-tenure system, which evolved through time to serve as the basis upon which the people met subsistence needs, reduced risk, and fulfilled religious, social, and trade obligations.

IIPR/TRR encompassed the multiple dimensions of access and use rights in relationship to the various forms of tenure, which ultimately depended upon the communal nature of the land holding and management by the community. Adults in good standing in the community (i.e., current on their county taxes and communal duties) had the right to make permanent and temporary land claims, and all residents could use the communal lands for firewood collection, mushroom hunting, gathering of medicinal plants, fishing, and hunting.

Permanent usufruct lands involved claims in perpetuity for individual house lots, agricultural fields, and pastures. These lands primarily included the county's better, flatter lands that were most suitable for continuous productive use. For practical purposes, permanent usufruct constituted a form of private property because these parcels could be exchanged, inherited, or sold among residents. Residents prohibited nonresidents from acquiring land, thus the people reserved land rights for community members and maintained control over their land.

Temporary usufruct lands were comprised of communal forest areas that served intermittently for cultivation of maize and beans. Farmers requested an area for temporary agriculture; they cleared forest by slash-and-burn methods, cultivated the land for several years, and then abandoned it to fallow with declining soil fertility and erosion. When cultivation ceased, the land returned to the commons. Under this system, lands cycled through different property rights and uses, through stages of forest, clearing, planting, and fallow to forest regrowth.

Historically, most of the county land remained free of permanent individual claims and was used communally. These common lands included areas protected by tradition as village woodlots and pastures, relatively marginal lands subject to periodic clearing and temporary usufruct, and extremely marginal lands that had few uses, especially steep slopes, rocky outcroppings, and canyons (cf. Netting 1976, 1982). The commons also included clay and sandbeds used for pottery production.

The municipality granted temporary and permanent usufruct to residents upon request. As a result of this policy, all farmers controlled their own parcels for production, and no farmer was landless. For the most part, only men requested usufruct, but occasionally unmarried women obtained land. People "paid" for their use of private and communal lands through local taxes, school fees, and municipal service. Their duties included communal labor obligations, such as marking borders, maintaining paths, fighting forest fires, cleaning public water sources, and assisting with the construction of public buildings. Community members who shirked their duties faced consequences that ranged from public criticism to fines and detention in the county jail (Tucker 1996: 229–238).

The land-tenure system served to meet community interests, such as protecting water sources. The common-property land also provided a foundation for shared identity. With the loss of the Lenca language during the twentieth century, shared lands and communal governance became principal elements uniting and defining people's ties to each other and the community (cf. Adams 1991:192). Even though disputes over land rights represent a recurrent element in interpersonal conflicts, the presence of common property supported social cohesion through related organizational and governance arrangements. The municipal government, composed of locally elected officials and representatives, offered the primary context for management and supervision of the common-property lands. Most adult men served on the council at some point during their lives, and any resident (although mainly males) could attend a council meeting to request use rights to a parcel of land, submit a complaint, or request mediation for a dispute.

IIPR/TRR and Land Tenure

The land-tenure system has provided a context in which IIPR/TRR could be practiced, and that has maintained traditional customs and beliefs. By permitting various forms of usufruct rights, and allowing every resident to use the commons, the land-tenure system has given every resident access to the natural resources integral to their livelihoods. With large forest areas retained as common pastures and woodlots, any resident can take advantage of the opportunity to track down dispersed and unpredictable resources such as edible mushrooms, medicinal plants, game animals, and fish. Certain individuals hunt honey produced by the native stingless bees (now nearly extinct), and some even capture bees to start their own hives. Traditional doctors and healers collect materials used for cleansing rituals, while nearly everyone understands how to use common medicinal herbs in poultices and teas. During the rainy season, people rise early to hunt mushrooms, taking advantage of at least a dozen edible fungi. No individual or minority within the community has been permitted to monopolize a natural resource. Joint land rights have provided the context that permits inhabitants to exercise their knowledge of the natural resource base and share it with new generations.

Land-use practices also relate to traditional beliefs about beneficent and vengeful spirits thought to inhabit the rivers and springs, hilltops, forests, and the claybeds. While it is difficult to gauge how these beliefs influence land use and protection of natural resources, residents commonly believe that spirits are associated with each resource, and unwise use of water, clay, or forest resources will anger the spirits and cause the transgressor to fall ill. When a person suffers from illnesses that Western medical attention or herbal treatments cannot remedy, the family may resort to special healing rituals to mollify the spirits, under the leadership of a traditional healer. These rituals have become rarer, and younger people increasingly doubt their efficacy. Under severe criticism by the Catholic Church, believers in these rituals rarely discuss them, and will only conduct the rituals in secret under cover of night.

The land-tenure system has been critical for protecting the resources needed for pottery production. The land-tenure system has defined the sources of clay, sand, and colored soil (used for painting) as common property in perpetuity. According to county laws, the resources cannot be enclosed or claimed privately, nor used by nonresidents. Farmers who work land adjacent to these resources are required to respect the numerous paths that enter the areas, and to leave space open around them. Occasional attempts to enclose these communal resources or their access routes have met with rapid sanctions by potters and the municipal council (Tucker 1996: 251–252).

The technologies of pottery making and the patterns used for decoration continue to be passed from mother to daughter and teacher to student. Even with increasing de facto land privatization, the majority of the people support communal rights to pottery materials. Pottery production represents one example of the close ties that can exist among land rights, land tenure, indigenous knowledge, and art. For many households, pottery production provides a major contribution to their income, and it has been particularly important for women who produce most of the pottery and usually control the proceeds from its sale. La Campa's pottery has been distributed widely through trade networks that appear to have pre-Hispanic origins, and more recent market connections (Castegnaro de Foletti 1989: 260–262; Ardón Mejía 1989). The art has survived and flourished; today buyers go to La Campa to purchase pottery for museums and tourist shops as far away as Tegucigalpa and San Pedro Sula.

Processes of Change in Traditional Land Tenure

While the principles of the traditional land-tenure system endure, it has experienced notable transformations through the latter half of the twentieth century, and particularly through the 1980s and 1990s. The primary transformations have included an increase in the area of land claimed permanently for private uses of communal land and a restructuring of ownership rights under a national land-titling program. The processes of de facto privatization of land rights relate to changes in agricultural technology, population growth, and closer ties to the market. Moreover, residents' experiences with national policies and programs have led to changes in their relationships to the land and with each other, with implications for IIPR/TRR.

De facto privatization of common lands has been occurring gradually. Population growth represents one factor, as each generation augments the demand for agricultural land. The county's mountainous land restricts the area suitable for agriculture; by the 1960s farmers began adopting inputs and techniques to intensify agricultural production. Oxen-drawn plows, fertilizers, and herbicides have resulted in higher yields and extended the time that fields can be cultivated. With increased use of plows, slash-and-burn methods have become less common. In the present, farmers rarely abandon fields, and temporary usufruct has become rare (Southworth and Tucker 2001).

While farmers' permanent land claims for agriculture have been an important factor in privatization, residents have also claimed forests for private woodlots and pastures. This form of privatization apparently became more common in the 1980s as a reaction to logging contracts approved by the Honduran Corporation for Forestry Development (COHDEFOR). Between 1974 and 1987, COHDEFOR sold rights to sawmills to log La Campa's communal forests. COHDEFOR limited residents' rights to harvest trees for tempering pottery and construction; it also prohibited agricultural clearings on forested land. Residents became increasingly irate over the restrictions and the degradation of their forests. In 1987, La Campa ousted COHDEFOR and prohibited logging (Tucker 1999). The experience with COHDEFOR made residents aware of the insecure status of their common lands relative to governmental intervention. The council ceased to enforce a rule that residents must clear forest from land to claim it. Residents who were able to afford the costs of fencing began to claim parcels of forest to secure their access to forest resources and obtain a reserve against future land shortages. Although private forests comprise a small portion of the forested land in La Campa, their emergence represents a shift in preferences toward private holdings, at least among the better-off residents in the community.

Privatization of land also relates to expansion of coffee production for the market. Although coffee has evidently been grown in the region for generations, it was traditionally grown for household consumption. During the 1960s, early innovators adopted new coffee strains for market production, but, with high start-up costs, few people were willing or able to risk the investment. In the 1980s, government programs provided economic incentives for coffee production and sponsored programs to teach farmers about proper use of chemical inputs and the adoption of modern coffee hybrids. Farmers with adequate resources to afford the inputs began to claim new lands in the higher elevations. While the mountainous lands had always been favored for agriculture due to slightly higher precipitation, the majority of the area remained as common forests. In the early 1990s, however, coffee prices soared (IHCAFE 1997). Lacamperos responded by claiming land in common forests for permanent usufruct intended for coffee plantations. The county council, which included several prospective coffee growers, apparently supported this transformation in hopes of furthering county development as well as their own interests. The processes of de facto privatization have reduced the communal forest area available for residents' exercise of TRR such as firewood collection and mushroom gathering.

The Land-Titling Program

Within this context of ongoing transformations, the Honduran government initiated a land-titling program in the 1990s to rationalize land tenure in areas that had not been affected by earlier land-titling programs (cf. Jansen and Roquas 1998). Ejidos represented a priority, because these titles did not carry the same legal standing as a private title. For example, a farmer on ejidal land could not use the land as collateral, nor could the land legally be bought or sold (although in practice, the land was saleable, and people held locally recognized titles). The program contained several options to replace ejidal titles with alternative types of land titles. Landholders or recognized claimants could choose to purchase a private land title outright. Indigenous communities were granted special status, so that they could choose to retain communal lands under a village title. At the same time, indigenous people could opt to purchase a private title to their individual land claims. The government aimed to increase land security and increase access to credit for individuals or groups by granting land titles that could serve as collateral.

The land-titling program appeared to raise serious threats to the traditional land-tenure system and IIPR/TRR. People expressed misgivings as to whether the information provided by government representatives explained the program in sufficient detail and worried about its implications for communal resources and their permanent usufruct parcels. Doubts were exacerbated by conflicting interpretations of the programs' rules and requirements. Residents suspected that the program intended to limit the number of parcels that they could own or permit privatization of the communal areas upon which nearly everyone depended for firewood, construction materials, and pottery making. Several farmers informed the researcher that they would have to give up usufruct to parcels outside their village of residence under the new program. Others surmised that they would have to participate in land councils in each of the villages where they owned land, which was seen as unreasonable. Yet they feared that if they did not accept the titling program, their land would be subject to expropriation by the government or outsiders.

The municipal council decided to approve the program after a process that many residents considered inadequate. But residents did accept the decision, and a critical element was the support of representatives of the

National Organization of Indigenous Lenca People of Honduras (Organización Nacional Indigena Lenca de Honduras, ONILH) who lived in the county and adjacent communities. ONILH members had received orientation on the land-titling program from the National Agrarian Institute (INA). One ONILH representative in La Campa promoted the program because it offered greater land security and improved access to credit programs. He reassured people that the program allowed conservation of communal resources under the new titles. Recalling La Campa's struggle to retain forest control from COHDEFOR, he argued that the new land titles provided better legal protection should the government ever again decide to appropriate communal forest resources.

Few people in La Campa opted to purchase individual land titles. The cost represented an obstacle for many, while community sentiment favored joint titles and the maintenance of communal lands. Those who purchased private titles tended to be better-off residents who were more individualistic and less dependent on social support networks than the rest of the community.

The new program devolved the titles traditionally held at the county level to villages. Each land title comprised all of the people who held land within a village territory, as well as common lands such as public woodlots. Decision making and control over this land was entrusted to village councils. This change caused consternation for the county council, which lost its authority over land governance. The only titles that remained under county council governance were the lands purchased under communal titles. This did not include the clay and sandbeds used by potters; these communal resources were titled to the villages in which they fell.

As the program progressed, INA provided orientation to village representatives concerning the formation and operation of village councils. The information evidently provided enough content for the village to adopt their new land management responsibilities with a degree of confidence. Moreover, the villages already had existing councils to manage local affairs. In practice, these councils took on the duties regarding new land titles and oversight. Many village authorities already had experience with debating and mediating land distribution and associated conflicts through their participation in the county council; some had served as elected county officials. As a result, management of the new land titles and village land governance built upon residents' previous experience.

The village councils tended to adopt the principles of the system practiced at the county level, and this has helped to protect IIPR/TRR associated with communal lands. Pottery-making resources have remained common property to which all county residents have de facto use rights. Each village has maintained at least one area as a communal woodlot and pasture, and there are also some unclaimed common forests available for the next generation to claim for private usufruct.

The village title system has posed several challenges for Lacamperos. Most farmers held fields in multiple areas spread through the county, now falling under different village land titles. Farmers were loath to consolidate land holdings because traditional practices reduced risk by dispersing agricultural fields. In principle, all landowners were expected to attend meetings in every village in which they held land. In practice, a high potential for scheduling conflicts existed, and landowners did not want to be obligated to attend meetings in multiple villages. Village councils came to the uniform decision that all landowners would be invited to attend meetings, but only those who actually resided in the village were required to attend.

The village councils also discovered that the new structure did not provide for a means to negotiate land disputes across village boundaries. Previously, the county council served as the principal entity for conflict mediation. Soon after the new village titles had been finalized, a conflict arose as residents in one village claimed a continuing right to use of a communal forest assigned to a neighboring village's territory. The county council intervened, and the mayor served as the mediator between the two villages' factions. The council's response set a precedent that reconfirmed its traditional role for land dispute mediation, if only for cases in which villages could not resolve conflicts.

Discussion

In a context of processes of change that have transformed the land-tenure system and influenced traditional agriculture and market relationships, IIPR/TRR have experienced some changes but thus far they have endured and adapted. The land-titling program compelled a major restructuring of the land-tenure system, yet Lacamperos managed to perpetuate common rights to certain resources, particularly forests, woodlots, and raw materials for pottery production. Thus far, the majority of farmers in La Campa continue to have usufruct rights to land. Despite initial shortcomings and doubts, the program permitted sufficient flexibility that the people were able to adapt it to their needs, traditions, and collective resource rights.

The progressive transformation of common lands into permanent agricultural fields and private forests began prior to the land-titling program, and the process may be undermining social cohesion. Protection of communal resources endures, but communal labor projects have declined in recent years. Obligatory group labor projects have largely been replaced with remunerative labor performed by poorer residents. As a result, people have fewer opportunities to work as a group, share common knowledge, and affirm their commitment to common goals. This may bode poorly for the future of collective practices and activities, but village councils provide some compensation as a space in which residents meet to discuss shared problems and interests.

As better-off community members depend more on monetary incomes and export crop production, their dependence upon reciprocal social networks and collective land rights is likely to become less important. Enforcing rules for resource management and equitable access to forest resources is likely to become more difficult if increasing social heterogeneity leads toward inequitable distribution of resources. With private forests and coffee fields making incursions on formerly common lands, the area available to people for subsistence agriculture and collection of forest products has decreased (Southworth and Tucker 2001), increasing the risk of overexploitation of remaining communal lands. Meanwhile, increasing market ties and availability of material goods pre-sent opportunities for assimilation and identification with the dominant Honduran society, particularly among the young people. All of these processes pose challenges to the maintenance of IIPR/TRR, which cannot be resolved or reversed solely by international accords, legislative acts, or even new protections for traditional systems, although these could be helpful.

La Campa represents but one case in which the land-tenure systems, land rights, and TRR/IIPR are intimately related. The traditional land-tenure system has accommodated changes in agricultural technology and market integration over the past half century and experienced the imposition of the new land-titling system that changed the structure of local land governance and management. The new land titles nevertheless allowed some flexibility, and the people made adaptations that reflected their traditional arrangements as well as their emerging relationships with the market and the national economy.

The situation offers promise as well as cautionary aspects for the future of indigenous knowledge and TRR/IIPR. Processes of privatization and expanding market involvement appear linked to increasing social heterogeneity, which in turn may undermine traditions of joint land management, cooperative decision making, and communal resource use. The new titling program was one of several change processes that contributed to transformations in La Campa's social fabric and land tenure, which may eventually undermine IIPR /TRR. The community has thus far proven to be relatively successful in maintaining certain aspects of its traditional land-tenure system and associated TRR, such as those related to pottery production.

The Honduran government showed flexibility by recognizing that indigenous communities should be permitted the option of communal land titles, even though the requirements forced changes in traditional land tenure in La Campa. Lacamperos' prior experience with collective land management contributed to their ability to work through the land-titling process and the redistribution of decision-making responsibilities to villages, while preserving traditional land-tenure elements important for their IIPR/TRR. At the same time, processes of market integration, reductions of communal land areas, and young people's increasing acceptance of the dominant Honduran culture appear to threaten local IIPR/TRR. La Campa continues to face the challenges of preserving its cultural heritage, improving the livelihoods of the impoverished majority, and maintaining its natural resources for future generations. These problems have wide relevance for traditional rural populations and indigenous peoples throughout the world.

The need for improved respect and legal protections for IIPR/TRR and their associated land-tenure systems represent only part of the challenge for the future of indigenous populations. In the face of globalization and powerful economic incentives, indigenous peoples' rights to self-determination include the rights to adopt new market activities, transform traditions, and acquire new knowledge and skills that may displace certain facets of traditional knowledge. These choices, however, must not be the only ones that offer the possibility of improved livelihoods and well-being. If the entire range of indigenous rights—to IIPR/TRR, land rights, traditional land-tenure systems, religious beliefs, and alternative resource management practices—is protected and respected, then indigenous peoples will have the option of achieving their own development goals through the control and development of their own knowledge and resources. This possibility may well be the most promising alternative for the protection of IIPR/TRR and the conservation of cultural and biological diversity in the world.

References

Adams, Richard
Strategies of Ethnic Survival in Central America. In *Nation-States and Indians in Latin America*, edited by Greg Urban and Joel Sherzer, 181–206. Austin: University of Texas Press, 1991.

Agarwal, Bina
Environmental Action, Gender Equity and Women's Participation. *Development and Change*, vol. 28 (1997): 1–44.

Ardón Mejía, Mario
Panorama de la Alfarería Tradicional de La Campa, Honduras. *Folklore Americano*, vol. 48 (1989): 69–80.

Behar, Ruth
The Presence of the Past in a Spanish Village: Santa María del Monte. Princeton: Princeton University Press, 1986.

Berkes, Fikret
Common-Property Resource Management and Cree Indian Fisheries in Subarctic Canada. In *The Question of the Commons*, edited by Bonnie McCay and James Acheson, 66–91. Tucson: University of Arizona Press, 1987.

Berkes, F., D. Feeny, B. J. McCay, and J. M. Acheson
The Benefits of the Commons. *Nature*, vol. 340 (1989): 91–93.

Bromley, Daniel
Commons, Property, and Common-Property Regimes. In *Making the Commons Work*, edited by Daniel Bromley, 3–16. San Francisco: Institute for Contemporary Studies Press, 1992.

Brush, Stephen
Whose Knowledge, Whose Genes, Whose Rights? In *Valuing Local Knowledge: Indigenous People and Intellectual Property Rights*, edited by Stephen Brush and Doreen Stabinsky, 1–21. Washington, D.C.: Island Press, 1996.

Castegnaro de Foletti, Alessandra
Alfarería Lenca Contemporánea de Honduras. Tegucigalpa: Editorial Guaymuras, 1989.

Chapman, Anne
Los Hijos del Copal y la Candela: Ritos Agrarios y Tradición Oral de los Lencas de Honduras. Tomo I. México: Universidad Autónoma de México, 1985.

Cox, Paul Alan
Will Tribal Knowledge Survive the Millennium? *Science*, vol. 287 (2000): 44–45.

Dodds, David
Assessing Indigenous Deforestation in Eastern Honduras. Paper presented at the Annual Meetings for the Latin American Studies Association, Chicago, Illinois, 1998.

Fandino, Mario
Land Titling and Peasant Differentiation in Honduras. *Latin American Perspectives*, vol. 20, no. 2 (1993): 45–53.

Fernández, J. W.
Decline and Recommitment in Asturias, Spain. In *The Question of the Commons: The Culture and Ecology of Communal Resources*, edited by Bonnie J. McCay and James M. Acheson, 266–289. Tucson: The University of Arizona Press, 1987.

Ford, Richard I.
Ethnoecology Serving the Community. In *Ethnoecology: Situated Knowledge/Located Lives*, edited by V. Nazarea, 71–87. Tucson: University of Arizona Press, 1999.

Greaves, Thomas
IPR: A Current Survey. In *Intellectual Property Rights for Indigenous Peoples: A Sourcebook*, edited by Thomas Greaves, 1–16. Oklahoma City: Society for Applied Anthropology, 1994.

Hamp, Eric P
The Last Lenca. *International Journal of American Linguistics*, vol. 42, no. 1 (1976): 73–79.

Hardin, Garrett
The Tragedy of the Commons. *Science,* vol. 162 (1968): 1243–1248.

Instituto Hondureño del Café (IHCAFE)
Boletín Estadístico 1970–1996. Tegucigalpa: IHCAFE, 1997.

International Alliance of the Indigenous-Tribal People of the Tropical Forests
http://iaip.gn.apc.org/chart/char1.html. Last accessed on January 5, 2004.

Jansen, Kees, and Esther Roquas
Modernizing Insecurity: The Land Titling Project in Honduras. *Development and Change,* vol. 29, no. 1 (1998): 81–106.

Jodha, N. S.
Common Property Resources: A Missing Dimension of Development Strategies. World Bank Discussion Paper No. 169. Washington, D.C.: The World Bank, 1992.

Johns, Timothy
Plant Constituents and the Nutrition and Health of Indigenous Peoples. In *Ethnoecology: Situated Knowledge/Located Lives,* edited by Virginia Nazarea, 157–174. Tucson: University of Arizona Press, 1999.

Kincaid, Douglas
"We are the Agrarian Reform": Rural Politics and Agrarian Reform. In *Honduras, Portrait of a Captive Nation,* edited by Nancy Peckenham and Annie Street, 135–147. New York: Praeger, 1985.

Lagrotteria, Marta, and James M. Affolter.
Sustainable Production and Harvest of Medicinal and Aromatic Herbs in the Sierras de Córdoba Region, Argentina. In *Ethnoecology: Situated Knowledge/ Located Lives,* edited by Virginia Nazarea, 175–189. Tucson: University of Arizona Press, 1999.

Lapper, Richard, and James Painter
Honduras: State for Sale. London: Latin American Bureau (Research and Action) Limited, 1985.

La Prensa
Particulares no podrán comprar tierras de indígenas y garífunas. La Prensa on the Web at: www.laprensahn.com; last accessed August 18, 1999.

Indígenas preparan movilización contra ratificación de artículo 107. La Prensa on the Web at: www.laprensahn.com; last accessed August 24, 1999.

Congreso no ratificará el artículo 107 constitucional. La Prensa on the Web at: www.laprensahn.com; last accessed October 13, 1999.

Maybury-Lewis, David
Voices from the Commons: Evolving Relations of Property and Management. Editorial. *Cultural Survival Quarterly*, vol. 20, no. 1 (1996): 3.

McCay, Bonnie J., and James M. Acheson
Human Ecology of the Commons. In *The Question of the Commons: The Culture and Ecology of Communal Resources*, edited by Bonnie J. McCay and James M. Acheson, 1–36. Tucson: The University of Arizona Press, 1987.

McKean, Margaret A.
The Japanese Experience with Scarcity: Management of Traditional Common Lands. *Environmental Review,* vol. 6, no. 2 (1982): 63–88.

Success on the Commons: A Comparative Examination of Institutions for Common Property Resource Management. *Journal of Theoretical Politics,* vol. 4 (1992): 247–281.

McKean, Margaret A., and Elinor Ostrom
Common Property Regimes in the Forest: Just a Relic from the Past? *Unasylva*, vol. 46, no. 1 (1995): 3–15.

Morgan, Ronald J.
Garífuna Communities Stand to Lose Lands. *NACLA Report on the Americas*, vol. 32, no. 5 (1999): 49–50.

Nazarea, Virginia
Introduction: A View from a Point: Ethnoecology as Situated Knowledge. In *Ethnoecology: Situated Knowledge/Located Lives*, edited by V. Nazarea, 3–20. Tucson: University of Arizona Press, 1999.

Netting, Robert McC.
What Alpine Peasants Have in Common: Observations on Communal Tenure in a Swiss Village. *Human Ecology,* vol. 4, no. 2 (1976): 135–146.

Territory, Property and Tenure. In *Behavioral and Social Science Research: A National Resource, Part II*, edited by Robert Adams, Neil J. Smaller, and Donald J. Treiman, 446–502.Washington, D.C: National Academy Press, 1982.

Newson, Linda
El Costo de la Conquista (The Cost of Conquest). Jorge Traviso, translator. Tegucigalpa: Editorial Guaymuras, 1992.

Organización Internacional del Trabajo (International Labor Organization; *hereafter* ILO)

C169: Indigenous and Tribal Peoples Convention (Convenio No. 169: Sobre Pueblos Indígenas y Tribales en Países Independientes 1989). Tegucigalpa: Editorial Guaymuras, 1994 (1989).

Ostergard, Robert L., Jr., Matthew Tubin, and Jordan Altman

Stealing from the Past: Globalisation, Strategic Formation and the Use of Indigenous Intellectual Property in the Biotechnology Industry. *Third World Quarterly*, vol. 22, no. 4 (2001): 643–656.

Ostrom, Elinor

Governing the Commons. Cambridge: Cambridge University Press, 1990.

Pineda Portillo, Noé

Geografía de Honduras. 2d ed. Tegucigalpa: Editorial ESP, 1984.

Posey, Darrell A., and Graham Dutfield

Beyond Intellectual Property: Toward Traditional Resource Rights for Indigenous Peoples and Local Communities. Ottawa: International Development Research Centre, 1996.

Rivas, Ramón D.

Pueblos Indígenas y Garífuna de Honduras. Tegucigalpa: Editorial Guaymuras, 1993.

Runge, C. F.

Common Property and Collective Action in Economic Development. *World Development,* vol. 14, no. 5 (1986): 623–635.

Shiva, Vandana

The Enclosure and Recovery of the Commons: Biodiversity, Indigenous Knowledge, and Intellectual Property Rights. New Delhi: Research Foundation for Science, Technology, and Ecology, 1997.

Southworth, Jane, and Catherine M. Tucker

The Influence of Accessibility, Local Institutions, and Socioeconomic Factors on Forest Cover Change in the Mountains of Western Honduras. *Mountain Research and Development,* vol. 21, no. 3 (2001): 276–283.

Stanley, Denise L.

Communal Forest Management: The Honduran Resin Tappers. *Development and Change,* vol. 22 (1991): 757–779.

Stevenson, Glenn
Common Property Economics: A General Theory and Land Use Applications. Cambridge: Cambridge University Press, 1991.

Suagee, Dean.
Human Rights and Cultural Heritage, Developments in the United Nations Working Group on Indigenous Populations. In *Intellectual Property Rights for Indigenous Peoples, A Sourcebook,* edited by Tom Greaves, 191–208. Oklahoma City: Society for Applied Anthropology, 1994.

Ten Kate, Kerry, and Sarah A. Laird
Biodiversity and Business: Coming to Terms with the "Grand Bargain." *International Affairs*, vol. 76, no. 1 (2000): 241–264.

Thorpe, Andy, Hugo Noé Pino, Pedro Jiménez, Ana Lucía Restrepo, Dagoberto Suazo, and Ramón Salgado
Impacto del Ajuste en el Agro Hondureño. Tegucigalpa, Honduras: Postgrado Centroamericano en Economía y Planificación del Desarrollo (POSCAE), 1995.

Tucker, Catherine M.
The Political Ecology of a Lenca Indian Community in Honduras: Communal Forests, State Policy, and Processes of Transformation. Ph.D. diss. Tucson: Department of Anthropology, University of Arizona, 1996.

Private versus Communal Forests: Forest Conditions and Tenure in a Honduran Community. *Human Ecology*, vol. 27, no. 2 (1999): 201–230.

Urban, Greg, and Joel Sherzer.
Introduction: Indians, Nation-States and Culture.In *Nation-States and Indians in Latin America*, edited by Greg Urban and Joel Sherzer, 1–18. Austin: University of Texas Press, 1991.

Utting, Peter
Trees, People and Power: Social Dimensions of Deforestation and Forest Protection in Central America. London: Earthscan, 1993.

White, T. Anderson, and C. Ford Runge.
Common Property and Collective Action: Lessons from Cooperative Watershed Management in Haiti. *Economic Development and Cultural Change,* vol. 43, no. 1 (1994): 1–42.

Wilson, Paul, and Gary Thompson.
Common Property and Uncertainty: Compensating Coalitions by Mexico's Pastoral *Ejidatarios. Economic Development and Cultural Change,* vol. 41, no. 2 (1993): 299–318.

CHAPTER 6

BENEFIT SHARING UNDER THE CONVENTION ON BIOLOGICAL DIVERSITY

Katy Moran

Those concerned with the conservation of bioresources recognize that when biodiversity-rich nations benefit from their sustainable use, conservation opportunities increase. The Convention on Biological Diversity (CBD) codifies this principle in its interrelated goals of (1) the conservation of biological diversity; (2) the sustainable use of its components, and (3) the fair and equitable sharing of the benefits arising out of its use. No longer are bioresources considered the "common property of mankind," as the CBD recognizes the sovereignty of nations over their bioresources and their rights to share in the benefits that accrue from commercialized bioproducts (United Nations International Convention on Biological Diversity 1992).

Since the CBD was introduced in Rio during the 1992 Earth Summit, 175 nations and the European Union have ratified the Convention, agreeing to enact legislation to implement provisions that represent national interests, yet do not impose restrictions that conflict with the objectives of the CBD. At the same time, commercial users of bioresources voluntarily attempt to comply with convention provisions in order to gain access to the raw bioresources that can be developed into bioproducts. Besides the risk of lawsuits and despoiling a company's commercial reputation, the legal search for biological resources protects future business strategies for companies to access raw bioresources. These arrangements have come to be called *bioprospecting*, or exploring biological diversity for commercially valuable genetic and biochemical resources (Reid et al. 1993; see also Moran, King, and Carlson 2001).

It is useful to examine how these practices, by both provider countries and user companies, are actually working today and offer examples to nations in the process of establishing legal frameworks to comply with the CBD. As of the end of 1999, some forty-two countries have introduced access and benefit-sharing regulations or have laws under development. Regional frameworks, which respond to the occurrence of biodiversity regionally, are also under consideration in the five States of the Andean Commission, the Association of South East Asian Nations (ASEAN), the Organization of African Unity (OAU), and the South Pacific Regional Environment Programme (SPREP).

But there are more stakeholders than provider countries, which include local, state, regional, and national government levels, and user industries, including both small and multinational companies. Many other interested parties are involved in bioprospecting relationships, often with competing agendas and conflicting interests. Major stakeholders include both the domestic and international research communities, including botanical gardens and universities. Their participation reflects the increasing commercial value of bioresources and spans a continuum from pure to applied research (Ten Kate and Laird 1999).

Also recognized as valuable to bioprospecting is the ethnobotanical knowledge of the forest-dwelling (or native, tribal, indigenous) peoples who live in or near tropical forests and possess information on the use of plants for medicinal purposes. Of the 120 active compounds isolated from higher plants and used today in Western medicine, 74 percent have the same therapeutic use as in native societies. This traditional knowledge is embedded in forest peoples' cultural systems and passed down generationally. Accumulated over millennia, traditional knowledge is as rich and diverse as tropical forests' biological resources, and as threatened (Moran 1997).

Nongovernmental organizations (NGOs) such as conservation, development, human rights, health, and other nonprofit organizations, foundations, pro bono law firms, and private consultants play growing roles as intermediaries in fostering, facilitating, and evaluating bioprospecting partnerships. To level the playing field in negotiating expertise, many countries and culture groups have successfully sought outside advice at different stages of bioprospecting negotiations from intermediaries that have some vested interest in promoting equitable arrangements. Many intermediaries speak the local language and have worked for many years and often lived in the community and earned its trust. They play many roles in access and benefit-sharing arrangements with source countries and other entities, often becoming partners in the relationship (Ten Kate and Laird 1999).

This chapter reviews three existing case studies on bioprospecting in Asia, Latin America, and Africa, focusing on the more important lessons regarding benefit sharing, the third goal of the CBD. Although there is a broad array of industrial uses for biodiversity, including biotechnology, cosmetics, crop protection, horticulture, and personal care industries, this chapter confines case studies and discussions to benefit sharing from pharmaceuticals and botanical medicines (Biotechnology in the Global Economy 1999). There are no "model" bioprospecting arrangements, as the case studies demonstrate. Rather, in one study the impetus came from a government research institute, another from an international environmental organization, and another was primarily initiated by a small company. Since one of the most contentious questions of bioprospecting regards the use of indigenous knowledge in the discovery of new medicines, each case study includes indigenous participants, so as to best illustrate and compare such arrangements (Case Studies on Access and Benefit Sharing 1998).[1]

Case Studies

India

Rich in biological and cultural diversity, India houses over 45,000 species of plants, 30 percent that are higher plants, and 400 unique ethnic groups, 75 percent of which are tribally organized. India's proposed Biodiversity Act strictly regulates international access to bioresources for both research and commercial use with heavy fines for breach of the act.

The Tropical Botanic Garden and Research Institute (TBGRI) was established by the government of Kerala, India, in 1979. In 1987, the TBGRI held an ethnobotanical field study in the forests of the Western Ghats in southwest India. These forests are home to the Kani tribe, nomadic traditional collectors of nontimber forest products, who now lead a primarily settled life in tribal hamlets. The Kanis use a wild plant species for energy that they called "arogyapacha," which was identified as *Trichopus zeylanicus* by the TBGRI. It provided a lead to the development of the drug "Jeevani" (giver of life) after the TBGRI transferred the manufacturing license to a major Ayurvedic drug company in India. The Aryavaidya Pharmacy Coimbatore Ltd. licensed Jeevani as a tonic to bolster the immune system and provide energy for a fee of Rs. 10 lakhs (approximately US$25,000). The TGBRI agreed to share 50 percent of the license fee and the 2 percent royalty on profits with the Kani (Anuradha 1998, 2000).

Traditional systems of the Kanis have eroded and been replaced by those of nontribal local communities. Rather than governance by a tribal chief (Mootha Kani), today's system, referred to as the Panchayati Raj, is based on the principle of devolution of administrative powers to the local village level under the Constitution of India. The predominantly nontribal Panchayat's decision-making body is elected by members.

Kanis, with a population of under 17,000, live in different areas and have differing opinions on the arrangement with the TBGRI, which has interacted primarily with the Kanis from one area. This group of Kanis support and appreciate the role of the TBGRI. However, Kanis in other Panchayat areas are offended that the TBGRI only works with one group. Some feel the benefit-sharing arrangement is superficial, since most Kanis are not involved in the process. In September 1995, a group of nine Kani medicine men wrote to the Chief Minister of Kerala, objecting to the sale of their knowledge to a private company.

The TBGRI acknowledged it has not reached out or communicated to all members of the Kani tribe, so, with the help of NGOs a trust was established and registered. The TBGRI reported in 1998 that the trust has over 500 members, but some critics feel this number falls far short of adequate representation of the Kani. In March 1999, *Science* reported that the first payment of $21,000 would be made and shared by the tribal community and the institute (Bagla 1999).

Dr. P. Pushpangadan, former director of the TBGRI, reports that arogyapacha, a perennial undergrowth, was cultivated to ensure a regular supply of the raw drug to the manufacturer (personal communication, Dr. P. Pushpangadan to author, 1998). But the TBGRI scientists learned that the medicinal qualities of the plant are lost, unless grown in natural forest settings. So the TBGRI organized fifty Kani families that live inside the forest to cultivate and preprocess the plant under the supervision of the TBGRI scientists. This plan, writes Pushpangadan, generates employment, as leaves of the plant are bought from the Kani who manage the semiwild crop. Each family has one or two acres of arogyapacha under cultivation in the first year of the project and earns about Rs. 30,000 per acre. This income is expected to increase in subsequent years, as it is anticipated that the production of leaves will increase and last for twenty to thirty years. Since the plant can be grown only in the natural forest habitat to maintain its medicinal qualities, it seems the Kani are in an effective bargaining position to regulate and control its harvest. Pushpangadan describes arogyapacha as "forest friendly" because it is grown under the shade of the natural forest canopy, but he does not refer to any sustainability studies on its management. Although it contributed no men, material, or finances to the effort, Pushpangadan writes, the State Forest Department now demands a share of the license fee and royalties on the grounds that the plant material is collected within a forest area.

Discussion

In all fairness, it must be remembered that the TBGRI process for benefit sharing with the Kanis evolved in a policy vacuum, well before the CBD was introduced. The lessons learned from mistakes made in this case study did not have the luxury of precedent, or of guiding legislation by the national government, but developed procedures in an ad hoc manner gradually over a dozen years. This occurred despite the fact that all project participants were nationals and did not involve any international trade, companies, or institutions. When governments enact restrictive regulations, it inhibits scientific research, whereas simple, flexible access laws discourage "biopiracy," encourage innovations, and minimize the transaction costs of bioprospecting for all.

Likewise, the absence of an intact traditional system of governance by the Kani crippled the decision-making processes that are enjoyed by culture groups with a lesser degree of acculturation. The trust fund that was initiated after complaints from the Kanis about equity cannot be considered legitimate unless the people who contributed to the process from which revenues are generated are the same ones who control the funds to some degree. Since wealth and technology are as concentrated in the North as poverty and biodiversity are in the South, what is "equitable" in the bioprospecting process is difficult to define. Equity is a relative term and can be determined only by the participants in the process. It means not only equitable compensation, but equal standing among participants in making decisions about what form benefits should take. Even though the Kani are quite powerless in relation to a large Indian government research institution, their uncontested right to deny access to bioresources or traditional knowledge would have supplied strong leverage during access negotiations, had the bioprospecting arrangement been negotiated today. The right to deny access is widely recognized and these processes are now undertaken well before any bioprospecting activities begin. No collecting permits are issued until such contractual agreements are negotiated, after the prior informed consent process. There must be a written understanding among all relevant stakeholders of rights, obligations, roles, and ownership, of who shares how much in what kinds of benefits, when. It defines exactly who the state and/or national authority is, whether it be the State Forest Department, the TBGRI, or some other entity that can make a claim as a stakeholder (Moran 1997).

In its wording, the CBD lumps together "indigenous and local communities," even though there are several anthropological criteria that clearly differentiate indigenous peoples from being defined simply as local communities. This case study demonstrates the dangers of assuming that the indigenous Kani and local communities share the same values, traditions, and methods of governance (Moran 2002).

Another question concerns the sustainability of the present system of sourcing arogyapacha, since there is no information on sustainability studies connected to methods of managing and harvesting the plant. Clearly, environmental impacts on the forest, as well as sustainability studies, are required if it is anticipated that the need for arogyapacha will increase and last for twenty to thirty years (King et al. 1999).

Suriname

The International Cooperative Biodiversity Group (ICBG) was launched in 1991 with funding from the U.S. government, sponsored by the National Institutes of Health (NIH), the National Science Foundation (NSF), and the U.S. Agency for International Development (USAID). Three interrelated goals of the ICBG include health improvement through the discovery of new drugs from natural sources, conservation of biological diversity, and sustainable economic development. By 1994, ICBG projects were held in Suriname, Costa Rica, Argentina, Chile, Mexico, Peru, Cameroon, and Nigeria (Guerin-McManus et al. 1998).

Suriname is located in the center of a two-billion-year-old Precambrian formation known as the Guayana Shield. This region of northern South America is the most extensive and least disturbed major tropical wilderness, with more than 90 percent of its original forests still intact. The interior of Suriname is covered with undisturbed neotropical Amazonian forest and largely uninhabited. With a land area of 166,000 square kilometers and a human population of 412,000, Suriname is one of the least densely populated countries in the world.

The Suriname ICBG's bioprospecting program was first proposed by the Suriname office of Conservation International (CI), an international nongovernmental organization and the Saramaka Maroons. Maroons are descendants of escaped African slaves who have lived in the Suriname forest for nearly three centuries. Although they are not indigenous to the area, the Saramaka Maroons meet several anthropological criteria in definitions of "indigenous" including forest dwelling, use of a local language, and tribal social organization (Price 1976). The cooperative partnership also includes the Virginia Polytechnic Institute and State University, Missouri Botanical Garden, Bristol-Myers Squibb Pharmaceutical Research Institute, and Bedrijf Geneesmiddelen Voorziening Suriname (BGVS), a pharmaceutical company owned by the Surinamese government.

Through a Statement of Understanding, the Suriname ICBG established a benefit-sharing plan with a US$60,000 total advance payment from Bristol-Myers Squibb Pharmaceutical Research Institute into the Forest Peoples' Fund (FPF), with additional contributions of $20,000 a year as the ICBG is renewed. The FPF is a mechanism, which CI Suriname helped broker, through which "up-front" benefits and future royalties from new drugs developed can be returned to the Saramaka people. Along with compensating the Saramaka Maroons for their ethnobotanical contributions, the FPF creates conservation incentives, finances sustainable management projects, provides research and technology exchanges, and supports other socially and environmentally sound projects. A board of directors consisting of two representatives from the Indian community (one Saramaka and one Amerindian), two from CI Suriname, and one from Suriname's Department of Interior was created to review proposals for ways to spend the advance payment and any future royalties from drug sales. It was agreed that funds would be used for projects involving community development, biodiversity conservation, and health care. If any products are commercialized from ethnobotanical collections, 50 percent of Suriname's share of any future royalties will go to the FPF and the other 50 percent will go to various ICBG partners in Suriname. If a drug is derived from random collections, the FPF's share is reduced to 30 percent, while 70 percent goes to other ICBG partners.

E. C. Green (1998), a consultant who speaks both Saramakan and SrananTongo, evaluated the Suriname project during a site visit in 1998. He learned that before the project began, Saramaka leaders held numerous palavers (*kutus*), after which their paramount chief and local chiefs (*Kapitenis*) voted for Saramakas to participate in the project. They considered ways to use the donated funds that supplied ongoing income generation to benefit whole communities. CI (Suriname and Washington) played a crucial guiding role in this, although the by-laws of the fund were written by Surinamese participants and are governed by the laws of Suriname. About half the available $60,000 funds was spent on local income-generating projects. The FPF purchased outboard motors and developed a canoe taxi service to transport people and goods upriver to Saramaka territory. Other funds were used to train local people to cater food for ecotourism; to purchase sewing machines and train women to sew school uniforms for sale to parents; and to supply tools and training for a commercial gardening project. Another project trained people in woodcarving, carpentry, and furniture making. A community-based organization called Afinga helped to coordinate these microenterprise initiatives. All of these small-scale projects have the potential to generate much-needed cash for the Saramakas of the upper Suriname River area where the ICBG is implemented.

Originally, according to Green, the ICBG agreement held no special provision for royalty sharing with traditional healers, an important consideration of ethnobotanical drug discovery. In Suriname, virtually all ethnobotanical knowledge made available to the ICBG project was supplied by healers rather than from general or popular plant knowledge. While fully supporting local development initiatives, traditional healers expressed a preference for being paid a small amount for their participation as ethnobotanical collecting developed. Since it was locally recognized that the ICBG and the FPF came to Saramaka territory because of the wisdom of local healers, the presence of the ICBG project, and especially the funds made available through the FPF, increased the healers' prestige in the community.

Discussion

Bioprospecting is complicated (Mays, Duffy-Mazan, Cragg, and Boyd 1997). It involves the development of drugs by megacompanies in faraway countries, use of alien technologies, complicated and time-consuming legal and governmental approval processes, and highly complex relationships between a bewildering array of public and private organizations, both foreign and domestic (Green 1998). Some communities need significant help from intermediaries to participate in the process. The lesson from the Suriname case study is how smoothly the bioprospecting process can move along when time and resources have been spent beforehand and when the stated goals of all partners are not in conflict, but interrelated. In Suriname, for example, the drug discovery process creates economic value for biologically diverse organisms, which in turn creates development funds and incentives for conserving biodiversity, satisfying the goals of all stakeholders.

Conservation International (at http://www.ci-suriname.org) helped pioneer the use of trust funds to target specific revenues for communities or projects in many countries. In Suriname, the Saramaka have a social and cultural identity distinct from the dominant society. They are geographically and linguistically isolated, which makes them particularly vulnerable to outsiders. Management of the FPF, however, is independent of outsiders, allowing the communities to determine how to use their benefits through their own cultural institutions without outside interference.

The question of individual compensation arises and is dealt with here. Typically, acknowledgment of the contribution of healers from indigenous societies in the discovery of new medicines that have historically benefited humankind is missing. This recognition is important because it enhances the prestige of individual healers within indigenous communities, countries, and internationally, just as it does for Western scientists. And formal recognition of the healers' contributing role generates pride in the Saramaka culture and motivates its conservation.

Nigeria

Today, Africa has one of the highest rates of deforestation in the world. The continent is estimated to have about 216,634,000 hectares of closed forest areas and an annual deforestation rate calculated at about 1 percent. Located in West Africa, the Federal Republic of Nigeria is the continent's most populous nation. It suffers an annual deforestation rate of 5.0 percent, compared to a global rate of 0.6 percent. To contend with such statistics, Nigeria modified its national parks law to attract and encourage conservation funding by establishing biodiversity prospecting requirements.

The Nigerian population, estimated as over 100 million in 1995, includes over 250 distinct ethnic groups, some numbering fewer than 10,000 people. Most are concentrated in specific geographic areas. The Hausa and Fulani (or Peul) in the north, the Yoruba in the southwest, and the Igbo in the southeast comprise about 65 percent of the population. Traditional leaders, such as chiefs, healers, and clan and lineage heads, are a major social force in communities, where numerous community development associations provide fora for citizens to identify, discuss, and prioritize problems and to seek means to solve them (Iwu 1996).

The oldest component of the Nigerian health sector consists of traditional healers and birth attendants, who are the de facto providers of primary health care in Nigeria, estimated to serve about 80 percent of the population. Healers provide client-centered, personalized health care that is culturally appropriate, holistic, and tailored to meet the needs and expectations of the patient. Since healers share the cognitive understandings and cultural values of those they treat, they serve a function broader and more complex than their medical counterparts in the modern sector. Nigerian healers are not strictly "traditional," however. The term *traditional*, in this case, refers to healing practices that have endured over time because of their continuing usefulness. Traditional healers in Nigeria are adaptive, incorporating into their healing repertoire modern components that adhere to their cultural values. Most healers want to learn how to treat illness more effectively, so they are highly motivated to cooperate with the modern health sector (Moran 1998).

The Bioresources Development and Conservation Programme (BDCP) is a multiethnic international NGO based in Nigeria that builds technical skills so that bioresources are a viable vehicle for improved health care and sustainable development (BDCP website, 2004).[2] The BDCP views science and technology as useful tools to be adapted to the local cultural framework, rather than as a modern alternative to the contributions of community members. One of the objectives of the BDCP is to use local bioresources and knowledge to target therapeutic categories for tropical diseases suffered in Nigeria such as malaria, leishmaniasis, and trypanosomiasis.

In 1990, Shaman Pharmaceuticals, Inc., established a research relationship with Nigerian scientific institutions, and the BDCP became the focal point for collaborative research. Shaman is a small San Francisco company that uses ethnobotany as well as isolation and natural products chemistry to discover and develop novel pharmaceuticals (Shaman Botanicals, 2004).[3] Nigerian scientists proposed initial discussions with healers and traditional leaders to talk about a collaborative relationship with Shaman for bioprospecting. The BDCP visited communities where members had worked for several years. Typically, each community or village state is autonomous, with its own chief and government. Their community decision-making process includes the village chief, his advisors, traditional healers, and the elders. Before bioprospecting began, discussions covered topics such as the intentions and goals of the project; how and where the plants would be analyzed; and their potential for commercialization and benefit sharing. After lengthy discussions over a year, the groups felt that Shaman shared a common purpose with them consistent with their cultural values concerning human health and agreed to collaborate through an Agreement of Principles.

Four ethnobotanical field expeditions were conducted. By choice of Nigerian collaborators, immediate and medium-term benefits from the expeditions took the form of workshops and training programs on public health, botany, conservation, and ethnobotany; support for a medicinal plant reserve; supplies for village schools; botanical collection supplies for a herbarium; laboratory equipment for scientific research on plants that treat parasitic diseases prevalent in West Africa; and support for Nigerian scientists to apply modern analytical techniques. Fulfilling company policy, immediate and medium-term benefits, such as those above, totaling over US$200,000 have been distributed through programs to the various stakeholders in the collaboration as the expeditions occur. The company regularly reports laboratory results to participating communities, and general literature on the project is published with both Nigerian and U.S. authors (Carlson, Iwu, King, Obialor, and Ozioko 1997).

At the time of its incorporation in 1990 as a for-profit corporation,

Shaman founded the Healing Forest Conservancy (the Conservancy), an independent nonprofit foundation. The Conservancy was established specifically to develop and implement a process to return long-term benefits to Shaman's collaborating countries and cultures, after a product is commercialized. Through the Conservancy, Shaman will donate a percentage of profits from commercial products to all company collaborators (some thirty other countries and culture groups) for as long as Shaman has a profit. The Conservancy will distribute these long-term benefits, equally, to all the countries and cultures that are Shaman collaborators, regardless of where the plant sample or traditional knowledge that was commercialized originated (Richter and Carlson 1998).

On October 20, 1997, in Abuja, Nigeria, the BDCP launched the Fund for Integrated Rural Development and Traditional Medicine (FIRD-TM) during an international workshop on medicinal plants. The FIRD-TM is the vehicle to receive and channel benefits in an equitable and consistent manner from many contributors, including the ICBG, which the BDCP is a member of. Funds are directed to source communities from which commercially useful bioresources and ethnobotanical knowledge are derived. The BDCP facilitated the establishment of the Fund and is its sponsoring entity. The Fund, however, has an independent board composed of leaders of traditional healers associations, senior government officials, multiethnic representatives of village councils, and technical experts from scientific institutions. Diverse culture groups in Nigeria will receive resources from the Fund through traditional healers organizations and villages consistent with their governing customs. Town associations, village heads, and professional guilds of healers are empowered to make decisions regarding use of the funds for projects in their localities. Those funded will follow the criteria of promoting conservation of biodiversity and drug development, as well as the socioeconomic development of rural cultures.

At the Fund's inauguration, the Healing Forest Conservancy donated $40,000 to the FIRD-TM for a pilot project, to test the efficiency and efficacy of the trust fund process, using a step-by-step process to assess the feasibility of future trust funds for benefit sharing. During the inauguration ceremony, the Association of Indigenous Pharmaceutical Manufacturers and the Orange Drug Company of Nigeria pledged additional monies to complement the Conservancy's donation.

The pilot Conservancy project generated a twenty-one-page constitution, which supplies a legally enforceable mechanism, under domestic law, for a trust fund, written pro bono, by Morrison & Foerster, Ltd., in Washington, D.C. Under the Constitution, trustees of the fund, as a collective entity, may institute legal proceedings in their capacity to achieve trust fund objectives. The Conservancy Constitution is a template to use for the benefit-sharing actions of the Conservancy in many different countries that is flexible enough to respond to unique conditions in countries where Shaman collaborates. It supplies a legal mechanism to widely disburse financial resources, over a long time frame, and within varied sectors of society.

The constitution provides for the distribution of benefits to all stakeholders in accordance with the following guidelines:

1. At least 50 percent, but not more than 70 percent, of available funds shall be distributed to traditional healers organizations and community development funds.
2. At least 10 percent, but not more than 15 percent, of available funds shall be distributed to national universities and other national institutions that share a commitment to the aims and objectives of the Fund.
3. At least 10 percent, but not more than 15 percent, of available funds shall be distributed to the sponsoring entity for its furtherance of conservation and development activities.

After 10 years and $170 million, in early 1999 Shaman Pharmaceuticals abandoned attempts to take any of its discoveries through the Food and Drug Administration regulatory process, as future time and costs for additional clinical trials proved prohibitive (Moran 1998). ShamanBotanicals.com was incorporated as a private, wholly owned subsidiary of Shaman Pharmaceuticals to leverage the company's research and development by launching its first botanical dietary supplement, SB Normal Stool Formula on August 1, 1999 (*The Economist* 1999). The product delivers a standardized extract from the sap of Sangre de Drago, the *Croton lechleri* tree, to prevent fluid loss and promote normal stool formation in the intestine to those suffering from side effects of HIV therapies, cancer therapies, and irritable bowel syndrome (at www.ShamanBotanicals.com). ShamanBotanicals.com is selling SB Normal Stool Formula through existing retail channels, including mass market (food, drug, and mass stores), multilevel marketing, and the Internet. This and future products will be differentiated by their origins, their quality, and Shaman's continuing commitment to benefit sharing, sustainability, and conservation.

For many years, Shaman invested in studies on managing and harvesting Sangre de Drago in Latin America, as the source of a future product. Ecological and distribution studies, as well as studies on yield and sustainability, totaled US$1 million at sites from Mexico to Paraguay (Holodniy 1999).

Discussion

A major lesson of this case study is the time, costs, and risks associated with drug discovery, a burden shouldered primarily by the company, but with critical implications for benefit sharing to source countries and culture groups. Spreading the risks and benefits among all stakeholders increases opportunities for benefits and lessens risk. Royalties may never materialize due to the tremendous costs, long time frame, unpredictability and volatility of the market, and the many other potential pitfalls of drug discovery. Some sort of up-front benefits, monetary or nonmonetary, as well as "milestone" payments such as those that went to Nigeria, are essential. Shaman Pharmaceuticals, Inc., was restructured due to costs of future clinical trials for the company's first drug, which consequently was launched as a dietary supplement, not a pharmaceutical. In the case of Shaman, however, the company's benefit-sharing principles are still intact and considerable revenues can be generated from the botanical income stream, while pharmaceutical research continues. In 1997, for example, the U.S. dietary supplement market for herbals or botanicals was nearly $4 billion, with a $5 billion 1998 projection and compounded yearly growth rate of 15–25 percent (King et al. 1999).

The BDCP goals of discovering and marketing bioproducts for diseases important to Nigeria is itself a lesson in opportunities brought about through bioprospecting. Too often, when the importance of biodiversity conservation is discussed for its value to human health, it refers to the health of residents of industrialized nations. The attitude is that biodiversity must be preserved to enlarge the pharmacopoeia of Western medicine, which provides therapeutics primarily for Western societies. Less discussed is the vitality of biodiversity to the health of 80 percent of the world, populations that depend solely on medicinal plants for their primary health care. Preserving biodiversity for the benefit of human health means preserving it for those in the tropics already using it, as well as for distant populations that may know it only in some refined or synthetic form at some unspecified future date.

This case study also demonstrates how biodiversity-rich yet financially poor tropical nations, such as Nigeria, can increase conservation and research funding and gain valuable training and technology. Since the economic values of biodiversity are seldom accountable in market valuations, strategies like bioprospecting bring added financial support for conservation. Countries can choose whether to supply natural products in the form of extracts, rather than raw unprocessed material, to foreign investors or to establish their own medicinal plant, phytochemical, or pharmaceutical industry.

Lessons and Conclusion

Monetary and Nonmonetary Benefits

Benefit sharing can take financial, conservation, social, and scientific forms and must be decided during the prior informed consent process before any bioprospecting permits are issued. As case studies demonstrate, opportunities for financial compensation include up-front payments and medium-term benefit sharing as research progresses. Many companies offer stakcs in equity, profit sharing, and joint venture opportunities. Royalties occur only if and when a drug is marketed, but it is risky to rely only on resources that may never materialize.

Cases that supplied support for conservation activities illustrated how cultural, as well as environmental, conservation can be accomplished. Acknowledging the contribution of healers supplies proof of the continuation of a traditional profession. It promises an economic future from preservation of the cultural patrimony by which healers train and pass on their heritage to future generations of practitioners.

In Nigeria, significant social benefits include development of low-cost phytomedicines and conserving the primary source of health care in the country. Participation of nationals in research on tropical diseases through technology transfer, training, and joint research publications builds the technical capacity of nationals during the discovery process.

Training and Technology Transfer

The Kani benefit from training and sourcing agreements to cultivate high-value raw material for processing into phytomedicines. Such training supplies income-producing opportunities to rural communities that are best located to manage, collect, and protect species. Inventories that describe local use can be undertaken in the local language, which protects ethnobotanical information from outsiders and leaves a documentation of cultural knowledge within the community. Training also generates employment by outsiders who are interested in bioprospecting and increases the capability of gene-rich countries to perform these services.

National governments benefit from training programs by gaining a technological infrastructure for science and commerce, yielding jobs and taxes. Fees can be charged to outsiders with commercial or research interests, allowing debt-ridden tropical nations to forgo short-term profits from logging, cattle-grazing, and monoculture development projects that destroy forests. There are several entry levels, including collecting procedures, inventories, bioassays, re-collection, harvesting, herbarium specimen storage, taxonomic identification, cataloguing, and management of collections. Training increases the capacity of biodiversity-rich countries to assess and evaluate their resources, to generate biological databases, and to enter into the natural products industry if they choose to do so.

Trust Funds

While trust funds are now widely recognized as the method of choice to distribute benefits, it is important to acknowledge the consent and support of each host country government for the activities of the fund. This minimizes the risk that trust funds are perceived as a threat to the sovereign right of the host country government to exploit its own natural resources. However, this acknowledgment should not be viewed as undermining the independence of trust funds and their autonomous operating authority as a nongovernmental organization. Their precise legal status will depend on laws of the host country where the fund is established. It is important that the fund be able to obtain the benefits normally associated with nonprofit and charitable entities, such as exemption from taxation, so it can offer the added value of attracting other sources of funds. Its NGO status reinforces the independence of the fund from the host government and permits it to participate in other NGO fora.

Acknowledgments

I gratefully acknowledge the critical input to this chapter from Marianne Guerin-McManus of Conservation International; Ted Green, private consultant; Maurice Iwu, the BDCP and its collaborators in Nigeria; Lisa Conte and Steve King from Shaman Pharmaceuticals, Inc.; and Tom Mays of Morrison and Foerster, LLP, Stas Burgiel of Bionet, and all other members of the Nigerian Trust Fund Pilot Project Committee.

Reprinted by permission with minor alterations from Katy Moran, "Bioprospecting: Lessons from Benefit-Sharing Experiences," *International Journal of Biotechnology* 2, nos. 1/2/3, 2000.

Notes

1. Katy Moran is Executive Director of the Healing Forest Conservancy. The information presented in each of the following case studies comes directly from the work she did with each group in a consultant capacity. While these cases date back to 1998, many of them are currently in operation today, and more information may be found for each case study online. See http://www.biodiv.org/doc/case-studies/default.aspx for listings of case studies worldwide, including the cases illustrated in this chapter.
2. More information on BDCP may be found at http://www.bioresources.org.
3. Shaman Pharmaceuticals is now known as Shaman Botanicals. More information can be found at http://www.shaman.com.

References

Anuradha, R. V.

Sharing with the Kanis: A Case Study from Kerala, India. Secretariat to the Convention on Biological Diversity, Fourth Meeting of the COP, Bratislava, Slovakia, May 1998.

Sharing the Benefits of Biodiversity. The Kani-TBGRI Deal in Kerala, India (Tropical Botanical Garden and Research Institute). *Journal of International Wildlife Law and Policy* 3:2, 2002.

Bagla, Pallava
Model Indian Deal Generates Payments. *Science* vol. 283. March 12, 1999: 1614–1615 (in News of the Week).

Bioresources Development and Conservation Programme (BDCP)
Available at: www.Bioresources.org.

Biotechnology in the Global Economy
Available at: www.cid.harvard.edu/cidbiotech/homepage.html, 1999; last accessed on January 1, 2004.

Carlson, T. J., M. M. Iwu, S. King, C. Obialor, and A. Ozioko
Medicinal Plant Research in Nigeria: An Approach for Compliance with the Convention on Biological Diversity. *Diversity,* vol. 13, no. 1 (1997): 29–33.

Case Studies on Access and Benefit Sharing
Available at: http://www.biodiv.org/doc/case-studies/default.aspx; last accessed on January 1, 2004.

Conservation International (CI)
Available at www.ci-suriname.org; last accessed on January 1, 2004.

The Economist
Shaman Loses its Magic. 21 February 1999.

Green, E. C.
Ethnobotany, Intellectual Property Rights and Benefit Sharing: The ICBG Project in Suriname. Paper presented at SfAA Symposium on coming to terms with IPR, San Juan, Puerto Rico, April 23, 1998.

Guerin-McManus, Marianne et al.
Bioprospecting in Practice: A Case Study of the Suriname ICBG Project and Benefits Sharing under the Convention on Biological Diversity. Secretariat to the Convention on Biological Diversity, Fourth Meeting of the COP, Bratislava, Slovakia, May 1998.

The Healing Forest Conservancy
Available at: www.shaman.com/Healing_Forest.html; last accessed on January 1, 2004.

Holodniy, M., J. Koch, M. Mistal, J. M. Schmidt, A. Khandwala, J. E. Pennington, and S. B. Porter
A Double-Blind, Randomized, Placebo-Controlled, Phase II Study to Assess the Safety and Efficacy of Orally Administered SP-303 for the

Symptomatic Treatment of Diarrhea in Patients with AIDS. *American Journal of Gastroenterology*, vol. 94, no. 2 (1999): 3267–3273.

Iwu, M. M.
Biodiversity Prospecting in Nigeria: Seeking Equity and Reciprocity in Intellectual Property Rights through Partnership Arrangements and Capacity Building. *Journal of Ethnopharmacology*, vol. 5, no. 1 (1996): 209–219.

King, S., E. Menza, F. Ayala, L. E. Forero, M. Pena, V. Zak, and H. Bastein.
Croton lechleri and the Sustainable Harvest and Management of Plants in Pharmaceuticals, Phytomedicines and Cosmetic Industries. In *International Symposium on Herbal Medicines,* edited by D. Wozzniak, S. S. Yuen, M. Garrett, and T. K. Shuman. San Diego, Calif.: International Institute for Human Resources Development, College of Health and Human Services, San Diego State University, 1997.

King, S. R., E. Menza, T. Carlson, J. Chinnock, K. Moran, and J. Borges
Issues in the Commercialization of Medicinal Plants. *Herbalgram*, no. 47 (1999): 46–51.

Mays, T., K. Duffy-Mazan, G. Cragg, and M. Boyd
A Paradigm for the Equitable Sharing of Benefits Resulting from Biodiversity Research and Development. In *Biodiversity and Human Health*, edited by F. Grifo and J. Rosenthal, 267–280. Washington, D.C.: Island Press, 1997.

Moran, K.
Returning Benefits from Ethnobiological Drug Discovery to Native Communities. In *Biodiversity and Human Health*, edited by F. Grifo and J. Rosenthal, 243–263. Washington, D.C.: Island Press, 1997.

Mechanisms for Benefit-Sharing: Nigerian Case Study for the Convention on Biological Diversity. Secretariat to the Convention on Biological Diversity, Fourth Meeting of the COP, Bratislava, Slovakia, May 1998.

Indigenous Peoples and Local Communities Embodying Traditional Lifestyles: Definitions Under Article 8(j) of the Convention on Biological Diversity. In *Ethnomedicine and Drug Discovery,* edited by M. Iwu and J. Wootton, 181–189. New York: Elsevier Science B.V., 2002.

Moran, Katy, Steven R. King, and Thomas J. Carlson
Biodiversity Prospecting: Lessons and Prospects. *Annual Review of Anthropology,* vol. 30 (2001): 505–526.

Price, R.
The Guiana Maroons. Baltimore: Johns Hopkins University Press, 1976.

Reid, W., S. Laird, C. Meyer, R. Gamez, A. Sittenfeld, D. Janzen, M. Gollin, and C. Juma
Biodiversity Prospecting. Washington, D.C.: World Resources Institute, 1993.

Richter, K. R., and T. S. J. Carlson.
Reporting Biological Assay Results on Tropical Medicinal Plants to Host Country Collaborators. *Journal Of Ethnopharmacology*, vol. 62 (1998): 85–88.

Shaman Botanicals (formerly Shaman Pharmaceuticals, Inc.)
Available at: www.shaman.com; last accessed on January 1, 2004.

Ten Kate, K., and S. Laird
The Commercial Use of Biodiversity: Access to Genetic Resources and Benefit-Sharing. London: Earthscan Pubs. Ltd., 1999.

United Nations International Convention on Biological Diversity
1992. Available at www.biodiv.org

CHAPTER 7

OWNERSHIP OF INDIGENOUS LANGUAGES: A CASE STUDY FROM GUATEMALA

Judith M. Maxwell

Language is a definitional part of being human. Human beings speak and/or sign languages. Every normal human if exposed to language will acquire language. Language is quintessentially an intellectual attribute. It may be written down, audiotaped, digitally recorded, but it arises in the human mind. Language is also intimately related to culture. Cultural concepts are expressed in and through language. Language reflects history, the contacts among cultures, the development of institutions, the creations of artists, the political and religious hegemonies. But do speakers of a language own that language? And if so, what does this ownership entitle them to?

Do speakers of a language have the right to use that language? To speak it in the home, in public, in schools, in government offices, in courts of law? To write the language? To determine how the language is to be written, what symbols will be used, how words will be divided? To educate and be educated in their language? To have technical and artistic writings available in their language?

The United Nations has a series of conventions that speak to some of these rights. The Universal Declaration of Human Rights (1948) holds that everyone has the right to education and that parents may determine the kind of education that is appropriate, which could be construed as including the language of that education. The Convention on the Rights of the Child (1960) affirms that "[e]ducation should foster respect for parents, cultural identity, language and value." . . . It further states that "[c]hildren of minority communities and Indigenous populations have the right to enjoy their own culture and to practise their own religion and language." In Article 27 of the United Nations International Covenant on Civil and Political Rights (1966) the rights to language use were affirmed, but circumscribed to within the community: "[i]n those states in which . . . linguistic minorities exist, persons belonging to such minorities shall not be denied the right, in community with the other members of their group, . . . to use their own language." The United Nations Committee on Elimination of Racial Discrimination in their 54th session declared that peoples should be guaranteed the right to study and communicate in a chosen language.

The Organization of American States has made stronger affirmations of the rights of Indigenous peoples to their languages. In the Draft American Declaration on the Rights of Indigenous Peoples approved by the Inter-American Commission on Human Rights in 1997, Article 2 affirms the right of Indigenous peoples to use their languages. Article 7 holds that states must recognize and respect . . . Indigenous . . . languages. Article 8 proclaims that Indigenous languages along with the philosophy and cosmovision they entail should be respected and disseminated. It charges the state to provide for radio and television broadcasting in Indigenous languages and to support the creation of Indigenous radio stations and other media. Article 9, section 2, affirms that Indigenous peoples should be given the option of having education available in their own languages as well as the official language(s) and to have educational curricula include Indigenous content. Article 16, section 3, provides for equal protection under the law, including consuetudinal law and, where necessary, use of their language.

A much broader set of rights is envisioned by the Universal Declaration of Linguistic Rights, a convention drawn up in Barcelona in June 1996. This declaration lists rights of speech communities and individual speakers. Among these are the right to use one's own language both in private and in public, the right to the use of one's own name, the right for one's own language and culture to be taught, the right of access to cultural services, and the right to receive attention in their own language from government bodies and in socioeconomic relations. Signatories of this declaration are not governments, but organizations (many of them PEN [international writers association] Centers and individuals who work with languages in multilingual contexts). To members of hegemonic groups these rights may seem so self-evident as to be presupposed.[1] To members of nonhegemonic language groups these rights may represent ideals whose attainment is far from certain.

Guatemala is a multilingual, pluricultural nation. The government recognizes twenty-one Mayan languages within its borders and in the Constitution of 1985, as reformed in 1993, it affirms the right of Indigenous communities to their languages and customs. Nonetheless, the Indigenous struggle for control of their languages has not yet been won. To understand this struggle we must quickly review the history of Indigenous language use, codification, and politics in Guatemala. With this overview in place, we can then examine the current conflicts in three areas: (1) standardization, (2) bilingual education, and (3) publication.

A Brief History of Control of Mayan Languages in Guatemala[2]

In preinvasion times, Mayan languages were the dominant languages of the Guatemalan landscape, though not the only ones. Communities of Xinca and Lenca speakers existed. There were pockets of Pipil speakers as well in the southern highlands. By the 1500s the Mayan languages had diversified to approximately their current number, eighteen to twenty-three within Guatemala. There is some evidence of the use of an elite language spanning linguistic groups (Houston, Robertson, and Stuart 2000), but the extent to which this language was used at all in the highlands of Guatemala, or spoken in any venue, is uncertain. It appears to have served the purpose of extending a medium of literacy throughout the Mayan lowlands and possibly into important administrative centers of the highlands. There is linguistic evidence of borrowing between highland and lowland languages before contact (Justeson, Norman, Campbell, and Kaufman 1985), primarily relating Tzeltalan languages with the Ch'olan and Yucatecan languages of the lowlands. As early as 1973, Floyd Lounsbury suggested K'iche'an influence on lowland scripts in the phoneticism of the Ben Ich glyph, which seemed to represent highland rather than lowland morphemes. There was active trade throughout the Maya zone and beyond (Smith and Berdan 2000). Marriage ties often linked polities (Schele and Miller 1986; Schele and Freidel 1992). In the *Annals of the Kaqchikel* (Hill and Maxwell forthcoming), many of the founding fathers of the K'iche' and Kaqchikel lineages have non-K'iche'an names, showing links with other highland Mayan groups and with Central

Mexican peoples. When Alvarado began his march south toward Guatemala, Moctezuma sent a warning to the Kaqchikels and to the K'iche's (Hill and Maxwell forthcoming). During this early period as speakers of Mayan languages spread out through the highlands of Guatemala and Chiapas, through the Huasteca and the Yucatan peninsula of Mexico, and through the Mayan lowlands and foothills of El Petén, Belize, Salvador, and Honduras, their speech forms diverged leading eventually to twenty-eight to thirty-one distinct languages; however, economic, social, and political ties continued to bind the groups together. These interconnections are evinced in the spread of linguistic features (innovations such as the noun classifiers, discontinuous deictics, and different forms of ergative split), the borrowing of lexical items, and tracings of lineage names.

Once the Spanish arrived in Guatemala, a struggle for linguistic hegemony ensued. Following crown policy, before a community was attacked by Alvarado or divisions of his army, a proclamation was read out, urging the inhabitants to submit peacefully and pledge allegiance (and tribute) to the Spanish crown. Those who failed to surrender, when thus advised, lost their rights to freedom, and so they as well as their holdings could be taken as chattel; they could be enslaved. Naturally, though Alvarado traveled with Nahuatl-speaking mercenaries and interpreters, this ultimatum was not delivered in Nahuatl (a language with which Guatemalan Mayan elites had some familiarity due to trade and kinship ties), but in Spanish. For eight years, Spanish armies campaigned to pacify the Maya of Guatemala. By 1535 they felt themselves to have established control of the country. They were exacting tribute from established elites; they had concentrated dispersed populations in town centers so they could be counted and held liable for levies of labor and tribute. Maya resistance continued (Pablo 1987), but the linguistic landscape was irrevocably changed. While priests made efforts to document and learn Indigenous languages to facilitate the process of proselytization (de Coto 1983; Pantaleón de Guzmán 1984; de Varea 1705; Ximénez 1993), crown policy with regard to languages its New World subjects spoke vacillated. Priests were alternately exhorted to learn the languages rapidly and well and then abjured from doing so. The Council of Trent 1545–1546 curtailed the production of dictionaries and grammars of Indigenous languages, holding that these languages were inadequate for proper use in religious education, catechism, conversion, biblical study, or translation. Nonetheless, the autochthonous languages were seen as practical tools for communicating with the indigenes, recruiting their souls to the Catholic church, their labor to public works, and their tribute to the crown coffers. The national university in Guatemala, Universidad San Carlos, required all students to study Kaqchikel, the Mayan language spoken in the vicinity of the first three Spanish capitals of the vice-royalty.

Nahuatl gained currency during the early period of the colony. While documents in Mayan languages could be accepted in civil and criminal courts in Guatemala in support of claims of entitlement, land ownership, bequests, and the like, these languages were not considered official and were not acceptable for correspondence to address the crown. Nahuatl, however, had semiofficial standing. Letters to the king in Nahuatl would be received. Many Mayan towns filed wills, land transfers, and church records in Nahuatl during this period. Petitions from Mayan towns drawn up in Nahuatl were forwarded to the crown. Dakin (1996) has suggested that a written Nahuatl lingua franca served Mayan as well as Pipil communities at this time. Matthew suggests that Nahuatl and Nahuatl-speaking people partially controlled access to officialdom during the colonial period. Place-names on the modern map of Guatemala reflect this period of Nahuatleco influence. Most large cities have Nahuatl names; Mayan settlement names, if present at all on maps, tend to be relegated to aldeas. Thus, the country is known as Guatemala from Cuauhtemalan; the country's second largest city is Quetzaltenango, rather than Xelajub' (No'j). Table 7.1 lists a few of the towns of Guatemala, with their Mayan and Nahuatl names as seen on maps and the literal meanings of each.

Table 7.1. Mayan/Nahuatl Place-Names

Mayan Name	*Gloss*	*Nahuatl Name*	*Gloss*
Xelajub' (No'j)	at the foot of (the mountain)	Quetzaltenango	at the walled city of the quetzal
B'oko'	shield	Chimaltenango	at the walled city of the shield
Chi Xot, Chi q'a'l	at the comal/tile, at the carbon	Comalapa	at the comal river/water
Chinab'jul	marimba cave/hole/grotto	Huehuetenango	at the walled city of the drum
Meq'enya'	hot water, hot springs	Totonicapan	at the place of the hot water
Chwi Lay	above the stinging nettle	Chichicastenango	walled city of the stinging nettle

Nahuatl borrowings in central highland languages attest to their heavy interaction during this period. Today the word for town in K'iche', *tinamit,* and in Kaqchikel, *tinamït,* comes from Nahuatl *tenamitl,* meaning walled city. The influx of new referents, particularly domesticated animals, put pressure on Mayan lexicons to come up with new terms. Many went through a series of marking reversals, first naming the new item as a Hispanic version of the New World analogy, then as the Hispanic animals became the more prevalent, they became the most common, so they became the default setting and the New World animals came to be lexicalized as wild versions. Berlin (1972) and Laughlin (1975, 1979, 1988) provide examples from Tenejapa Tzeltal. See table 7.2.

Such reversals are attested in languages of highland Guatemala as well. In Kaqchikel, we find examples such as those in table 7.3.

That Nahuatl was an important language in the area at this time can be seen in the importation of Nahuatl loans to replace the Mayan words, once the original names have been taken over by the Spanish referents. Thus, *kej* was precontact Kaqchikel for deer. However, the arrival of the horse and its subsequent use as a mount and a beast of burden made it more salient and the term *kej* in modern colloquial (nonritual) Kaqchikel means horse. Kaqchikel borrowed the term *masat* from Nahuatl *maz_tl* to mean deer.

In the first century of the viceroyalty of Guatemala, Nahuatl and Mayan languages interplayed with one another. Nahuatl had the prestige benefit of being accepted by the Spanish crown as well as the viceroyal courts. Nahuatl scribes served actuarial purposes in Mayan communities. Nahuatl may have had some further uses as a lingua franca. Still, Mayan elites in the central highlands produced documents, town records, wills, and histories in their own languages. Maestros de canto in the Catholic Church composed and compiled songs in a variety of Guatemalan lan-

Table 7.2. Marking Reversals in Tenejapa Tzeltal

Precontact	*Gloss*	*Early Use of New Domesticate*	*Gloss*	*Later Stage, Once Import Had Spread*	*Gloss*
chij	deer	tunim chij	sheep, lit. cotton deer	te'tikil chij	deer, lit. woods sheep
chitam	javalí	kaxtilan chitam	pig, lit. Spanish javalí	wamal chitam	javalí, lit. wild pig

Table 7.3. Marking Reversals

Precontact	*Gloss*	*Early Use of New Domesticate**	*Gloss*	*Later Stage Once Import Had Spread*	*Gloss*
äk'	turkey	kaxtilan äk'	chicken	äk'	chicken
				qo'l	tom turkey
				pi'y	hen turkey (onomatopoeia from calls)
aq	javalí	kastilan aq	pig	juyub'al aq	mountain pig

*These forms are attested in the Annals of the Kaqchikel (Hill and Maxwell forthcoming)

guages, Nahuatl, Spanish, and Latin (Stevenson 1964, ms. 1). Native speakers of Mayan languages were literate in these languages using Latin-based alphabets. They were producing documents for their interactions with the Spanish legal system and with the Catholic Church, and possibly for lineage internal affairs.

However in 1646 Spain sent a Royal Visitor to Guatemala, Don Antonio de Lara. He was charged to enforce the proscription on Indigenous languages and to promote the use of Spanish. Specific new policies were to be enforced. In all Indian towns, children between the ages of five and eight were to receive daily Spanish instruction. Indians were to adopt Spanish naming practices. Courts were to take testimony only in Spanish. All public speech was to be in Spanish. Only those who learned Spanish could wear Spanish dress or ride a horse. The last four of these directly relate to Indigenous rights to their language, so I loosen the chronological flow to bring the trajectory of these policies up to date.

Spanish Naming Practices

All indigenes were to take or be given Spanish surnames and were to adopt Spanish naming practices. The application of this ruling was uneven across the Guatemalan countryside, reflecting the intensity of Spanish presence and pressure. The *Annals of the Kaqchikel* (Hill and Maxwell forthcoming) documents this time, as lineage heads are baptized and given new Spanish names. In the first years of this transition, period leaders are mentioned with both their names, Kaqchikel first, then Spanish. But the dual-naming system cedes rapidly to single designation by the Spanish surname. In other areas where contact with the Spanish was more sporadic, naming practices differed. In Nebaj, the largest of the Ixil municipios, the dual-naming practice persisted up through the 1970s. My coauthor for the Ixil-language textbooks prepared for the Proyecto Lingüístico Francisco Marroquín (PLFM) from 1973 to 1976 was Domingo Sanchez Brito, or Ku' Tz'u'ch. Further north and west in Guatemala, the Q'anjob'alan and Chuj areas adapted Spanish forenames to their own naming system. Thus a child was given his own forename followed by that of his father and then that of his mother. In San Sebastián Coatán, a Chuj town, I worked with brothers, Juan Gaspar Juan and Pascual Gaspar Juan. Their father's forename was Gaspar; their mother's Juan(a). There are Mayanized equivalents for these forenames, so that when speaking Chuj, Juan Gaspar Juan would be X[3]un Kaxin Xun. In San Mateo, Ixtatán, a Chuj town that early in the colonial period had a resident priest and then later had regular visits, Spanish surnames were successfully introduced, but only as a patronym. Thus, in San Mateo a child receives his own forename (often a repeat of that of a grandparent, but possibly that of any older kin), his father's surname, and his mother's forename. My San Mateo coauthors were Gaspar Mendoza Diego and Francisco Santizo Mateo II. Francisco Santizo Mateo I is II's older brother. After 1646, governmental birth registries were to be kept only in Spanish, though some ecclesiastical, especially cofrade registries of births, baptisms, marriages, and deaths, continued to be recorded in Indigenous languages. Gradually Spanish took over within the church and its associated brotherhoods for official record keeping. As children and adults were baptized and given Hispanic names, María became an extremely common forename for women. So much so that in colloquial Guatemalan Spanish, Indigenous women are often referred to as las Marías. The Mayan doublets of Hispanic names were not written down in official records. They passed into oral tradition and community internal usage. Some groups lost the practice of giving Mayan names to their children, though they might earn sobriquets or be called by kinship terms. However, in the late 1970s and early 1980s, some Mayan educators, linguists, and writers in the central regions, where the dual-naming practice had weakened, began to take Mayan names of their own and wished to give Mayan names to their children. They took names from two main sources, the 260-day ritual calendar, which served as the source of names for Mayan rulers from at least 890 AD, and from the historical record. They published articles in the press, limited run linguistic studies, and gave papers at international and national meetings using their Mayan names as a prename to their Hispanic names, but their papers and passports showed the Hispanic names. Attempts to register children, however, failed as Hispanic registrars refused to write down the Mayan names indicated by the parents, and if the parents refused to proffer an Hispanic alternative, they were simply given one. However, in 1985 a new constitution was drafted that guaranteed the rights of Indigenous peoples to the use of their languages. The publication of the new constitution did not immediately change the practice of registrars, but test cases of Marcos Kuxin and Pakal B'alam established a precedent. In 1986 Marcos Kuxin tried for three months to get his daughter's name registered in Kaqchikel, before succeeding, writing the name out for the registrar. Pakal B'alam was able to register his son with only two visits, though it required bringing a hard copy of the constitution on the second trip. Though the practice has had to spread municipio by muncipio, registry of Mayan names is now possible. Names chosen are being drawn from more sources. The 260-day calendar typically provides 260 names for men, since boys are given the name of their birth day and its numeral coefficient; but only 20 names for girls, since they normally take just the day name plus the female prefix. Today parents are giving attribute names, using Mayan doublets, and borrowing calendar names from other languages, both Maya and non-Maya. A few of those adults who use their Mayan names professionally have legally changed their names, so that they no longer need the Spanish designation. However, many Maya continue to use their Spanish names and to give their children only Spanish names. The change of surname is viewed as particularly dangerous, since they hold land titles that record the Spanish last names.

In 1987, Governmental Accord 1046-87 established official orthographies for the Mayan languages of Guatemala. The spelling conventions so designated differed from standard Spanish writing practice in several regards. For example, the voiceless velar stop was to be spelled **k** in all environments, rather than as in Spanish **qu** before **i** and **e** and **c** before **a**, **o**, and **u**. The voiceless dental fricative was to be spelled **s** everywhere, rather than as in Spanish **c**[4] before **i** and **e**, and **z** before **a**, **o**, **u**, or, as in colonial practice, **ç**. **Q** represents a voiceless postvelar stop. Glottalization is represented by an apostrophe. A scare campaign was run in 1987 and 1988 in an attempt to repeal the officialization of the new orthography. People in the countryside were told that they would lose the title to their lands with this new writing system made the legal standard, since their papers showed their names spelled by Spanish conventions. A suit was brought to the Human Rights Ombudsman, de León Carpio, claiming that the new writing system violated the human rights of Mayas. The case was dismissed. Nonetheless, spelling reform has not been applied to Mayan surnames. The names **Kej** and **Katu'**, important Kaqchikel family names before, during, and after the colony, are still spelled **Quiej**[5] and **Catu**.

Spanish in Court Testimony

Don Antonio de Lara, interpreting the crown's desires for the colony, denied testimony in court being given in Indigenous languages. No systematic provision was given for interpreting testimony or writing out translations of testimony to be entered into the legal record. Documents in Indigenous languages could still be submitted to substantiate a claim, but oral argument had to be in Spanish. Cribs or full translations of Indigenous documents came to be submitted. As certification of true translations became common, the submission of original family documents, histories, wills, and town records in Mayan languages withered. Schwartzkopf (2000) in canvassing the nineteenth-century holdings of the Archivo General de Centroamérica (AGCA) and the Archivo Histórico Arquidiocesano in Guatemala City found few documents with any Indigenous language use at all; some labels for illustrations, maps, and a few short statements comprise the official record by the 1800s.[6]

With the signing of the third point of the Accord for a Firm and Lasting Peace in Guatemala on March 31, 1995, Indigenous peoples were guaranteed the right to due process and to understand the language of a court proceeding in which they were involved. It was envisioned that interpreters translating Spanish into the language of Mayan participants and Mayan languages into Spanish would facilitate this understanding. Pursuant to ratifying this convention, the Guatemalan government provided initial funds for the training of court interpreters. The Universidad Rafael Landívar at their Quetzaltenango campus began a degree program in court interpretation. They provide training in the four Amajority Mayan languages: K'iche', Mam, Kaqchikel, and Q'eqchi'. The initial cohort had to learn the laws and legal concepts in Spanish, translate these ideas into their languages (often devising neologisms), interpret the neologisms and the concepts foreign to Mayan consuetudinal law for potential clients, and identify places of conflict between local practice and the de jure law. The first class graduated in 1999. Meanwhile a small, but growing number of Mayas have completed legal training at the Universidad San Carlos and so are titled lawyers. They can assist clients from their language communities, speaking to them in their language and addressing the court in Spanish, with or without an interpreter.

However, there is no requirement that the judge be able to understand any Indigenous language or be able to interact directly with Indigenous plaintiffs or defendants. Seventeen Mayan languages have no legal interpreter training programs, nor access to the materials developed for the Big Four.

Initiatives to study consuetudinal law, record practices, and so provide guidelines for respecting community custom and common law started before signing of the Accords. An International Seminar on the Judicial System of the Original Peoples of América convened by the Centro de Estudios de la Cultura Maya (CECMA) July 15–17, 1993, in Guatemala. They recognized a body of law having the characteristics of (1) being largely unwritten, (2) based in customary practice, (3) subscribed to voluntarily as a reproduction and representation of community values, (4) but with the sanctioning force of the community. This seminar labelled this set of usages *el sistema jurídico Maya* "the Maya Judicial System," preferring this term to "*Consuetudinal Maya Law.*" Licenciatura theses at the Universidad San Carlos, at Universidad Rafael Landívar, and at Universidad Mariano Gálvez have been written on consuetudinal law in Mayan communities. But there is no governmental integration of these findings into policy.

The Mayan languages encode the legal relationships recognized within Mayan communities and the responsibilities appertaining thereto. These designations when translated into Spanish are not recognized as legal terminology and do not enter into official legal proceedings. Kaji' Kawoq Esquit Choy (1993) in his licenciatura thesis explores the sociolinguistic and pragmatic import of the vocabulary used in ceremonies leading up to marriage within the Kaqchikel community of Patzitzía, Guatemala. He examines the *k'utunïk* "the petition," a series of visits/negotiations between the families of the bride and groom, mediated by experts in ritual speech. He notes that the several discourses of the *k'utunïk* spell out the responsibilities of the bride and groom to their natal families and to the future in-laws, as well as to each other. They also spell out the involvement of the marriage sponsors. A set of formal addresses within the wedding proper *pixa'* Acounsel spell out traditional roles and expectations for each spouse. Esquit Choy points out that these expectations form the marriage contract, and the families, sponsors, and witnessing community subscribe to this contract as well, bringing sanctions to bear to ensure fulfillment of obligations thus entailed. The Mayan wedding ceremony, though establishing the couple within the Maya community, is not legally recognized by the state. To be legally wed, the couple must go to the town hall and pay to have the marriage legally recorded, signing the town registry.

Mayan languages are no longer banned from the courts, but they are still not the basis for legal actions, for contracts, or for official records. Lawyers and judges are aware of consuetudinal law, but have not developed precedents for integration of the Maya and the state judicial systems. Four Mayan languages of Guatemala have a nascent legal literature to facilitate interpretation of court proceedings for their speakers. Seventeen lack trained interpreters to guarantee the right to understand the language of the court proceedings.

Public Speech in Spanish

Antonio de Lara also set about enforcing the edict that all forms of public speech be in Spanish. Priests were told not to deliver homilies in Indigenous languages, nor to allow singing of hymns in languages other than Spanish and Latin. Even catechism was to shift to Spanish only. Public announcements, requirements for community service, work levies, and so on would be given only in Spanish. Children in schools were expected to speak to the teachers in Spanish only. Among themselves, in the classroom or on the school grounds, they were allowed to speak Spanish only. The ban on public use of Indigenous languages was again differentially effective. Some priests continued to give religious education in local languages; many parishes had Indigenous catechists to further evangelization. Public announcements might be translated by precinct leaders so that their neighborhood's responsibilities could be met, but as the colony gave way to the Republic, use of Indigenous languages by non-Indians (outside the Q'eqchi' area) diminished and Indigenous languages retreated from public spheres of interaction to the home.

In the 1980s and 1990s, surveys by Summer Institute in Linguistics (SIL) linguists found that even languages of the Big Four were seldom used in public places (Lewis 1996; Powell 1989). Lewis (1996: table 4, summary) found that:

> [t]he domains in each community which show the lowest levels of K'iche' maintenance are, as might be expected, the domains which are most formal and public. In all of the communities (except possibly Joyabaj) there is a clear break between those domains which are more intimate, and thus most likely to be associated with K'iche' use and those which are more public and associated more generally with Spanish. While Home, Street, Play, Market and Work are clearly K'iche' domains, Religion, Stores, Media, School and Government Offices are all domains which show markedly lower levels of K'iche' use.

Powell's findings for Kaqchikel are similar; if anything, Kaqchikel was strong in fewer domains, as the work, the street, and even the market when vendors from other towns were involved fell out of the Kaqchikel usage domains. I have observed Kaqchikel women speak to one another in Kaqchikel, then turn to a vendor, also Kaqchikel but from another community, and carry out their bargaining in Spanish. When I asked my friends, who were bilingual teachers committed to fostering Kaqchikel, to explain to me why they used Spanish for the transaction, they replied that they did not know the vendor. When I persisted, protesting that they knew she spoke Kaqchikel, they just shrugged and said yes.

Throughout the 1980s and until 1999, I found non-Mayan educators teaching in Mayan towns reporting to me that they did not allow the children to speak Mayan languages in the classroom or on the school grounds. In 1999 the Reforma Educativa (Educational Reform) initiative began a series of seminars for school principals and visitations to rural schools. One of the objectives of these seminars was to increase the respect for Indigenous cultures and languages. The Peace Accords and 1960 Convention of the Rights of the Child hold that all children have a right to their own cultures and languages. Teachers in Indigenous communities were being asked to acquire or use fluency in the local languages to enhance the classroom experience. The Programa Nacional de Educación Bilingüe-Bicultural (PRONEBI) was made a permanent branch of the Ministry of Education, changing its name to Dirección General de Educación Bilingüe-Bicultural. More materials for use in bilingual programs were made available. Teachers who did not speak any Mayan language were to have three years to learn the language of their students. Most non-Mayan teachers protested this requirement. Many threatened to quit. None has been dismissed for noncompliance, as no means of instruction in the languages has been provided. Still, principals are now enjoined from punishing the use of Mayan languages on the school grounds and many communities have established schools of their own, where Mayan languages are the primary languages of instruction. Over forty such schools have sprung up in Kaqchikel towns since 1990. Twelve normal schools have been founded since 2000.

Mayan languages are finding their way back into public spaces. On June 14, 1991, at the ceremony for the printing of Dr. Demetrio Cojti' Cuxil's book *Configuración del Pensamiento Político del Pueblo Maya*, Dr. Cojti' declined to visit with friends and family in Kaqchikel before the ceremony, explaining afterward that it was necessary at such official functions for his Spanish to be pristine, showing no cracks to the non-Mayas present. In 1997 Dr. Cojti' Cuxil inaugurated the First Congress of Mayan Studies at the Universidad Rafael Landívar with an opening statement in Kaqchikel. It is noteworthy as well that Dr. Cojti's first publications use his Spanish name exclusively. His works since 1997 appear with his Mayan name listed first (Waqi' Q'anil).

In the last presidential campaign (1999–2000), the front-runners' television campaign featured spots in Q'eqchi'. The last two sets of mayoral elections have put Indigenous leaders into offices in their home communities. Some of these men have given parts of their public speeches in their own languages. In Sololá, where tradition had maintained a dual municipal government, one locally empowered (referred to as the Indian municipality) and one recognized by the central government (the civil municipality) the last elections placed Indigenous leaders in all offices of both structures. There are now thirteen Indigenous members of the Guatemalan Congress; an address in Q'eqchi' has been given on the floor of the Congress.

Some radio stations have been giving Indigenous languages blocks of time for as many as twenty years. Often the times have been predawn hours; but more daily programming is evolving in Mayan languages. Tecpán now has a local radio station, playing largely Christian music; Kaqchikel is the language of commentary, advertising, and announcements for most of the day. Radio IGER (Instituto Guatemalteco de Radiofónica) initiated by the Catholic Church has sponsored literacy programs in both Spanish and Indigenous languages for twenty years.

Print media are beginning to employ Mayan languages. *Siglo XXI* runs Mayan language supplements monthly. These supplements provide regular news coverage, opinion columns, and feature stories in the language of the month. Mayan writers and entrepreneurs ran their own newspaper, *El Regional*, for several years in the 1990s, though most of the articles were written in Spanish.

Bilingual education has brought the Mayan languages, both orally and in written form, into the schools.

The Peace Accords provided for possibility of making Indigenous languages official, either within their communities, or at a national level. The failure of the 1999 popular referendum that was to have provided enabling legislation for the various provisions of the Accords, coupled with the lack of consensus between and within the governmental committee studying officialization and that of the Academia de las Lenguas Mayas de Guatemala, the semiautonomous organ of the Guatemalan government charged with safeguarding and promoting the autochthonous languages, has resulted in no action being taken to officialize Mayan languages regionally or nationally. Nonetheless, they are reappearing in public spaces. Speakers of Mayan languages are reclaiming domains once ceded to Spanish.

Spanish Language as a Prerequisite to Spanish Dress

Antonio de Lara also published the edict that in order to wear Spanish attire or to ride a saddled horse, one had to speak Spanish. Given the beauty, durability, and climatic adaptation of Mayan attire, it would seem that there would have been little desire to change to Spanish garments. Horses could be ridden with cloths and could be used to carry cargo without the necessity of Spanish. However, one could not hold public office unless one wore Spanish attire. So unless one spoke Spanish, one could not hold public office, at the municipal level or above. To become enfranchised, one had to give up ethnic attire.

Today few men retain their traditional garb as everyday attire, though they may dress in Mayan raiment for ceremonies and special occasions. Many more women dress daily in clothes that mark them as Mayan. During the late 1970s and early 1980s, Mayan men in public positions, scholars, and writers began experimenting with emblematic attire; they were looking for something they could wear that would acknowledge their group membership, while not requiring that their families begin large-scale weaving projects. Some men tried wearing sandals to work in their offices. Sandals were noted in the trait list of the 1950 Guatemalan census as one of the criteria for identifying an Indian as such. However, as Q'uq'ulkan Guaján Rodríguez confided (personal communication) the ridicule by fellow office workers made this option a constant struggle. At the Taller Maya in Quetzaltenango in 1989, a group of these leaders, men and women, gathered sample jackets from meeting participants and tried out design modifications that would mark them as Mayan. The result was a solidarity jacket. The original designs were a dark blue cotton cloth,[7] with narrow embroidered panels along the front zipper and a day sign patch over the heart. Thereafter, Mayan men could wear Western clothing, slacks, T- and/or long-sleeved shirts, but still mark their allegiance to their ethnicity by the use of the jacket.

At the June 2000 ceremony for the repatriation of de Varea's *Calepino de Lengua Cakchiquel* (sic), Kaqtijax Anastasio Guarcax Guarcax, President of the Kaqchikel Cholchi', the Kaqchikel branch of the Academia de las Lenguas Mayas de Guatemala, appeared in full *traje*[8] for the ceremony hosted by the Universidad Rafael Landívar. Kaqtijax was not the only Mayan man present. Several were present in the audience, in solidarity jackets; one other, who wore a three-piece tailored suit, shared the platform, but Kaqtijax alone wore his complete attire.

The legal ban on Mayan dress has been lifted. Dress is recognized in the Peace Accords and in the Guatemalan Constitution as a protected right of the Mayan communities and not tied to language use or ability. Still, use of Mayan attire, even by women, is declining in many areas. In part this is due to economic pressures to enter the wage labor force, reducing the amount of time that a woman can spend weaving. In part, it is due to the relative cost of Western garb versus the traditional Mayan clothing. Mayan daily wear is much more expensive. Some women substitute plain commercial fabric, folded and sewn in *huipil*-like fashion,[9] for blouses. The ultimate marker of ethnicity in women's dress is the *corte*, or skirt-length. When a woman takes off her corte, switching to skirts or slacks, others in the community question her allegiance to group values. At the same time, the spread of a pan-Mayan ideology is leading some women to increase the diversity of their wardrobe, not by switching to Western dress, but by adding huipils in the styles of other communities. Individual Mayan communities have identifiable huipil styles, characterized by type of weave, color, and motifs. Recently women have been acquiring and wearing huipils from other towns. In 1987, Valeriana Cu' (personal communication) assured me that I had not recognized her at first (having not visited her community for two years) because she wasn't like this before. She had begun wearing other huipils, in addition to her own from San Antonio Aguascalientes. She saw the change as a fundamental ideological commitment, presenting a new face to the world, one I had failed to recognize. Carol Hendrickson (1995) notes that Mayan women are constantly weaving new images of self within a frame of identity set by expectations of their communities. This social construction identity now includes articles of Western manufacture as well as local artisanry for both men and women, but the legal tie to language has been severed. Economics and ideology play themselves out in the Mayan wardrobe today.

Summary of the 1646 Edicts

After the arrival of Antonio de Lara as Royal Visitor in 1646, crown policy became explicitly assimilatory. Indigenous peoples could be loyal subjects and would be, once they became Spanish speakers, adopting Spanish dress and the Catholic religion.

When Guatemala became an independent republic, the assimilationist ideology continued. Skinner-Klee (1954) noted that the founders of the Guatemalan republic saw Spanish as the unifying principle of the state. The Constituent Congress affirmed Spanish as the national official language, characterized the Indigenous languages as incomplete and imperfect, and charged the parish priests to devise means of speedily extinguishing the autochthonous tongues.

While government policy remained assimilatory, means varied. Jorge Ubico was President of Guatemala from 1931 to 1944. He sponsored legislation for universal public education, requiring that in Indigenous communities education be bilingual. While the legislation passed, sufficient enabling budgetary steps were not taken to reach all Indigenous communities, or to train a cadre of bilingual teachers. Arévalo, President after Ubico, continued the push to establish schools in rural Indigenous communities. Arévalo also favored bilingual education, but again failed to introduce a systematic program for its implementation. In 1965 the Organic Education Law was passed. This law specified that Spanish was the official language of education, but that Indigenous languages could be used in the first year(s) of school to facilitate transition to Spanish-language competence and instruction. UNESCO provided some bilingual teacher training. Bilingual castillianization classes for children and adults were established in thirteen of the twenty-one Mayan language areas of Guatemala by 1982.

Governmental policy still aimed a creating a united state by bringing the Indians into the Spanish-speaking fold. However, the 1985 constitution recognized the Indigenous cultures and languages as part of the patrimony of the country. The 1993 constitutional reforms recognized pluriculturality and the right of the cultures and languages to persist, develop, and enrich their communities and the nation now and into the future. To understand how Indigenous peoples have exercised their intellectual rights in their language to these goals, let us examine (1) standardization, (2) bilingual education, and (3) publication.

Standardization

Standardization is the process of establishing a norm for the proper use of a language. In English, standardization is achieved through use of dictionaries (themselves compiled by lexicographers who scour print sources documenting language use), grammar books, and manuals of style provided by publishing houses and journals; by teachers; and by prestigious newspapers and their columnist language mavens. Our spelling system developed through literate usage, with some nationalist tweaking by Noah Webster.[10]

In preinvasion times, there appears to have been standardization of the glyphs used to write the Mayan languages. The hieroglyphic writing system was used throughout an area that today is home to six different language groups. Within the system itself there were some variations, both regional (Bricker 2000) and artistic; there was variation between codical style writing and monumental inscriptions. However, as discussed earlier, once the Spanish arrived, hieroglyphic writing dwindled. Mayan languages were written in the early colonial period using a writing system based on the Latin alphabet, with some accommodations to the new phonemes. This writing system was standardized too. In that, many priests used the conventions devised by Father Parra. There was some regional variation as well. Yucatec Mayan writing used the digraph **dz** to represent the glottalized voiceless dental affricate. This sound was represented by **q** in the languages of highland Guatemala. There was considerable stylistic variation in the representation of /w/. Within a single document, this labiovelar glide might be written as **hu**, **uh**, **u**, or **v**. Likewise **j**, **i**, and **y** alternated. Some authors were redundant in phonetic features such as voicelessness for word final liquids in K'iche'an language by writing **h** after these segments; others were not; yet others were so sporadically. The writers of documents in Mayan languages during the early colonial period were often priests, seeking to teach other clerics Indigenous languages and tropes to further evangelization, or documenting parish events; but there were also many native authors. They wrote historical annals, recorded dynastic succession, and witnessed political and legal happenings in their communities. However, once Indigenous languages of Guatemala were suppressed by the Council of Trent and the edicts of 1646, less was recorded in Indigenous languages. Emphasis shifted to Spanish literacy.

Little was written in Mayan languages of Guatemala during the next 250 years. Some European travelers and scholars collected colonial manuscripts, studied them, wrote studies of the languages, and produced glossaries (cf. Seler ca. 1900, 1990–1998; Berendt 1869, 1866–1877; Stoll 1888–1896). But this was writing on the Mayan languages for an audience of international scholars, not production of materials in Mayan languages for speakers of those languages.

When William Cameron Townsend arrived in Guatemala in 1919, there were few literate Mayas. Townsend envisioned a worldwide campaign to bring the Gospels to all the peoples of the world. To do this they would have to be written in all the languages of the world and all the peoples of the world would have to be literate in their languages in order to read the writings. In 1934, in an Arkansas farmhouse, he began training people to become linguists and undertake this work. The first language he worked with was Kaqchikel. The methodology he developed, as refined by Dr. Kenneth Pike and others, has facilitated the study of 1,576 languages around the world, development of practical orthographies for them, and production of texts in these languages. These texts often include school primers, tracts on hygiene and agriculture, as well as the four books of the Gospel. As literacy is a requisite for having access to the printed words of the Gospel, SIL has also developed techniques for teaching reading and writing skills (Wendell Vanderzee 1989). However, the goal of this literacy is to provide access to the Scriptures. Other publications are secondary to the production of an adequate translation of the Gospels.

In developing alphabets for writing the Mayan languages of Guatemala, SIL linguists did not take into account early writing practices, neither glyphic nor colonial. They saw literacy in Mayan languages as transitional to an ultimate literacy in Spanish. They adapted Spanish spelling conventions to represent the phonemes of the Mayan languages. SIL served as an advisory body to the government of Guatemala from the mid-1940s until the mid-1980s. The SIL contract allowing them to work and publish in Guatemala expired in 1998. For forty years, SIL linguists set the norms for writing in Mayan languages. In order to make the Gospels readily accessible, they held that books should be written in the local variety of a language; thus, there was no attempt to develop a uniform standard for a language, rather each dialect should receive its own version of materials. Limitations on time and resources militated against dividing material production within townships, but for three of the Big Four more than one set of materials, texts, Gospels, and dictionaries were developed. Speakers of Mayan languages in many communities learned to read in their languages using SIL materials. Many homes have Bibles or New Testaments in their native tongue thanks to the efforts of SIL linguists. SIL has produced Bible stories in neoliterate friendly forms, such as comic books (Itzol Gómez 1981). SIL was effective in developing orthographies and materials for the Mayan languages of Guatemala.

However, SIL was not alone in studying Mayan languages. The Benedictines in Guatemala had long wanted to have a program that would teach speakers of Mayan languages to read and write in their languages, but that would go further and empower those speakers to produce their own materials, their own texts in these languages. In 1971 they contracted with Robert Gersony to establish the Proyecto Lingüístico Francisco Marroquín (PLFM). This organization was to be a lay institution and was meant to train speakers of Mayan languages in technical linguistics and in pedagogical materials production so that Mayan communities could direct the development of written linguistic resources. Gersony, seconded by Tony Jackson of OXFAM, set up a program whereby U.S. linguists sponsored by the Peace Corps would train cadres of Mayas chosen by their communities. The first two years of the project saw work begin with K'iche' and with Mam. In 1973 the PLFM expanded to include Kaqchikel, Q'eqchi', Ixil, Tz'utujiil, Awakateko, Q'anjob'al, Akateko, and Chuj. In 1975 Popti' was added, along with Ch'orti', another variety of Mam, and more Ixil. Orthographic principles applied by PLFM linguists were based on three criteria: (1) phonemic adequacy; (2) one phoneme–one graphemic realization; and (3) ease of mechanical reproductions (no symbols not found on a standard typewriter keyboard were to be used). Again neither colonial nor precolonial practice served as models.

The orthographies developed by the PLFM differed in few details from those already in use by SIL. The main differences resided in not incorporating Spanish orthographic practices where these led to a violation of the principle of one phoneme– one graphemic representation, and in not using diereses over consonants.

Other organizations were also at play in the field of writing. Individual scholars within the Catholic Church and within Protestant groups began to write Guatemalan languages. In Alta Verapaz, Father Esteban Haeserijn (1979, 1966, and 1972) meticulously studied and documented Q'eqchi'. He published bilingual dictionaries as an aid to those wanting to learn Q'eqchi' and as a resource for Q'eqchi' seeking to master Spanish. He produced mimeographed sketches of grammar as an aid to the Q'eqchi' in learning about the structure of their language. His writing system retained some elements of colonial practice as well as some modern Spanish accommodations. Haeserijn intended his codification to be of use to outsiders wishing to learn Q'eqchi' or learn about it, but also to be useful to Q'eqchi' speakers, though often as an aid to their Spanish.

James Mondloch (1978) wrote a basic K'iche' grammar, using an alphabet much like that of SIL, with diereses over short vowels. His grammar is directed to English-speaking scholars and is intended to facilitate non-Mayas' learning K'iche'.

Don Adrián Inéz Chávez, a K'iche' scholar, also developed an orthography for writing his language and suggested that its principles be extended to other Mayan languages. His alphabet was based largely on modern Spanish spelling conventions, but he made a few modifications, marking the distinctiveness of K'iche' and other Mayan languages. He advocated superimposing the **t** on **z** for representation of the glottalized voiceless dental affricate, **tz'** in the PLFM and SIL orthographies. He suggested a sun sign, ☼, for the glottalized postvelar voiceless stop. This sound is the initial consonant of the word for sun in K'iche'. He also suggested an asterisk-like star sign, *, for the glottalized alveopalatal voiceless affricate, the initial consonant in the K'iche' word for star. He founded an academy for the K'iche' language to regulate the development of the language and materials within it and to promote its use. This academy continues today alongside the K'iche'an branch of the Academy of Mayan Languages. The Association of Mayan Writers, headquartered in Quetzaltenango, also counts Don Andrián Inéz Chávez among its intellectual forebears. Some writers within this group and others under the K'iche' Academy continue to use Chávez' alphabet, or elements of it, rather than subscribing completely to the officialized alphabets.

In the 1960s and 1970s several organizations were involved in the government's literacy campaign, seeking to teach both adults and children to read and write. First language literacy was viewed as an effective tool for successful transfer to Spanish language literacy. Local literacy workers often invented nonce systems for writing the Indigenous languages.

In 1980 the Guatemalan Ministry of Education decided to extend bilingual education beyond preschool. They wanted a uniform and official orthography for use in the Big Four languages of the pilot program, but in theory extendable to the rest of the languages of Guatemala. In 1984 the Instituto Indigenista Nacional convoked an international congress on the alphabet question. The objective was to derive a single orthographic system that could be employed to write all the Mayan languages of Guatemala. Individual languages might make use of proper subsets of the symbols, but the value of those symbols was to be uniform and transferrable. Participants convoked included foreign linguists working with the SIL, various clergy who were teaching literacy, Mayan linguists trained by the PLFM, literacy workers from various governmental and nongovernmental programs, bilingual education instructors and materials developers, and leaders of Indigenous communities. All participants were allowed to express their opinions, suggest options, and debate. Only Indigenous participants were allowed to vote on the proposals. The Indigenous scholars voted to ratify the PLFM proposals with one modification. The symbol **7**, which the PLFM used to represent a glottal stop,[11] was replaced with an apostrophe. The Indian participants also chose a central cadre of trained linguists from the PLFM and community leaders to continue the work of standardization of Mayan languages, moving beyond the question of simply what graphemes should represent the sounds, but to answer questions of word division, punctuation, capitalization, and usage. All members of the convocation pledged to adopt the new alphabet and promote its usage.

SIL, however, had several publications already in the works. They would have had to make several global search-and-replace sweeps to amend their publications in accord with the new guidelines. Seven years after the Congress on Alphabets, SIL published a dictionary of Central Cakchiquel (sic) (Ruyán Canú and Coyote Tum 1991) with the SIL orthography in bold print and the official spellings below and in italics. Other groups were also sporadic in their use of the agreed-on orthography.

Meanwhile the cadre of linguists and community leaders working together since the Congress on Alphabets gained governmental support for the establishment of an Academy of Mayan Languages of Guatemala (ALMG). The ALMG was confirmed as a semiautonomous organ of the government in 1987. The first official act of the ALMG was to seek congressional approval of the unified alphabet established by the 1984 convocation. This unified alphabet was officialized in 1987 by Governmental Accord 1046-87. This accord laid out the phonological inventories of the twenty-one Mayan languages that the government recognized; it specified how these phonological distinctions were to be rendered in writing. It did not give sanctions for lack of compliance or provide mechanisms for transposing existing documents into the new orthographies or for the training of speakers and writers in the new practices; nor did it envision modifications in the inventories of either graphemes or languages.

In 1988 the ALMG received a budget to begin the work of developing representation for each of the Mayan linguistic communities of Guatemala. Since that time they have established committees within the twenty-one officially recognized language communities. The presidents of these committees meet regularly in Guatemala City to determine priorities for the fostering of Mayan language use in both written and spoken domains. As the body legally charged to represent speakers of Mayan languages, the ALMG undertook a two-year study from 1995 to 1997 concerning the possible officialization of (a) Mayan language(s). Local committees have been involved in projects sponsored by UNICEF to develop neologisms in Mayan languages for use in grades 1–4 of elementary schools. In 1994–1995 Kaqchikel Cholchi', the Kaqchikel branch of the ALMG, spearheaded a project to propose vocabulary for the social science, natural science, language, and mathematics curricula of grades 1–4 for seven of the K'iche'an languages (UNICEF 1995a, b, c, d). This neologism project did not simply provide glosses for Spanish concepts that appear in the national school textbooks; it also sought to systematize and document the correlative concepts for those domains in the Mayan languages. Thus the neologisms texts not only record words for root and square root in Mayan languages, they also review the base twenty system of Mayan mathematics. The natural sciences texts give words for the Linnaean divisions: amphibian, reptile, mammal, bird, fish. They also list the taxa used by Mayas based on ways of biting and food required. The social science lists the modern divisions of the state (often with revitalized colonial forms that had fallen out of usage) and also the traditional hierarchies within communities. Language materials include equivalents for the traditional grammar categories, such as subject and verb, but also include linguistic designations for properties peculiar to the Mayan languages, such as ergative, absolutive, positional, relational noun, and numeral classifier.

As Mayan linguists continue to work on their languages, they have come to new understandings. Many Mayan linguists, including K'iche' linguists, are not happy with the official representation of their vowel system, which uses diereses over short vowels. The linguists of Oxlajuuj Keej Mayab' Ajtz'iib' (OKMA), a Mayan research group, have repeatedly taken the stand that the long vowels should be written double and short vowels written as a simple grapheme without dieresis, as in the name of their organization. Writers and Mayan linguists working in other languages have also found problems with their official writing systems. The use of **nh** in Chuj as a digraph for the voiced velar nasal has led to difficulty distinguishing this phoneme from the series **n** followed by **h**. Q'anjob'al authors have begun to use the grapheme **h** as a place-holder in addition to, or instead of, a representation of a voiceless glottal fricative.

Moreover, understandings of what constitutes a language group or community are shifting. Many speakers of Akateko, a Q'anjob'alan language of northwestern Huehuetenango, identify themselves as speakers of Q'anjob'al rather than of a separate language. As Q'anjob'al is a larger language and has materials developed by PRONEBI/DIGEBI, the many Akatekos want to proceed with bilingual education under the auspices of Q'anjob'al and with Q'anjob'al teaching resources, since materials in Akateko could be years away. However, Akateko has a separate language committee and a community president who represents them in the ALMG and runs small programs for children in San Miguel Acatán.

Similarly some Achí linguists, notably Juliana Sis Ib'oy (López and Sis Iboy 1993), argue that Achí is a dialect of K'iche' rather than a separate language, though politically the Achi's are fiercely independent of K'iche' associations.

Conversely, speakers of Teko, a variant of Mam officially, are declaring their independence of the body of the Mam community, claiming that materials developed for the majority dialects of Mam are unintelligible to their speakers. They wish theirs to be recognized as a separate language.

Less controversially, Jakalteko speakers wish their language and their language community to be recognized by their own designation rather than the term Jakalteko, which is an Hispanicized rendition of the Nahuatl place-name of the largest town within the community. They say they speak Popti' and wish this term to be the official name of the language. The ALMG has granted this wish internally; however, it has not moved to ask the Congress to ratify the change in designation.

Nor have any of the spelling/orthography reforms suggested by member communities been officially promulgated through the ALMG. The national congress has not been asked to change any elements of the language specific orthographies, nor its count of the number of Mayan languages that exist. Conversations in 1998 and 1999 with members of the executive board indicated that the ALMG was not likely to seek such congressional action in the future. There was a general fear that the gains that had been made might be wiped out were the ALMG to return to the congress with further requests, especially requests that might be construed as errors in previous proposals.

The government likewise has made no concerted effort to bring all subsidiary units into alignment. In 1993, seven years after the officialization of the alphabets of Mayan languages and three years after the ratification of the names of these languages rendered in the new unified system,[12] the National Museum of Ethnology and Anthropology had not changed the signage on the linguistic map displayed to the public. Towns and natural features on official maps not only retain Nahuatl or Spanish names rather than appearing with their Mayan designations, but those settlements, rivers, and mountains that have Mayan names have these names spelled in Spanish orthography. The ALMG has erected welcome signs along highway entrances to towns that host the linguistic community centers. These signs do use the unified alphabet and the Mayan placenames.

Without congressional modification of the enabling legislation, the ALMG pursues its goals of fostering Mayan language use. It provides periodic training seminars for local committees and Mayan educators. However, members of the ALMG, even executive board members, often publish statements in their languages through local or national presses that themselves do not follow the official spelling and orthographic practice guidelines of the academia. The ALMG has not the ability to censor the publications of other organizations or of individuals. Kaqchikel Cholchi' offers its services as proofreaders, hence style/norm setters, for those writing in Kaqchikel and even in related K'iche'an languages, notably Sakapulteko and Sipakapense; but submissions are voluntary. *Kukuy*, a children's magazine published in Kaqchikel, does submit copy to be proofed, when the production schedule permits and Chochi' staff are available. Likewise, *Kaqchi' Wuj*, a magazine for adults, typically is passed through Cholchi' review, so long as printing deadlines allow. As a result, Kaqchikel publications are among the most uniform in terms of spelling conventions, punctuation usage and strategies of word division and capitalization. But, by no means do all publications flow through Cholchi' hands.

Aside from the ALMG, what other mechanisms of standardization are available? Many of the languages have dictionaries available, either those published by the PLFM, Universidad Rafael Landívar, or Cholsamaj (all of which use the official unified alphabet) or those published by SIL (which uses the old alphabet). These dictionaries, however, are bilingual. Almost all provide glosses running from the Indigenous language to Spanish, with no reverse concordance section. Blair et al. (1969) made a trilingual Kaqchikel dictionary, with English and Spanish reference sections. However, these dictionaries are of primary utility for speakers of English or Spanish seeking to find an Indigenous phrase. The PLFM dictionaries do provide some notes on usage, mentioning regional differences, gender associated traits, and some levels of formality. The PLFM dictionaries also offer occasional synonyms and antonyms. They set the standard for spelling. While usage comments are common and literary citations are lacking, these dictionaries, though bilingual, do provide native writers with a window on standardization.

OKMA and the Universidad Rafael Landívar have provided manuals of style for writers in Mayan languages. In the 1980s Rafael Landívar hired a group of linguists (often associates of the PLFM) to tailor a boilerplate text on writing in Mayan languages to their specific languages. These books were published with the generic title *Escribamos X* (*Let's Write X*), where X could be replaced with the name of the Mayan language in question. Then in 1993 they published pedagogical grammars, written by OKMA linguists. These grammars were published for Kaqchikel, K'iche', Tz'utujiil, Poqom, and Mam. And in 1994 OKMA linguists brought out editing manuals, published by Cholsamaj, for these same languages. These materials on writing self-consciously set out to determine proper spellings, word divisions, capitalizations, punctuations, and formatting. They are all written in Spanish, with only examples from the Mayan languages whose usage they seek to regulate, but they describe these structures from the vantage point of a profound understanding of the grammar and praxis of the language. The linguistic and literary vocabulary employed to describe and prescribe are all Spanish, but neologists have developed the vocabulary to make such technical discussions possible in Kaqchikel and sister languages. OKMA has envisioned future projects calling for monolingual dictionaries in Mayan languages and monolingual texts on linguistics, language use, and literature.

Bilingual Education

Guatemala has a long history of bilingual education, both public and private. To recapitulate briefly, prior to the Spanish invasion there was bilingualism (or multilingualism) at least among members of the elites. Scribes recording dynastic histories in glyphs or drawing out codices for regulating ritual celebrations mastered a writing system, which served as a lingua franca, overarching the local languages. Contact with the polities of Central Mexico produced some Nahuatl–Maya bilingualism; whether languages were taught directly in the schools for young nobles is not known. Once the Spanish arrived, priests established classes in Spanish and in Latin, often while promoting the use of Mayan languages as a tool of evangelization. The Council of Trent and the edicts of 1646 ended the fostering of Mayan languages. Spanish-language instruction was prescribed for all Mayan children between the ages of five and eight. Throughout the colonial period the crown strove to castellanize the Maya, making them good subjects by making them good speakers of Spanish. The philosophy of the Republic of Guatemala was likewise to foster unity through use of a common language, and that language was to be Spanish. In the early 1900s, successive governments passed universal education acts and opened more and more schools in rural, highland areas of the country, Mayan areas. Under Ubico, education in Indigenous areas was meant to be bilingual, but lack of teachers and materials thwarted this vision. Arévalo also supported bilingual education, and though a few new schools were opened, bilingual teachers were still too few and materials lacking. In the 1960s UNESCO sponsored training programs for bilingual teachers. The government sponsored several literacy programs in the countryside, including Socio-educativo Rural and CONALFA (Comisión Nacional de Alfabetización). Many of the teachers in these programs used the Indigenous languages as an aid to literacy, whether initial literacy was to be in Spanish or the Indigenous language. Bilingual promoters were assigned as teachers' aides for thirteen of the twenty-one language communities. In 1965 teaching in Indigenous languages was introduced in a Head Start–like program to ready young Mayan children for first grade. Grade school, however, was to be taught in Spanish. In 1980, with two-thirds funding from USAID, the Guatemalan Ministry of Education extended bilingual education beyond preschool. The plan was to phase out instruction in Mayan languages so that by grade 3, children would be ready to enter a monolingual Spanish classroom. The pilot project was run in test schools within the areas of the Big Four: K'iche', Mam, Q'eqchi', and Kaqchikel. In 1984, the pilot program was evaluated and found to be a success. Not only were levels of academic achievement higher in the bilingual schools, but drop-out rates were lower as well. Parental satisfaction was higher. The Guatemalan government took on more of the financial responsibility for the program and established PRONEBI.

PRONEBI increased the number of schools reached within the Big Four language areas and expanded the Mayan curriculum through fourth grade. It also gradually increased its language coverage to include Q'anjob'al, Ixil, Poqomchi', and Tz'utujiil.

Despite the measures of success of PRONEBI, bilingual education was not without its critics. Luis Enrique Sam Colop (1983) found that the all existing programs in Guatemala were assimilationist in ideology. The goal was transition to Spanish, whether transition in first, third, or fourth grades. There were no programs aimed at fomenting the use of Mayan languages, maintaining them in their communities of origin and fostering understanding of Indigenous cultural concepts and values. Shortly thereafter, Dr. Demetrio Cojti' Cuxil in a report for the Ministry of Education stated that while there were many systems of bilingual education—direct castellanization, subtractive/indirect castellanization, additive abstractionist, additive functionalist, juxtaposed bilingualism—they were all necessarily assimilationist. He concludes:

> Por eso, hemos subtitulado este ensayo: desde el bilingüismo etnocida hasta el bilingüismo etnocida, porque no hay bilingüismo no etnocida escolar excepto él de y para los individuos y círculos sociales pudientes y dominantes.
>
> *Therefore, we have subtitled this essay: from ethnocidal bilingualism to ethnocidal bilingualism, because there is no bilingualism that is not scholastic ethnocide except that of and for the powerful and dominating individuals and social circles.* (1987: 35)

PRONEBI took the concerns of these scholars to heart. While expanding their programs to over 400 schools, they modified their materials from suppletive texts, designed to lead to monolingual instruction in Spanish, to parallel texts, presenting Mayan and Spanish content in tandem. Math lessons would be given both in base ten as in monolingual Spanish classrooms, but also in base twenty in Mayan languages. Support for the new duality was not universal. Some parents felt that their children needed no help with their native language, but needed Spanish to get ahead economically. They worried about class time being taken from crucial instruction in Spanish and in

Western curricula that would govern admission to the urban workplace. Many teachers also felt unsure of the new materials, or unsure of their own fluency in the local language.[13] In surveys of teachers in Kaqchikel and K'iche' area schools, students at Mariano Gálvez found that most did not give the prescribed time allotment to instruction via Mayan languages. Many reported that they seldom used the materials at all, as they lacked enough time in the school day to adequately present even the traditional curriculum, much less its double. PRONEBI countered these problems by running workshops and seminars in the communities, demonstrating the effectiveness of bilingual education. PRONEBI supervisors traveled constantly around a circuit of schools, introducing teachers to the new materials, observing classrooms, answering questions, offering suggestions, and making sure that teachers did split their days among the languages.

Mayan support for bilingual education grew. In 1993, Alfredo Tay Coyoy[14] became minister of education. He felt that PRONEBI was not Maya enough, rather it hastened Westernization by allowing facile translation of Western concepts into Mayan languages (CECMA 1992). He fostered a program for grassroots schools to be started in Mayan communities, run by Mayan teachers with Mayan curricula and accredited by the state. At first, start-up funds were available to help communities bootstrap schools, but Arzu's minister of education discontinued this program. Nonetheless Mayan schools continue to develop. UNICEF has contributed funds to this initiative. The Mayan schools have confederated and associated with the Centro de Documentación e Investigación Maya (CEDIM). These grassroots schools design their own curricula and often their own texts, but they also use materials developed by PRONEBI and by the Linguistic Institute of Universidad Rafael Landívar. The focus of these schools is Mayan education for the Maya by the Maya. CEDIM (1994) envisions the curricula as containing some Spanish, for example Spanish as a second language or Spanish literature, but proposes that 70–90 percent of the instruction in the Mayan schools be in the local Mayan language. Drs. Julia and Michael Richards in reviewing the impact of the Mayan schools conclude: "What is of paramount importance, however, is that the efforts of the Escuelas Mayas are fundamentally a matter of Maya themselves controlling the education of Maya children" (Richards and Richards 1996: 221).

Meanwhile PRONEBI schools have responded to the call for more Mayan content in classes. In 1996 the PRONEBI became DIGEBI. This name change signaled a strengthening governmental commitment to bilingual education. By 1998, Guatemala reported to the United Nations Commission on Human Rights that through DIGEBI "[t]here are 5,960 schoolteachers currently employed by DIGEBI . . . working in 1,277 schools attended by 330,000 boys and girls in 12 of the country's 22 geographical departments. They use 14 of the 21 languages spoken in Guatemala: Pokoman (sic), Ch'orti (sic), Q'eqchí (sic), Poqomchí (sic), Achí (sic), Kaqchikal (sic), Tz'utujiil, K'ochee (sic), Ixil, Mam, Q'anjob'al, Awakateko, Popti (sic) and Sipakapense" (UN Commission on Human Rights, Session 54 1998).[15] DIGEBI has been working in the past three years to increase the number of languages covered and to strengthen Mayan curricular content. The introduction of bilingual and heavily Mayan curricula in new communities has met with resistance as new groups of parents are introduced to concepts of non-Spanish-based education, but DIGEBI has developed new training programs for teachers and for community organizers to explain the motivations for bilingual education, to review academic achievement records of extant programs, and to establish common goals with parents and students so that education can be tailored to the felt needs of the communities. DIGEBI, currently headed by Raxche' Demetrio Rodríguez Guaján, is committed to making DIGEBI schools as Mayan as the Mayan schools, providing cutting-edge technological training within the cultural framework of the Mayan worldview (Raxche', personal communication 2001, 2002, and 2003).

Education is far from universal in Guatemala, and Mayan areas lag behind non-Mayan, nonrural communities. The National Plan for the Development of the Mayan People of Guatemala (Q'uq'kumätz 1999) reports that 82 percent of Mayan women are illiterate and in Mayan areas only 44 percent of school-age children actually attend schools. Nevertheless, as Mayan schools spread through Mayan areas and parents support their children's school attendance, school desertion is tapering off. More Mayan students now have schools available in the home communities; more of these schools go beyond third grade (the former rural standard). Once in schools, students and their cultures are treated with respect. Basic literacy rates are increasing; adult education programs continue. The majority of programs are Maya run; curricula are Maya developed; goals are set by Maya. Children within these schools are learning to read and write in Mayan languages. The materials designers of DIGEBI and of the

Institute Rafael Landívar subscribe to the official alphabets, as revised by continuing work of Mayan linguists, notably those of OKMA and the ALMG. Standardization of the norms suggested by these bodies is becoming normalized through the schools.

Publication

Fishman (1991) identifies publication in threatened languages, availability not only of something to read but also of outlets for written expression as an important factor in reversing language shift or language extinction. Indeed, in many cases, writers in nonhegemonic languages have been key forces in the standardization and promulgation of the languages, providing through their writings models for usage.

In the 1960s there were few outlets for writings in Mayan languages. SIL was publishing pamphlets and biblical works in Indigenous languages. The government's castellanization programs were printing primers in Mayan languages, with Spanish subtitles. In 1974 the PLFM began to put out small mimeographed runs of collections of stories aimed at schoolchildren in Mayan areas. But original works by Mayan authors had limited circulation. In 1975 Juan Yool Gómez wrote a Kaqchikel history but could find no publisher. The PLFM ran a few mimeographed copies of this work. The Linguistic Institute of Rafael Landívar University with USAID funding began to develop reading materials for Mayan children. At first their Mayan authors recorded traditional stories (Yool Gómez and Fong 1990), but then they developed original compositions (Giracca de Castellanos 1993a, b; Lima 1993). The publications of the Linguistic Institute were distributed free to educators in Guatemala upon request. But they were not systematically distributed to all schools within Mayan linguistic communities. Conditions of the USAID support prohibited sale of these materials, which further limited exposure to these works. But a body of children's literature was growing in Mayan languages.

Reading material for adults was more limited. SIL's treatises on sanitary outhouses, use of pesticides, and combating the medfly were intended for adults. The constitution of 1985 was translated into the Big Four languages. The World Health Organization appealed to the ALMG for aid in getting anticholera propaganda translated into Mayan languages. The U.S. Army put out comic book pamphlets warning against poppy cultivation.

Mayan authors did compose original literature. Humberto Akabal published poems that gained international acclaim. Though a Kaqchikel speaker, he composed his poetry in Spanish. In 1995, five years after his first collection of poems, *El Animalero,* appeared, Akabal brought out a bilingual version, *Ajyuq: El Animalero.* But his subsequent publications remain monolingual in Spanish. In 1992 Gaspar Pedro González, a Q'anjob'al author, published *La Otra Cara: la vida de un Maya*, the first Mayan novel. This novel was subsequently translated into English, in a 1995 edition. And then in 1996 the novel appeared in the author's own language, Q'anjob'al, a bilingual (Q'anjob'al–Spanish) edition. Victor Montejo, a speaker of Popti' and a professor at University of California—Davis, has written four works of fiction and two testimonial histories of the violence in Guatemala. One of his original works has been issued in bilingual edition: *Q'anil, el hombre rayo : una leyenda de Jacaltenango 'Komam Q'anil, ya' k'uh Winaj : yik'ti'al xajla'.*

Several presses have been founded to provide an outlet for the expression of Mayan authors and Mayan concerns. Cholsamaj and Nawal Wuj are allied publishing houses in Guatemala City. They publish primarily works by Mayan authors, but also works by others on Mayan topics. They also produce Mayan notebooks, folders with Mayan motifs, flashcards of Mayan numerals, games with Mayan motifs for schoolchildren, and posters. Saqb'e maintained a small press in Chimaltenango for six years, publishing only Mayan materials. The newspaper *El Regional*, which folded after a ten-year run, was Mayan owned and operated, though published largely in Spanish. The ALMG publishes materials in Mayan languages, as does the PLFM, often in conjunction with the Linguistic Institute of Rafael Landívar University. Yaxte' Press, founded by Fernando Peñalosa, though based in the United States, includes Gaspar Pedro González on its executive board and distributes its publications in Guatemala, as well as among the swelling Mayan population of the greater Los Angeles area. Yaxte's publication list contains over thirty titles. Many of its works are by Mayan authors, although non-Indigenous authors writing on the Maya are also published. Eight of the titles are bilingual editions in Indigenous languages and Spanish.

There are now outlets for written expression in Maya. The national newspaper *Siglo XXI* publishes news supplements in a variety of Mayan languages on a rotating basis. Mayan authors, such as Enrique Sam Colop, are regular columnists for the Prensa Libre, though their contributions are in Spanish, with token phrases in Mayan languages. The Kaqchikel branch of the ALMG publishes a feature magazine, *Kaqchi' Wuj*. This publication is exclusively in Kaqchikel, though authors are often identified by both their Mayan and Spanish names. Maya are writing, both in their native languages and in other languages, including Spanish and English. There are several presses dedicated to producing Mayan literature and Mayan studies. The Maya are expressing themselves, and they, as well as non-Maya, are reading and learning from these expressions.

Conclusion

What are the rights of speakers in their languages? First of all, do they have the right to speak in their languages in all domains and walks of life? This had not been the case in Guatemala. Legally, Indigenous languages were prohibited in public spaces during the colonial period. During the Republican period, Indigenous language use in the classroom was tolerated only as a means to achieve Spanish fluency, and in the late 1900s, schoolchildren were still being punished for speaking in their own languages in the schoolyard. In 1985, language rights won constitutional backing. The 1995 Peace Accords provided further guarantees and stimulated the training of legal translators to provide equal protection under the law. Mayan languages were back in the legal system. They were to be not only tolerated, but also fostered, in the schools. Evangelical churches ordained speakers of Mayan languages and encouraged them to preach in their native languages. The Catholic Church gave more attention to placing Mayan priests in towns where they spoke the language and encouraged non-Mayan priests to acquire fluency. Mayan languages were again part of institutionalized religion. Moreover, the Peace Accords affirmation of the Mayan cosmology and the resurgence of the 1980s and 1990s brought forth a public flourishing of traditional Mayan religious practices. Mayan daykeepers (once reviled as witches and driven underground) presided in public over mass ceremonies. The UN Decade of the Indigenous Peoples was inaugurated by twenty daykeepers at K'aminaljuyu'. The 2000 Waqxaqi' B'atz' (Mayan New Year) rites at Iximche' were performed before thousands of spectators. Mayan ritual speech has also emerged from the shadows. Individuals within the workplace may still enjoin their

Mayan coworkers to speak Spanish, or be "Christian," or to joke about the postvelars and glottalized consonants in the language. But the right to use the language in the workplace is established. The bulk of public speech is still in Spanish. The vast preponderance of writing is in Spanish, even by Mayan authors, but the amount of publicly visible and audible Mayan language is increasing. Whereas bilingualism has always been an onus placed on the Mayan population,[16] non-Maya are now feeling the need to learn a Mayan language. The Department of Anthropology of the Universidad del Valle has required a Mayan language of its students for fifteen years. The law school of the national university, Universidad San Carlos, began offering its students Kaqchikel in 2000. Graduates of the School of Linguistics of the Universidad Mariano Gálvez are required to have fluency in at least one Mayan language. The Maya of Guatemala, after centuries of having their languages repressed and suppressed, have won back the right to speak.

Second, as owners of their languages, speakers have the rights to establish the rules for proper usage, in both spoken and written form. Speakers of a language have the right to set the language standards. During the years of language suppression, only outside scholars studied Mayan languages systematically, and when literacy projects were initiated in the 1900s, outsiders used their own best judgment as to expediency of symbols, pedagogy, and orthography practice. With the linguistic training programs begun by the PLFM and then furthered by the School of Linguistics of the Universidad Mariano Gálvez and the Linguistic Institute of the Universidad Rafael Landívar, Mayas gained technical linguistic training enabling them to study their languages scientifically and make informed decisions about their structures and the representations thereof. OKMA, a cadre of PLFM-trained Mayan linguists, continues technical linguistic studies of Mayan languages as well as applying their findings to pedagogy and language prescription. Educators working with schoolchildren and adult literacy learners brought their experience with pedagogy to bear in collaboration with the curriculum developers of PRONEBI and DIGEBI, with the aid and assistance of UNICEF and USAID, to develop effective curricula for teaching children the norms of a standard(izing) language.

Third, speakers of a language have a right to maintain its traditional art forms and to develop new ones through literary expression. Traditional oral practices are making a comeback in Mayan areas. The *k'utunïk* described by Kaji' Kawoq Alberto Esquit is reappearing as part of wedding procedures in many communities that had largely foregone the elaborate exchange of visits, replacing these community affirmations with a series of counseling sessions with a priest followed by religious and civil services. Formal prayers in Mayan languages may now inaugurate public events, such as the opening ceremonies of K'amol B'ey, a nonpartisan political organization sponsored by Rigoberta Menchú. Carvings of Mayan glyphic writing now adorn furniture, clocks, and office structures, as Mayan artisans turn to classic sculptures for inspiration. New literary traditions are emerging more slowly. Authors often write in Spanish to reach larger audiences and translations may turn to English, other European languages, or Japanese first, in an attempt to reach more readers. Nonetheless, authors who write in Mayan languages do now have outlets. The linguistic market, both Bourdieu-an and monetary, has yet to make writing a viable vocation for Mayan authors; but the market is expanding.

The Maya have wrested back their linguistic destinies. They can now assert their intellectual property rights over their languages. However, there are still battles to be won. Mopan and Itzaj have less than 500 speakers all told. In 1991, Charles A. Hofling published a collection of Itzaj texts. He writes, "[t]here are perhaps several dozen speakers left in San José. They lament the loss of the language and the old ways, but generally recognize that the changes are now irrevocable and that the Itzá Maya language and culture preserved in these texts will soon perish" (3). Even the Big Four languages are not safe from the specter of language death. The language shift documented by McKenna Brown in the late 1980s has continued, though slightly abated by the successes of the vigorous programs of Kaqchikel Cholchi'. Have Maya won the right to control their language only to see the maelstrom of globalization swirl them off into Spanish monolingualism or Spanish-English bilingualism? A writer for *Kaqchi' Wuj*, Lu' Pedro Morejón (2000), poses this issue to his Kaqchikel readers:

> Wakami ya'on q'ij chi qe, pa qaq'a' röj Kaqchikela' k'oj wi. Wakami niqanimirisaj ruk'ojlem ri qach'ab'äl; wi k'a niqach'ab'ej tiqatijoj qi' chi re rutz'ib'axik, wi man niqach'ab'ej ta chïk tiqakanoj achike nik'utun chi qawäch. K'oj na wi jun q'ij ri qach'ab'äl xtib'erujunamaj ri' ruk'in ri' kaxlan ch'ab'äl, ruma ri' k'oj ta chi ja röj niqaya' ri quchuq'a'.

> *Today the opportunity is given to us, it is in our hands, we the Kaqchikel people. Now we can raise the stature of our language; so then if we speak (the language) let us learn how to write it, if we don't speak it, then let us find a way to teach ourselves. A day is coming when our language will compete with Spanish, therefore we must give it our strength.* (p. 4)

Speakers of a language have ultimate rights in and to that language, including the right to speak or not to speak. The Maya of Guatemala having won the right to speak their languages at school, at church, in the courts, and at home and to determine the sounds and shapes of their languages, spoken and in print, and gaining access to media of public artistic expression will decide what language(s) they will bring into the twenty-second century.

Notes

1. But recall that it was illegal to speak English before Norman lords in England for approximately 300 years.
2. For purposes of this discussion, I avoid the term *pre-Columbian*, or the more Guatemalan-specific term of *pre-Alvarado-an*, using instead a translation of the phrase current in Mayan discussions of the era: *preinvasion*.
3. The grapheme **x** in the official unified alphabet represents the voiceless alveopalatal fricative often written **sh** in English.
4. Note that in standard peninsular Spanish, these graphemes **c/z** represent a retroflex voiceless fricative, rather than the plain voiceless dental fricative of standard Guatemalan Spanish.
5. Thc palatalization indicated by the **i** is phonetically predictable and so is not written in the official orthography, which is morphophonemic.
6. It should be noted that many of these documents were written by non-Indians sent to Indigenous communities to oversee censuses or liquor taxation or to investigate claims.
7. This cloth, *morga*, is typically used for women's skirt lengths. The blue dye originally was a vegetable dye requiring a saline mordant.
8. Mayan clothing is referred to as *traje* in local Spanish.
9. *Huipil* is the local Spanish word, borrowed from Nahuatl, for the Indigenous-style woman's blouse or chemise.
10. Webster advocated spelling reforms to create an American language independent of British English (Peters 1968: 291).

11. The International Phonetic Alphabet representation of glottal stop is [?], without the base dot.

12. Legislative Decree 65-90 specifies the spellings of the twenty-one officially recognized Mayan languages.

13. Prior to PRONEBI, the Ministry of Education had assigned teachers to schools without regard for the language of the students. Most teachers assigned were non-Indians, monolingual in Spanish, or bilingual in Spanish and another European language. While there were two government-certified schools training Indigenous teachers, less than 10 percent of the graduates were placed in government schools. Indigenous teachers who were placed were often sent to communities with languages different from their own, so that their native language fluency was of little use. PRONEBI did place speakers within their own language areas, but often individual settlements have local language variation.

14. Tay Coyoy thus became the first Maya in Guatemalan history to hold a cabinet position.

15. Legislative Decree 65-90 ratifies the following spellings for these languages: Poqoman, Ch'orti', Q'eqchi', Poqomchi', Achi, Kaqchikel, Tz'utujiil, K'iche', Ixil, Mam, Q'anjob'al, Awakateko, Jakalteko, and Sipakapense. Note that while the government report to the UN fails to get the new spellings right, it does make an attempt on most languages and in fact the spelling K'ichee for K'iche' reflects the current feeling among K'ichee' linguists that the final vowel should be long (though followed by a glottal stop). Moreover, the government report has acceded to the speakers' request to have the name Jakalteko be superceded by the Maya name Popti', though again the report replaces the vowel followed by glottal stop with an acute accent over the vowel.

16. The Q'eqchi' area is a notable exception, where non-Maya, both Guatemalans and immigrant German coffee plantation owners, traditionally have learned Q'eqchi' as the language of wider communication.

References

Akabal, Humberto

El Animalero: poemas. Guatemala: Ministerio de Cultura y Deportes, 1990.

Ajyuq: el Animalero. Guatemala: Cholsamaj, 1995.

American Declaration on the Rights of Indigenous Peoples (Draft) (1997). Available at: http://www.dialoguebetweennations.com/OASdeclaration/dintro.html; last accessed on January 1, 2004.

Berendt, Carl Hermann

Diccionario de la lengua maya, por d. Juan Pio Perez. Mérida, México: J. F. Mólina Solis, 1866–1877.

Analytical alphabet for the Mexican & Central American languages. New York: American Ethnological Society, 1869.

Berlin, Brent

Speculations on the Growth of Ethnobotanical Nomenclature. *Language in Society*, vol. 1 (1972): 51–86.

Blair, Robert W., John S. Robertson, Larry Richman, Greg Sansom, Julio Salazar, Juan Yool, and Alejandro Choc

Diccionario Español-Cakchiquel-Inglés. Provo, Utah: Brigham Young University, 1969.

Bricker, Victoria R.

Bilingualism in the Maya Codices and the Books of Chilam Balam. *Written Language and Literacy*, vol. 3, no. 1 (2000): 77–115.

Brown, R. McKenna

Language Maintenance and Shift in four Kaqchikel towns. Ph.D. diss., Latin American Studies, Tulane University, 1991.

CECMA (Centro de Estudios de Cultura Maya)

Hacia una Educación Maya: Primer Encuentro Taller de Escuelas Con Programas de Cultura Maya. Guatemala: Cholsamaj, 1992.

CEDIM (Centro de Documentación e Investigación Maya)

Marco conceptual y modelo educativo de las Escuelas Mayas. ms, 1994.

Chacach, Kab'lajuj Tijax, et al.

Rukemik K'ak'a' Taq Tzij. Kaqchikel Cholchi': Iximulew (Guatemala), 1995.

Chávez, Adrián Inéz

Kí-Chè Zib: escritura Kí-Chè y otros temas. Guatemala: Libería, 1992.

Constitución Política de la República de Guatemala

Con reformas de 1993 (Reformada por Acuerdo legislativo No. 18–93 del 17 de noviembre de 1993), 1985. Available at: www.georgetown.edu/pdba/Constitutions/Guate/guate93.html; last accessed on January 1, 2004.

Convention on the Rights of the Child (1960)

Available at http://www.unhchr.ch/html/menu3/b/k2crc.htm; last accessed on January 2, 2004.

Cuxil, Demetrio Cojti'
Ensayo Sobre las Variedades de Enseñanza Bilingüe: desde el Bilingüismo Etnocida hasta el Bilingüismo Etnocida. Report to Ministerio de Educación Pública, Prodeprir/BID 707-SF-GU, 1987.

La Configuración del Pensamiento Político del Pueblo Maya. Quetzaltenango, Guatemala: El Estudiante, 1991.

Ri Maya' Moloj Pa Iximulew: el Movimiento Maya (en Guatemala). Guatemala: Chojsamaj, 1997.

Dakin, Karen
"The Characteristics of a Nahuatl Lingua Franca." Texas Linguistic Forum, 18:55–68 (1981).

El nahuatl de las *Memorias*: los rasgos de una lingua franca indígena. In *Nuestro pesar, nuestra aflicción*, edited by Karen Dakin and Christopher Lutz, 167–189. México: Universidad Nacional Autónoma de México, 1996.

de Coto, Fray Thomás
Thesaurus Verborû: vocabulario de la lengua Cakchiquel v[el] Guatemalteca, nueuamente hecho y recopilado con summo estudio, trauajo y erudición. Edited by René Acuña. México: Universidad Nacional Autónoma de México, 1983.

de Guzmán, Fray Pantaleón.
Compendio de Nombres en Lengua Cakchiquel. Edited by René Acuña. México: Universidad Nacional Autónoma de México, 1984.

de Varea, Fray Francisco
Calepino en Lengua Cakchiquel. Photostat of ms. from holdings of American Philosophical Society, repatriated to Guatemala in 2000; 1705.

Esquit Choy, Kaji' Kawoq (Alberto)
Análisis del Discurso Matrimonial Kaqchikel de Patzicía, Departamento de Chimaltenango. Licenciatura Thesis Universidad Rafael Landívar, 1993.

Fishman, Joshua
Reversing Language Shift: Theoretical and Empirical Foundations of Assistance to Threatened Languages. Bristol, Penn.: Multilingual Matters, 1991.

Giracca de Castellanos, Anabella
Yin Yitikïr yib'e'ok. Guatemala: Instituto Lingüístico, Universidad Rafael Landívar, 1993a.

Eleq'anel taq Achïk'-Kitzijonik taq Ala's. Guatemala: Instituto Lingüístico, Universidad Rafael Landívar, 1993b.

González, Gaspar Pedro

La Otra Cara: la vida de un Maya. Guatemala: Ministerio de Cultura y Deportes, 1992.

A Mayan Life. Rancho Palos Verdes, Calif.: Yaxte' Press, 1995.

Sb'eyb'al Jun Naq Maya' Q'anjob'al. Rancho Palos Verdes, Calif.: Yaxte' Press, 1996.

Haeserijn, Esteban

Ensayo de la gramática del K'ekchi'. Guatemala: Imprenta Suquinay: Purulhá, B.V., 1966.

Guía para aprender a hablar, a leer, y a escribir el K'ekchi'. Guatemala: Mimeografiado: San Juan Chamelco, A.V., 1972.

Diccionario K'ekchi'-Español. Guatemala: Piedra Santa, 1979.

Hendrickson, Carol

Weaving Identities: Construction of Dress and Self in a Highland Guatemala Town. Austin: University of Texas Press, 1995.

Hill, Robert and Judith M. Maxwell

Annals of the Kaqchikel, Kiwuj Xajila'. Manuscript under review at University of Texas, forthcoming.

Hofling, Charles Andrew

Itzá Maya Texts with a Grammatical Overview. Salt Lake City: University of Utah Press, 1991.

Houston, Stephen, John Robertson, and David Stuart

The Language of Classic Maya Inscriptions. *Current Anthropology*, vol. 41, no. 3 (2000): 321–356.

Itzol Gómez, María Teresa

Félix y ri elek'oma'. Guatemala: SIL, 1981.

Justeson, John S., William M. Norman, Lyle Campbell, and Terrence Kaufman

The Foreign Impact on Lowland Mayan Language and Script. Middle American Research Institute (MARI) Publication 53. New Orleans, La.: MARI, 1985.

Laughlin, Robert M.

The Great Tzotzil Dictionary of San Lorenzo Zinacantán. Washington, D.C.: Smithsonian Institution Press, 1975.

Notes from the Underground. In *Papers in Mayan Linguistics,* edited by Laura Martin, 15–49. Columbia, Mo.: Lucas Brothers, 1979.

The Great Tzotzil Dictionary of Santo Domingo Zinacantán with Grammatical Analysis and Historical Commentary (with John B. Haviland). Smithsonian Contributions to Anthropology, No. 31. Washington, D.C.: Smithsonian Institution Press, 1988.

Lewis, M. Paul

Language Maintenance in Seven K'iche' Communities. In *Summer Institute in Linguistics Electronic Working Papers.* Accessed at: gamma.sil.org/silewp/1996/002/SILEWP1996–002.html; last accessed on November 1, 2003.

Lima, Ricardo

Ixkab', jun xti xtän xb'erila' ri ch'umil chuqa' ri kikotemal. Guatemala: Instituto Lingüístico, Universidad Rafael Landívar, 1993.

López, Manuel Antonio and Juliana Sis Iboy

Gramática del idioma Achi / autores, Manuel Proyecto Lingüístico Francisco Marroquín: La Antigua Guatemala. Guatemala, 1993.

Lounsbury, Floyd

On the Derivation and Reading of the Ben-Ich' Prefix. In *Mesoamerican Writing Systems*, edited by Elizabeth P. Benson, 99–143. Washington, D.C.: Dumbarton Oaks, 1973.

Mondloch, James

Basic Quiche Grammar. Albany, New York: Institute for Mesoamerican Studies, State University of New York, 1978.

Montejo, Victor

Q'anil, el hombre rayo : una leyenda de Jacaltenango: Komam Q'anil, ya' k'uh Winaj : yik'ti'al xajla' . Rancho Palos Verdes, Calif.: Yaxte', 1999.

Morejón, Lu' Pedro

Ruk'a'tz ri Ch'ab'äl. Kaqchi' Wuj 12: 4. Cholsamaj/Nawal Wuj: Guatemala Ms 1 (1570–1635). Microfilm copy of No. 1 Santa Eulalia M. Md. 1, Latin American mss. B, Guatemala Music, held in the Lilly Library of Music, Indiana University, Bloomington, 2000.

Nuk'ulem, Chi Rij Kib'anikil, Chuqa' Kich'ojib'al Ri Achamaqi'

Acuerdo sobre Identidad y Derechos de los Pueblos Indígenas. Guatemala: Cholsamaj, 1995.

Pablo, Fortunato
Quienes somos? Lecture to Oxlajuj Aj. July 26, 1987. Antigua, Guatemala, 1987.

Peters, Robert A.
A Linguistic History of English. Boston, Mass.: Houghton Mifflin Company, 1968.

Powell, Patricia
Language Maintenance and Shift: Kaqchikel Case Study. Guest Lecture to Oxlajuj Aj, Antigua, Guatemala, July 1989.

Q'uq'kumätz-Menmagua
Plan Nacional de Desarrollo del Pueblo Maya de Guatemala. Guatemala: Programa de Naciones Unidas Para el Desarrollo, 1999.

Richards, Julia Becker, and Michael Richards
Maya Education: A Historical and Contemporary Analysis of Mayan Language Educational Policy. In *Mayan Cultural Activism in Guatemala*, edited by Edward F. Fischer and R. McKenna Brown, 208–221. Austin: University of Texas Press, 1996.

Rodríguez Guaján, José Obispo.
Rutz'ib'axik ri Kaqchikel/Manual de Redacción Kaqchikel. Guatemala: Cholsamaj, 1994.

Ruyán Canú Déborah and Coyote Tum Rafael
Diccionario cakchiquel central y español. Jo Ann Munson L., comp. Guatemala: Instituto Lingüístico de Verano de Centroamérica, 1991.

Luis Enrique Sam Colop
Hacia una Propuesta de Ley de Educación Bilingüe. Licenciatura thesis at Universidad Rafael Landivar, Guatemala, 1983.

Schele, Linda, and David Freidel
A Forest of Kings: The Untold Story of the Ancient Maya. New York: Quill/W. Morrow, 1992.

Schele, Linda, and Mary Ellen Miller
The Blood of Kings: Dynasty and Ritual in Maya Art. Fort Worth, Tex.: Kimbell Art Museum, 1986.

Schwartzkopf, Stacey
Preliminary prospectus for dissertation in anthropology at Tulane University, 2000.

Seler, Eduard

Chronologie der cakchiquel-annalen. pamplet collection. New Orleans, La.: LAL, ca. 1900.

Collected Works in Mesoamerican Linguistics and Archaeology. Edited by J. Eric, S. Thompson, and Francis B. Richardson; Frank E. Comparato, general editor. Culver City, Calif.: Labyrinthos, 1990–1998.

Sexto censo de poblacion, Abril 18 de 1950

Guatemala: Imprenta Universitaria, 1953.

Skinner-Klee, Jorge.

Legislación indigenista de Guatemala México: Instituto Indigenista Interamericano, 1954.

Smith, Michael E., and Frances F. Berdan

The Postclassic Mesoamerican World System. *Current Anthropology*, vol. 41, no. 2 (2000). Available at: www.journals.uchicago.edu/CA/journal/issues/v41n2/002803/002803.html; last accessed on November 1, 2003.

Stevenson, Robert

European Music in 16th Century Guatemala. *The Musical Quarterly*, vol. 50, no. 3 (1964): 341–352.

Stoll, Otto

Die Maya-sprachen der Pokom-gruppe. Vienna: A. Hölder, 1888–1896.

Summer Institute of Linguistics International (SIL)

Brief History of SIL. Accessed at: www.sil.org/sil/history.htm; last accessed on November 1, 2003.

UNICEF

K'ak'a taq Tzij Nokisäx pa Retamab'alil Kajulew. Guatemala: UNICEF, 1995a.

K'ak'a taq Tzij Nokisäx pa Retamab'alil Ajilab'äl. Guatemala: UNICEF, 1995b.

K'ak'a taq Tzij Nokisäx pa Retamab'alil B'anob'al. Guatemala: UNICEF, 1995c.

K'ak'a taq Tzij Nokisäx pa Retamab'alil Ch'ab'äl. Guatemala: UNICEF, 1995d.

United Nations Commission on Human Rights, Session 54

Accessed at: www.hri.ca/fortherecord1998/documentation/commission/e-cn4-1998-77.htm#IC; last accessed on November 1, 2003.

United Nations International Covenant on Civil and Political Rights

1966 (date refers to the first signing the covenant). Available at: http://www.unhchr.ch/html/menu3/b/a_ccpr.htm; last accessed on November 1, 2003.

Universal Declaration of Human Rights (1948)
Text available at http://www.unhchr.ch/udhr/; last accessed on January 1, 2004.

Universal Declaration of Linguistic Rights
Accessed at: www.linguistic-declaration.org/decl-gb.htm; last accessed on January 2, 2004.

Wendell Vanderzee, Margaret M.
Literatura sin muletas: la expresión de los pueblos ágrafos. Guatemala: Instituto Lingüístico de Verano, 1989.

Witkowski, Stanley R., and Cecil H. Brown
Cultural Importance, Linguistic Marking, and Lexical Change. ms. Copy, 1981.

Ximénez, Fray Francisco (O.P.)
Arte de las tres lenguas, Kaqchikel, Kíche´ y Tzútujil. Edited by Rosa Helena Chinchilla. Guatemala: Academia de Geografía e Historia de Guatemala, 1993.

Yool Gomez, Juan, and Fong, Myra.
Ri Kinimaq'ij ri Chikopi' Guatemala: Instituto de Lingüística, Universidad Rafael Landívar, 1990.

Part Three

ACCESS AND CONTROL

CHAPTER 8

INTELLECTUAL PROPERTY RIGHTS AND INDIGENOUS PEOPLES' RIGHTS AND RESPONSIBILITIES

Maui Solomon

Ko Te Awa Inganga Te Awa (Te Awa Inganga is my river)
Ko Manukau Te Whenua Tapu (Manukau is my sacred lands)
Ko Te Awapatiki Te Kopinga (Te Awapatiki is the sacred meeting place)
Ko Te Kopinga Te Marae (Te Kopinga is our meeting house)
Ko Rekohu Te Motu (Chatham Islands is the island)
Ko Tame Horomona Rehe Te Rangatira (Tommy Solomon is my grandfather)
Ko Rongomaiwhenua Te Karapuna (Rongomaiwhenua was the founding ancestor on Rekohu)
Ko Moriori me Kai Tahu nga Iwi (Moriori and Kai Tahu are my tribes)
Tihei Mauri Ora! (I sneeze the breath of life)
Ko tenei te mihi ki a koutou, te hau kainga, nga tangata whenua o tenei motu.
He mihi hoki ki a koutou katoa e huihui mai nei Tena koutou katoa (Greet ings to you the local Tangata Whenua [people of this land] and to other peo ples present at this meeting)

This chapter discusses the efforts being made by a number of Maori tribes in Aotearoa to have their cultural rights and values recognized and protected. There are a number of different ways in which this is occurring, but the most significant case in terms of seeking protection of traditional knowledge is the claim currently before the Waitangi Tribunal.[1] This chapter also examines from a Maori perspective their notion of Indigenous peoples' rights and responsibilities and how they are at odds with existing intellectual property systems, and explores how some of the Maori claimants consider that their rights should be acknowledged, respected, and protected and the inevitable obstacles that must be confronted and overcome before this can happen. Finally, this chapter considers the implications of Article 8(j) of the Convention on Biological Diversity and related provisions and how they impact on the struggle by the Maori to have their rights and obligations recognized and protected within Aotearoa/New Zealand.

My own Moriori tribe from Rekohu (Chatham Islands) and Maori tribes from Aotearoa (New Zealand) are as much concerned about their obligations to one another and to the natural world at large as they are concerned with asserting their cultural rights. But without access to their rights, they cannot exercise their responsibilities. Such is the relationship of respect and reciprocity. This is mainly true of Indigenous and traditional peoples all over the world.

Maori View of Their Natural World

Like most other Indigenous traditional peoples, Maori have a unique relationship with their natural world. They view themselves as part of and not dominant over their natural flora and fauna. The people, the land, the sea, the forest, and all living creatures are all members of the same family.

In the beginning was *Te Kore,* or total darkness. There was no life, only potential. *Papatuanuku*, the Earth Mother, and *Ranginui*, the Sky Father, were locked together in an embrace that stifled all growth. Their children, desperate for light, devised a plan to forcibly separate their parents. This job fell on the shoulders (literally) of one of the children, *Tane Mahuta*, God of the Forests. Binding to his mother below, he pushed upward with his legs and all his strength and pushed his father apart from the earth.

Into the light created between *Papatuanuku* and *Ranginui* sprang the raging winds of *Tawhirimatea* (God of the Winds), the swirling seas of *Tangaroa* (God of the Sea) and all his progeny, and the towering forests of *Tane Mahuta* and all his progeny and the varieties of cultivated and uncultivated crops. *Tane Mahuta* fashioned the first human, *Hine-ahu-one,* from the clay of his mother. He slept with her and begat a daughter, *Hinetitama*. With *Hinetitama*, *Tane* begat other children. Discovering her father and lover were the same, *Hinetitama* fled to the underworld, where she lives still in the name of *Hine nui ite po*. The spiritual home of the Maori, the home of their gods and of creation is known as:

Hawaiiki nui
Hawaiiki roa
Hawaiiki pamaomao.

The Maori name for Indigenous people is *Tangata Whenua*. This literally means "peoples of the land." My own Moriori people of Rekohu claim to have sprung from the earth (*no ro whenua ake*). Legends tell of different *waka,* or canoes, arriving on Rekohu and Aotearoa from Hawaiiki in various migrations from about 900 AD. They named every landmark, stream, rock, mountain, and other natural feature in the landscape, including the flora and fauna they found there. Maori regard themselves as one with their natural world. Maori have a direct *whakapapa,* or genealogical connection, to the land through their ancestress *Papatuanuku,* the Earth Mother; to the sea and its marine creatures through their ancestor *Tangaroa*; to the forest and all its inhabitants through their ancestor *Tane Mahuta;* and to the heavens and its entire celestial domain through their ancestral Sky Father, *Ranginui.*

During the period of 1,000 years of occupation, the ancestors of the Maori developed complex rituals and protocols for regulating behavior between themselves and the environment they found themselves in. But the Maori world was not a perfect one. Like all cultures, mistakes were made by Maori in their interaction with their environment. Some species, such as the large flightless Moa bird found by Maori on their arrival in Aotearoa, were hunted to extinction. Lessons learnt were incorporated into traditional practices. Thus, as populations grew and pressures became intense on scarce resources, *rahui,* or prohibitions on the taking of certain species at certain times of the year, became commonplace.

Homage was also paid to the spiritual guardians of land, the sea, and the forests. In order for Maori to survive and prosper from the land and sea, they had first to acknowledge and respect the deities and the gods of those places. Ritual *karakia,* or blessings, were spoken and permission sought before cutting down a tree for canoe building or taking fish from the sea to feed their families. This reciprocity of respect and caring between the people and their creator gods was central to the relationship. By demonstrating caring and respect for the *kaitiaki,* or ancient guardians, they in turn would ensure that the needs of the people were satisfied. There were rights to access and utilize resources within a tribal territory but only after observing the ritual obligations of reciprocity and respect.

Intellectual Property Rights (IPR) versus Indigenous Peoples Rights and Responsibilities (IPRR)

Acknowledging the spiritual dimension of their universe and respecting the *mauri,* or central life force of every living thing, was fundamentally important to the Maori worldview. In other words, the reciprocity of obligations was balanced against the right to use and exploit. This can be contrasted with the notion intellectual property rights, which focuses on the economic right to exploit for profit and financial gain. The needs of the individual, and corporate legal personalities such as multinationals, are preferred to the collective good.

Under this capitalist model, resources are viewed entirely as a means of exploitation for economic gain. There is little or no reciprocity or respect for the integrity of the resources as living and breathing entities with their own *mauri,* or life force. Thus, there can be seen a fundamental clash between the ideological underpinnings of the *intellectual property rights system* and the philosophical underpinnings of what I have termed *Indigenous peoples rights and responsibilities.*

For example, a Maori elder may look at a native totara tree and pay homage to an ancient member of his *whanau,* or family. A scientist or geneticist may look at the same tree and think of ways to alter its genetic programming so that instead of taking 1,000 years to grow to maturity, the tree can reach maturity in 100 years. They consider ways to improve the tree by the application of modem technology. This approach is justified under the rationale of progress and technological advancement in a modern society.

Many Maori regard the genetic modification of flora and fauna as the interference or tampering with their *whakapapa* (genealogy). In a Maori context, modifying or mixing the genes of the same or different species is analogous to genetic experiments on one's own family members. The issue is really one of respect, respect for the fact that Maori and Indigenous peoples everywhere have a special kind of relationship with their natural world. Before economists and scientists go too far down the track of exploiting or reengineering what the gods created, these relationships and values must be acknowledged and respected.

Maori people are not against development and exploitation. But they do insist that the Crown (the government and all of its various agencies), local authorities, and commercial enterprise stop to consider the issues from a Maori perspective. Unfortunately, in New Zealand society today there is only lip service paid to acknowledging Maori cultural values.

In Aotearoa, Maori knowledge of their environment was ignored and their spiritual healers *(Tohunga)* were banned from practicing. In 1909, the Crown passed the Tohunga Suppression Act in an attempt to stamp out these practices. Sadly, *Tohunga* became the subject of ridicule even among their own people, who were encouraged to forget about the past and taught to become "Brown Pakeha."[2] But Maori tribes are resilient. The traditional healing practices were forced underground but have continued to the present day, albeit in a much reduced form. Sadly, a vast amount of this knowledge has been lost as the older generations have died out and the Indigenous institutions, capable of passing on this knowledge, have been denied legitimacy.

An example of the contrast between Indigenous attitudes toward healing and medicine and Western attitudes was apparent from the powerful and moving evidence given by one of the elders for Ngati Wai to the Waitangi Tribunal. This woman was in her late eighties and had practiced *rongoa Maori* (traditional Maori healing using native plants) for more than seventy years. This knowledge had been passed down to her by her father.

During the two days she was questioned, she fasted and would only drink water because of the *tapu* (sacred) nature of the evidence she was giving. When talking about the *ngahere* (native bush or forest), it was as though she was talking about her own *whanau,* or family. She knew the plants and the animals and they knew her. She knew the exact time to go into the bush, the seasons, the days, the type of plants, and what side of the plant to take and in what quantities. She used her knowledge to help peoples from all walks of life (Maori and Pakeha) but would never request payment for her services. Her reason is that she regarded her healing powers and knowledge as gifts that had been bestowed on her by the creator. To use those gifts for profit would only dilute the healing power. But as is common in Maori society, she would accept *koha,* or gifts, exchanged to her for her help. These might include food or reciprocal services or could even include money. But it was up to the giver to determine the nature of the *koha* to be given.

This Maori woman, although eighty-seven years old, looked and acted thirty years younger. She had a healthy body, a sharp intellect, and a wonderful sense of humor. She attributed her good physical and mental health to the fact that she had never in her life taken conventional medicines. She had only ever used traditional healing methods and natural remedies. She described how as a nurse in the 1940s and later, her traditional knowledge and practices were frowned upon in the mainstream system, but from time to time she would secretly employ her *rongoa Maori* knowledge to help patients when conventional medicines would not work. On the final day of her evidence, she was joined by her eighty-nine-year-old sister and her seventy-eight-year-old brother who had also been brought up with the knowledge of *rongoa Maori*. Between them they had a combined total of 254 years knowledge of traditional healing practices.

The Treaty of Waitangi

The early Maori recognized the many benefits that interaction and trade with the English settlers would bring for their society. They were a highly inventive and adaptive people. From Captain Cook's first arrival in Aotearoa in 1769 through to 1840 when the Treaty of Waitangi was signed, Maori actively traded with the British settlers and for the most part provided food, protection, and in many instances land for the newcomers. There was also intermarriage with many early colonists to cement relationships between Maori and Pakeha.

In 1840, the Maori population numbered about 115,000 people. This compared with a British migrant population of approximately 2,000 people. The Treaty of Waitangi[3] (go to www.legislation.govt.nz, type in Treaty of Waitangi to find TOW Act 1975, Schedule 1) was signed in both Maori and English. In effect, there are two versions of the treaty. Most Maori Chiefs signed the Maori version. The terms of the two treaties are, in certain respects, conflicting. For example, in Article 1 of the English version, the Chiefs and tribes ceded their sovereignty to Queen Victoria. But Article 1 of the Maori version refers to a grant of *kawanatanga* (a missionary transliteration of the word "governorship"). Article 2 of the Maori Treaty reserved to the Chiefs and tribes their *tino rangatiratanga o ratou wenua o ratou kainga me o o ratou taonga katoa*. By this, the Chiefs understood that their full chiefly authority to manage their own affairs in relation to their lands, treasures, and people would be retained. The equivalent under the English version of Article 2 is just as robust:

> Her Majesty the Queen of England confirms and guarantees to the Chiefs and Tribes of New Zealand and to the respective families and individuals thereof the full exclusive and undisturbed possession of their Lands and Estates, Forests, Fisheries and other properties which they may collectively or individually possess so long as it is their wish and desire to retain the same in their possession.

As one northern Chief who signed the treaty observed afterward when explaining his understanding of the treaty: "Ko te atukau o te whenua i riro ia te kuini, ko te tinana o te whenua i waiho ki nga Maori" (Only the shadow of the land is to the Queen, but the substance remains to us).

But it was not long before Maori realized that the new colonizers did not intend to honor the terms of the Treaty—either the English or Maori version. By the 1860s the immigrant population had exploded and there were increasing pressures for land. Maori were subject to dubious land purchase deals and began resisting continual encroachment by settlers and the Crown. This led to invasion by Crown military forces to expel Maori from their lands and naturally, as a warrior people, Maori responded by defending their lands.

Although mostly outnumbered and facing the best that the British Empire had to throw at them, the Maori responded brilliantly. Their military tactics and defense works were inventive and greatly underestimated by the Crown forces. They adapted their traditional fighting *Pa* (fortified villages) to counter the British cannon barrages, which would sometimes go on for days. They survived these assaults by constructing elaborate underground defense works and tunnel systems. These new fighting *Pa* were built deep in the dense New Zealand bush (forests) where they would lead the unwitting soldiers. Colonial troops were often baffled when they mounted a ground assault only to find that the enemy numbers had hardly been affected by the bombardment. Maori were the first to develop this system of defensive earthworks, which were used (but not with the same effect) during the First World War.

In many cases, Maori tribes prevailed over the superior Crown forces. The true extent of their military genius is only now being appreciated by New Zealand historians. However, by sheer weight of numbers and military firepower, the colonizers eventually prevailed. Invasion and military defeat were followed by massive confiscations of land in the 1860s. In the Taranaki region alone (East Coast of the North Island), 1.5 million acres were confiscated by the Crown. In the Waikato, about 3 million acres was taken. This often included land of tribes who had not been involved in the fighting or had even, in some cases, fought on the side of the Crown. This confiscated land was used for settlers and military resettlement.

The system of parliamentary representation imposed on Maori after 1840 was based on the monocultural dominance of British constitutionalism. From 1856 to 1868, Maori representation was at the pleasure of the governor. In 1868, Maori were represented through four seats in the Parliament (increased to five seats in the 1999 election and now standing at seven seats) and were powerless to prevent the framing of legislation and policies that continued the confiscations of land and ignored the aspirations of Maori.

By 1877, in the infamous case of *Wi Parata v. The Bishop of Wellington,* Prendergast declared the treaty to be a "simple nullity." He could not accept that Maori had "any kind of civil government" or "any settled system of law," and certainly were not capable of entering into an international treaty. In 1901, the Privy Council in *Nireaha Tamaki v. Baker* rejected the argument that "there is no customary law of the Maori of which the Courts can take cognizance." But any cognizance that was taken was in the context of the all-encompassing assumptions of the British common law, where Maori customary law is treated as analogous to "local custom" in England. The custom is easily supplanted by statute and is usually only given recognition where the relevant statute specifically requires it to do so. Being politically powerless to influence the law-making process, Maori customary law and practices were marginalized.

At the beginning of the twentieth century, Maori were regarded as a doomed race. Population numbers had plummeted, most were living in severe poverty, and health was very poor. In effect, Maori had become third-class citizens in their own country. But Maori never gave up on the hope that one day the treaty would be honored and they continued to discuss and debate it among themselves on *marae* (traditional meeting places) around the country. But for Pakeha New Zealanders, the treaty had become a distant relic of the past. They had got what they wanted and that was that. New Zealand was portrayed internationally as a model of how race relations should be—with Maori and Pakeha living and working in harmony as one people. But just beneath the surface there lurked a deeper reality; a reality understood by Maori but completely ignored by most Pakeha.

For the past 100 years, successive policies of assimilation and integration have failed to substantially improve the socioeconomic circumstances of Maori. They continue to top the statistics for unemployment, poor health, smoking, low education, and crime—statistics mirrored in every other country where Indigenous and traditional peoples have been colonized. But despite their ravaging effects on Maori, these policies have failed to completely homogenize Maori culture and destroy their identity as a people. Today, Maori now comprise 15 percent of New Zealand's population of 3.9 million people. Despite the ravages that Maori have had to endure, there has always been the beacon of hope and strength kept alive on the various tribal *marae* around Aotearoa. Today, the younger and more educated Maori generation have begun to reclaim their heritage and identity guided by the wisdom of their elders.

Renaissance of the Treaty of Waitangi

In the 1970s, protest groups such as *Nga Tama Toa* (Young Maori Warriors) began to stage organized protests over the broken treaty promises. Maori lands were still being confiscated for public works and other community needs and Maori began staging land occupations and other forms of nonviolent protests. This eventually led to a land march being staged from the tip of the North Island (or the tail of *Te Ika a Maui*, the Fish of Maui) down to the seat of government in Wellington (some 1,200 kilometers distant). This march was led by an elderly *Kuia,* the late Dame Whina Cooper, who was in her mid-seventies when she led the march. The marchers stopped at every *marae* along the way until they had reached Wellington. This took place in 1974 and eventually led to the passage of the Treaty of Waitangi Act in 1975. That act established the Waitangi Tribunal as a body comprising an equal number of Maori and Pakeha members who could receive and inquire into claims from Maori that the Crown had breached principles of the Treaty of Waitangi. As noted by Chief Judge Eddie Durie:

> The Waitangi Tribunal is unique in the world insofar as it is comprised of an equal number of both the Indigenous people and of those who came from Europe and other countries. Elsewhere most of these issues tend to be determined by Courts in which the aboriginal or Indigenous

> people are not represented. The Tribunal operates in an entirely different way. It has both Maori protocols and English law protocols. It has an equal number of Maori to Pakeha. It includes people of standing within the community, of historical and anthropological backgrounds, so it does not rely purely on lawyers. It is inter-disciplinary and bicultural, which is seen as an interesting precedent. (Durie 1994: 26)

In 1985, the Waitangi Tribunal was given retrospective powers to hear claims dating back to February 6, 1840, the date upon which the treaty was signed. There are now over 1,000 claims registered with the Waitangi Tribunal ranging from lands, fisheries, forests, geothermal, language, radio spectrum, and of course the claim commonly referred to as the Indigenous flora and fauna claim, Wai262.

Many of these claims have focused on the protection of fishing reefs, harbors, rivers, and lands from the adverse environmental consequences of development. Sadly, the news media in New Zealand are fixated with highlighting Maori claims as a continued grab for resources rather than portraying a balanced and fair view of the claims process. Consequently, vast numbers of New Zealanders have a negative view of the Treaty of Waitangi process and a woeful knowledge of Maori culture. Most have little or no knowledge of the real issues other than what they read in the newspapers, which most often present an unbalanced view. As one of the most important social issues facing our country today, this attitude is at best irresponsible and at worst biased. The New Zealand government and the news media have a responsibility to ensure that its citizens are better informed and educated about the history of their own country.

The Waitangi Tribunal only has powers of recommendation to the Crown. They are not binding on the Crown and are often simply ignored. Although the tribunal was given certain binding powers in relation to Crown-owned forests and state-owned assets (in many cases being sold off to foreign-owned companies), subject to claims, the Tribunal has never exercised those powers. A previous minister of justice threatened to repeal those powers if they were ever exercised! But the influence of the Waitangi Tribunal and its many reports has had considerable influence on both the judicial and political landscape of Aotearoa. Maori have been able to use the tribunal process and findings as leverage in negotiations with the Crown and/or as a springboard for further litigation in the ordinary courts. However, in recent years, the Crown has shown a greater tendency to ignore the findings of the Waitangi Tribunal and there is a growing level of political (and public) opposition to recognizing and protecting Maori rights

While the tribunal only has the status of a Commission of Inquiry (as opposed to an ordinary court), its process of hearing evidence from tribal claimants and the Crown and the making of legal submissions is rigorous and robust. The process is also unique as the tribunal can invoke *tikanga Maori* (Maori customary protocols) when hearing traditional evidence on *marae* and evidence can be given in Maori. The norm is for the tribunal to sit on *marae* when they are hearing historical claimant evidence. The usual course is for claimant counsel to make opening submissions outlining the nature of the case and the evidence to be brought. This is followed by elders and other tribal experts giving their evidence (which can be traditional and contemporary).

The Crown lawyers then have an opportunity to question the witnesses as do the members of the tribunal. There are usually between three and five members on the tribunal who have a mixture of *tikanga Maori*, legal, historical, and anthropological skills. Traditional witnesses are followed by professional, academic expert testimony that is subject to more rigorous cross-examination from Crown lawyers. The Crown then presents its evidence and calls witnesses who are also subject to cross-examination by claimant counsel. There may be more than one claimant group in any one hearing and each counsel has the right to cross-examine.

The tribunal may also call its own evidence at the hearing. In the case of Wai262, the tribunal has commissioned five major research reports on different aspects of the claim, for example, all Crown policy concerning management of the environment and treaty-related issues from 1840 up to the present day. These reports can often run into thousands of pages. Finally, the claimants and the Crown make their closing submissions and the tribunal adjourns to write its report and issue its findings and recommendations.

Sadly, due to a lack of adequate funding for the Waitangi Tribunal and its work, claims can often take years to be heard and more years to be reported on. As regards the Wai262 claim, it was filed in 1991, the hearing began in 1997, and it is still ongoing. The six Iwi or tribal claimants have all presented their traditional and expert evidence. In 1998, the tribunal heard evidence from overseas experts on traditional knowledge and intellectual property rights, including the late Dr. Darrell Posey. In 2002, the tribunal heard evidence from a range of experts on Maori spiritual values and beliefs, institutional structures, Maori medicine, and environmental and conservation management policies in New Zealand dating from 1840. It now remains for the Crown to present its evidence and an opportunity will also be given to third parties including pharmaceutical companies, nurseries, and intellectual property companies to make submissions to the tribunal.

Resource Management Act 1991 and Conservation Act 1987

The Treaty of Waitangi and Maori cultural values are also given recognition in the Resource Management Act 1991 (RMA), which deals in a comprehensive way with the management of our environment. The main purpose of the act is sustainable management. There was considerable consultation with Maoridom in the development of the legislation and therefore much hope that Maori would have a greater role in environmental decision-making processes. Sadly, after twelve years experience under the RMA, this is not the case. In 1993 the Waitangi Tribunal ruled that the Resource Management Act was "*fatally flawed*," because the treaty protections contained within the RMA were too weak. The Crown, once again, ignored these findings.

Local authorities, who have delegated authority from the Crown to manage the natural resources and issue resource consents to developers, largely pay lip service to their obligations to Maori under the RMA. Much-touted provisions to enable local authorities to delegate responsibilities to local tribal authorities for managing natural resources (with which the tribes have a traditional association) have not been exercised by any of the local authorities. Indeed, there is still a reluctance to involve Maori in meaningful consultation, let alone grant control over issues that affect their environment. While there are heavy expectations on Maori to fulfill their obligations as *kaitiaki* (guardians) of the environment, they have neither the funding nor the resources available to fulfill their customary obligations. The other major piece of legislation relevant to the environment is the Conservation Act 1987. The Department of Conservation (DOC) is the single largest owner and manager of lands in New

Zealand. Historically, DOC has displayed a patronizing attitude toward Maori and their traditional knowledge of the environment. This attitude is gradually beginning to change as a consequence of Maori assertiveness and a growing acceptance from DOC that they have no option but to work in partnership with Maori tribes—just as the treaty had foreseen. Although the Conservation Act 1987 contains a strong treaty protection provision, the Courts have applied a minimalist interpretation of this section and in doing so have demonstrated a failure to comprehend Maori customary rights to their resources.

Claims to the tribunal (such as the Wai262 claim) often focus on the relationship between Maori and DOC, and this has had a considerable influence on DOC's responsiveness to Maori concerns. But this is a double-edged sword for Maori. While Maori are forced to go through the long and expensive process of having their claims heard (with the prospect of a report not available for another few years), the Crown is proceeding to develop and implement policies and legislation that impact on the claim. A recent example was the amendments to the Trade Marks Act, which give limited protection to the use of Maori names in trademark applications but fall far short of the protections being sought by the Wai262 claimants. The difficulty is that such changes are made at the Crown's pace and within the context of the Crown's own agenda.

General Public Attitudes to Treaty and Maori Issues

Common refrains often heard from Pakeha New Zealanders is that "We can't go back to 1840; why should we be blamed for what our ancestors did?" Or, "When is it all going to end?" There is a hankering by many to return to the days when the assimilationist policies were at their height and New Zealanders "were all one people." Others maintain that Maori culture has no relevance for them or their children in modern-day New Zealand. Across New Zealand society, these sentiments are not unfamiliar. In 2004, the main opposition political parties in New Zealand have signaled their intentions to focus on race-related issues and what they have described as "special privileges" for Maori. This, of course, ignores the fact that the treaty was a charter for protecting Maori property rights. It seems that in New Zealand's democracy, property rights are sacrosanct, but less so if you are Maori.

The average Kiwi (New Zealander) has very little knowledge of the treaty apart from what he or she reads in the newspapers or sees on television which more often than not present a superficial and slanted perspective of the issues. Politicians are also ready and willing to play the "race card" in order to improve their showing in the polls. Perhaps if people were better informed and educated about the issues, many of their fears and prejudices would lessen. Maori identity and culture have benefits for all New Zealanders, not just Maori.

For example, Maori culture makes New Zealand unique from the rest of the world. On most occasions when there are international leaders visiting New Zealand, Maori are called upon to undertake the welcoming ceremonies and cultural performances. Televised news reports showed a leading Maori elder from the *Ngati Whatua* tribe giving a traditional *hongi* (pressing of noses) greeting to former U.S. President Bill Clinton when he arrived in New Zealand for the Asia-Pacific Economic Co-operation (APEC) conference in 2000. Maori images, icons, and symbols are regularly used to promote New Zealand internationally by tourist companies and major corporates, including Air New Zealand and Telecom New Zealand.

However, that is often as far as it goes. The recognition is usually superficial and undertaken without consultation or the consent of the people concerned. Unfortunately, New Zealanders will often avail themselves of Maori culture and identity when it suits their purpose but when it comes to sharing the benefits of that exploitation, it is another matter. But there are also increasing numbers of Pakeha New Zealanders who are strongly supportive of the Treaty of Waitangi and *Kaupapa Maori* (Maori cultural objectives). They have no fear of acknowledging Maori culture because they can see that it can only strengthen New Zealand's identity as a nation both at home and internationally.

Maori insist that in terms of their culture, *matauranga* (knowledge), and intellectual heritage rights, they should be in control of their own destiny. They want recognition and effect given to their *tino rangatiratanga,* or full chiefly authority. Some say that this is going back to the past. But Maori are a forward-thinking and -moving people. For Maori, it is about applying traditional values within a modern-day context. This has benefits for both Maori and Pakeha.

The Wai262 Claim to Indigenous Flora and Fauna and Cultural and Intellectual Heritage Rights and Obligations

Concerned over the increasing loss of native plants and animals, the destruction of ecosystems, and the continuing erosion of *matauranga Maori* (traditional Maori knowledge), a group of Maori elders got together in 1988 to formulate a claim to the Waitangi Tribunal. The claimants are from the following tribes: Ngati Kuri (Mrs. Saana Murray), Te Rarawa (Mrs. Hema Nui-a-Tawhaki Witana or Del Wihongi), Ngati Wai (Mr. Witi McMath), Ngati Porou, and Ngati Kahungunu. I represent the three claimants from Ngati Kuri, Te Rarawa, and Ngati Wai.

The claim is founded upon the rights guaranteed in article 2 of the Treaty of Waitangi, which guaranteed to Maori the "*full, exclusive and undisturbed possession of their lands and estates, forests, fisheries and other properties which they may collectively or individually possess*" (English version). In the Maori version of the treaty, the guarantee was in relation to their *tino rangatiratanga* over all of their *taonga,* or treasured things.

The Statement of Claim, which was filed in 1991 with the Waitangi Tribunal and amended in 1997, states as follows:

2.0 THE CLAIM

2.1 The claim relates to te tino rangatiratanga o te Iwi Maori in respect of Indigenous flora and fauna *me o ratou taonga katoa* (and all their treasures) including but not limited to matauranga, whakairo, waahi tapu, biodiversity, genetics, Maori symbols and designs and thcir use and development and associated Indigenous, cultural and customary heritage rights in relation to such taonga. 'Taonga' in this claim refers to all elements of a tribal group's estate, material and non-material, tangible and intangible.

2.2 Reference to 'Indigenous, cultural and customary heritage rights' in this claim is deemed to include all rights (including intellectual and property rights) past, present and future in relation to taonga o te Iwi Maori.

2.3 Te tino rangatiratanga o te Iwi Maori is the authority residing within and exercised by te Iwi Maori o Aotearoa me te Waipounamu/Rekohu prior to the arrival of the colonial government which includes but is not limited to the full and exclusive rights and responsibilities of manaakitanga, kaitiakitanga and tapu and the development of these rights.

2.4 Te tino rangatiratanga a te Iwi Maori incorporates a right of development which permits the Iwi to conserve, control, utilise and exercise rights over Indigenous flora and fauna *me o ratou taonga katoa.*

2.5 Te tino rangatiratanga a te Iwi Maori incorporated and incorporates:

(a) Decision-making authority over the conservation, control of, and proprietary interests in natural resources including Indigenous flora and fauna *me o ratou taonga katoa;*

(b) The right to determine Indigenous cultural and customary heritage rights in the knowledge and use of Indigenous flora and fauna *me o ratou taonga katoa;*

(c) The right to participate in, benefit from, and make decisions about the application of existing and future technological advances as they relate to the breeding, genetic manipulation and other processes relevant to the use of Indigenous flora and fauna;

(d) The right to control and make decisions about the propagation, development, transport, study or sale of Indigenous flora and fauna;

(e) The right to protect enhance and transmit the cultural, medicinal and spiritual knowledge and concepts found in the life cycles of Indigenous flora and fauna;

(f) A right to environmental well-being dependent upon the nurturing and wise use of Indigenous flora and fauna;

(g) The right to participate in benefit from and make decisions about the application, development, uses and sale of *me o ratou taonga katoa;*

(h) The right to protect, enhance and transmit the cultural and spiritual knowledge and concepts found in *me o ratou taonga katoa.*

2.6 The exercise of te tino rangatiratanga a te Iwi Maori as it relates to Indigenous flora and fauna *me o ratou taonga katoa* was and is a recognition of an Iwi interest in the continued existence of flora and fauna and cultural taonga as particular species and as interconnected threads of te ao turoa.

2.7 That such recognition vested in Whanau, Hapu and Iwi all rights and responsibilities relating to the protection, control, conservation, management, treatment, propagation, sale, dispersal, utilisation and restrictions upon the use of Indigenous flora and fauna and the genetic resources contained therein.

2.8 Indigenous flora and fauna includes the genetic resources contained therein and the environment in which they reside.

2.9 *Me o ratou taonga katoa* includes but is not limited to whakairo, rongoa Maori, waahi tapu, pa sites and Maori cultural images, designs and symbols and associated Indigenous, cultural and customary heritage rights in relation to such taonga.

2.10 The claimants say that they are or are likely to be prejudicially affected by ordinances, Acts, regulations, Orders in Council, proclamations, notices and other statutory instruments, and the policies, practices, acts or omissions adopted by or proposed to be adopted by or on behalf of the Crown and further as set out in this statement of claim.

2.11 The claimants further claim that all of the ordinances, Acts, regulations, orders, proclamations, notices and other statutory instruments, and the policies, practices, acts or omissions adopted by or on behalf of the Crown referred to are and remain inconsistent with the principles of Te Tiriti o Waitangi/Treaty of Waitangi.

The claim also includes reference to native species of flora and fauna and to the Crown's obligations to Maori in relation to international treaties and conventions. In that context, the claimants argue that the New Zealand government should not make commitments under international treaties and protocols without the prior consultation and agreement of Maori where these treaties impact on Maori rights under the Treaty of Waitangi.

Sadly for the claimants, the claim is taking far too long to be completed. The tribunal suffers from a shortage of funds for the prompt hearing of evidence and for adequate research. The adversarial manner in which the claims are increasingly handled also means that solutions are more difficult to find. Compounding the delays is the appalling lack of funding support for the claimants. In many cases, the claimants and their immediate families are left to carry the financial burden themselves.

The claimants are people who care deeply about their environment and the degradation that is occurring. The following is a poem written by one of the claimants, Mrs. Haana Murray of Ngati Kuri, in the 1960s, describing the pain, love, and suffering for her land and people and her feeling of cultural oppression:

MY OWN BLOOD AND BONES
Dreams though unreal
Always appearing like ghosts to steal
My tormented spirit away
Haunting, till break of day
I watch spellbound
As slowly a coffin arises out of the ground
It opened before my unbelieving eyes
O mother! mother! I cried
Give me time! Give me time!
I've tried and tried, but all in vain
Our lands to reclaim
How much longer must I bear these pains?
So on and on I dream
of the Maori lying at death's door
Dying landless like our Ancestors before
Under the country's merciless laws
I hear scratching on bare wood
And trembling where I stood
Hands appeared from under the coffin lid
Mother, dear mother, please remain
Where you are, in God's domain
I couldn't bear
to see you dying again
In this world I'll fight for you
And your wishes to pursue
Then, like a devil possessed,
I crushed my enemies with my bare hands
Why should I profess
that the White Man is better than I am?
Tossing and turning I awake in cold sweat
Vowing never to forget
All treaties are binding beyond death
Even our mixed blood and race
But truly no man owns the land
It's only ours to command
So let the Maori go free

And ratify the Treaty of Waitangi
Please release me from this oath
The Maori or Pakeha, I cannot disown
I love them both
They are my own blood and bones.

This poem also reflects the reality for many Maori that they also have shared Pakeha ancestry. It is not surprising that those who are a mixture of Maori and Pakeha descent almost invariably identify more strongly with their Maori side. Perhaps it is the sense of belonging to the land and the spiritual connectedness that explains this deep sense of feeling for being Maori—qualities that are inherent in all Indigenous and traditional cultures but sadly lacking in our modern Western society. This is not to say that Pakeha cannot and do not feel a spiritual connection with the land, but that Pakeha can never state that his or her connection and cultural relationship with the environment has been actively suppressed.

Without the rights of *tino rangatiratanga* (including rights of ownership, control, and decision making), Maori are unable to exercise their obligations of *kaitiakitanga* (guardianship and protection) and *manaakitanga* (sharing and providing for others). How can Maori care for the land and its resources if they are denied ownership or control over it?

For example, of the 66 million acres of land in New Zealand, some 64 million acres have passed from Maori into Pakeha ownership. This is a result of confiscations, dubious purchases, the operations of the Native Land Courts (designed to "Europeanize" customary Maori land title), and compulsory acquisition under the Public Works legislation. Without their land, the Maori are nothing. Without their land they are cut off from their links to the past, the rich tapestry of who they are and where they came from. Today, gradual steps are being taken to return land to Maori tribes through the government's treaty settlement process. As one tribe has stipulated, "*as land was taken, so must land be returned.*" But these settlements are achieved at a huge cost to the tribes concerned, not so much for what they are receiving but for what they are being asked to give up. As one tribal negotiator lamented, "*settlements are not about fairness and justice but about what is politically acceptable to the non-Maori majority who elect Governments.*" Most of the settlements to date have returned to Maori the financial equivalent of between 1 and 3 percent of the total loss based on present-day values.

What Are Maori Seeking?: A Tikanga Maori Framework of Protection (TMFP)

It is critically important to the claimants that any remedies are built on a foundation of *tikanga Maori*, or Maori customary values. Just "tweaking the edges" of the existing legislative regime and IPR system will not be acceptable to the claimants. It is true that aspects of the IPR system can be accommodated within a *tikanga Maori* framework. However, because of the ideological differences between IPR and Indigenous peoples' rights and responsibilities discussed earlier, we need to start from first principles. That means viewing any system of protection from a Maori cultural viewpoint, not something imposed from the outside.

A *tikanga Maori* framework of protection would have some or all of the following features:

- The system should be developed by Maori.
- The system should be based in *tikanga Maori*, reflecting Maori cultural values and ethos.
- Inherent in this system will be the acknowledgment, protection, and promotion of rights and obligations to manage, utilize, and protect resources in accordance with Maori cultural values and preferences.
- Flexibility will be very important. Whatever structure or structures are chosen will need to be flexible enough to take account of issues that affect Maori in a national sense as well as at the regional and local *marae* level. The structure must also accommodate the rights of individuals such as Maori artists, carvers, musicians, and designers.
- How such a framework is mandated by Maori will be a vital and challenging ingredient. In New Zealand today there are many national bodies that represent Maori, including Maori Congress (an Iwi or tribal-based organization), New Zealand Maori Council (a statutory body), Maori Womens' Welfare League, the Confederation of United Tribes (based on the 1835 Declaration of Independence), and others. There are also

various Iwi organizations and bodies, Land Trusts, Maori Incorporations, and *marae* trustees, to name a few. Indeed, one of the most challenging issues confronting Maoridom is the issue of mandate. Who speaks for the people? In a political sense, in terms of achieving unity within Maoridom, tribalism is a double-edged sword. On the one hand, tribes are fiercely protective of their individual cultures and identities. On the other hand, the same tenacity of character can be a barrier to achieving unity at a national level. This lack of unity has often played into the hands of successive governments, who have been adept at employing the tried and true strategy of "divide and rule."

- In terms of the resourcing of the framework, the claimants would seek an allocation of funds from the Crown (as part of their remedies package), to undertake nationwide consultation with tribes and urban Maori to discuss the formation of a structure. Funding would also be needed to implement and administer the new body on an ongoing basis.

- Finally, there are considerations of enforceability. In order to enforce compliance with this new regime, some form of legal recognition and protection will be necessary within the current New Zealand legal system. But there may also be nonlegal codes of ethics, and protocols containing rights and obligations, designed to educate and persuade voluntary compliance with the TMFP.

The TMFP might be responsible for:

- acting as a referral body to *Iwi* (tribes), *hapu* (subtribes) or *whanau* (families), or individuals, once it is determined at which level of Maori decision making the relevant issue is most appropriately advanced. Where it was obvious that certain issues affected particular tribes, the issue would be immediately referred to that tribe to deal with. So, for example, if someone wanted to research the *Pupu Harakeke* (flax snail), they would have to deal with the Ngati Kuri people of the Far North. If it was a matter that affected Maori at a national level, then a national body could deal with and undertake research at that level;

- acting as a support agency for Maori tribes and organizations in the undertaking of their own research;
- liaising with mainstream government departments;
- being a consultative body with Maoridom. This would be a key component of the TMFP. Hui and consultation with Maori would need to take place on a regular basis;
- assisting Maori in the formulation of policies to aid them in their role as *kaitiaki* of their various *taonga* (treasured things). Policies might deal with issues of respect for cultural values, access, and use and where appropriate (and sanctioned by the tribe), commercial exploitation. Such policies themselves would have to be flexible to take account of the different *tikanga* and relationship that each tribe or *hapu* has with the *taonga* within their own *rohe* (tribal territories);
- acting as a principal point of contact for those wishing to access and exploit traditional Maori knowledge of native flora and fauna for commercial gain;
- promoting education about Maori cultural values and their application within a modem-day context. This might include the general public, government agencies, and the corporate sector.

Benefits to Aotearoa/New Zealand

Many more businesses in New Zealand are beginning to appreciate the "added value" and marketing opportunities that a distinctive Maori identity, Maori place-names, and traditions give to New Zealand businesses operating in the international market. As one New Zealand marketing strategist has observed:

> In worldwide research on New Zealand, "sheep" and "green" are the only two icons that stand out . . . we can actually add value using our Indigenous products. It will come from our Maori people, our artists, our playwrights and designers. . . . Maori custom and culture is absolutely wonderful. There is potential for developing Maori icons to our culture. . . . I would love to see New Zealand borrow from Maori elements and use

> them in a modern context, because they help to position us worldwide. . . . By drawing on Maori culture and referencing, we could produce the most stunning textiles and fabric. Nobody yet has exploited Maori graphics and upholstery and curtaining fabrics etc. (Richards 1994: 209)

Maori culture and imagery is a powerful branding tool for New Zealand. But Maori want to have control over how and to what extent this should happen. They do not want their culture or values denigrated or portrayed in an offensive manner. The misuse of Maori names, traditions, and imagery in computer games by Microsoft and Sony are two recent international examples where Maori cultural property rights have been used for commercial purposes without their knowledge or consent. Accurate and culturally appropriate portrayal of Maori values or traditions will not only protect those values but also will enhance the commercial value of any product it may be associated with. But it is for Maori to finally determine what is and what is not appropriate for commercial exploitation and how the benefits of that are to be shared.

Maori self-determination of their own destiny, in dialogue and cooperation with their treaty partner (but on an equal basis), would be beneficial for Maori but also would enable Maori to make a greater collective contribution to New Zealand society as a whole. This is perhaps what Chief Judge Eddie Durie intended when he said:

> My vision for Maori is of a very strong people with their own economic base, not dependent upon government, with the ability to manage their own resources in their own communities in their own way, and yet totally tied into the national structure. Not standing apart from it, but making a contribution to the nation as Maori. We can make a far stronger contribution to the nation as Maori than as individuals. I believe we have a whole new dimension to offer the country. (Durie 1994: 24)

The Convention on Biological Diversity (CBD), Article 8j, and World Intellectual Property Organization (WIPO)

The maintenance of cultural diversity is now regarded by the world at large as necessary to the maintenance of biological diversity. Even though Article 8j talks about *respecting, preserving and maintaining traditional knowledge as it relates to sustainable use of biological diversity* and that this must be done with the *approval and involvement of the holders of such knowledge*, these worthy sentiments are overridden by the caveat that such protections are *"subject to national legislation."* In other words, each contracting party (national government) is only obliged to respect and maintain such knowledge *as far as possible and as appropriate* to their own country's circumstances.

The voices of Indigenous peoples are invariably marginalized because they do not get to vote in the decision-making processes of the CBD. One could argue if Indigenous, traditional, and local communities are responsible for the preservation of 90 percent of the Earth's biological diversity, that those people should be given greater standing in the decision-making process. Until Indigenous peoples are given a greater role in the decision-making processes, the longer it will take to achieve what are the most important objectives of the CBD—namely the conservation of biological diversity and the sustainable use of its components (Article 1).

Having said that, there are some positives that have emerged from the CBD process in recent years. The most obvious is the establishment of the Ad Hoc Open-Ended Inter-Sessional Working Group on Article 8(j) and Related Provisions ("the Article 8(j) Working Group"). But, although the work of that group is to be commended, there is still a feeling that ultimately the destiny of traditional knowledge holders is in the hands of those who are parties, as opposed to those (such as Indigenous and traditional peoples) who are just observers at the Conference of the Parties (COP).

Article 15.1 of the CBD is a sobering reminder that sovereign rights over natural resources rests with the parties, not with Indigenous peoples. However, for Indigenous peoples their rights and obligations are inseparable from ownership of genetic resources. In this regard, it is pleasing to note from the Report of the Panel of Experts on Access and Benefit Sharing (UNEP\CBD \COP\5\8, 2 November 1999, paragraph 131[c]) that they identify:

> a need to ensure that granting intellectual property rights does not preclude customary use of genetic resources and related knowledge;

and further at paragraph 133(b):

> making provision to ensure the continued use of genetic resources and related knowledge

in relation to IPR and Access and Benefit Sharing Agreements.

Similar sentiments are expressed by the World Intellectual Property Organisation (WIPO) in their statement to the Article 8(j) Working Group at Seville, Spain, March 27–31, 2000: "WIPO's exploratory work in 1999 has shown that traditional knowledge is a rich source of creativity and innovation" (Statement, page 4).

While the observations by the Panel of Experts, and the work of WIPO in particular, are welcome advances, there are nevertheless some fundamental issues of conflict that remain to be addressed. The first is that it is not just customary use but also ownership and control that are important to Indigenous and traditional peoples and local communities.

The next major point of conflict is that the rights and obligations of Indigenous peoples are philosophically at odds with the Western concept of resource exploitation and intellectual property rights. For example, within the tribal territory of Ngati Kuri in Parengarenga Harbour in Northland, Aotearoa, silica sands are being mined and commercially exploited for the making of glass. The magnetism of the silica sands attracts and guides the *kuaka* migrating from Siberia to Aotearoa. Practically all her life, Mrs. Saana Murray has been fighting to protect those sands from overexploitation and proving the importance those sands have for the surrounding ecosystems. The sands also have importance because of Ngati Kuri's customary relationship with the *kuaka*. These are all treasured *taonga* to Mrs. Murray and her people. The government and its agencies grant the licenses for the exploitation of these resources and the Indigenous and local communities can do little about it. Even the Resource Management laws in Aotearoa (which are by world standards quite advanced) have proven largely inadequate to adequately protect traditional and customary rights of Maori.

It seems that Indigenous and traditional communities are expected to preserve and maintain the Earth's biological diversity (as they have done for thousands of years), but only to the extent that governments and multinationals will allow them to do so.

It makes logical sense to involve international organizations such as WIPO in the implementation of the CBD and Article 8(j) in particular. But how do WIPO and COP (and more importantly Indigenous peoples) propose to deal with what may be seen as an inherent conflict in WIPO (and WTO) driving this process? For example, as noted in the Introduction to the WIPO statement to the Seville meeting of the Working Group on Article 8(j):

> WIPO's mandate is the promotion and the protection of intellectual property (IP) throughout the world through co-operation among States and, where appropriate, in collaboration with any other international organization.

It goes on to note that the definition of "intellectual property" is defined in the Convention Establishing the World Intellectual Property Organization, 1967, and includes rights relating to:

- literary, artistic, and scientific work;
- performances of performing artists, sound recordings, and broadcasts;
- inventions in all fields of human endeavor;
- scientific discoveries;
- industrial designs;
- trademarks, service marks, and commercial names and designations;
- protection against unfair competition; and
- all other rights resulting from intellectual activity in the industrial, scientific, literary, or artistic fields.

There exists an apparent conflict between the roles of WIPO on the one hand to promote and protect the existing IPR systems while at the same time taking a lead role in the development of mechanisms for the recognition and protection of traditional knowledge. Although it is arguable that the definition of "intellectual property" could be extended to include aspects of traditional knowledge and Indigenous value systems, this is to put a much-strained interpretation on that definition. The definition under the convention could be amended to specifically include "traditional knowledge systems and cultural values." However, this does not address the central argument that the two systems of IPR and IPRR would appear to be fundamentally and philosophically at odds with each other. A key concern is that outcomes are *not* being driven by the "needs and expectations" or with the "approval and consent" of the holders of traditional knowledge (TK), but by the needs and expectations of members states and the multinationals and research institutions who have a vested interest in the eventual outcomes.

WIPO is working in close collaboration with the secretariat for the CBD and FAO in its work on TK and intellectual property (IP) issues. An Inter-Governmental Committee (IGC) comprising member states was formed in 2000 and there have been five IGC meetings to date. The IGC has studied a range of legal measures for protecting traditional knowledge through existing intellectual property mechanisms and through systems specifically designed for that purpose. However, the current emphasis within the IGC appears to be toward adapting TK to conform to existing IPR instruments rather than undertaking a thorough analysis of alternative options for protecting TK including sui generis and customary methods of protection that take account of the great diversity of knowledge and practices within traditional communities.

The IGC is undertaking a study of the legal protection of traditional cultural expressions that analyzes current intellectual property rights and new options. Future work will include consideration of the possible development of model provisions for national laws and the international protection of traditional cultural expressions.

Lack of Effective Participation by Indigenous Peoples in the IGC

The IGC is open to member states of WIPO. Other United Nations members, intergovernmental organizations, and accredited NGOs may participate as observers. Approximately 175 accredited NGOs take part in the IGC's discussions. However, nongovernmental Indigenous groups have only a limited voice and no power within this process, which has resulted in some Indigenous groups walking out of WIPO meetings. Given the fundamental importance of the issues being dealt with by the IGC that will have far-reaching implications for Indigenous peoples, it is critical that the presence and profile of Indigenous groups is raised within this process. There is also a lack of any sustained critical analysis by Indigenous groups of the work being undertaken by the IGC.

As a result of submissions from Indigenous groups, the IGC is considering ways to enhance the participation of local and Indigenous communities in its work, including the establishment of a voluntary fund to assist Indigenous participation at these WIPO meetings. However, enhanced participation does not necessarily translate to more *effective* participation in terms of decision-making processes and assurances that the Indigenous voice is being listened to by member states.

A major issue for Indigenous peoples was the following announcement by WIPO in September 2003:

> Member states of the World Intellectual Property Organization (WIPO) decided today to push forward with work relating to the intellectual property aspects of traditional knowledge, folklore and genetic resources. The General Assembly, meeting from September 22 to October 1, 2003, decided on an extended mandate for the WIPO Intergovernmental Committee on Intellectual Property and Genetic Resources, Traditional Knowledge and Folklore (IGC). The mandate requires the IGC to accelerate its work, and to focus in particular on the international dimension of intellectual property (IP) and genetic resources, traditional knowledge (TK) and folklore. *The new mandate excludes no outcome for the IGC's work, including the possible development of an international instrument or instruments in this field.* (WIPO Press Release September 29, 2003, Geneva)

As noted above, this should not be at the expense of exploring in more detail the interface between customary law and Western IP law in order to seek a better understanding of how existing customary law practices and sui generis regimes can be used to protect and utilize traditional knowledge. Although there is evidence that many Indigenous groups are utilizing IP tools such as copyright and trademarks to protect and facilitate commercialisation of their traditional knowledge, this is due to the limited or nonexistence of other legal alternatives to ensure protection of that knowledge.

The current IPR system cannot protect the *underlying value systems* of Indigenous peoples. It was not designed to do so and without major adjustment, it is incapable of doing so. Yet despite the overwhelming calls by Indigenous peoples for strengthening of existing customary law systems and development of new frameworks or regimes for protecting their traditional knowledge systems—as opposed to simply imposing the IPR system on them—these calls are being largely ignored.

This is not to argue that *aspects* of the IPR system are not useful for the protection of traditional knowledge and values. The main point is that it must be Indigenous peoples who are driving this process and deciding for themselves what is and is not necessary for the protection of their knowledge and the granting of access to it. To have it any other way would be to have the tail wag the dog.

Conclusion

Maori support the call for a new approach for the recognition and protection of their rights and obligations. For this reason, they are likely to support the recommendations of the Article 8(j) Working Group, in relation to the development of sui generis and other appropriate systems for the protection of traditional knowledge. However, they will insist on being directly involved in any decision-making processes to develop and implement such systems for protection of *matauranga Maori* in Aotearoa/New Zealand. These accord with the requirement under Article 8(j) that the application of traditional knowledge be undertaken with the "*approval and involvement of the holders of such knowledge.*" It is not acceptable for the Crown to implement its own policy agenda in this area while at the same time the Wai262 claimants face the prospect of yet further delays in completing their already long-running claim.

On a global level, the issues are larger and even more complex. However, the Wai262 claim can be seen as a microcosm of the global struggle confronting Indigenous and traditional peoples seeking protection, not just of their traditional knowledge, but of their whole cultural values system. Just as the Wai262 claimants are confronted with delays, there will, at the current rate of progress, continue to be delays in implementing protection mechanisms for traditional knowledge under the CBD process. In this respect, the decision of the sixth meeting of the Conference of the Parties held in April 2002 to proceed with preparation of a composite report on the status and trends worldwide of traditional knowledge and what is being done to protect and promote it at national and regional levels is a positive step forward. It may be hoped that this is the beginning of a process that will result in greater national and international recognition and protection for Indigenous and traditional knowledge systems and, more importantly, the greater involvement and participation of Indigenous peoples in the framework and design of these measures of protection.

Notes

1. The Waitangi Tribunal is a quasi-judicial body established in New Zealand in 1975 to inquire into claims by Maori against the New Zealand government for alleged breaches of the principles of the Treaty of Waitangi signed between the Maori Chiefs and the English Crown in 1840. The treaty purports to grant sovereignty to the British in exchange for the guarantee to Maori of their *tino Rangatiratanga*, or full chiefly authority.

2. The term *Pakeha* is a Maori word meaning a New Zealander of English/European descent.

3. The text of the Treaty of Waitangi (in both English and Maori) is available at http://www.publicaccessnewzealand.org/files/treaty_text.html; last accessed on January 1, 2004.

References

Durie, Eddie
Not Standing Apart. Kaupapa, New Zealand: Vision Aotearoa, 1994.

Richards, Brian
Using the Chisel of the Mind. Kaupapa, New Zealand: Vision Aotearoa, 1994.

CHAPTER 9
BIOCOLONIALISM AND ISOLATES OF HISTORIC INTEREST

Marie Annette Jaimes Guerrero

Genetic Research and Biocolonialism/ Biopiracy

This chapter is intended to provide correlations of the linkages with genetic research and argues in the context of the legacy of conquest and colonialism in the United States. This critical analysis includes, in this context, a eugenics movement that had its hiatus at the turn of the nineteenth century. Today, this is inherent in what is being called a case for "biocolonialism." In this context, the new genetic engineering research is shown to be a portent to a new strain of eugenics inherently specific in what is being called the Human Genome Diversity Project (HGDP) (indicated as the Diversity Project in this work). This project is presumably distinct from the overall Human Genome Project, which is sampling the human DNA of all human populations worldwide. This Diversity Project, on the other hand, targets over 700 Indigenous peoples and their respective cultures worldwide, as objectified subjects that leading geneticists insensitively refer to as "isolates of historic interest" (Geneticists' Summary [GS] 1992). This position argues that the Diversity Project is a covert or "invisible" genocide that takes place in the context of *biocolonialism* linked with *biopiracy,* which are entrepreneurial enterprises for the genetic patenting of Indigenous knowledge, referred to as "Indigenous knowledge systems (IKS)." These genome agendas raise serious questions of bioethics, which includes the "informed consent" issue and involves the patenting of plants, animals, and humans for pharmaceutical consumerism. Both these terms, biocolonialism and biopiracy, are used to counter the advocacy for *bioprospecting*, as the corporate agenda for profit-driven genetic patenting of Indigenous knowledge in the commercial commodification of plants, animals, and humans, in what the geneticists term "biomedical discoveries" from this reductionist mindset.[1] This chapter, therefore, is intended to build a case for biocolonialism and biopiracy of Indigenous knowledge, which includes human DNA as well as nonhuman subjects.

Such denigrating genome agendas erode further the rights of Indigenous peoples and their respective cultures and are countered in this chapter with the advocacy for *biodiversity*—meaning the recognition of the relationship between biology, including humans, with the bioregional landbase and the natural environment as Nature. Inherent in the meaning of biodiversity is also the recognition of the reciprocal relationship between humans, and other biological entities (i.e. plants, other animals, nonhuman features), with the land as an Indigenous habitat and homeland, and how this is integrated in their respective land-based cultures and traditional kinship and ceremonies. This can also be philosophically interpreted as the conceptual meaning of *indigenism*, which literally means to be born of a place, but that also implies to be in reciprocal relationship with that place: as a sense of being-ness or identity with a sense of place and homeland, as part of an emerging Indigenous movement for basic human rights of Indigenous peoples.

A crucial intent of this work is also to make contextual connections to the historical treatment of peoples native to the Americas, and particularly to focus on the American colonialist legacy of native genocide and the U.S. colonialism that followed in the aftermath of the Indian-settler wars for empire building. This legacy of colonization and genocide, under the banner of "manifest destiny" by the Euro-Americans, has been documented by a discourse on native genocide in the Americas (Pearce 1965; Horsman 1981; Drinnon 1990; Stannard 1992; Churchill 1993, 1997), which is still practiced today by way of sociopolitical hegemony and the institutionalization of racism against American Indians in U.S. society. Yet a more insidious agenda, with roots in institutionalized racism, has dire portents for the future survival of Indigenous peoples worldwide. The DNA blueprinting by the Human Genome Diversity Project, in particular, lends itself to the commodification of Indigenous peoples as natural human resources for genetic engineering and biomedical profiteering by megacorporate pharmaceuticals and other companies. As noted earlier, the advocates of this biomedical research prefer to use the term *bio-prospecting*, while its critics in protest, among Indigenous peoples and their allies, call it *biocolonialism* linked with *biopiracy*.[2] As a native critic of the impact of the "new sciences" in genetics and biomedicine on Indigenous peoples and their respective cultures, I deem it important to make the connection between this kind of genetic determinism as *genocide* (as a biological or physical decimation of a communal people) that is linked with *ethnocide* (as cultural and economic erosion or decimation) as well as *ecocide* (as environmental erosion or decimation of an ecosystem, as a bioregional homeland for biodiversity) among land-based groups. I use the descriptor "erosion" to be linked with genocide, ethnocide, and ecocide, since this destruction can be seen as a devastating process, as well as the act of an intentional decimation to a people, their respective culture, and the natural environment that is the habitat upon which they reside, the latter as a landbase for their respective Indigenous homeland.

The Diversity Project, therefore, is focused on the patenting of human DNA among about 700 Indigenous peoples worldwide, as well as natural resources in their designated habitats.[3] A major premise of this research is that this scientific racist ideology is now manifesting and being "justified" within the genetic discourse and "scientific rationale" of what it means to be "objective" in a "pure science." As a case in point, the state of Vermont recently passed legislation to sanction "DNA certification" of its mixed-blood native population, arousing concerns on how this genetic blueprinting will be used.[4] The Biodiversity Convention(s) that came out of the international 1992 Earth Summit, to which the United States under the Bush administration did not send any representatives and refused to sign, calls for the input of targeted Indigenous peoples regarding the "bioprospecting" enterprises. This has resulted in native protests and resistance to the biopiracy of environmental and natural resources among Indigenous peoples and their respective cultures. It should be noted, however, that the so-called Biodiversity Conventions are not directly connected with the Diversity Project, since "humans" as commercial subjects were ruled out in the conventions. While the biodiversity conventions and consequent Indigenous peoples' responses are not in the scope of this chapter, it is important to show the movement of genetic science from Indigenous plant and other nonhuman DNA sampling and collection to human subjects among Indigenous peoples. I explain the organizational structure of the Human Genome Diversity Project in the following section and its intent in today's genetic research (refer to the chart attachment of the genome projects; *Cultural Survival Quarterly* 1996).

In the larger framework, this work is also interested in how the genome agendas can be perceived within a discourse of native genocide in the Americas. The more comprehensive non-native authors to write on this subject are: Harvey Pearce (1965), Reginald Horsman (1981), and Richard Drinnon (1990), who wrote on genocidal campaigns against American Indians in the early history of U.S. conquest and colonialism. Later, David Stannard (1992) wrote about an "American Holocaust," as a more current contribution to this genocidal discourse. Native scholars have also been putting forth their treatises on the "cultural imperialism" perpetrated upon native peoples and their cultures, and focusing on more contemporary times; most notable among these is the senior scholar Vine Deloria Jr.[5] Hence, it is my intent to link this body of writing on other forms of genocide, such as ethnocide and ecocide, among those Indigenous peoples targeted by the Diversity Project.

This chapter is an overview of the construction of the Human Genome and the distinct Diversity Project, which presents a case for a racialized genetics in what can be called genetic racism premised on the turn-of-the century legacy of "scientific racism." It can be perceived in the historical context of the turn-of-the-nineteenth-century eugenics ideology as biodeterminism, called "scientific racism" (Kuhl 1994) in a genocidal legacy, which can be seen as a portent for a "new age eugenics" in contemporary genetic research that is targeting Indigenous peoples for DNA data banks. Therefore, it is important to provide an overview to make this link with the contemporary situation to the genocidal and colonialist practices of the past. There are also Indigenous responses and criticisms to the Diversity Project, as biocolonialism and biopiracy, as an Indigenous challenge that highlights native women's organizations and leadership, such as the Indigenous Women's Network (IWN) in alliance with the Indigenous Environmental Network (IEN), in raising concerns about genetic research. In collaboration with other Indigenous delegations, representing the membership of these nongovernmental organizations (called NGOs), both IWN and the IEN have put forth the significant *Declaration of Indigenous Peoples of the Western Hemisphere,* with its demand for a global moratorium before the United Nations. There is expanding criticisms leveled at the Diversity Project by spokespersons, as biocolonialism linked with biopiracy, which is quoted in this chapter. There is also a call for more legislation and education, to counter the pitfalls of Western colonization, and for an anti-biocolonialist campaign that ensures an Indigenous peoples' future. My concluding remarks are derived from my own critical analysis of the current state of affairs regarding the genetic research, as genome agendas, that is targeting Indigenous peoples and their respective cultures.

This criticism also involves the patenting of Indigenous knowledge by Indigenous delegations before the United Nations and other international human rights forums. Therefore, this chapter is a call for an interdisciplinary and integrated *Indigenous Global Studies,* and toward a resolution that would present the Indigenous perspectives and values in both theory and practice. Such a curriculum would advocate for (1) political accountability; (2) cultural integrity; (3) economic self-sufficiency with environmental sustainability; and (4) a bioethics for ecological preservation and restoration of Indigenous landbases, as "ecocultures," also called "applied ethics" in the humanities context.

The set of questions that have been formulated from this research, as a general inquiry that poses these queries to the geneticists and others who advocate these genome agendas, is as follows: (1) What criteria are being used by these geneticists to target these Indigenous peoples while not others? (2) What do Indigenous peoples targeted gain or benefit from this genetic research? (3) What are the profit-driven enterprises behind such an agenda for commercial commodification, and in the context of the language terms (i.e. "isolates of historic interest," called "genome diversity," etc.) used in the scientific language as rhetoric? (4) How does this genetic research affect or impact Indigenous peoples not targeted, as well as nonIndigenous peoples? (5) What are the bio-ethical implications in terms of basic human rights being raised about these genome agendas? (6) What is the prospectus for the future in regards to the long-term consequences of this genetic research and these biotech enterprises? In this overall inquiry is the underlying critical query: Whose genes are these in the first place? (Crisite 1996; Lioqula 1996), of which native peoples already know the answer, in order to challenge what a core group of geneticists are determining as "threatened peoples" that they call "isolates of historic interest." As one observer succinctly put it, regarding the most important question of the Gene Age, we should not be asking "How?" but "Why?" (Abate 2000).

MARIE ANNETTE JAIMES GUERRERO

An Overview of the Human Genome/Diversity Projects Construction—As Genetic Racism

> Native American Identity, past and present,
> is linked with a vision of *Indigenism*
> that is formed in the context of the environment
> and our natural relationship with it,
> as a "Native Land Ethic"
> as "ecocultures"
>
> —(M. A. Jaimes, quoted in Churchill 1992/93)

The focus of this chapter is on the scientific agenda of the Human Genome Diversity Project and its impact on targeting Indigenous peoples, being objectified as "isolates of historic interest" by a core group of leading geneticists for genetic DNA sampling. An overview of the Diversity Project, in its overall construction, is followed by a discussion of the historical legacy of the 1900s eugenics movement, which is relevant to the reductionist genetic mind-set that prevails in this new genome agenda. In this vein, I criticize the way in which this genetic research is being conducted by leading geneticists who are advocating a controversial plan in the pursuit of biomedical discoveries. In its organization, the Diversity Project is sponsored by private corporations that purport to be separate from the government-sponsored Human Genome Project,[6] which is collecting human DNA samples from the human population at large for a larger data bank. It should be noted that the same Diversity Project players are also key participants in the broader Genome Project. It is also evident that these projects offer these participating scientists opportunities to personally benefit from their results, both professionally and financially. Both projects are tied in with what is called the internationally based "Human Genome Organization" on the overall organizational chart (*CSQ* 1996).[7] However, a critical distinction is that the Diversity Project was originally advocated for and funded by private corporations, which represent big pharmaceuticals interested in profit-driven biomedical discoveries, as well as research scientists with genetic engineering interests.

There is also the issue of "DNA certification," with the state of Vermont (noted earlier) to first pass legislation advocating this requirement and its implications, as to who can identify him- or herself as an "American Indian" or "Native American." Such an established precedent will most likely influence other states as well, regarding the genetic identification of its Indigenous populations. This racialized mind-set has its roots in "blood quantum" criteria established by the U.S. federal government since the mid-1800s, to determine a policy of "federal Indian identification" for tribal and Indian "benefits" (the subject of my 1990 doctoral thesis). This kind of reductionist research, as scientism, can also be correlated to the early racist doctrines of "scientific racism" as a science of bigotry espousing eugenics. This objectifying thinking referred to Indigenous peoples, as well as *all* women, as "inferior," physically and intellectually, as a result of cranium size compared to northern and western male Europeans. This pseudoscience, as it directly related to the "inferiority" of native populations and regardless of gender, was known as *Crania Americana* (Gould 1981). Today these new genetic schemes, under the guise of "diversity," imply unethical and immoral aims by way of a duplicitous rationale for genetic research in biotech and biomedicine. One of its major objectives is to patent the data accumulated as genetic resources called "intellectual property" by geneticists and other scientists, and in collaboration with both government and corporate sponsors, continuing the objectification of Indigenous peoples into the present day.

In the current genome scheme of the Diversity Project, Indigenous peoples are being targeted worldwide for genetic research through the sampling of individual members for DNA blueprinting of a particular group; such a selection is made by the Diversity Project geneticists who consider this group to be a distinct genetic and cultural entity. There are scientists who claim they are interested in the targeted group's preservation for future study, so they solicit DNA data sampling and collection from human subjects among their group membership. At the same time, these same scientists do not seem concerned with the alleviation of the physical demise of these peoples (as genocide), and also as a distinct culture (as ethnocide) with unique bioregional knowledge for biodiversity (as ecocide) that is manifested in their respective Indigenous communal ways.

A report issued by a team of geneticists, who came together in the Washington, D.C., area (from February 16, 1993, to February 18, 1993) contains a summation of results conducted by a group of leading genetic researchers on the Diversity Project. This gathering was held on the campus of the National Institutes of Health, in Bethesda, Maryland, where geneticists were participating in a third workshop that came to be called the "Washington Meeting." Such workshops also generated a list of about 700 Indigenous groups worldwide, attached to their report, to be targeted subjects (and with about 70 located in North America, the United States and Canada). This document also indicated that a data bank of this genetic research was being considered for location at Los Alamos, N.M.[8]

Such a list raises many more questions as to what groups are targeted, why, and where by the participating geneticists. The geographic breakdown for "DNA collection" among these targeted peoples, as reported by Debra Harry, is as follows: Africa, 165; Asia, 212; Oceania, 101; South America, 114; North America, 107; Europe, 23; totaling 722 (Harry, quoted in *CSQ* 1996). It is also interesting to note that most of these Indigenous groups are non-European and are located in parts of Africa, Asia, and South America as well as throughout the hemispheric Americas. This could read like some kind of contest, as to what Indigenous groups made this list and which ones, for whatever reasons, did not, since the criteria for those listed are neither clearly indicated nor discussed. Hence the critical questions are why these groups are targeted and not others, and some even in close bioregional proximity to each other; as in the case of Yaqui communities on both sides of the U.S. and Mexico border, with Yaqui communities on the U.S. side not on the list while the Yaquis on the Mexico side initially listed. It is answers to such queries that the geneticists who made this selection[9] have been evasive about, while they skirt around the question of what criteria were established to determine this selective list in the first place.

This Maryland workshop on the Diversity Project was formatted into three roundtable discussions, which claimed to focus on "an exploration of the ethical and human-rights implications" of the Diversity Project:

> (1) The ethical concerns raised by this Project are both real and significant. Although no participant stated that those concerns are so serious that the Project should not go forward, the participants agree that careful attention must be paid in designing and executing the Project in order to minimize the risks of harm; . . . (3) the Project should be designed and executed with help from the populations to be samples as far as feasible, although the participants realize that there will often be enormous

> logistical barrier to such assistance; . . . (7) Some people will almost certainly attempt to misuse the Project's data and findings in support of racist or nationalist ends. . . . Whether that misuse would have any significant consequences is unclear, but the participants believe the Project has a duty to try to minimize the effects of such misuse; . . . and finally (11) There is no reason to believe that the ethical concerns raised by this Project are insurmountable. . . . The value of this research and the urgency caused by the continuing disappearance of isolated human populations makes the ethical concerns all the more important. If the Project does not proceed carefully and properly, it could spoil the last good opportunity to obtain some of this data.[10]

In scrutinizing this genome agenda, a case can be made that their overall conclusions, as put forth regarding the ethical and human rights implications of their genetic research focus, mask a hidden agenda, on which this chapter intends to shed light from an Indigenous response and critique of the Diversity Project.

The federal government has since announced that it will contract out to private corporations to take over the research for the broader Human Genome Project that is sampling the U.S. population at large.[11] There is evidence that this development is setting a precedent to privatize such genome research in other countries as well, and that will impact national citizenry among both Indigenous and non-Indigenous populations. Such commercially engineered entrepreneurial genome agendas, with little or no political accountability, also raise the tax question, as to what are nationalist citizens actually paying their federal governments, in these corporate takeover times, with a globalizing "new world order" underfoot?! Eugenics "experts" have already experimented with the genetic engineering of plants and animals,[12] which even involves the controversy over human cloning today. Therefore, one of the most contested issues is around the patenting of and privatization of "Indigenous knowledge systems (IKS)" as "intellectual property issues (IPI)" (Harry, quoted in *CSQ* 1996).

A recent report from the Rural Advancement Foundation International (RAFI), titled "Phase II for Human Genome Research—Human Genetic Diversity Enters the Commercial," warns that there are rapacious financial stakes involved in the escalating race to find and commercialize human genetic variation, which is taking place in the absence of public debate and government action. The report notes that "the human rights abuse of research subjects has worsened, and governments and intergovernmental institutions have fallen all over themselves trying to sidestep responsibility for this complex ethical and medical conundrum." The RAFI Executive Director, Pat Mooney, is quoted, "In 1993, we first warned that the collection and management of human diversity research was taking place in an almost total policy and regulatory vacuum. . . . That the vacuum still exists is cause for outrage" (RAFI 2000).

RAFI, as a "watchdog" organization, is described as such: "an international civil society organization headquartered in Canada, and it is dedicated to the conservation and sustainable use of biodiversity, and to the socially responsible development of technologies useful to rural society. It is also concerned with the loss of agricultural biodiversity, and the impact of intellectual property on farmers and food security." However, it is already evident that genetic research is operating under the guise of a theoretical "virtual reality," which is at the expense and exploitation of native peoples as distinct cultural and biological entities for genetic research and experimentation, and with an agenda for commercial aims and corporate monopolies that can be called "corporate fascism." A part of this discussion is about how these participating geneticists are contextually defining "culture" and "diversity," as well as the racialized implications of these targeted Indigenous groups as separate biological entities.

There are growing concerns and voices of protest among many native human rights activists who are referring to this genetic sampling as the "Vampire Project" (Harry, quoted in *CSQ* 1996), since the most efficient way to get a DNA sample is from the subject's blood. Brian Tokar, in his 1998 paper for the Edmonds Institute titled "Indigenous Communities and the Commercialization of Science," quotes John Liddle, Director of the Central Australian Aboriginal Congress: "Over the last 200 years, non-Aboriginal people have taken our land, language, cultures, health—and even our children. Now they want to take the genetic material that makes us Aboriginal people as well." Tokar follows this with more on Indigenous opposition, stating, "From the very first announcements of the HGDP in scientific circles, representatives from Indigenous nations around the world began to express serious misgivings and outright opposition to its undertaking." Debra Harry, coordinator of the Indigenous People's Coalition on Biodiversity, cites 16 separate resolutions passed by Indigenous people's gatherings around the world that question the social, economic, political and ethical implications of the Project. From Brazil to the South Pacific, and in many parts of North America, Indigenous subjects of genetic research have voiced their objections to scientific activities that promote the patenting of genes and the appropriation of traditional knowledge (p. 7–8; among targeted Indigenous subjects). Tokar notes the World Trade Organization's (WTO) aggressive role in these genome schemes, to purport:

> Each of these activities respresents (sic) the same disregard for Indigenous people's biological and culture integrity, the same patronizing attitudes in the name of scientific, technological and economic 'progress,' and a continuation of the Western legacy of colonialism and conquest. In many cases, medical research, the identification and patenting of genes, and bioprospecting for commercially useful plants and other products from native lands are all being undertaken by the same people and the same thoroughly unaccountable institutions (p. 8–9; on the Diversity Project's genome agenda).[13]

In a similar vein (that makes the same points about biocolonialism linked with biopiracy), this chapter criticizes the Diversity Project as a "global genocide" impacting Indigenous peoples targeted by the Human Genome Diversity Project. Such biocolonialist schemes are often sponsored by international and transnational corporations, and especially in the interest of corporate pharmaceuticals with the financial backing of government-sponsored genetic scientists. A critical point of this chapter is that scientists can no longer hide behind the claim of "neutrality" or assert that science is not political or elitist, as a criticism that is referred to as scientism. Also at issue are the group or collective rights of distinct cultural entities, or what are traditionally called communal rights and later tribal rights as a result of colonialism, in contrast to individual rights of citizenry. Hence, these collective or communal rights are being denied those Indigenous peoples targeted by the geneticists. This is an ongoing debate that also involves whether Indigenous peoples are "peoples" or "populations" before the United Nations (Harry, quoted in *CSQ* 1996) and other international forums. Yet megacorporations and scientific projects do make their own claims for collective rights, and in the name of the "common good," which actually favor profit-driven markets and other privileged domains that operate more and more transnationally and globally at the expense of accountability to the national domain and its majority of tax-paying citizenry.

The organizational structure of the Human Genome Diversity Project is said to be different from the overall Human Genome Project that is sampling all nation-state populations with the backing of the nationalist governments; both entities at present are being privatized to ensure a maximum of profitable enterprise as well as enable noninterference in secrecy from public attention. It has been speculated that since the broader project is interested in determining human dispositions toward certain kinds of diseases, and indicated in their "DNA blueprinting," there is interest in determining the degree of environmental radiation in a individual's genetic makeup.[14] The Diversity Project workshop, featuring leading geneticists (noted earlier), focused on the "ethical and human rights issues" that were being debated by critics and was headed up by the internationally renowned geneticist Dr. Luca Cavelli-Sforza. Ironically, this team of geneticists decided to go ahead with this research, offering recommendations to take into consideration the ethical and human rights considerations of their subjects—the targeted Indigenous groups who were not even present or represented at this meeting.[15]

In telling terms, these geneticists have used dehumanizing language to define their "human subjects," for example (as noted earlier) in the use of *"isolates of historic interest,"* a term established in a report by the organizing committee of an earlier workshop in 1992. The specific quote from the introduction is thus:

> many populations around the world, especially isolates living traditional lifestyles, will soon disappear as independent units, because of disease, economic or physical deprivation, genetic admixture, or cultural assimilation. In this report, we refer to such groups as "isolates of historic interest" because they represent groups that should be sampled before they disappear as integral units so that their role in human history can be preserved. . . . The organizers have attempted to use terminology in this report that is as sensitive as possible in this regards. Undoubtedly, errors have been made. There is no attempt to make judgments about the inherent values of any people or populations, cultures, languages, and the like. The ethics review mechanisms of the Project will be designed to protect, to the extent that it is possible, against any such sensitivities.[16]

Therefore, what is implied in this report is a eugenicist assumption that "genes equal people," and that threatens the self-determination for survival among these groups (which is discussed later in this chapter). Also inherent in this scientific jargon is the blatant disrespect for human life by implying that these Indigenous peoples are already on their way out as extinct cultural entities and therefore warrant this kind of commercial exploitation; this involves the commodification of their respective Indigenous knowledge, which now includes their human DNA for human posterity, but with no or little intent in assisting them with their survival in the twenty-first century. Yet these Indigenous peoples have valuable knowledge—in the way of human origins and biomedical discoveries—that these geneticists are interested in enough to want to patent the discoveries in their own names, which raises questions of commercial (as in pharmaceutical drugs as "biomedical discoveries") self-interest and corporate opportunism.

It is evident that in such understated language these geneticists are attempting to rationalize the neutrality of their scientific attitudes at the expense of the assumed extinction of these targeted peoples, among Indigenous populations and cultures worldwide; also indicative is their condescending concern for the consequences of their decisions as well as their inhumane attitudes to their subjects as human guinea pigs. Hence, there remain many unanswered questions as to what is really behind these genome agendas, and to what purpose they will be put in the long run once these groups have disappeared by way of physical or cultural extinction.

In these genome workshops, however, neither Indigenous peoples nor their representatives are present or have input into these portentous decisions being made about their physical survival. These genome agendas are also about the posterity of these peoples' genetic makeup, once their respective culture and they, themselves, have physically disappeared, as "endangered species"! The geneticists' language is clever in this kind of duplicitous rationale, as in how they use the term *diversity* to imply an interest in "cultural diversity," but this is really a guise for racialized genetics as genetic racism. This is what I have earlier referred to as circular reasoning in a "Catch-22" in regards to who or what group is monopolizing the discourse, in both theory and practice, among the so-called experts. I have noted in my earlier work that: "One cannot identify as an American

Indian or Native American unless one has 'federal recognition.' However, one cannot have 'federal recognition' unless one is identified as an American Indian or Native American" (Jaimes 1994).

In a more recent scenario of this "reasoning," the Yuchi (Euchee) people of Oklahoma where among those targeted in the United States for DNA testing in these genome schemes. However, their spokespersons stated they would not cooperate unless they were granted "federal recognition," which they had been striving for. Since their petition was denied for this tribal status, this illustrates the glaring hypocrisy of the "Diversity" agenda in that this population is good enough for genetic research but not good enough to attain "federal recognition." One spokesman, Corky Allen, is quoted: "Our DNA is regarded as a vital, irreplaceable of the global heritage of humankind, yet we are denied federal acknowledgement which would give us a political standing, more clout, in the fight to keep our language, our culture." The author of this article, R. A. Grounds, points out, "The discussion of these issues within the Yuchi context presents a microcosm of the larger controversy" (1996: 64–68). This case, therefore, indicates the legislative ironies and legal issues that are raised in regards to subject rights in the targeting of Indigenous peoples for genetic research. Therefore, it is often stated that the Diversity Project came after the fact and in order to "counter racism," as Luca Cavelli-Sforza purports, with an interest in preserving the "diversity" among those Indigenous peoples targeted. Such language is stated in the genome agendas of the Diversity Project and can be perceived to be a kind of rhetorical subterfuge for obfuscation of the Diversity Project's real intent.[17] Yet it is evident that these genome agendas, which make claims of advocating for "diversity," are not really as much interested in the preservation of either cultural diversity or biodiversity as they are interested in racializing genetics in these profit-driven biomedical schemes as well as tracking human origins among Indigenous peoples.

There is also the rationale of the Diversity Project proponents, among these geneticists who assert an urgent need for the research because these targeted groups are being "threatened" with extinction, in the language of the geneticists,[18] since these targeted groups cannot keep up with modernization brought on by the new technologies in this "new world order." Therefore, this is assumed to create the need for biomedical discoveries for human health and survival from which the Indigenous subjects themselves will not be around to benefit. Even if there were those who were able to survive the onslaught of these hypermodernist times and the technological revolution, these groups would most likely not be able to afford such biomedical discoveries. This is a result of patents to privatize the biotechnological products by these scientific teams of geneticists that are in collaboration with the profit-driven pharmaceuticals and corporate interests for monopolies of such "discoveries." Behind these genome agendas is actually a hidden agenda—the corporate greed of a team of elitist geneticists who rationalize their actions for the greater good of humanity while they pursue patents to make themselves even more wealthy with these monopolizing biomedical schemes underway, called "corporate fascism."

Hence, the bigger picture of these genome agendas reveals the subterfuge and obfuscation behind their rhetoric and scientific rationales that use "biological determinism" to claim these targeted Indigenous subjects are *"isolates of historic interest,"* as "endangered species" that are being labeled as if they were already history! Meanwhile, this scientific campaign is continuing the history of genocide instead of supporting the survival of Indigenous peoples worldwide. There are cases in point of the actual profit-motive and corporate schemes that are behind these genome agendas, as in the case of the first attempt by a U.S. team of scientists to patent the DNA of the Hagahai peoples in Papua, New Guinea. This team of medical scientists, including geneticists, claimed the attempt to patent was actually to protect these people from AIDS; there is debate over the consent issue. The case went before the World Courts, since the New Guinea government took issue with the U.S. efforts as a violation of their sovereignty over these Indigenous peoples, but there was little representation from these peoples themselves. When information was finally forthcoming as to the real interest of the geneticists, to genetically sample this group, it was discovered that these isolated peoples, numbering about 200 members, had an immunity to leukemia and other degenerative diseases (refer to*CSQ* 1996: 37).[19] The Hagahai case has similarities to the infamous "El Dorado" case, among the Yanomami in the Brazilian rainforest, which is still being investigated for demonstrating a lack of medical bioethics.[20] There are also the legal implications in the Yuchi case (earlier illustrated above), in Oklahoma.

In these above scenarios, the U.S. scientists appear in collaboration with transnational pharmaceutical corporations (i.e., the now-defunct Shaman Pharmaceutical, based in San Francisco, California) and others to gain a lead and an eventual monopoly in biomedical "discoveries" for biotechnology and genetic engineering. All of these credentialed individuals are considered to be among the leading "genetic experts," and several are affiliated, ironically, with the National Institutes of Health. These same individuals, as well others, often show up in similar circles around the Diversity Project agenda. Among them is Luca Cavelli-Sforza (noted earlier), a leading designer of the initial master plan for the Diversity Project.

Luca Cavelli-Sforza, touted as a liberal humanitarian, is a renowned academician and a professor of genetics, emeritus, at Stanford University, who presented a paper to UNESCO, under the auspices of the United Nations (Geneva, Switzerland), in Paris, France, on September 21, 1994. He is quoted regarding his academic position, and in an obfuscatory literary style, in a fund-raising ploy that advocates for the implementation of the Diversity Project:

> The Human Genome Diversity Project (HCD Project) is an international anthropology project that seeks to study the genetic richness of the entire human species. This kind of genetic information can add a unique thread to the tapestry of our knowledge of humanity. Culture, environment, history, and other factors are often more important but humanity's genetic heritage, when analyzed with recent technology, brings another type of evidence for understanding our species' past and present. The Project will deepen our understanding of this genetic richness and show both humanity's diversity and its deep and underlying unity. I have spent most of my career studying human genetic diversity, and I am the chair of the International Executive Committee of this (Diversity) proposed Project. In my talk, I will briefly discuss the Project's history, describe the Project, set out the core principles of the Project, and demonstrate how the Project will help combat the scourge of racism.[21]

The overall orientation of Cavelli-Sforza's paper was to solicit international corporate and private support, in partnerships and funding, as well as national/federal institutional assistance, to carry on this genetic research and in continuation of already established funds (i.e., U.S. National Science Foundation (NSF); National Institutes of Health (NIS); U.S. Department of Energy). His paper also notes that the Diversity Project he advocates for was estimated to cost its corporate sponsors a mere $3 million over a five-year period. This is an extremely optimistic estimate considering the timeline in his report, and compared to the overall Genome Project, sampling varied mainstream populations worldwide with federal government sponsorship, estimated to cost a whopping $30 million to the year 2003. The Diversity Project was therefore estimated to cost about 10 percent of the overall Genome Plan.[22] However, UNESCO did not follow up with an endorsement for the United Nation's oversight of the Diversity Project at that time, despite Cavelli-Sforza's effort; it is presumed that the agency wanted more time to look into this genetic area (Hanley 1996). Cavelli-Sforza has also noted, in regards to regional meetings in the Americas, that a North American committee, under the leadership of professor Kenn Weiss of Pennsylvania State University, "is the only region so far to have proposed bylaws for its functioning." A South American Committee has also been formed, as well as European regional ones and a Chinese Committee. The North American Committee has since met twice at Stanford University, in January and August 1994.[23]

In a National Indian Health Board issue brief on "Genetic Research and Native Peoples," Brett Lee Smith is quoted by Larry Shelton on this issue under the category of "genetic diversity projects":

> Since Indigenous populations represent a significant portion of the world's human diversity, they are also priority subjects for scientific curiosity. To a scientist, the best samples of genetic material from an Indigenous population group are as genetically "pure" as possible, to ensure that the sample is "untainted" by the genes of other ethnic groups. Therefore, "full-bloods" [my quotes] provide the ideal samples. Further, it is better if members of a family all provide samples, across several generations and across several degrees of relations (as in biological kinship relations). (Shelton 1998)

This analyst also describes two of the more prominent projects focusing on the need for diversity in human genome samples and describes the Environmental Genome Project, whose goal is "to discover connections between genetic susceptibility to diseases and environmental factors . . . the Project personnel claim that better intervention strategies for individuals and populations should eventually be the result" (Shelton 1998). The other project is the Human Genome Diversity Project, which is the focus of this chapter; both projects have the same agenda in the area of biomedical discoveries from genome research that involves human subjects for commercial as well as medical interests.

It is my contention that the promotional spin for medical intervention is not thoroughly factual, since such rhetoric in the advocacy of genetic research is deliberately vague and evasive, and even contradictory in parts. Even Cavelli-Sforza points out, in one such glaring inconsistency in the Diversity Project, and as pointed out by Lee Smith's statement (quoted earlier):

> The truth is that there is no documented biological superiority of any race, however defined. Nowhere is there purity of races, except in plants and in some domestic animals that have undergone a special inbreeding process for laboratory purposes. Even in these cases there in no absolute "purity," which is very difficult to achieve. No damage is caused in humans by racial mixture. Humans thrive by remaining individually different one from another. In fact, the concept of race can hardly be given a scientific, careful definition.[24]

Yet the "superiority" of one race over another is often correlated with Social Darwinian interpretations of genetic "natural selection" and "survival of the fittest," both of which imply the "superior" groups' high degree of survival and longer mortality over more interracial "inferior" types. This can be referred to as "Darwinian economics," working in tandem with "Newtonian scientism" from the Cartesian philosophical hegemony. Also, nineteenth-century eugenicists subscribed to this notion of the "superiority" of Anglo-Saxons and others, and in the context of a "purity principle," which sometimes even advocated inbreeding among its aristocracy, despite known deleterious effects in children produced from incestuous relationships. At the same time, this "white race" was contrasted to other denigrated racialized groups among "people of color," who were seen as "mixed-blood" and mongrel-types as a result of their interbreeding or exogamy in terms of their degree of miscegenation; these groups were called "mulattos," "mestizos," and "metis," and other miscegenation labels (Jaimes 1994; Gould 1981).

My work in this area is interested in the hidden agendas of these genetic research plans, as in what is behind the propaganda that is campaigning for huge taxpayer dollars while most people go unaware of the implications and portents to their lives and their children in the not-so-distant future. It is, of course, expected that miraculous biomedical discoveries, involving what is being called "gene therapy" with the potential to someday even reverse the aging process, will be made. Yet, at what cost to those as research guinea pigs, and to our greater humanity in terms of the commercial appropriation, reification, and exploitation of human beings as "natural resources," as profit-driven privatization and corporate monopolies underfoot? It is also necessary to comprehend such methods that are being employed in this new scientism of biotech genetic engineering, in determining the promotional aims and intents of those engaged in these genome campaigns. The RAFI Report (cited earlier) further summarized the issues on privatization and corporate monopolies with genetic interests:

> With computer-assisted DNA sequencing machines running faster and more cheaply than its originators ever imagined, researchers are now turning from the crude "genetic map" of the Human Genome Project to its inevitable Phase II—the drive to plunder, patent, and privatize the commercially-important bits of variation found in individuals, Indigenous peoples, disease and disability groups, and ethnically-distinct communities (referring to the Diversity Project). "What has changed since RAFI first reported on the subject, is the intensification of research on human genetic diversity and its commercialization," notes RAFI's Director of Research, Hope Shand, [who adds] "The genomics companies are working hand-in-hand with the Gene Giants, and the rush is on to claim exclusive monopoly patents on even the tiniest bits and pieces of the human genome." The real money in human diversity mapping lies in identifying and patenting single nucleotide polymorphisms (SNPs or "snips") that code for specific traits including diseases. The Gene Giants are hoping to patent SNPs in order to develop diagnostic kits, monitoring instruments, and even "designer drugs" tagged to the specific DNA of wealthy customers. Hundreds of millions of dollars are being spent in the effort to find and control SNPs but the long-term profits will be in the billions and could ultimately restructure the entire health care industry. (RAFI 2000)

As an inter/transnational case in point, the RAFI communiqué illustrates:

> Were the commercial value of human genetic diversity research ever in doubt, those misgivings were unambiguously laid to rest when Iceland sold its genetic heritage to the genomics company deCODE, who in turn hawked the human data to Hoffman LaRoche of Switzerland for

> US $200 million. The spectacular and controversial deal turned genomics research overnight from an obscure biotech niche industry into a mainstream commercial venture. Suddenly, almost unheard of genomics companies like Millennium (US), Genset (France), and Axys (US), are patenting diversity studies into a multi-billion-dollar commercial product strategy aided and abetted by researchers at universities and even some governments. The extension of patentability by the US Patent and Trademark Office to . . . SNPs (as the smallest unit of genetic variability) has further galvanized commercial pharmaceutical enthusiasm for the new industry. SNPs are the genetic basis upon which diversity researchers define their investigations and distinguish individuals and human populations from one another. (RAFI 2000)

There is also interest (as noted earlier) in the native origins of Indigenous peoples to the Americas, which is a hotly contested arena of controversy and debate, among native groups themselves as well as non-Indigenous peoples. I refer to this arena as a "Native Genesis," which hypothesizes a "cradle of civilization" among the ancient Pueblo cultures of what is now the U.S. Southwest and parts of Central and Latin America. Since crucial issues over ethical and human rights considerations have surfaced, such as issues about "hereditary meritocracy," a "biological underclass," and "genetic discrimination" in the overall genome agendas (Shattuck 1996: 210–217, 215), the U.S. government, as a leading player in these genetic campaigns, has only recently negotiated the broader Genome Project under private corporate contract, and it seems to ward off potential taxpayers' curiosity and concerns regarding the costs and objectives. This move seems to give the government less direct accountability for this national and globalizing plan, and with U.S. capitalism as the vehicle. It has been additionally criticized for its own interest in these profit-driven schemes, in collaboration with corporate interests and monopolies, as Big Business in biogenetic research for biomedical discoveries. Another distinction is that the national Genome Project is interested in sampling individuals for population profiles, while the Diversity Project is targeting Indigenous peoples as distinct genetic and cultural groups; at the same time these groups are discouraged from organizing themselves and their interests in the plan as a collective entity. It is also interesting to note that the United States has the "National Center for Human Genome Research" under its Department of Health and Human Services, while the

Diversity Project has a much wider international agenda, which includes Japan, France, the UK, and others along with the United States, and it is linked with the Department of Energy as well as an International Executive Committee (*CSQ* 1996: refer to organizational charts, p. 23).

Protests and criticisms of the Diversity Project have been noted in this chapter, as Indigenous responses in opposition, which include the IWN as well as the IEN, as signers of the *Declaration of Indigenous Peoples to the Western Hemisphere*, are calling for a worldwide moratorium on these genome agendas (*CSQ* 1996: 63). There is also the conservative National Congress of American Indians (NCAI), which supports this call for a moratorium and is therefore in direct opposition to those few tribal entities brokering for negotiations in "shareholding" interests, in regards to whatever profit is made from such genome enterprises (RAFI 2000). Such significant declarations, among Indigenous organizations and their respective delegations to the United Nations human rights forums, mainly the "Working Group on Indigenous Populations/ Peoples," are challenging what I refer to as the outcome of Global Genocide. Hence, what is emerging is an Indigenous Movement that is inter-American, international, transnational, and global, as a result of biocolonialism and biopiracy, in the exploitation and commodification of Indigenous peoples and their cultures worldwide. A focus has also been on the genome differences between men and women, (wittily illustrated in the political cartoon, "Below the Beltway").[25]

This movement for Indigenous human and cultural rights also had native representatives and Indigenous delegations at the confrontation with the World Trade Organization (WTO) in the recent Seattle, Washington, Washington, D.C., and European protests, which the media failed to find newsworthy. In this transnational and global movement, native women are key players in the leadership and activism through their Indigenous organizations, among others in the inter-American and international theaters before human rights forums, as in the case of nongovernmental organizations (NGOs) before the United Nations Working Group on Indigenous Populations/Peoples, in Geneva, Switzerland (*CSQ* 1996: including p. 63). These protests have emerged as an international and even transnational Indigenous movement that challenges and counters, by advocating for Indigenous biodiversity rights, these human genome agendas in the further genocidal denigration of Indigenous peoples by today's leading geneticists. Such agendas are therefore also linked to Indigenous ethnocide and ecocide with the use of genetic racist language that inhumanely labels these targeted Indigenous peoples as "IHIs," to mean *"isolates of historic interest."*

To end on a bittersweet note as to the state of affairs to date, such Indigenous delegation protests in alliance with grassroots activism, among those peoples targeted, have in fact been able to shed light and concerns on these human genome agendas, and by advocating for more information and education on these genetic enterprises as megacorporate genome schemes, the latter would focus on Indigenous perspectives as Indigenous global studies. They have even been effective in breaking up the monolithic entity known as the Human Genome Diversity Project as well as shutting down corporate pharmaceuticals, such as the San Francisco-based and ironically named Shaman Pharmceuticals.[26] However, this has established smaller human genome projects and agendas, which claim to address issues of human rights, environment, and genome ethics, called *bioethics*. Yet, this core of elite geneticists continue to pursue their profit-driven biomedical monopolies via patents for self-interest and exploitation of others, at the immediate expense of Indigenous peoples and the predictable long-term costs to non-Indigenous peoples.[27] The latest development in these genome schemes is called the "Rifkin Initiative," in which the author, Jeremy Rifkin, is calling for "The Treaty To Protect the Genetic Commons." It has been criticized as another ploy, in the launching of this "global campaign affecting Indigenous issues *without* (emphasis added) Indigenous peoples."[28] Again, one has to deconstruct the language to determine the meaning of a "genetic commons," in the context of who will benefit and at whose expense this "treaty" will serve, if taken seriously. And there are those who are already calling it "legal biopiracy," under the rhetoric of a "gene pool trust,"[29] as yet another form of colonialist exploitation—biocolonialism linked with biopiracy.

Thus, this work further sheds light on the conflict between Indigenous peoples and their allies in protest and resistance to the geneticists and their corporate brokers. In conclusion, inherent in the Human Genome Diversity Project is a genetic racism under the guise of "diversity" that targets its subjects, among Indigenous peoples, for their human DNA. In these genome schemes, as genetic blueprinting with a profit motive, it remains to be seen how far these scientists and their collaborators, in both the corporate world and political arena, will go in this continuing biocolonialist saga of genocide, ethnocide, and ecocide of Indigenous peoples worldwide—to the ultimate loss to future generations and our greater humanity.

Notes

1. The theme of "Biocolonialism and Biopiracy," was the title of a 1998 conference that focused on the Human Genome Diversity Project, held on the Flathead Indian Reservation of the Salish-Kootenai Confederated Tribes, in Polson, Montana; this author was among the presenters.

2. See Harry 1995a, 1995b; Shiva 1997. In a broader scope, the construction of the Indigenous argument also shows a linkage with the past, and especially in the context of what is termed *cultural anthropology* in the continuing objectification, commodification, and today's commercialism for the further exploitation of Indigenous peoples and their cultural and ecological knowledge; the latter is what I later conceptualize to counter this subordinate hegemony as "ecocultures."

3. Jaimes 1992. My analysis of this genome agenda culminates in an Indigenous philosophical and spiritual argument on basic human and sacred rights. In my earlier work, I address the related issue of "federal Indian identification" as racialized formulas that include "blood quantum" criteria to determine who is an "American Indian" and therefore "eligible for federal Indian services."

4. This legislation was cited on an e-mail memo as Internet news, 2000.

5. Vine Deloria Jr., Native Colonization as Cultural Imperialism, as the final statement in *Integrateducation, Special Issue on American Indian Education,* vol. 19, nos. 1–2 (Winter–Spring 1981): 58–63.

6. Refer to *CSQ* 1996, special issue, Genes, People, and Property: Furor Erupts over Genetic Research and Indigenous Groups (note the telling use of the term "Group" in title rather than Peoples), as an Introduction by *CSQ* guest editor, John Friedlaender.

7. Refer to Organizational Charts, *CSQ* 1996, special issue, p. 23.

8. Geneticist's Summary (GS) Report on 3rd Workshop called "Washington meeting," convened in Maryland May 17, 1993; with cover letter by Jean Doble (to Pat Mooney, International Development Research Centre, RAFI, Ottawa, Ontario, Canada), assistant director for Morrison Institute for Population Resource Studies, at Stanford University, Palo Alto, California.

9. GS Report on 3rd Workshop, May 17, 1993.

10. GS Report on 3rd Workshop, May 17, 1993, 1–3.

11. See *CNN News* Broadcast 1998, on the U.S. government "privatizing" the Human Genome Project by contracting it out to the private sector.

12. See Shiva 1997.

13. Brian Tokar, on Indigenous Communities and the Commercialization of Science, for the Edmonds Institute, Institute for Social Ecology, Plainfield, Vermont, 1997: 7–9; also citing Debra Harry in Indigenous People's Opposition to the HGDP, for Indigenous People's Coalition Against Biopiracy. Available at: http://www.ipcb.org; last accessed April 30, 2001.

14. For more information on radiation connection, see Sharon Begley, "Decoding the Human Body," *Newsweek,* April 10, 2000, 50–57.

15. GS Report on 3rd Workshop, May 17, 1993.

16. GS Report on 2nd Workshop, held at Pennsylvania State University, State College, Pennsylvania. Not published—internal documents (unpublished workshop documents). October 29–31, 1992: 8–9.

17. GS Report on 3rd Workshop, May 17, 1993; Luca Cavelli-Sforza's paper is titled The Human Genome Diversity Project, pp. 1–19; this ringleader in genetics circles is a professor of genetics, emeritus, at Stanford University, Palo Alto, California, who presented this position paper before the United Nations UNESCO, in Paris, France, on September 21, 1994.

18. Cavelli-Sforza, September 21, 1994, pp. 1–19.

19. Case of the Hagahai People in Papua, New Guinea, Indigenous Person from Papua New Guinea Claimed in US Government Patent, RAFI press release, *CSQ* 1996: 37. (This case is also illustrated in the video documentary titled *Gene Hunters,* ZEF Productions Ltd., Luke Holland, producer [subtitled version] RX February 11, 1991, Film for Channel Four and sponsored by The Ford Foundation and Television Trust for the Environment, among others; as an overview on the targeting of Indigenous peoples, as "endangered species," by the Human Genome Diversity Project for biotech genetic engineering ventures and the lack of scientific ethics.)

20. Case of the Yanomami people in the Brazilian rainforest, citing a recently released book, *Darkness in El Dorado,* by Patrick Tierney, Norton Books, New York, 2000.

21. Cavelli-Sforza, September 21, 1994, pp. 1–19.

22. Cavelli-Sforza, September 21, 1994, pp. 1–19.

23. Cavelli-Sforza, September 21, 1994, pp. 1–19.

24. Cavelli-Sforza, September 21, 1994, p. 16.

25. Mike Peters, "Below the Beltway" (as a political cartoon on genome and gender), *Sunday Examiner & Chronicle*, 9 July 2000.

26. *Gene Hunters*, Pt. 1, February 11, 1991. There is also the video documentary, titled *DNA Hunters: The Power over Life*, Pt. 1, Alligator Films Video Production, Markku Fink, 1991 (i samarbeid med TV2), as an internationally independent producer, on specific cases of Indigenous peoples being targeted

by the Human Genome Diversity Project and corporate pharmaceuticals for biomedical research, as in the case of the Hagahai people in New Guinea, and the U.S. agenda, pending before the World Court, to patent their human DNA.

27. *Gene Hunters*, Pt. 1, February 11, 1991; *DNA Hunters: The Power over Life*, Pt. 1.

28. The "Rifkin Initiative," proposed by author Jeremy Rifkin, for a "Treaty To Protect the Genetic Commons," as a "New Initiative for Rio + 10: A Global Campaign Affecting Indigenous Issues without Indigenous Peoples," sent by email memo by Indigenismo El Mundo (Indigenous World), April 4, 2001.

29. "Rifkin Initiative," April 4, 2001.

References

Abate, Tom
Bioscope. *San Francisco Chronicle,* 26 June 2000, B1–2.

Begley, Sharon
Decoding the Human Body. *Newsweek* (2000, April 10): 50–57.

Churchill, Ward
Struggle for the Land: Indigenous Resistance to Genocide, Ecocide, and Expropriation. Monroe, Maine: Common Courage Press, 1992/93.

A Little Matter of Genocide. San Francisco, Calif.: City Lights Bookstore, 1997.

Crisite, Jean
Whose Property, Whose Genes? *Cultural Survival Quarterly (CSQ).* Special Issue, vol. 20, no. 2 (summer 1996): 34–6.

Cultural Survival Quarterly (CSQ)
Special Issue, vol. 20, no. 2 (summer 1996).

Drinnon, Richard
Facing West: The Metaphysics of Indian-Hating and Empire Building. New York: Schocken Books, 1990.

Geneticists' Summary (GS)
Report on 2nd Workshop, on Oct. 29–31, 1992: 8–9.

Gould, Stephan Jay
The Mismeasure of Man, on "Morton's Skulls." New York: Norton Books, 1981.

Grounds, R. A.
The Yuchi Community and the Human Genome Diversity Project: Historical and Contemporary Ironies. *Cultural Survival Quarterly (CSQ)*, special issue, vol. 20, no. 2 (summer 1996): 64–68.

Hanley, Charles
Genes Project Send Drums Beating. *The Cairns Post*, Cairns, Australia, June 14, 1996, 8.

Harry, Debra
The Human Genome Diversity Project and Its Implications for Indigenous Peoples. *IPR Statement #6* (January 1995a). [Also in Genes, People, and Property: The Furor over Genetic Research on Indigenous Groups. *Cultural Survival Quarterly (CSQ)*, special issue, vol. 20, no. 2 (summer 1996).]

Patenting of Life and Its Implications for Indigenous Peoples. *IPR Info #7* (January 1995b). [Also in Genes, People, and Property: The Furor over Genetic Research on Indigenous Groups. *Cultural Survival Quarterly (CSQ)*, special issue, vol. 20, no. 2 (summer 1996).]

Horsman, Reginald
Race and Manifest Destiny: The Origins of American Racial Anglo-Saxonism. Cambridge, Mass.: Harvard University Press, 1981.

Jaimes, M. A.
Federal Indian Identification Policy: An Usurpation of Indigenous Sovereignty in North America. In *The State of Native America*, edited by M. A. Jaimes, 123–38. Boston, Mass.: South End Press, 1992.

American Racism: The Impact of American Indian Identity and Survival. In *Race*, edited by S. Gregory and R. Sanjek, 41–61. New Brunswick, N.J.: Rutgers University Press, 1994.

Kuhl, Stefan
The Nazi Connection: Eugenics, American Racism, and German Nationalist Socialism. New York: Oxford University Press, 1994.

Lioqula, Ruth
Value of Life. *Cultural Survival Quarterly (CSQ)*. Special Issue, vol. 20, no. 2 (summer 1996): 42–45.

Pearce, Harvey
Pearce, Roy Harvey. *Savagism and Civilization: A Study of the Indian and American Mind.* Baltimore, Maryland: Johns Hopkins Press, 1965 (1967 Printing).

Rural Advancement Foundation International (RAFI)
News Release on watchdog organization RAFI Report, January 21, 2000. Available online at: http://www.etcgroup.org/; last accessed on January 9, 2004.

Shattuck, Roger
Forbidden Knowledge. New York: Harcourt Brace & Co., 1996.

Shelton, Larry
National Indian Health Board Issue Briefing on Genetic Research and Native Peoples and the Human Genome Project, February 18, 1998, p. 2 (1–11); citing Brett Lee Smith's unpublished paper.

Shiva, Vandana
Biopiracy: The Plunder of Nature and Knowledge. Cambridge, Mass.: South End Press, 1997.

Stannard, David
American Holocaust: Columbus and the Conquest of the New World. New York: Oxford University Press, 1992.

CHAPTER 10

INDIGENOUS KNOWLEDGE AND TRADITIONAL PLANT RESOURCES OF THE SECWEPEMC (SHUSWAP) NATION

Kelly P. Bannister

Ethnobotany is IN!

—Richard I. Ford (1994: viii)

A seemingly insatiable public interest in plant-based medicines has provided impetus for widespread industrial exploration of the largely untapped potential of the world's biological resources for drug discovery. This exploration is fueled further by aspirations to concomitantly protect biological diversity by establishing the economic value of intact forests and other ecosystems, which if protected (it is reasoned) may provide humanity with a wealth of new medicines and other products for health improvement. Inventorying and screening some 300,000 existent plant species for innumerable useful biological activities, however, is clearly a costly undertaking. Hence, many research programs take a systematic approach to plant selection, based on criteria believed to maximize cost-effectiveness.

The recent ethnopharmacological and phytochemical literature indicates that targeting medicinal plants used by Indigenous societies is an increasingly popular means of finding biologically active constituents of medical significance. Some research programs have relied largely on medicinal plant knowledge of Indigenous cultures as criteria for plant selection (King and Tempestra 1994; Cox 1994; Towers et al. 1997), while other research programs that have generally adhered to a random approach in plant selection are giving priority to medicinal plant-based collections "when reliable information is available" (Cragg et al. 1994: 188).

Ethnobotany, a discipline that seeks to understand direct interrelations between plants and humans (Ford 1994), is viewed as one means of uncovering such plant knowledge. In fact, much of the published ethnobotanical literature on plant medicines is now collated in easily accessible databases, for example the NAPRALERT (NAtural PRoduct ALERT) database (Loub, Farnsworth, Soejarto, and Quinn 1985). Furthermore, there is a sense of urgency about intensifying ethnobotanical field research to gather Indigenous cultural knowledge and plant resources before the irreversible effects of acculturation and ecosystem destruction take their toll (Schultes 1994). However, ethnobotanical studies that document information on plant species, preparation methods, and medicinal uses by Indigenous peoples usually form part of a broader, context-dependent framework that is necessary to understand the often complex reciprocal relationships that exist between plants and humans. Thus ethnobotany does not so much involve finding *products* as it involves finding *out about processes*. Ethnobotany also involves both *promotion* and *protection* of those plants, peoples, and interrelationships that it seeks to understand. There are concerns within the field about the "economically motivated search for new drugs" (Berlin and Berlin 1994: 247) since drug discovery "cannot be divorced from the broader objective of promoting the survival of biological and cultural diversity" (Martin 1994: 228).

Current widespread interest in commercial exploitation of plant knowledge and resources of Indigenous cultures has, ironically and perhaps unwittingly, positioned ethnobotanists as perfect agents for cultural appropriation. Through academic publication and other modes of dissemination, cultural knowledge of Indigenous peoples has been gradually brought into the public domain and become freely available for use by others. It is increasingly apparent that appropriation and commodification of Indigenous cultural knowledge and traditional plant resources are of major concern to Indigenous peoples worldwide. These concerns have been made explicit in several recent international declarations and statements,[1] although at local levels many Indigenous people remain largely unaware of how their cultural knowledge is being appropriated.[2] Furthermore, adequate means to address these collective concerns are often lacking.

As interest in ethnobotany and its exploitative potential for drug discovery has increased, so have uncertainties as to whether ethnobotanical research will ultimately help or hinder the populations of plants and peoples upon which the research depends. This presents a serious ethical dilemma that merits consideration. Ethnobotanists are bound by an academic imperative to share the outcomes of publicly funded research with the wider public. While this imperative may be seen as consistent with *promotion* of biocultural diversity, there is also a moral commitment within the discipline to uphold trust relationships and *protect* the biocultural integrity of plant-people relationships. The dilemma emerges when *promotion and protection conflict*. For example, conducting and publishing research on traditional medicines of Indigenous societies can be seen as a double-edged sword. While it may establish the sophistication of traditional knowledge and the importance of Indigenous knowledge systems to the integrity of cultural and biological diversity, publication also makes that knowledge accessible for appropriation and commodification by third parties—who may not be compelled to respect the original contributors nor acknowledge their contributions to applications, developments, or further discoveries based on Indigenous knowledge. Furthermore, such dilemmas may be exacerbated within the academic setting by current university ownership policies, funding and advancement criteria, and ethics review systems, none of which typically acknowledge added complexities surrounding research involving cultural knowledge of Indigenous societies (Bannister 2000; Laird, Alexiades, Bannister, and Posey 2002; Bannister and Barrett 2004).

In this chapter, I present a specific example from ethnobotanical and phytochemical research on traditional foods and medicines of the Secwepemc (Shuswap) Nation (Bannister 2000) as a case study to explore ethical issues and complicating factors involved in current medicinal plant research. Effectiveness of available measures for redress, including research agreements, intellectual property rights mechanisms, and professional codes of conduct, are discussed in parallel with the role of academic publication in promotion and protection of Indigenous claims to intellectual property.

First, however, it is necessary to provide some context for the example that will be described, as this research comprises one part of a much larger ethnobotanical study with and within the Secwepemc (Shuswap) Nation.

The Secwepemc Ethnobotany Project

The Secwepemc (Shuswap) Nation is composed of seventeen Aboriginal bands and is one of seven Interior Salish cultural groups located in southern-central British Columbia (the western-most province of Canada). "Shuswap" is the anglicized word for "Secwepemc," which means "the spread-out people" (Ignace 1998: 216), and this is an appropriate description considering that Secwepemc traditional territory extends over approximately 180,000 km. This area is located in what is known as the Interior Plateau region (between the coast and Rocky Mountain ranges), and includes several biogeoclimatic zones, making it one of the most botanically diverse traditional territories in British Columbia. In 1991, a collaborative, interdisciplinary research program focusing on Secwepemc plants, language, and culture was initiated in consultation with and with the support of the Shuswap Nation Tribal Council,[3] the Secwepemc Cultural Education Society, and Secwepemc elders and researchers from various Secwepemc communities.

The initial purposes of the Secwepemc Ethnobotany Project (1991–1994)[4] included comparison of Secwepemc plant names and associated knowledge of plants from different ecological and dialect regions of Secwepemc territory. Subsequently (1994–1998),[5] the project expanded to include the role of plant resources in the life-ways of Secwepemc peoples, past and present, by incorporating a combination of anthropological, archaeological, ecological, linguistic, nutritional, and biochemical approaches. The combined data and experiences resulting from this project were intended to provide a base of information and training for applications within community education, resource management, treaty negotiations for land and resources, and health care regimes for Secwepemc peoples.

My biochemical research on the nutritional and medicinal properties of one plant (i.e., balsamroot), which was part of the Secwepemc Ethnobotany Project, will serve as the basis for subsequent discussion of issues pertaining to recognition and protection of Indigenous claims to intellectual property.

The Balsamroot Story

In Secwepemctsin,[6] it is called *tset'selq,* which translates as "the head, or the chief" (Marianne Ignace 1996, personal communication to Peacock as cited in Peacock 1998: 145). In botanical Latin, it is *Balsamorhiza sagittata* (Pursh) Nutt., referring to the balsam-like aroma of its root and the sagittate or "arrow-shape" of its leaves (Parish, Coupé, and Lloyd 1996; Hitchcock and Cronquist 1973), and it is assigned to the aster family (Asteraceae). Commonly, it is referred to as "sunflower," "spring sunflower," or most often, "balsamroot" (Turner and Ignace in preparation). Balsamroot (figure 10.1) is known by the Secwepemc, as well as other Interior Salish peoples, as an important food and medicine. In fact, it has been referred to as "one of the most versatile food plants used by the peoples of the southern interior" of British Columbia due to its edible roots, root crowns, young shoots, and seeds (Turner 1997: 93), and Secwepemc elders have indicated it as "the plant to end all plants" (Turner and Ignace in preparation).

Balsamroot as Food

In the past, the root was an important food staple for Secwepemc and other Interior Salish peoples. At first glance, however, the root seems a

A B

Figure 10.1. Balsamroot, *Balsamorhiza sagittata*, or *tset'selq*. Figure 1A shows flowers and arrow-shaped leaves in early spring. Figure 1B shows a root harvested for medicine in late summer.

perplexing choice of plant for a staple food source. The deep-growing taproot of this herbaceous perennial requires a significant effort to dig, develops a thick, woody barklike outer layer (which is both difficult and time consuming to peel from raw roots), and is mainly composed of the carbohydrate inulin and related oligofructoses—which happen to be *indigestible* by humans. While the chemical structure of inulin is essentially based on chains of fructose units, the sugars are linked together in a way that makes them resistant to the normal hydrolytic cleavage of enzymes found in the human gastrointestinal tract (Roberfroid 1993; Avigad and Dey 1997; Wang and Gibson 1993).

An explanation for this apparent contradiction is found within the chemistry of traditional processing methods of balsamroot. Prior to consumption, the roots typically underwent a long, slow cooking process in an earth oven, an age-old technology known as pitcooking. Recently, Peacock (1998) demonstrated that pitcooking of inulin-containing roots in earth ovens increases their digestibility for humans. However, Peacock's (1998) reconstructions of traditional Interior Salish cooking pits also indicated that careful attention to the details of the traditional "recipes" was required for successful chemical conversion, including adequate temperature, moisture, and acidity. When these conditions are met, pitcooking can result in the cleavage of much of the inulin into fructose units, thus making the root both highly palatable and readily available for digestion and energy metabolism. In fact, carbohydrate analysis of the raw and pit-cooked roots showed that the pit-cooking process converted over half of the inulin to fructose or oligofructose, and increased by 250 percent the energy available through consumption of digestible carbohydrate (Peacock 1998; Mullin, Peacock, Loewen, and Turner 1998).

Interestingly, other recent studies on the health-promoting functions of inulin and dietary fructans suggest that the inulin remaining in pit-cooked roots may also have beneficial roles. These include addition of fiber to the diet, a sweet taste with low calorific value, and the ability to stimulate colonic health by serving as a preferential substrate for the growth of beneficial intestinal bacteria (e.g., *Bifidobacterium* spp.), which subsequently out-compete potentially pathogenic species (e.g., *Escherichia coli*) in microbial colonization of the human colon (Gibson, Beatty, Wang, and Cummings 1995; Wang and Gibson 1993; Van Loo, Coussement, De Leenher, Hoebregs, and Smits 1995).

The traditional role of balsamroot as a staple food has now been superseded by easier and faster foods—understandably, since in addition to root collection, pit construction, and the preparation of food stuffs, pit-cooking itself typically took twenty-four to forty-eight hours! However, to this day, balsamroot remains an important Secwepemc medicine. Interestingly, as in traditional processing of balsamroot for food, the preparation of balsamroot as a medicine also requires a heating process.

Balsamroot as Medicine

As a Secwepemc medicine, the resinous roots are used to treat a variety of skin ailments, including infections. Secwepemc elder Dr. Mary Thomas (Nesconlith) recommends digging the roots after flowering, in midsummer, when the medicinal qualities of the root are believed to be highest. Then the roots are boiled in water and left to stand until a layer of pitch collects at the surface. The pitch is applied directly to infected areas while the cooled pitchy water can be used as a soaking solution or wash (Mary Thomas, personal communication, 1996; Turner and Ignace in preparation).

The medicinal applications of balsamroot imply that the roots could have antimicrobial properties (i.e., the ability to prevent the growth of bacteria, fungi, and/or viruses that cause or exacerbate disease). Consistent with this, both antibacterial and antifungal activity have been reported in standard laboratory bioassays of methanolic extracts of dried, raw roots (McCutcheon, Ellis, Hancock, and Towers 1992; McCutcheon, Ellis, Hancock, and Towers 1994), and an antibacterial compound referred to as Thiophene E has been isolated and purified from raw roots (Matsuura, Saxena, Farmer, Hancock, and Towers 1996).

These published data seem consistent with the traditional use of balsamroot as a topical treatment for skin infections, except for the fact that Thiophene E was detected in *methanol* extracts of *raw* root samples, whereas Secwepemc instructions on the medicinal preparation of balsamroot involve heat treatment in the form of boiling in water. As the solubility properties and stability to heat treatment of Thiophene E were undetermined, its presence in medicinal preparations (i.e., in the pitch and/or cooled pitchy water used as medicine) was not known.

As part of the Secwepemc Ethnobotany Project, roots were harvested and pitch was collected from the roots by boiling, according to elder Dr. Mary Thomas's instructions outlined earlier. Assays in vitro indicated that the pitch did have antibacterial activity, as did the cooled pitchy water used as a soaking solution. Furthermore, chemical analysis by gas chromatography-mass spectroscopy (GC-MS) confirmed that Thiophene E was present and active in the pitch, as were numerous other antimicrobial compounds that are presently being isolated and purified for chemical identification (Bannister 2000). These results suggest that Thiophene E may indeed play a role in the medicinal properties of balsamroot when prepared as described by Secwepemc elders to treat skin infections. However, these results also indicate that the antimicrobial nature of the pitch is chemically complex and cannot be attributed solely to the activity of Thiophene E.

This emerging picture of the importance of traditional methods of root processing provided an opportunity to address an important concern regarding the nutritional and medicinal duality of balsamroot. Thiophenes are generally noted for their wide-ranging biological toxicity to a number of different organisms (Champagne, Arnason, Philogene, Morand, and Lam 1986; Hudson, Graham, Chan, Finlayson, and Towers 1986; Towers, Page, and Hudson 1997; Dojillo-Mooney, Page, Isman, and Towers 1999), and due to their potential toxicity to humans, interest in commercial development of this class of compounds for antibiotic applications has been low. However, given that: (1) Thiophene E (in addition to the other, as of yet unidentified compounds) retained antibacterial activity after heat treatment by boiling, and (2) Thiophene E was originally isolated from *whole* roots rather than pitch, it seemed likely that these compounds would be present in pit-cooked roots and thus would have been consumed with the carbohydrate and other nutrients in traditional diets. Further research on pit-cooked roots was undertaken to address concerns about the routine consumption of antibiotic-like and/or toxic compounds, which would presumably have a significant impact on the ecology of human intestinal microflora.

Analysis of pit-cooked roots by laboratory bioassays in vitro revealed that antibacterial activity was present, but it was reduced to negligible levels by removal of the outer barklike covering after pitcooking (Bannister 2000). Cooking appears to draw the pitch out of the edible portion of the root where it hardens onto the inner wall of bark, which is removed prior to consumption (Bannister 2000). Consistent with this, GC-MS analysis confirmed that Thiophene E was present in pit-cooked roots but was localized to the barklike covering (Bannister 2000). Thus, it appears that the inner *edible* portion of the root does *not* have antibacterial properties when prepared for consumption using traditional Secwepemc methods.

When Promotion and Protection Conflict

The cumulative data resulting from the Secwepemc Ethnobotany Project underscore the sophistication of past and present Secwepemc plant knowledge and have contributed toward a deeper understanding of the meaning of plants within Secwepemc culture. In the balsamroot example outlined above, combined studies on a traditional food and medicinal plant have shown the importance of heat as a differential processing method—essentially creating multiple uses for a single plant part. In this case, heat is crucial in both medicinal and nutritional applications, albeit apparently for different reasons. As medicine, heat applied by boiling *made available* heat stable and pitch-soluble antibacterial compounds for treatment of skin infections (Bannister 2000). As food, an *edible* carbohydrate was created from an *inedible* root by chemical degradation of inulin (Peacock 1998) and removal of undesirable antibacterial compounds (Bannister 2000). An understanding of the utility of balsamroot as both food and medicine, and the "discoveries" of antibacterial properties of the processed bark and pitch would not have been possible without the guidance of Secwepemc elders who shared knowledge of their traditional preparation methods and uses. Indigenous knowledge, then, has been key to these laboratory findings.

The wider interest in these and other findings generated through Secwepemc ethnobotanical research has been unpredictably high. For example, inulin-containing plants are receiving increased attention in North America for their value as "functional foods" and already have an established market in Japan and other parts of Asia and Europe (Mullin et al. 1998: 770). Thus, partly as a result of the balsamroot studies, researchers at Agriculture Canada have initiated an investigation of the local and international market potential of balsamroot as an "exotic" native vegetable or as a possible commercial source of short-chain inulin. Field trials to determine feasibility of large-scale growing and harvesting of balsamroot for these purposes are in progress (John Mullin, personal communication, 1998).

The original research on antimicrobial properties of balsamroot, which resulted in the first reported isolation of Thiophene E from this plant, was sponsored by a federal Centre of Excellence called the Canadian Bacterial Diseases Network (CBDN). The ongoing mandate of the CBDN includes discovery of patentable antibiotics or useful lead compounds from plants native to Canada. The selection of plants for antimicrobial activity screening is guided largely by the published ethnobotanical literature (McCutcheon et al. 1992; McCutcheon et al. 1994; Matsuura et al. 1996; Towers et al. 1997). After Thiophene E was isolated from balsamroot (Matsuura et al. 1996), no further CBDN-sponsored phytochemical research was carried out on this plant. However, the phytochemical data generated through the Secwepemc Ethnobotany Project (Bannister 2000) has contributed to renewed interest in the antimicrobial properties of balsamroot, as well as in other Secwepemc plants.

The results of research on Secwepemc food and medicinal plants are apparently seen as beneficial by a variety of agencies and individuals, based on the interest expressed in this work by local herbal companies, herbalists, wild-crafters, and even the Canadian Broadcasting Corporation Radio Network—rather startling considering the data have yet to be published. The research data remain unpublished at the time of this writing precisely because of the high level of third-party interest in it, and consequent uncertainties surrounding biocultural impacts of publication.[7] For example, how will publication of medicinal plant data affect Secwepemc control of traditional plant knowledge and access to traditional plant resources? While publication may serve to *recognize* Indigenous claims to intellectual property, can it also serve to *protect* them?

The welfare of Indigenous culture is linked with the integrity of Indigenous cultural knowledge and traditional biological resources. Concern for the integrity of biocultural diversity thus requires consideration of direct or indirect impacts of ethnobotanical research on Indigenous cultures. In light of widespread and increasing public and private interest in appropriation and commodification of cultural knowledge of Indigenous peoples, especially in the area of plant medicines, dissemination of such knowledge through publication should be an important point for discussion among and between ethnobotanists and Indigenous peoples.

The following section assesses the influence of publication on protection of the cultural knowledge of Indigenous or traditional societies using legal and moral mechanisms such as research agreements, systems of intellectual property rights (IPR) and professional codes of conduct.

Influence of Publication on Protection Mechanisms

Research Agreements

As previously mentioned, research within the Secwepemc Ethnobotany Project has taken place in consultation with and with the approval of the appropriate governing bodies of the Secwepemc Nation. Furthermore, as is required for all research involving humans conducted in Canada, individual academic researchers were required by their respective institutions to undergo a formal ethical review process to gain approval of their research proposals.[8]

A mandatory part of this ethical review process involves submission of a written Letter of Consent that must outline various items of concern and be completed by the "subjects"[9] of the study (i.e., in this case, individual Secwepemc participants and the Secwepemc Cultural Education Society). These policies and procedures are intended to protect the rights of the researchers, their sponsoring institutions, the "subjects" involved in the research, and the wider public for whose benefit publicly funded research is ultimately conducted.

However, the academic setting in which the phytochemical research on Secwepemc traditional food and medicines was conducted led to uncertainties in legal ownership of data resulting from the research—only a point of contention if the research led to potentially useful products, which was possible, but not the goal of the research. Thus it was agreed by the contracting parties that my Letter of Consent governing chemical research would also include an explicit statement of ownership of Secwepemc knowledge and provisions for future use as follows: "the Secwepemc Nation has control over access to the traditional plant knowledge, as well as to potential development of any marketable products (such as drugs or pharmaceuticals) that may be discovered as a result of the traditional knowledge shared during the course of this research" (Bannister and the Secwepemc Cultural Education Society 1997: 2).

Subsequently, the research agreement represented by this Letter of Consent was critiqued as a contractual approach to protecting knowledge, as part of a case study analysis on the use of IPR for protection of

Indigenous knowledge in Canada (Mann 1997). Mann's analysis highlighted the important issue of third-party use of the original data once it is published. It advised that without formal links to legal mechanisms of IPR protection (such as patent, trademark, copyright, and licensing arrangements), after publication the rights of ownership of the Secwepemc Nation were left open to definition by third parties. It stated further that: "a considerable reliance on the acknowledgement by others of Aboriginal rights in the subsequent uses of traditional knowledge is implicit in this provision for its full operation to be effective in the manner it appears to have been intended" (Mann 1997: 37), and concluded that "the longer term impacts of these arrangements will unfold in time" (Mann 1997: 37).

Mann's (1997) informative (but rather discomforting) analysis compelled us to consider whether formal links to legal mechanisms of IPR protection are *feasible* in this case, and if so, are they *appropriate*?

Intellectual Property Rights Mechanisms

Patents are probably the most common means of intellectual property protection for chemical compounds of economic value discovered from plants. While a compound such as Thiophene E in balsamroot would not qualify for patent protection because it had previously been identified from another plant in the same plant family, *Ambrosia chamissonis* (Less.) Greene (Balza et al. 1989), it has yet to be determined whether other antibacterial compounds found in the pitch of balsamroot are novel. If this were the case, and if the tri-criteria (i.e., novelty, utility, and inventive ingenuity) for obtaining a patent in Canada were met for one or more of these compounds, then a patent would only be valid if the "invention" was not made public before the patent application was filed.[10] Thus, publication of the chemical structures, functions, and/or the processes for obtaining them prior to patent application would preclude obtaining patent protection for these (World Wide Legal Information Association [WWLIA] 1995).

In fact, precisely because of this, publication could be used strategically to block others from obtaining a monopoly through patent protection—a process termed "defensive publication" (Crucible Group 1994; Posey and Dutfield 1996). However, subsequent public disclosure of the invention is a mandatory *requirement* of obtaining patent protection so that patented inventions may serve as starting points for future innovation.[11] Given that approximately 90 percent of patents are for improvements to existing patented inventions (WWLIA 1995), public disclosure of data (be it as a requirement of patent protection, through defensive publication, or by other means) still serves as a valuable resource for exploitation by third parties.

Trade secrets have also been proposed as a means of protection of formulae, methods, techniques, and other commercially valuable know-how related to medicinal plant knowledge (Barton 1994; Posey and Dutfield 1996; Peteru 1997; Stephenson 1999). Confidentiality is a key element, however, and this implies that the entire ethnobotanical knowledge base shared among researchers and community members within the context of the Secwepemc Ethnobotany Project over several years is likely already disqualified from this sort of protection, even without publication. Peteru (1997: 98) comments that "establishing a trade secret may be elusive in a culture that emphasizes common over private property." Indeed, it would appear antagonistic in an environment where reviving, rebuilding, and celebrating language, culture, and traditional life-ways are priorities.

Licensing agreements have been suggested as potential means of employing IPR protection for medicinal plant knowledge (Barton 1994; Stephenson 1999) as they effectively grant rights without relinquishing ownership. However, establishing a form of IPR (e.g., patent or trade secret) is obviously prerequisite to the licensing of IPR.

Thus, it appears that with or without investing the necessary time and expense to employ formal means of legal protection, Secwepemc traditional plant knowledge and resources would still be largely left unprotected from appropriation, commodification, and perhaps monopolization of derived knowledge by enterprising individuals or organizations who chose not to acknowledge Aboriginal concerns in subsequent uses. And these concerns are, of course, far deeper and more complex than can be portrayed by a discussion limited to chemical properties of plants. Thus, the *feasibility* of employing IPR protection to Secwepemc medicinal plant knowledge and resources is a related but nevertheless separate issue as to whether these means are seen as *appropriate* in the first place. While this chapter can address the former to some degree, it cannot determine the latter, which (to my understanding) has yet to be resolved by Secwepemc peoples themselves. And surely it must be a difficult question to resolve. The threat of privatization or inappropriate commercialization of shared cultural knowledge and teachings deeply mars the spirit of sharing and poses a serious problem—*are Indigenous peoples being forced (often prematurely) into considering IPR protection mechanisms simply as a defensive strategy to prevent others from employing them first?*

It is all too apparent that an intercultural chasm exists in terms of the concepts of "ownership" and "value" of knowledge and resources. The framework underlying the legal and economic protection afforded by IPR regimes is suited to protection of inventions or discrete expressions of intellectual creativity with commercial potential. It is ill-equipped, however, to encompass the long-term, communal concept of guardianship and the concomitant protection of knowledge and resources as integral parts of cultural identity and life-ways. The significance of plants such as balsamroot to Secwepemc culture cannot be measured only in terms of uses and economic potentials for inulin and antibacterial pitch compounds—nor do these products alone represent the importance of chemical research on traditional processing methods of balsamroot. Any such products can attest to only *one of many* valuable aspects of the traditional knowledge shared, and the process of sharing by and with Secwepemc peoples. Ironically, it is the *products* and perhaps certain *technical* aspects of knowledge that qualify for protection under current legal regimes—even if to the detriment of the underlying relationships, processes and knowledge systems upon which the "discoveries" are based.

Moral Incentives

A lack of compatible legal mechanisms to address protection of knowledge outside of the parameters of research agreements or contracts means that protection largely rests on moral imperatives and compliance with ethical standards. Many professional societies have developed Codes of Ethics for education and assistance in decision making when faced with ethical choices or conflicts. Some relatively recent guidelines for ethical research conduct attest to an increasing awareness of the importance of intellectual property issues surrounding ethnobotanical research. These include, for example, the Code of Ethics and a (Draft) Code of Conduct of the International Society of Ethnobiology,[12] and a Guidelines of Professional Ethics of the Society for Economic Botany.[13] Although these particular documents may approach ethical issues in botanical research with Indigenous peoples from divergent perspectives, in both cases there is consideration of the ethical conflicts imposed by trying to meet obligations to multiple stakeholders, and concern about dissemination and use of research findings. Related to the latter, it has been suggested that publications could contain an explicit statement informing readers of the origins of the knowledge, the conditions under which it was shared, and moral obligations for further use (Elisabetsky and Posey 1994; Posey and Dutfield 1996). While such statements may entail no legal obligation (Barton 1994), their widespread use could potentially set a standard and culminate in significant moral suasion. This could have a pronounced effect if subsequent use could be monitored, for example, through legal requirements to disclose and credit sources of cultural knowledge upon which patents are based. At the academic level, editorial policies of journals could include a requirement that the source of all cultural knowledge be adequately acknowledged (whether it was obtained directly from communities or indirectly through the literature), and literature-based databases could likewise include this information (Bannister and Barrett 2001).

How to proceed in light of uncertainties regarding the effects of publication on protection of Secwepemc knowledge and resources is not clear. Yet publication is not only a reasonable expectation for publicly funded research, but is an academic requirement for doctoral degrees (of which this research is a part) and career advancement. Publication of ethnomedicinal data, then, could be seen as a compromise between *protecting* Indigenous interests and rights to traditional knowledge and resources, and *facilitating access* to these—which is, in essence, a serious compromise between promoting the importance of culture knowledge and serving as an instrument for cultural appropriation.

The issues and dilemmas raised by publication of Indigenous knowledge of plant medicines stem from a lack of clarity on the foreseeable impacts of knowledge dissemination on Indigenous communities whose value systems, priorities, and conduct differ from those of the academic community engaged in the research. It is accepted that the impacts of research, be they positive or negative, cannot always be foreseen at the time the research is initiated, and it is expected that a reasonable effort will be made to foresee, forestall, and disclose adverse effects. More difficult, or even impossible, is prediction of all downstream effects that might arise as a direct or indirect consequence of the original research, and problems that do arise are likely to be case specific. In this regard, Brown (1998: 200) comments that "the Law of Unintended Consequences reigns supreme; there will always be unforeseen effects, both good and bad, when information enters the public domain." However, rather than serving as *rationalization*, Brown's (1998) observation above can be taken as an *invitation* to acknowledge and address the powerful role that publication can play in issues of control. This is particularly pertinent as mounting evidence suggests that Indigenous peoples are increasingly uncomfortable with the sharing of cultural knowledge outside of traditional routes due to uncertainty in what dissemination of that knowledge will mean in the longer term. Thus, guidelines are needed to acknowledge the social, cultural, political, and economic complexities involved in dissemination of cultural knowledge, and to assist in ethical decision making in light of the uncertainties presented by publication.

A Precautionary Approach to Publication: *in dubio pro natura?*

A useful framework that is increasing in repute for guiding decision making in the face of uncertainty is provided by the precautionary principle. This ethical and legal principle was originally founded in German environmental policies (Boehmer-Christiansen 1994) but has since gained widespread international application[14] and support in areas of biodiversity and human health (Research and Information System on Non-Aligned and Developing Countries [RIS] et al. 1999), biological conservation (Backes and Verschuuren 1998), ecological restoration (Noss 1998), agricultural biotechnology (Barrett 1999), and in ethnobiological research (Bannister 2000; Bannister and Barrett 2001; Laird et al. 2002; Bannister and Barrett 2004).

The precautionary principle embodies a "when in doubt, err on the side of caution" approach wherein measures to prevent damage or harm may not be deferred on the grounds that insufficient scientific evidence exists about the effects of a particular activity (Backes and Verschuuren 1998). From this it has been inferred that in many situations an activity should only be allowed when there is scientific certainty that this activity has no detrimental effect—i.e., the principle of *in dubio pro natura.*[15] Consideration of the precautionary principle in the area of ethnobotanical research and publication of cultural knowledge may have relevance, in light of uncertainties and perceived risks in dissemination of knowledge, and consequences of these for formal Indigenous claims to IPR or general concerns about knowledge and resource protection.

The precautionary principle does not lay out a set of specific rules to be followed; rather it offers a framework to assist in decision making, based on a set of guiding principles that include: (1) protection of the environment and recognition of intrinsic value; (2) recognition of potential harm and persistent uncertainty; (3) proactive and anticipatory action; (4) open and inclusive decision-making processes; (5) reversal in burden of proof; and (6) assessment of alternatives. An in-depth application of these principles to ethnobiological research and publication issues has been discussed elsewhere (Bannister 2000; Bannister and Barrett 2004). However, the essence of points (2), (3), and (6) are of particular relevance to the publication issues raised, that is, acknowledgment that consequences of our actions cannot always be predicted, anticipation of harmful outcomes, and proactive approaches to preventing harm through alternative action rather than reliance on compensatory measures after harm has occurred.

For example, benefit sharing and compensation are recognized as important components in ethnobotanical research. However, an obligation to share benefits accrued from research based on cultural knowledge typically results only when *direct* links between Indigenous communities and researchers exist. Research based on published ethnomedicinal studies are often perceived free of obligation, even if Indigenous knowledge was key to subsequent findings, since the knowledge was already in the public domain. In this way, publication serves to circumvent the spirit and obligations of benefit-sharing.

Similarly, publication circumvents third-party accountability and just compensation for harm. Without engaging in direct interaction with Indigenous communities, how would a third-party even be aware of harms stemming from knowledge appropriation? While harm cannot always be accurately predicted in advance of initiating research, a commitment to ongoing interactive dialogue would be invaluable in better understanding the forms that harm can take, and thus would assist in prediction and prevention of similar harms in future (Bannister 2000; Bannister and Barrett

2001). Indeed, Battiste and Henderson (2000) uphold that the laws and norms of the Indigenous peoples who are the focus of the research should be the starting point for defining all aspects of the research process and outcomes.[16] If part of the current backlash regarding appropriation of Indigenous knowledge is understood as an accumulation of many harms unattended, perhaps the cumulative impact of foreseeing and addressing potential harms in future will likewise forestall future injustices.

Does a precautionary approach to ethnobotanical research and publication imply that no research or publication on traditional plant medicines should proceed unless or until there is conclusive proof that there are *no* adverse effects, be they direct or indirect? Taken to an extreme, of course, this approach could lead to a form of paralysis, and be reasonable grounds for dismissal (i.e., while we debate the pros and cons of our actions and inactions, the world waits for desperately needed medicines and other physical, social, and economical remedies). However, as Duthie (2001, personal communication) suggests, invoking the precautionary principle without a commitment to undertaking action that would eliminate uncertainties is an abuse of the principle. The merit of a precautionary approach is in its *action*-oriented nature, which first compels us to *acknowledge* problems or limitations and then challenges us to *seek out alternative approaches* for redress (i.e., in the interest of the greater good, the price for new medicines need not, and ought not, be borne unevenly by Indigenous peoples).

Alternative approaches to address the dilemma presented by publication of traditional medicinal knowledge could begin with insisting that publications include biological and cultural contexts, which are essential for an appreciation of broader knowledge systems. Inclusion of prominent statements in publications as to moral obligations stemming from further use of the data, such as proposed by Posey and Dutfield (1996) and exemplified by Elisabetsky and Posey (1994), may significantly raise awareness of the concerns of Indigenous peoples. Appropriate acknowledgment of sources goes without saying, but perhaps Indigenous contributions also merit coauthorship. With or without coauthorship, Indigenous partners in research should be entitled and encouraged to review and approve not only publications but research grant proposals and research records. For example, within the Secwepemc Ethnobotany Project, research agreements with the Secwepemc Cultural Education Society have specified that research grant proposals, field notes and other records, and publications including graduate student dissertations would all be subject to a review and approval (for accuracy of cultural information) process. Furthermore, researchers have worked to establish a publication avenue that is acceptable to Secwepemc sponsors and collaborators to disseminate the collective research of the Secwepemc Ethnobotany Project. Two forthcoming volumes on Secwepemc (Shuswap) Ethnobotany (editors N. Turner and M. Ignace; and K. Bannister and N. Turner) have been approved in principle by the Shuswap Nation Tribal Council for copublication by the Secwepemc Cultural Education Society (Turner and Ignace in preparation; Bannister and Turner in preparation), and the copyright of these publications will be jointly held by the publisher and the Secwepemc Nation through the Secwepemc Cultural Education Society.[17]

Supporting Indigenous rights to protect cultural knowledge will require challenging some academic policies that inadvertently encourage exploitation of Indigenous cultural knowledge—such as career advancement and other rewards based on publication, industrial partnerships that focus on applied or patentable research, and university ownership policies. Many academics still publish based on the concept of free exchange of information, without regard for the current corporate assault on the public domain. Until legal means exist for supporting Indigenous rights to *not* have knowledge and resources privatized (Posey 1999), publication in such ignorance may serve to further disadvantage protection of cultural knowledge. As Barton puts it, "the question is one of drawing a rational line between a scientific world of free exchange and a proprietary world of controlled exchange" (Barton 1994: 220), and it is a question that, as academics, we all ought to consider. We must be informed and honest about the state of the public domain so that Indigenous peoples can truly make an informed choice about what it means today to share cultural knowledge with the wider public.

Conclusion

It is important to acknowledge that concerns expressed by Indigenous peoples about current third-party access to traditional plant knowledge are deeply linked to both the past and the present. Addressing the present therefore necessitates acknowledgment of historical events and the significance of their impacts. In British Columbia, for example, the legacy left by colonization has been particularly challenging in that the complex issues of land-title questions and negotiating Aboriginal treaties are only now being addressed. This leads to significant uncertainties in what the future holds for *all* peoples of British Columbia and how present actions will affect the future. Thus, fears for loss of control of traditional knowledge and access to resources, which seem to be at the heart of concerns about appropriation and commodification, must be understood in a broader context than simply economic. An understanding will require a careful unraveling of the inner weavings of this broader context, and this will necessitate adequate *time* to enable decision-making processes—which will offer a further challenge to many of us to reexamine our own relationships to time.

Indeed, as the quotation of Ford (1994: viii) at the beginning of this chapter indicates, ethnobotany certainly *is* "in"—especially in the area of ethnomedicine. However, as Frank (1992: 74) reminds us, "Life is not just curing diseases; instead life continues around and in spite of the disease. In the extreme, curing the disease may interfere with other activities that are most fundamental to living." And so the latter might be argued, in terms of the current frenzied exploration of the world's biocultural diversity to find medical remedies while biological, cultural, social, political, and economic ills persist. However, the current interest in ethnobotany and the wide audience presently captivated by plant medicines of Indigenous societies also offer a unique forum to bring forward this important complex of issues. And perhaps *this* may be used as "a step in the transformative process of decolonizing our history, a start toward undoing the colonial legacies that still characterize the relationships between Native and non-Native people in this country. Too often researchers have heard these stories without listening, listened without acting, and acted without listening again. It is time to break that cycle" (Kelm 1998: xxiii). In our consideration of measures to recognize and protect Indigenous claims to intellectual property, perhaps rethinking the role of publication is a means to break this cycle.

Acknowledgments

This chapter is a revision of a paper presented at the 98th annual meeting of the American Anthropology Association, Chicago, 1999. Financial support during the revision was provided by Global Forest Science (Grant number: GF-18-2000-75). This chapter has benefited greatly from discussions with K. Barrett, M. F. Brown, and G. P. Nicholas, and from editorial comments by I. E. P. Taylor. I thank my Ph.D. supervisor, Dr. Nancy Turner, members of the Secwepemc Nation, the Shuswap Nation Tribal Council, and the Secwepemc Cultural Education Society for opportunities to both study some of the chemistry underlying interrelationships between Secwepemc plants and peoples and to appreciate many of the complexities involved in current ethnobotanical research. I offer a special thanks to elder Dr. Mary Thomas (Nesconlith) and Chief Ron Ignace (Skeetchestn), who have unceasingly shared their knowledge, their insights, their homes, and more—their pride in Secwepemc culture, concern for the environment, and fearless thirst for knowledge shall surely serve as timeless inspiration to all peoples.

Notes

1. For example: the Kari-Oca Declaration (1992), the Mataatua Declaration (1993), the Julayinbul Statement (1993), the Sabah Statement (1995), the Suva Statement (1995), and the Union of British Columbia Indian Chiefs Statement on Protecting Knowledge (2000).
2. Community-level awareness is certainly on the increase in British Columbia, as indicated by local statements such as the St'at'imc Nation Statement of Proprietary Rights Over All Species on our Territory (2000).
3. Shuswap Nation Tribal Council Chiefs Council Meeting, motion #04/10/93 of support.
4. Secwepemc Plant Knowledge: More Than the Sum of the Parts. Research grant from the Social Sciences and Humanities Research Council of Canada to Dr. N. J. Turner (Principle Investigator).
5. Secwepemc (Shuswap) Ethnobotany: Expanding Horizons. Research grant from the Social Sciences and Humanities Research Council of Canada to Dr. N. J. Turner (Principle Investigator).
6. Secwepemctsin is the traditional language of the Secwepemc.
7. My doctoral dissertation, which contains this data, has been placed in restricted access for a minimum period of five years to allow time for appropriate publication decisions to be made in consultation with the Secwepemc Nation and the Secwepemc Cultural Education Society.
8. Ethical standards and guidelines are set out by the Tri-Council Policy Statement on Ethical Conduct for Research Involving Humans, which governs all

such academic research at Canadian institutions, as well as federal funding supported by the Social Sciences and Humanities Research Council of Canada (SSHRC), the Natural Sciences and Engineering Research Council of Canada (NSERC), and the Canadian Institutes of Health Research (CIHR). Document available online at: pre.ethics.gc.ca/english/policystatement/policystatement.cfm; last accessed on September 16, 2003. At the time of writing, specific discussions on research involving Aboriginal communities and the policy-related concerns raised in this chapter are in progress by SSHRC.

9. "Subjects" is the antiquated language of the ethical review process and is not necessarily a term deemed appropriate in referring to current ethnobotanical research in which Indigenous peoples are research partners or participants.

10. In Canada, there is a one-year exception to this clause: if the inventor, or someone who learned of the invention from the inventor, publicly discloses the invention, then a patent application can still be filed within one year (WWLIA 1995).

11. In Canada, information concerning the nature and use of an invention becomes public eighteen months from the filing date of the patent (Canadian Biotechnology Advisory Committee [CBAC] 2001).

12. Documents available from the International Society of Ethnobiology website at: guallart.dac.uga.edu/ISE; last accessed on September 16, 2003.

13. Document available from the Society for Economic Botany website at: www.econbot.org/ethics/professional_ethics.html; last accessed on September 16, 2003.

14. Some examples of international applications of the precautionary principle include the following:

- United Nations Environment Program (1989)
- Nordic Council's International Conference on Pollution of the Seas (1989)
- Bergen Declaration of Sustainable Development (1990)
- Bamako Convention on Hazardous Wastes within Africa (1991)
- Rio Declaration on Environment and Development (1992)
- Convention on Climate Change (1992)
- Maastricht Treaty on the European Union (1994)
- Cartagena Protocol on Biosafety (2000)
- The main tenet is stated in the preamble of the Convention on Biological Diversity (1992).

15. This Latin phrase is translated in wildlife law applications as: whenever there are doubts about the consequences of a certain action on wildlife, the decision must always be in favor of the interests of wildlife ecology (Backes and Verschuuren 1998).

16. An increasing number of Indigenous communities in Canada and elsewhere are developing research protocols that outline customary laws and local expectations for research conducted in their territory. For examples that are available on the Internet, see the Community-University Connections website at: web.uvic.ca/~scishops/resources.htm (date of last access: September 16, 2003), or the First Nation Cultural Heritage in Canada website at: www.lawualberta.ca/research/aboriginalculturalheritage/; last accessed on September 16, 2003.

17. Publication is anticipated in 2004–2005.

References

Avigad, G., and P. M. Dey
Carbohydrate Metabolism: Storage Carbohydrates. In *Plant Biochemistry*, edited by P. M. Dey and J. B. Harborne, 143–204. San Diego: Academic Press, 1997.

Backes, C. W., and J. M. Verschuuren
The Precautionary Principle in International European and Dutch Wildlife Law. *Colorado Journal of International Environmental Law and Policy*, vol. 9 (1998): 43–70.

Balza, F., I. Lopez, E. Rodriguez, and G. H. N. Towers
Dithiacyclohexadienes and Thiophenes from *Ambrosia chamissonis*. *Phytochemistry*, vol. 28 (1989): 3523–3524.

Bannister, K. P.
Chemistry Rooted in Cultural Knowledge: Unearthing the Links between Antimicrobial Properties and Traditional Knowledge in Food and Medicinal Plant Resources of the Secwepemc (Shuswap) First Nation. Ph.D. diss., Vancouver, Department of Botany, University of British Columbia, 2000.

Bannister, K., and K. Barrett
Challenging the Status Quo in Ethnobotany: A New Paradigm for Publication May Protect Cultural Knowledge and Traditional Resources. *Cultural Survival Quarterly*, vol. 24, no. 4 (2001): 10–13.

Weighing the Proverbial "Ounce of Prevention" versus the "Pound of Cure" in a Biocultural Context: A Role for the Precautionary Principle in Ethnobiological Research. In *Ethnobotany and Conservation of Biocultural Diversity*, edited by T. Carlson and L. Maffi. *Advances in Economic Botany*, vol. 15. Bronx: New York Botanical Garden Press, 2004.

Bannister, K. P., and the Secwepemc Cultural Education Society
Letter of Consent for the Secwepemc Ethnobotany Project: Ethnopharmacology of Secwepemc Traditional Medicines. Submitted in partial fulfillment of Ethical Review by the Behavioural Sciences Screening Committee for Research and Other Studies Involving Human Subjects. Vancouver: University of British Columbia, 1997.

Bannister, K. P., and N. J. Turner
Secwepemc People and Plants: Research Papers in Shuswap Ethnobotany. Edited by K. P. Bannister and N. J. Turner. Kamloops: Secwepemc Cultural Education Society, in preparation.

Barrett, K.
Canadian Agricultural Biotechnology: Risk Assessment and the Precautionary Principle. Ph.D. diss., Vancouver, Department of Botany, University of British Columbia, 1999.

Barton, J. H.
Ethnobotany and Intellectual Property Rights. In *Ethnobotany and the Search for New Drugs*, Ciba Foundation Symposium 185, edited by D. J. Chadwick and J. Marsh, 214–221. Chichester: John Wiley and Sons, 1994.

Battiste, M., and J. (S.) Y. Henderson
Protecting Indigenous Knowledge and Heritage: A Global Challenge. Saskatoon: Purich Publishing, 2000.

Berlin, B., and E. A. Berlin
Anthropological Issues in Medical Ethnobotany. In *Ethnobotany and the Search for New Drugs*. Ciba Foundation Symposium 185, edited by D. J. Chadwick and J. Marsh, 240–265. Chichester: John Wiley and Sons, 1994.

Boehmer-Christiansen, S.
The Precautionary Principle in Germany—Enabling Government. In *Interpreting the Precautionary Principle*, edited by T. O'Riordin and J. Cameron, 31–60. London: Earthscan, 1994.

Brown, M. F.
Can Culture Be Copyrighted? *Current Anthropology*, vol. 39 (1998): 193–222.

Canadian Biotechnology Advisory Committee (CBAC)
Biotechnology and the Patenting of Higher Life Forms Consultation Document. Ottawa: CBAC, 2001.

Champagne, D. E., J. T. Arnason, B. J. R. Philogene, P. Morand, and J. Lam
Light-Mediated Allelochemical Effects of Naturally Occurring Polyacetylenes and Thiophenes from Asteraceae on Herbivorous Insects. *Journal of Chemical Ecology*, vol. 12 (1986): 835–858.

Cox, P. A.
The Ethnobotanical Approach to Drug Discovery: Strengths and Limitations. In *Ethnobotany and the Search for New Drugs.* Ciba Foundation Symposium 185, edited by D. J. Chadwick and J. Marsh, 25–41. Chichester: John Wiley and Sons, 1994.

Cragg, G. M., M. R. Boyd, J. H. Cardellina II, D. J. Newman, K. M. Snader, and T. G. McCloud
Ethnobotany and Drug Discovery: The Experience of the US National Cancer Institute. In *Ethnobotany and the Search for New Drugs.* Ciba Foundation Symposium 185, edited by D. J. Chadwick and J. Marsh, 178–196. Chichester: John Wiley and Sons, 1994.

The Crucible Group
People, Plants, and Patents: The Impact of Intellectual Property on Trade, Plant Biodiversity, and Rural Society. Ottawa: International Development Research Centre, 1994.

Dojillo-Mooney, J., J. Page, M. B. Isman, and G. H. N. Towers
Tolerance to Thiarubrines from *Ambrosia chamissonis* by the rare Moth *Lasionycta wyatti*. *Journal of Chemical Ecology*, vol. 25 (1999): 1369–1382.

Elisabetsky, E., and D. A. Posey
Ethnopharmacological Search for Antiviral Compounds: Treatment of Gastrointestinal Disorders by Kayapó Medical Specialists. In *Ethnobotany and the Search for New Drugs.* Ciba Foundation Symposium 185, edited by D. J. Chadwick and J. Marsh, 77–94. Chichester: John Wiley and Sons, 1994.

Ford, R. I.
Preface to the Second Edition. Ethnobotany—1994. In *The Nature and Status of Ethnobotany*, 2d ed., edited by R. I. Ford, viii–xxxii. Anthropological Papers, Museum of Anthropology, University of Michigan, No. 67. Ann Arbor: The Museum of Anthropology 1994.

Frank, A.
Commentary: "Normal" Non compliance. *Second Opinion* (January 1992): 74.

Gibson, G. R., E. R. Beatty, X. Wang, and J. H. Cummings
Selective Stimulation of Bifidobacteria in the Human Colon by Oligofructose and Inulin. *Gasterenterology*, vol. 108 (1995): 975–982.

Hitchcock, C. L., and A. Cronquist
Flora of the Pacific Northwest. An Illustrated Manual. Seattle: University of Washington Press, 1973.

Hudson, J. B., E. A. Graham, G. Chan, A. J. Finlayson, and G. H. N. Towers
Comparison of the Antiviral Effects of Naturally Occurring Thiophenes and Polyacetylenes. *Planta Medica*, vol. 6 (1986): 453–457.

Ignace, M. B.
Shuswap. In *Plateau, Volume 12, Handbook of North American Indians*, edited by D. E. Walker, 203–219. Washington, D.C.: Smithsonian Institution, 1998.

Julayinbul Statement
Julayinbul Conference on Intellectual and Cultural Property Rights, Jingarrba, Australia, 27 November 1993.

Kari-Oca Declaration and Indigenous Peoples Earth Charter
The World Conference of Indigenous Peoples on Territory, Environment and Development. Kari-Oca, Brazil, 25–30 May 1992.

Kelm, M.-E.
*Colonizing Bodies: Aboriginal Health and Healing in British Columbia 1900–50.*Vancouver: UBC Press, 1998.

King, S. R., and M. S. Tempestra
From Shaman to Human Clinical Trials: The Role of Industry in Ethnobotany, Conservation and Community Reciprocity. In *Ethnobotany and the Search for New Drugs*. Ciba Foundation Symposium 185, edited by D. J. Chadwick and J. Marsh, 197–213. Chichester: John Wiley and Sons, 1994.

Laird, S. A., M. N. Alexiades, K. P. Bannister, and D. A. Posey
Publication of Biodiversity Results and the Flow of Knowledge. In *Biodiversity and Traditional Knowledge: Equitable Partnerships in Practice*, edited by S. A. Laird, 77–101. London: Earthscan Publications, 2002.

Loub, W. D., N. R. Farnsworth, D. D. Soejarto, and M. L. Quinn
NAPRALERT: Computer Handling of Natural Product Research Data. *Journal of Chemical Information and Computer Science*, vol. 25 (1985): 99–103.

Mann, H.
Indigenous Peoples and the Use of Intellectual Property Rights in Canada: Case Studies Relating to Intellectual Property Rights and the Protection of Biodiversity. Report submitted to Industry Canada, Intellectual Property Policy Directorate, and to the Canadian Working Group on Article 8 (j) of the Convention on Biological Diversity. Sponsored by Industry Canada, Intellectual Property Policy Directorate, 1997.

Martin, G. J.
Conservation and Ethnobotanical Exploration. In *Ethnobotany and the Search for New Drugs*. Ciba Foundation Symposium 185, edited by D. J. Chadwick and J. Marsh, 229–239. Chichester: John Wiley and Sons, 1994.

Mataatua Declaration
The Mataatua Declaration on Cultural and Intellectual Property Rights of Indigenous Peoples. Whakatane, Aotearoa/New Zealand, 12–18 June 1993.

Matsuura, H., G. Saxena, S. Farmer, R. Hancock, and G. H. N. Towers
An Antibacterial Thiophene from *Balsamorhiza sagittata. Planta Medica* 62 (1996): 65–66.

McCutcheon, A. R., S. M. Ellis, R. E. W. Hancock, and G. H. N. Towers
Antibiotic Screening of Medicinal Plants of British Columbian Native Peoples. *Journal of Ethnopharmacology*, vol. 37 (1992): 213–223.

Antifungal Screening of Medicinal Plants of British Columbian Native Peoples. *Journal of Ethnopharmacology*, vol. 44 (1994): 157–169.

Mullin, W., J. S. Peacock, D. C. Loewen, and N. J. Turner
Macronutrients Content of Yellow Glacier Lily and Balsamroot; Root Vegetables Used by Indigenous Peoples of Northwestern North America. *Food Research International*, vol. 30 (1998): 769–775.

Noss, R.
A Broad Context for Restoring Ecosystems. Keynote Address presented at the Helping the Land Heal Conference on Ecological Restoration in British Columbia, Victoria. November 5–8, 1998.

Parish, R., R. Coupé, and D. Lloyd

Plants of Southern Interior British Columbia. Vancouver: B.C. Ministry of Forests and Lone Pine Publishing, 1996.

Peacock, S. L.

Putting Down Roots: The Emergence of Wild Plant Food Production on the Canadian Plateau. Ph.D. diss., Victoria, University of Victoria, 1998.

Peteru, C.

Indigenous Peoples Knowledge and Intellectual Property Rights Working Paper. *Proceedings of the Indigenous Peoples Knowledge and Intellectual Property Rights Consultation,* 85–133. 24–27 April, Suva, Fiji: Pacific Concerns Resource Centre, 1997.

Posey, D. A.

Comment on "The Development of Indigenous Knowledge." *Current Anthropology*, vol. 39 (1998): 242.

Safeguarding Traditional Resource Rights of Indigenous Peoples. In *Ethnoecology: Situated Knowledge/Located Lives,* edited by V. D. Nazarea, 217–229. Tucson: University of Arizona Press, 1999.

Posey D. A., and G. Dutfield

Beyond Intellectual Property: Toward Traditional Resource Rights for Indigenous Peoples and Local Communities. Ottawa: IDRC, 1996.

Research and Information System on Non-Aligned and Developing Countries (RIS), Kalpavriksh, and IUCN—The World Conservation Union

Recommendations from the Workshop on Biodiversity Conservation and Intellectual Property Rights, New Delhi, 29–31 January 1999.

Roberfroid, M.

Dietary Fiber, Inulin, and Oligofructose: A Review Comparing Their Physiological Effects. *Critical Reviews in Food Science and Nutrition*, vol. 33 (1993): 103–148.

Sabah Statement

Statement of the Asian Consultation Workshop on the Protection and Conservation of Indigenous Knowledge, TVRC Tamunan, Sabah, East Malaysia, 24–27 February 1995.

Schultes, R. E.

Amazonian Ethnobotany and the Search for New Drugs. In *Ethnobotany and the Search for New Drugs.* Ciba Foundation Symposium 185, edited by D. J. Chadwick and J. Marsh, 106–115. Chichester: John Wiley and Sons, 1994.

St'at'imc Nation Statement
St'at'imc Nation Statement of Proprietary Rights Over All Species on our Territory. St'at'mic Nation, Mount Currie, BC, Lil'wat Nation. 22 February. Presented at the Union of British Columbia Indian Chiefs Protecting Knowledge: Traditional Resources in the New Millennium Conference, Vancouver, British Columbia, Canada, 23–26 February 2000.

Stephenson, D. J.
A Practical Primer on Intellectual Property Rights in a Contemporary Ethnoecological Context. In *Ethnoecology: Situated Knowledge/Located Lives*, edited by V. D. Nazarea, 230–248. Tucson: University of Arizona Press, 1999.

Suva Statement
Final Statement of the Consultation on Indigenous Peoples' Knowledge and Intellectual Property Rights, Suva, Fiji, 24–27 April 1995.

Towers, G. H. N., A. R. McCutcheon, H. Matsuura, J. Page, G. Saxena, S. Farmer, E. Gibbons, T. E. Roberts, L. A. Babiuk, L. M. Thornson, R. W. Stokes, P. Sokol, and H. Klingemann
Antimicrobial Activities of Phytochemicals from British Columbian Medicinal Plants. In *Chemistry, Biological and Pharmacological Properties of Medicinal Plants from the Americas,* edited by K. Hostettmann, M. P. Gupta, and A. Marston, 125–142. Switzerland: Harwood Academic Publishers, 1997.

Towers, G. H. N., J. E. Page, and J. B. Hudson
Light-Mediated Biological Activities from Plants and Fungi. *Current Organic Chemistry,* vol. 1 (1997): 395–414.

Turner, N. J.
Food Plants of Interior First Peoples. Royal British Columbia Museum Handbook. Vancouver: U.B.C. Press, 1997.

Turner N. J., and M. Ignace
Plants of the Secwepemc (Shuswap) First People. Edited by N. J. Turner and M. Ignace. Kamloops: Secwepemc Cultural Education Society, in preparation.

Union of British Columbia Indian Chiefs Statement on Protecting Knowledge
Spirit of the Conference Statement. Protecting Knowledge: Traditional Resource Rights in the New Millennium, Vancouver, British Columbia, Canada, 23–26 February 2000.

Van Loo, J., C. Coussement, L. De Leenher, H. Hoebregs, and G. Smits
On the Presence of Inulin and Oligofructose As Natural Ingredients in the Western Diet. *Critical Reviews in Food Science and Nutrition,* vol. 35 (1995): 525–552.

Wang, X., and G. R. Gibson
Effects of the *in vitro* Fermentation of Oligofructose and Inulin by Bacteria Growing in the Human Large Intestine. *Journal of Applied Bacteriology*, vol. 75 (1993): 373–380.

World Wide Legal Information Association (WWLIA)
Canadian Patent Law. Canadian Intellectual Property Office. Hull: Industry Canada, 1995.

CHAPTER 11

INTELLECTUAL PROPERTY RIGHTS AND INDIGENOUS CULTURAL HERITAGE IN ARCHAEOLOGY

George P. Nicholas and Kelly P. Bannister

One topic that will likely figure prominently in anthropology in the twenty-first century is the relationship between knowledge and power. Anthropology will influence, and be influenced by, aspects of Indigenous sovereignty, rights to resources and intellectual properties, education, and social responsibility. Not surprisingly, these issues will also involve archaeology. Indeed, the frequent use of the phrase "Who owns the past?" in book and journal article titles (McGhee 1989; McBryde 1985) reflects a growing awareness by archaeologists of issues relating to material and intellectual property rights. This chapter focuses on the topic of intellectual property rights (IPR) within the context of archaeology and the degree to which these rights may be employed by Indigenous peoples as tools in the protection of their cultural heritage. It also examines the implications that IPR issues may have for archaeologists.

For many years the authors of this chapter have each worked closely with several First Nations in British Columbia, Canada. In addition, we have monitored the evolving relationship between Indigenous peoples and archaeology (Nicholas) or ethnobotany (Bannister) worldwide. A key concern that has emerged in these realms is the degree of participation in, and control of, research processes and outcomes that Indigenous peoples have today, and how these are affecting, or will affect, the status quo of the research environment.

In archaeology especially, much attention has been given to the concept of "working together" with Indigenous peoples, who are increasingly involved in identifying, interpreting, and protecting their own archaeological past. This involvement has increased in recent years to the point where the term *Indigenous archaeology* has become a widely recognized dimension of contemporary archaeology (Nicholas and Andrews 1997; Watkins 2000). These efforts have been very much directed toward involving Indigenous peoples in the *process* of doing archaeology; it is clear that Indigenous involvement represents an important element of all future archaeological study (Davidson, Lovell-Jones, and Bancroft 1995; Dongoske, Aldenderfer, and Doehner 2000). However, little attention has been paid to the *products* of doing archaeology, regardless of who is doing it. And it is here that we enter a realm in which rights to intellectual property and cultural heritage need to be carefully considered.

Rights to intellectual property (or the "creation of mind" that can be protected by legal means) as applied to cultural knowledge is a rapidly expanding topic, particularly in relation to biotechnology, medicine, and ecological or ethnobotanical knowledge (Bannister 2000; Bannister, chapter 10 in this volume; Brush and Stabinsky 1996; Dutfield 2000; Greaves 1994; Laird 2002; Posey and Dutfield 1996; Swanson 1995). The issue of owning culture has also been explored by Brown (1998) and others. However, most archaeologists have yet to consider how IPR may affect their research. While material property issues certainly have arisen in archaeology and been especially contentious in terms of repatriation and reburial (Bray and Killion 1994; Mihesuah 2000; Thomas 2000), the question of IPR has not yet appeared. Its absence in archaeology may be due to the complexity of the issues and to the challenges of defining "intellectual property" beyond the realm of technological innovation. However, archaeological sites and their contents, as well as types of information derived from archaeological research, potentially fall within the realm of *both* material and intellectual property.

Examination of trends in other disciplines may reveal a glimpse of what archaeology might expect in the coming years. For example, in ethnobotany, concern over the exploitation of medicinal knowledge of Indigenous peoples has been widespread and growing (see Bannister, chapter 10 in this volume). Although the search for cancer cures and other remedies may be seen as a noble cause, "bioprospecting" in its many incarnations has become big business. While notable exceptions are beginning to emerge, most bioprospecting is still perceived as market-driven and largely divorced from Indigenous participation and concerns.[1] If such developments in ethnobotany and related disciplines are any indication, then the descendants of the people responsible for the archaeological record are similarly likely to be concerned about the appropriation, misuse, and loss of control of knowledge, and loss of access to its products. On the other hand, researchers equally may be concerned about censorship of their work, loss of control over data, restrictions on use of knowledge, and suppression of academic freedom—all of which may affect academic/professional credentials, promotion, and continued research funding.

At the heart of these concerns is *loss of control* of knowledge. An obvious tension between the different actors exists in terms of the importance, potential utility, and *meaning* of knowledge. Within archaeology at least, we suggest this tension is better understood when "knowledge" is seen as both part of cultural *property* and integral to cultural *identity*. From this perspective, the appropriation and commodification of knowledge acquire added complexity, and control of knowledge becomes vital to cultural integrity.

In this chapter, we examine various types of IPR and their potential degree of influence in archaeology, a topic that we have also explored in greater detail elsewhere (Nicholas and Bannister [*forthcoming*]). The first part of this chapter examines the material and intellectual products of the archaeological record. We examine the mechanisms that may serve to protect such products, as well as examples of their appropriation and commodification. The second part identifies some of the concerns and responses of Aboriginal peoples in Canada and Indigenous peoples elsewhere about their material culture and intellectual property. We conclude by describing a recently initiated collaborative project involving intellectual property and protection of First Nations' cultural heritage in Canada that seeks to address some of the issues we raise.[2]

The Products of Archaeology

Since its beginnings in antiquarianism, archaeology has long been focused on the material record of past civilizations (Trigger 1989; Willey and Sabloff 1993)—the projectile points, potsherds, sculptures, and human remains that are the legacy of ancient lives. While the discipline has matured significantly with a greater emphasis on the people behind the artifacts—especially since the plea for a more anthropological archaeology was raised by Taylor (1948), Willey and Phillips (1958: 2), and others—archaeologists remain dependent upon material culture simply because it provides the only access to the past.

Material culture is thus the *means*; what we do with the artifacts is another matter. The product of artifact classification, faunal analysis, and other forms of archaeological research is scientific knowledge that enables us to understand the world in new ways. Indeed, as David Thomas has sagely noted (1998: 96), "it's not what you find, but what you find out"—a clear recognition that the intellectual dimension of doing archaeology is, in the end, what really counts.

Aside from unearthing artifacts, archaeology produces culture histories and chronologies and illuminates the processes by which things have changed. It can also have practical applications, ranging from studies that reveal the (in)effectiveness of both modern landfills (Rathje 1991) and efforts to restore the Atlantic salmon fishery (Carlson 1995) to the use of forensic archaeological methods to identity victims of warfare and natural disasters (e.g., Mann, Anderson, Holland, Rankin, and Webb 2003). The products of archaeology also reflect past Indigenous knowledge systems (e.g., Erickson 2000) and serve as symbols of cultural identity and worldview that are still important to many of the descendants of the sites' creators (e.g., the site of Great Zimbabwe [Ndoro 1997] from which the former Rhodesia took its new name). Archaeological sites thus represent both material culture and intellectual property in a variety of ways.

What types and levels of protection exist for this heritage? And to what degree do the descendants have rights over *intellectual* aspects of heritage? In Canada and the United States, the protection of archaeological materials is based exclusively on the notion of *physical* property. While legislation protecting *intellectual* property is extensive in both countries (see Neumann and Sanford 2001; Parks Canada 2000), and could offer additional protection to archaeological sites, no explicit protection for the intellectual component of the archaeological record exists under any federal, provincial, or state heritage policies. Most archaeologists, in fact, would not explicitly recognize an intellectual component at all. Even if they did, many would argue that the great age of most archaeological sites puts this information in the realm of shared heritage, in the same way that many academics and professionals view (and perhaps mistrust the integrity of) oral histories and medicinal folklore.

The situation is very different for communities with a vested interest in their own heritage sites. Aboriginal Australians, for example, have expressed the concern that cultural heritage laws focus on tangible cultural heritage (e.g., specific areas, objects, and sites), but the intangible aspects of sites (e.g., associated stories, songs, and dreaming tracks) are unprotected (Janke 1998: xxiv; also Janke 2002). Likewise, Battiste and Henderson (2000: 66–67) argue that: "Indigenous peoples construct their teachings around the belief that at certain places there is a sacred ambiance that can and does empower human consciousness and spirituality."

Does IPR legislation provide new avenues that Indigenous peoples can pursue to protect their cultural and intellectual property as *they* define these entities? What are the consequences? Our discussion here addresses two complementary dimensions of archaeological heritage—material culture and intellectual property—and identifies some of the threats they face.

Commodifying Material Culture

The appropriation and commodification of cultural knowledge and property—that is, taking and affixing a price to what many would consider inalienable and priceless—affects the cultural identity and integrity of contemporary Indigenous societies. This raises several complex questions for consideration. Should cultural and intellectual property be protected from such exploitation? If so, should protection be from outside interests only or from *all* users, including Indigenous peoples themselves? What if Indigenous groups want to exploit their own past for commercial gain? Should IPR be used discriminately to protect the past, to preferentially support Indigenous rights? What are the potential consequences of appropriation and commodification of material property? Does a *Homo erectus* skull belong as much to white-skinned descendants, as it does to the African paleoanthropologist who found it, or to the villagers in whose territory it had resided?

The collection and sale of antiquities has gone on for thousands of years (Trigger 1989: 27–72). In the recent past, Pompeii was mined for artifacts by Italians, the British bought the marble frieze from the Parthenon in Greece, the French collected antiquities from Egypt, and other empires gained similar trophies from the lands they colonized. Today, however, the antiquities market (in all of its guises) has reached an unprecedented level as it responds to growing market demands. Those participating in the collection, trade, and sale range from Missouri farmers who collect arrow points as they plow their fields to wealthy patrons of the arts who buy artifacts to "save" them from deteriorating in their place of origin. There are hobby clubs, artifact shows and sales, and websites (including eBay) where all varieties of items prized for their age, rarity, exoticness, or "Aboriginalness" can be bought or sold. Artifact prices can be found in collector's magazines (e.g., *Indian Artifact Magazine* [$20 for a certain projectile point]) to higher-end publications (*American Indian Art* [$80,000 for an Apache basket]). For those who can't afford the real thing, or who prefer replicas for ethical or other reasons, there are also many sources.[3]

Indigenous peoples also contribute to this, as evidenced by the activities of *huaqueros*, the often-impoverished Indigenous Central Americans who loot tombs and then sell the artifacts to support their families (Matsuda 1998). So-called subsistence digging also occurs in North America, including instances where the profits from artifact sales may provide the means of acquiring the knowledge or skills that allow Aboriginal people to improve their circumstances (Hollowell, chapter 3 in this volume; Staley 1993). Julie Hollowell-Zimmer (2003: 10) writes: "Once a young woman brought a newly-found artifact to show me, an ivory animal worth many thousands of dollars on the market. 'I know I shouldn't sell this, Julie,' she said, 'but it will help pay for my college education.'" Aboriginal people may also collect arrow points and other artifacts for the same reason as non-Aboriginal people—out of interest in the past or the innate human attribute of collecting things.

The appropriation and commodification of artifacts may take less obvious forms. Images of artifacts and sites, sometimes including those cherished or sacred to past or present Indigenous peoples, are appropriated in many ways, from international to local levels. Such images may be associated with national identity, such as the strong association of British identity with Stonehenge. They may appear in magazine ads, billboards, wine bottle labels, postcards, and other media, such as Sherwin-Williams's use of Upper Paleolithic rock art in advertising for house paint. Or Apotex Inc.'s use of a Haida totem pole in advertising a new health product called "Apo-Sucralfate" as "Distinctly Canadian." Across the world, appropriated images are often found on T-shirts and other tourist paraphernalia, as was the case for images of sacred petroglyphs on Gabriola Island, British Columbia, until the Snuneymuxw First Nation obtained legal protection for the images against commercial use.[4]

Even anthropologists and archaeologists, who presumably should be more sensitive than others to issues of cultural appropriation and commodification, may assume that ancient objects become divorced from contemporary cultural impacts once they enter the public domain. The illustration of a carved stone figurine bowl on the program cover of the 1992 Northwest Anthropology Conference raised the ire of several Native American conference attendees who considered it inappropriate since such bowls still have spiritual value to them. We suspect that privately held objections to such display are far more common than publicly expressed ones. It is our experience that many Indigenous peoples are hesitant to raise objections in public, even in circumstances in which they have been deeply offended. This appears to be most common with elders, perhaps in part because they may have already suffered much hardship or abuse through residential school systems and the like. It is ironic that some elders may be so hesitant to comment on the appropriateness of the casual public use or display of items of their heritage, given that they are typically the most knowledgeable individuals within their communities regarding their cultural traditions and spiritual values. One result is that archaeologists and others may not learn of the spiritual values of things or certain places, and thus potentially avoid future offensive behavior.

Archaeologists constantly use artifacts as illustrations in their publications, and generally seek permission only from the museums that "own" those items. The covers of many archaeological journals contain stylized or actual representations of a wide array of artifacts, rock art, and sites (e.g., *American Antiquity, Antiquity, Canadian Journal of Archaeology, Latin American Antiquity*). In most of these instances, the illustrations are used as a celebration of past cultures, but some Indigenous peoples may feel otherwise, as Amy Roberts (personal communication, 2001) noted regarding objections to the stylized naked human figures that grace the cover of the journal *Australian Archaeology*.

There are, of course, more blatant appropriations of aspects of Indigenous cultural heritage, such as the unauthorized use of Aboriginally produced images, whether ancient or modern. The commodification of Aboriginal designs has been widespread in Australia, particularly those created by contemporary Aboriginal artists (Johnson 1996). While legal cases concerning appropriated designs may be won by contemporary artists or their clans or initiation groups, the situation is significantly different with more ancient work. Worldwide, rock art images representing the ritual knowledge of past peoples appear in books and other media, but seldom with attribution to the descendants who still occupy that territory. Tracking down the traditional owners can be difficult. Furthermore, in those instances where permission to reproduce those images has been obtained from Indigenous individuals, it is not always clear whether that permission carries with it the approval of the larger community, tribe, or nation.

Regardless of the original intention of their creators, appreciation of artifacts and rock art was very different in the past than it is today, as images are more widely disseminated and easily altered with current technology. The following anecdote recounted by one of us (Nicholas) illustrates how easy it is to alter an idea expressed in tangible form, how little control we have over dissemination of the original idea, and how difficult it is to make proprietorial claims of an intellectual nature within various high-tech media:

> About ten years ago, I was preparing illustrations for a lecture on hunter-gatherer economy. I was thinking about "access to the means of production" and other ideas influenced by Karl Marx. In my whimsy, I pasted Marx's head onto the body of a !Kung hunter, and then onto an Upper Paleolithic "Venus" figurine [figure 11.1]. I sent copies of these hybrid images to a few colleagues, including one at the University of Massachusetts, where I had completed my Ph.D. Recently, I learned that my Venus/Marx figure appeared on a T-shirt prepared for the department's 25th anniversary. I was both amused and honored that this late night whimsy had found fame. But in thinking about copyright and ownership of ideas, I wondered where my intellectual creation might ultimately end up. Perhaps an enterprising person, seeing the shirt, will create a series of T-shirts featuring famous people on Venus figurine bodies. (Nicholas and Bannister forthcoming)

Appropriating Intellectual Property

There are parallels to intellectual property with what has occurred (or may yet occur) with the material property of Indigenous peoples. Cultural knowledge, once restricted within specific cultural systems, is now more widely available, but seldom due to the decisions of the communities themselves. Immense public interest in "things Aboriginal" has for centuries prompted collecting, scrutinizing, and even imitation of Indian

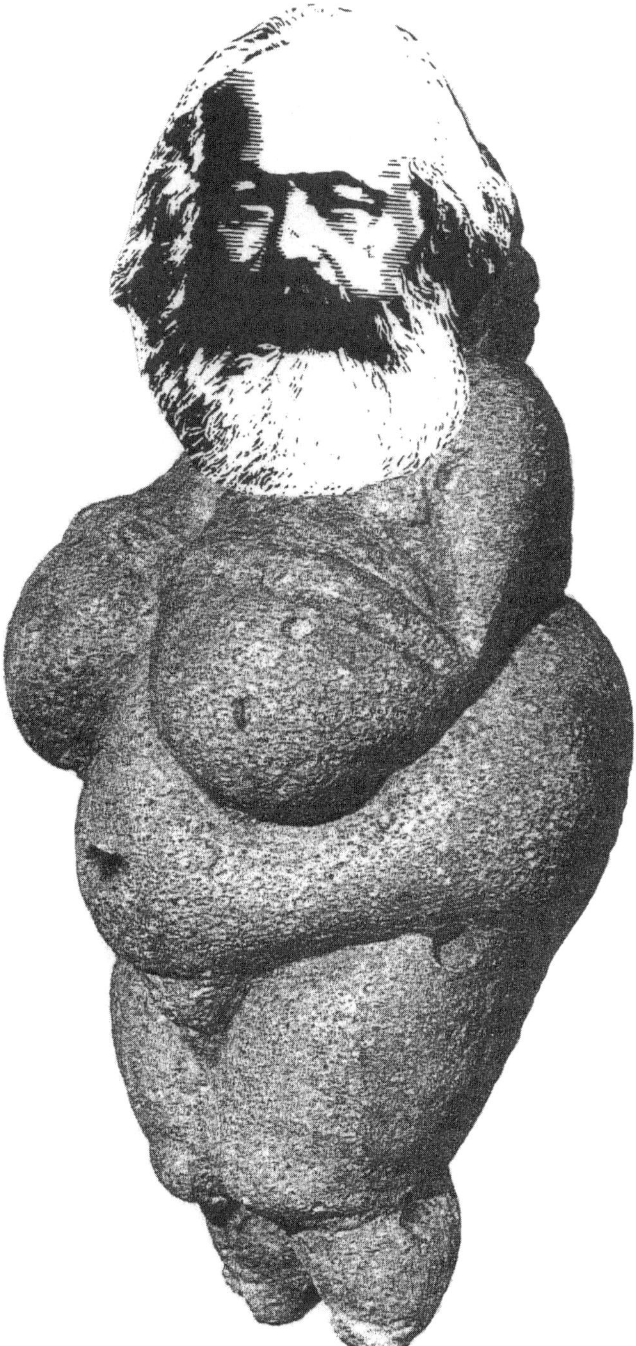

Figure 11.1. "The Venus Marx Figurine." Courtesy of George Nicholas. (Nicholas and Bannister *forthcoming*).

curios and life-ways. The lure of the North American Indian is by no means limited to North America, as evidenced by German Indian clubs (Calloway, Gmunden, and Zantop 2002), whose members attempt to create or re-create a Native American identity. Photographers Andrea Robbins and Max Becher have magnificently captured the essence of two such events called "Cologne Karnival" and "Karl May Festival" in photos that were on display in New York at Leslie Tonkonw Artworks and Projects (See figures 11.2, 11.3, and 11.4.).[5] As the photographers note:

> No country has more of a fascination with Native Americans than Germany. For more than a century, hobby clubs, open air theater festivals, fairs, and carnival costumes have been developing. Besides a deep-rooted romantic view of a pre-industrial past, and the imagery of Cowboy Western movies, the primary cause of this fascination is the work of the 19th century writer Karl May. Although he didn't visit North America until late in life, he wrote many novels about the Wild West, portraying Native Americans as heroes and whites as villains. (Robbins and Becher 1997/98)

While the type of cultural appropriation represented by these festivals, and by the hobby clubs, is interesting in its own right, they have a deeper, more disturbing history:

> Although the "pro-Indian" slant of Karl May can be understood as a progressive, anti-colonial message, his writings were also an important part of Nazi mythology. German fascists identified with the Indian as noble savage and as the victim of a modern, corrupt, overly intellectual world. The Nazis' home-spun victim mythology formed the basis for retaliatory aggression against those who they perceived as threats. Ironically, while Hitler was researching American Indian reservations as models for concentration camps, he made his generals carry around volumes of Karl May's writings.
>
> After World War II, the east-west division of Germany caused a split in the culture of Native American emulation. In East Germany Indian fan clubs increased because they were a legal opportunity to gather in large numbers and Karl May's anti-American/anti-capitalist messages conformed to eastern bloc doctrine. In West Germany, the influx of

Figure 11.2. "Blonde," from the series "Karl May Festival," by Andrea Robbins and Max Becher 1997/98. Included with permission of the photographers and courtesy of Sonnabend Gallery, New York.

Figure 11.3. "Chief," from the series "Karl May Festival," by Andrea Robbins and Max Becher 1997/98. Included with permission of the photographers and courtesy of Sonnabend Gallery, New York.

Figure 11.4. "Campfire," from the series "Karl May Festival," by Andrea Robbins and Max Becher 1997/98. Included with permission of the photographers and courtesy of Sonnabend Gallery, New York.

American popular culture expanded the imagery of the American West, but conflicted with Karl May's sympathetic descriptions of Indigenous Americans. Although an intense pro-Americanism developed after World War II, the notion of Americans as invaders, of course, ties in with the resentment felt during the U.S. military occupation. Also, postwar Germans, discouraged from nationalism and group ritual, sense a permission to find themselves in other ethnic groups. And, perhaps, criticism of atrocities against Native Americans also gives Germans some sense of relief from their own shame of the holocaust.

Karl May's birthday is celebrated annually in his hometown of Radebeul, near Dresden, by hundreds of Germans dressed as Native Americans. Loosely formed groups, called tribes, gather from all over the country. The local tribe is led by the self-proclaimed chief of this area, Old Bull, also known as Gerhard Fischer. Tourists stream through the two-day festival to witness the various encampments and lifestyle enactments. A

> broad range of Native American cultures are painstakingly researched in the belief that they are being perverted by modernity and in need of outside preservation. However, artifacts and customs are imaginatively combined, with little concern or explanation as to which specific nations they represent. (Robbins and Becher 1997/98)

Not surprisingly, intellectual aspects of cultural property and cultural identity have also been appropriated and sometimes commodified in various ways, including traditional land-use studies (see Markey 2001), use of human remains (e.g., a T-shirt featuring "Kennewick Man"[6]), and the re-creation of the past through tourism and museums (e.g., Jameson 1997). To take the last example, the appropriation of Indigenous life-ways through cultural tourism has become a significant industry worldwide. Many living museums include reenactments of life in the past, utilizing speech and people/actors/guides in period clothes to represent both the colonizers and the colonized. The "best" of these, such as Colonial Williamsburg in Virginia, include participant voices; the "worst" blatantly exploit and stereotype Indigenous peoples—especially when those re-creations don't include Indigenous guidance in their development or participation in their delivery. In North America, Africa, Australia, and the Pacific, however, there is now a proliferation of Aboriginal heritage parks, tours, workshops, and "experiences" that are Aboriginally conceived, developed, and run (see figures 11.5 and 11.6 for specific examples). The way that Aboriginal communities choose to present themselves is critical to whether the experience is perceived and appreciated as one of cultural education and sharing, or criticized as cultural "prostitution."

We can also look at the use of past knowledge rediscovered through archaeology to address modern-day problems. One example of new uses of ancient knowledge is archaeologist Payson Sheets's manufacture of obsidian blades as scalpels for use in eye surgery (Sheets 1989). The extremely sharp edge of flaked obsidian is up to 1,000 times sharper than surgical steel, a feature that hastens healing and reduces scarring. While stone blades were made by all past human societies, this technology was potentially patentable because it was a new use. Our search for patents in the U.S. Patent Office database, however, did not identify any patents. A second application of ancient knowledge is illustrated by the rediscovery and reintroduction of raised field farming techniques by archaeologists in

Figure 11.5. A guided canoe trip by Tla-ook Cultural Adventures, a First Nations-owned and -operated company in coastal British Columbia that invites customers to paddle with Nuu-chah-nulth guides aboard dugout canoes and learn about Nuu-chah-nulth culture and the environment. Courtesy of Jacqueline Windh, www.windhphotos.com.

Bolivia and Ecuador (Erickson 1998). Such highly productive, sustainable, and ecologically savvy techniques were once widely employed in Central and South America (Coe 1964; Parsons and Denevan 1967). Does the reintroduction of forgotten raised field farming represent intellectual property? If so, the question is *for whom*—the archaeologists or the descendants of the people who developed the technology in the first place?

Indigenous Concerns and Responses

We have argued that different forms of archaeological information about cultural heritage can be considered material and intellectual property. Our discussion now considers the means by which Indigenous peoples may seek control over the knowledge that this information represents, through existing legal rights and IPR mechanisms or other

Figure 11.6. Perpetuation and presentation of traditional activities through cultural tourism, Cook Islands Heritage Centre, Cook Islands. Courtesy of G. P. Nicholas.

strategies. In British Columbia, these range from the implementation of local Indigenous protocols to registering trademarks on traditional images or sacred names, to denying researchers access to sites and site data.

Cultural knowledge and cultural identity are integrally linked to, and reflected by, both a society's material culture and its intellectual traditions.

As stated at the onset, control over access to knowledge is thus situated at the core of the issue since this control helps to define or restore cultural identity for present and future Indigenous societies. It is something long a part of autonomous Aboriginal societies in North America and elsewhere. Whether during the historic or precontact periods, control of knowledge was expressed through family ownership of songs and religious ceremonies, for example. Only family members (or in other contexts, initiated individuals) could possess and employ the knowledge associated with songs, masks, and places (e.g., Harris 1997).

In similar fashion, archaeologists have controlled the dissemination of information derived from the past in a variety of ways. These include research and publishing practices (i.e., decisions as to what aspects of research will be pursued and/or published), restricting access of site location information to the public (the "uninitiated"), or using the authority of academic credentials to promote certain ideas and interpretations, often at the expense of others. While such "management" helps to preserve sites, there are potentially negative aspects (Nicholas, in press). For example, much archaeological information has been kept from Indigenous communities, often inadvertently. Since archaeologists are in the position to choose what they will or will not publish, information potentially useful to communities may simply not be available because it fell outside of the interests of the investigator and was not pursued. Access to knowledge is obviously the first of several key steps in more equitable control of knowledge.

Beyond relying on existing heritage protection legislation, is it possible to increase Indigenous control of cultural knowledge and property through legal tools such as IPR mechanisms? If so, what are the implications for future archaeological research? We offer a series of examples that may begin to elucidate answers to these complex questions.

Examples of Indigenous groups seeking to control access to or use of their past are on the rise in many parts of the country, and local protocols are increasingly used as the basis for research agreements between the communities and outside researchers. Protocols of various forms have been developed and articulated in writing by many Aboriginal groups in British Columbia. Some groups require their own heritage permit in lieu of one issued by the Archaeology Branch (the component of the Ministry of Sustainable Resources that oversees cultural heritage matters within the province). For example, the Sto:lo Nation states: "We hereby declare that all artifacts recovered from our traditional campsites, ceremonial sites, villages, burial grounds and archaeological sites are the rightful property of the Sto:lo" (Sto:lo Nation 1995). The Kamloops Band, Secwepemc Nation, have a more inclusive archaeological permitting system that requires anyone wishing to do archaeological research on their reservation to sign a protocol (Kamloops Indian Band 1997). The provisions of their archaeological permit refer only to physical property and research results; intellectual property is not mentioned. The Kamloops provision does, however, include "data" in listing the products of archaeological investigations. The term is not defined, which enables the Kamloops Band to interpret "data" very broadly, and *may* allow intellectual property to be included.

Should such permits explicitly include reference to intellectual property in future? If so, might a contemporary Aboriginal group lay claim to a prominent archaeological site and exert exclusive control over the site, name, images of the artifacts, or related items? What would this mean if there were competing interests due to overlapping territorial claims? These are just some of the difficult questions that have yet to be raised and addressed in archaeology.

Beyond contractual approaches to control Indigenous cultural and intellectual property, examples in archaeology or related fields that employ existing IPR tools such as copyright and trademark are beginning to emerge. For example, the Heritage Investigation Permit of the Kamloops Indian Band stipulates "joint copyright between the Permittee and the Band" for all resulting publications (Kamloops Indian Band 1997). Indeed, copyright may be one of the more commonly recognized and used forms of intellectual property protection. Although copyright represents an important principle in acknowledging authorship of creative works, the assumed degree of protection or control that it offers, especially in terms of research publications, is often overestimated.[7] For most published works, copyright is usually held by the publishers. With greater collaboration between archaeologists and Indigenous communities, publishers will need to accommodate more flexible copyright arrangements, something already underway in ethnobotany and some aspects of anthropology. For example: Bannister and Turner (Bannister, chapter 10 in this volume) sought a joint copyright arrangement for the Secwepemc Cultural Education Society on publication of collaborative ethnobotanical research;

Turner (1997, 1998) was able to change the copyright of two popular books containing ethnobotanical knowledge of First Nations groups to a shared copyright between the First Peoples Cultural Foundation and the British Columbia Royal Museum when the books were reissued;[8] and in Bierwert (1996: colophon), while copyright of "translations and other scholarly apparatus" is held by the publisher, it is stated that "the texts of Lushootseed stories are understood to be part of native cultural tradition, and therefore no claim of copyright is here made upon them."

Trademark is also gaining recognition as a potentially useful tool in the context of protecting Indigenous images, designs, and sacred names. As mentioned earlier, in 1998 the Snuneymuxw First Nation (British Columbia) successfully registered with the Canadian Intellectual Property Office at least seven ancient petroglyphs as "official marks" to *prevent* them from being copied and reproduced by anyone for any purpose, arguing the petroglyphs are sacred and copies for any reason are sacrilegious.[9] In the early to mid-1990s, the Cowichan Band Council (British Columbia) registered the words "Cowichan," "Genuine Cowichan," and "Genuine Cowichan Approved" as both official marks (noncommercial use) and certification marks (commercial use) with the Canadian Intellectual Property Office. These certification marks are used mainly in the marketing of handmade clothing created by Coast Salish knitters using traditional materials and methods (unprocessed, undyed, hand-spun wool) and traditional patterns (e.g., thunderbird, whale). Authentic wares may bear the words "Cowichan," "Genuine Cowichan," or "Genuine Cowichan Approved," and/or the certification mark.[10] While current usage for these marks is for the clothing market, there is potential to apply them in the protection or promotion of other aspects of cultural heritage. The Comox Indian Band (British Columbia), for example, has registered the word "Queneesh"[11] as an official mark, thereby protecting the place name of a sacred site.

Patents may seem fairly unrelated to archaeological research to date. Archaeological research at the molecular level, however, may involve recovery and analysis of ancient DNA. Access to DNA from contemporary populations is a very contentious issue (e.g., chapter 9, this volume; Christie 1996; Cordillera Peoples' Alliance 1994; Gibbs 1998; Kahn, 1994; NRC 1997), in part because it brings up serious issues related to privacy and informed consent, but also because the genetic information derived through analysis may be seen as a valuable commodity. In North America, DNA has been successfully extracted from preserved brain tissue from 8,000-year-old sites (Doran et al. 1986), and efforts are now underway to obtain it from Kwäday Dän Ts'ínchi, a 550-year-old individual whose frozen remains were found in northern British Columbia (Beattie et al. 2000). The full value and applications of these findings is still unknown, but human genetic material is patentable in many countries and so raises important issues involving cultural heritage and intellectual property rights.

Finally, an indirect means to controlling intellectual property is by restricting researcher access to archaeological data in the first place. In British Columbia, for example, we are aware of several cases in which researchers were not able to obtain information they had requested from First Nations bands, either because they were unable or unwilling to meet in person with them (as part of the protocol process), or were simply turned down. It is important to note, however, that Aboriginal groups may also not release requested information simply because they can't meet the demands placed on them. In many cases, the capacity and amount of resources available to meet the routine needs of the group are seldom adequate; with outside requests for information, a poor situation is made worse.

Protection and Repatriation of First Nations' Cultural Heritage in Canada

A new collaboration between a team of international scholars in law and anthropology and Aboriginal groups in British Columbia and Alberta, Canada, may offer answers and give direction to many of the questions and concerns raised in this chapter. The "Protection and Repatriation of First Nations' Cultural Heritage in Canada" project was designed by Professor of Law Catherine Bell, at the University of Alberta, and initiated in collaboration with Professor Robert Patterson (Faculty of Law, University of British Columbia), in response to a perceived need for an exhaustive critical analysis of legislation affecting ownership, protection, and control of First Nations' cultural heritage. The purpose of the project, which we are both participating in, is to critically examine existing Canadian legislation affecting First Nations' cultural heritage and develop strategies for reform and further protection. The research is informed by a series of case studies designed in close collaboration with (and largely controlled by) First Nations' partners to explore Aboriginal communities' concepts of property, customary laws, and heritage protection priorities. In addition, the research will include reviews of Canadian Aboriginal rights and property law; international laws and treaties on human rights, cultural property, intellectual property, and the rights of Indigenous peoples; and reform initiatives in jurisdictions with similar legal obligations such as Australia, New Zealand, and the United States.

This research project offers a timely new way of conducting legal research, placing First Nations' and Canadian laws and concepts of property on equal footing in law reform activity and valuing equally participation by First Nations' partners and scholars to foster incorporation of a diversity of approaches to legal theory and analysis. Resulting reports, publications, and reference libraries are expected to be valuable to Indigenous peoples and organizations engaged in cultural heritage issues, scholars of various disciplines, and government agencies engaged in self-government negotiation and law reform.

The social and cultural significance of the research is viewed with equal importance to the legal applications. Case studies are required to adhere to local community protocols and designed to assist First Nations' partners in recording and archiving their own cultural information that they deem important for preservation of oral history, survival of cultural identity, and education of future generations. The project will also employ and train First Nations' community interviewers, researchers, and interpreters as well as graduate and undergraduate students in law, anthropology, and sociology (Bell 2001). The research team hopes to produce curriculum materials for use by Indigenous and non-Indigenous educational institutions.

Aside from the important subject matter of this project, we see its greatest strength lying in the emphasis on participatory research methods, local capacity building, and explicit power sharing in terms of collaborative priority setting and decision making, from the research design to outcomes. In addition to potentially creating a wide range of resources of widespread interest and value, if successful, the project may set new ethical and practical standards in collaborative research with Aboriginal groups in Canada.

Conclusion

This chapter has sought to raise awareness of some emerging issues facing both archaeologists and Indigenous communities. How should we proceed from here? For one thing, we ought to look to other disciplines for examples and experiences relating to IPR. Differences are obvious between archaeology and such disciplines as ethnobotany in the types of information sought and how they are utilized. One could argue that archaeology and ethnobotany approach IPR issues from two opposite ends of a spectrum—archaeology from the *material* record of *past* culture, with supposed *limited* present use, and ethnobotany from the *intellectual* aspects of *living* peoples, with perceived *high* contemporary value (see Bannister, chapter 10 in this volume). In this light, perhaps archaeology and ethnobotany can mutually inform one another. Archaeology may be lagging behind other disciplines in acknowledging IPR issues, but archaeologists also have the potential to become leaders in dealing with these issues in their own field, in part by becoming aware of current debates in related disciplines and considering the implications for archaeology.

Is ownership of the past something that archaeologists truly need to be concerned with? Does raising the specter of IPR entering the archaeological realm, as we do here, pave the way for its occurrence? Our position is that raising awareness among our colleagues, Indigenous and non-Indigenous alike, is an early step toward resolving developments that are likely inevitable, whether we draw attention to them or not. Further, in broaching the topic of IPR in archaeology, we are not decidedly for or against use of IPR mechanisms for protecting cultural heritage; we do believe understanding their uses, potentials, and limitations is vitally important to making informed decisions for their appropriate applications. We heed Brown's (1998: 199) warning that IPR legislation serves primarily to "convert information into property" and misses the heart of the problem. As long as information is recognized as a commodity, means of control will be sought, whether by legal or other mechanisms, and whether for commercialization or to protect from commercialization. What is needed, Brown (1998: 199) notes, is "extensive discussion on the moral implications of exposing native people to unwanted scrutiny, on the one hand, and sequestering public-domain information, on the other." We support Brown's (1998: 202) call for "urgently needed public discussion about mutual respect and the fragility of native cultures in mass societies." Increasing the profile of the issues that have been raised here, we argue, is a step toward fostering such a dialogue in archaeology.

Today, none of the ethical statements of archaeological and heritage-related organizations contain any explicit mention of IPR. However, we predict that many will before the decade is over. We thus encourage careful consideration of these issues, from Indigenous and non-Indigenous perspectives alike, as they relate to archaeology. If, as is likely, more restrictions will be placed on the products of archaeological research, whether by Indigenous groups or others, there will be consequences—both positive and negative—for everyone. We suggest that it is in our best interest to work *cooperatively* and *proactively* with all those who have an interest in Indigenous cultural heritage, to identify, understand, and address conflicts that may emerge in laying claim to ownership of the past. This will require a deeper recognition of what archaeological knowledge means—and what *control* of that knowledge means—beyond simply economics or professional reward and advancement. Solutions will stem from recognizing ethical obligations, supporting participatory research, and enhancing the capacity of Indigenous communities to be the primary stewards of their past, so the past can be available to inform the future for all of us.

Acknowledgments

A version of this chapter was originally presented by George Nicholas in the session "Protection of Cultural Heritage and Intellectual Property Rights of Indigenous Communities: Current Opportunities and Challenges," organized by Kelly Bannister, for the World Indigenous Peoples conference, Kelowna, British Columbia, October 2001. This chapter has benefited from discussions with Michael Brown, Catherine Bell, John Jules (Kamloops Indian Band), and Amy Roberts. We are grateful to Mary Riley and to Rosalie Robertson (AltaMira Press) for the flexibility they have allowed us in meeting our obligation to this volume.

Notes

1. The exceptions refer to two cases where Indigenous communities are involved directly or indirectly in benefit-sharing agreements for profits that *may be* accrued from the commercialization of patented plant compounds derived from their

cultural knowledge: (1) The first example is the anti-AIDS compound "prostratin," which was derived from the Samoan plant *Homoalanthus nutans* (locally known as *mamala*) and "discovered" based on medicinal knowledge of Samoan healers that was shared with ethnobotanist Paul Cox. The National Cancer Institute has licensed prostratin to the AIDS ReSearch Alliance (a U.S. nonprofit group), who, in turn, developed a Profit-Sharing Agreement with the Samoan prime minister to ensure that money from the commercialization of prostratin will be shared with the Samoan government, the village where the plant was found, and the families of the now-deceased healers who assisted in the discovery (ARA 2001; Briscoe 2001; Langbein 2001). (2) The second example is the appetite suppressant "P57," which is made from a patented bioactive compound derived from the South African succulent plant *Hoodia gordonii*. The compound was found based on ethnobotanical information published in the 1930s that documented traditional use of the *Hoodia* plant by the San peoples. South Africa's Council for Scientific and Industrial Research (CSIR) holds the patent to P57 and licensed commercialization rights to Phytopharm (UK), who in turn sublicensed to Pfizer (USA). CSIR developed a Memorandum of Understanding in 2002 with the San Council as a commitment to develop a benefit-sharing agreement in anticipation of commercial benefits (CSIR 2002; Phytopharm 2002; Carroll 2003). A benefit-sharing agreement was announced in March 2003 that commits CSIR to pay the San 8 percent of all milestone payments from its licensee, Phytopharm, and 6 percent of all royalties that CSIR receives once the drug is commercially available. The potential monies will be deposited into a San Hoodia Benefit Sharing Trust, to be used for supporting development and training of the San community (CSIR 2003).

2. In this chapter, the terms *Aboriginal* and *Indigenous* are used relatively interchangeably. Our choice to use the term *Aboriginal peoples* within a Canadian context is a conscious decision to refer inclusively to First Nations, Metís, and Inuit peoples. We use the term *Native American* when referring to Indigenous peoples of Canada and the United States. We also use the convention of pluralizing Indigenous peoples to recognize the diversity among different groups.

3. It is even possible to obtain "authentic" replicas. Visitors/clients to the *Artifact Replicas* website (www.artifact-replicas.com) are greeted with the message, "The president of E-Nterprises, Inc.'s Great Great Grand Mother was a Full Blooded Cherokee Indian." This is accompanied with pictures of the many different replicated artifacts available, including some decidedly non-Cherokee kachinas.

4. Protection of the petroglyphs was accomplished through use of a form of trademark law, discussed in more detail subsequently. Reproduction of the petroglyphs, for commercial use or otherwise, is seen by Snuneymuxw elders as cultur-

ally offensive, if not potentially dangerous (Geraldine Manson, personal communication, 2002).

5. Reproduced here with permission from the photographers and courtesy of Sonnabend Gallery, New York.

6. See: www.tricityherald.com/news/1999/0729.html#anchor596920; last accessed on March 20, 2003.

7. For example, in our experience, copyright is often confused with (or incorrectly assumed to be equivalent to) rights to royalties. Further, as with other forms of IPR protection, the onus is on the copyright holder to enforce their right; most breaches of copyright go completely unnoticed.

8. Turner's (1997, 1998) examples underscore the importance of giving advance thought to who will hold copyright on a publication, given that the opportunity to change copyright of a book must await its reprinting. Applying her past experiences to the future, she notes that the Haida Gwaii Watchmen Programs will hold the copyright to a forthcoming book by Turner called "Plants of Haida Gwaii" (N. J. Turner, personal communication, 2003).

9. The seven petroglyph images can be found on the Canadian Intellectual Property Office website in the Trademarks Database at: strategis.ic.gc.ca/cipo/trademarks/search/html/help_e.html#criteria; last accessed on March 20, 2003.] None of the images has been reproduced here out of respect for the beliefs of Snuneymuxw Elders that any form of reproduction is inappropriate.

10. From the Canadian Intellectual Property Office website: strategis.ic.gc.ca/SSG/0792/trdp079217400e.html; last accessed on March 20, 2003.]

11. From the Canadian Intellectual Property Office website: strategis.ic.gc.ca/SSG/0908/trdp090857300e.html; last accessed on March 20, 2003.]

References

AIDS ReSearch Alliance of America (ARA)

AIDS ReSearch Alliance of America Announces Landmark Agreement to Share Drug Profits with Samoan Village Healers. West Hollywood: Prostratin Press Release, December 13, 2001.

Bannister, K. P.

Chemistry Rooted in Cultural Knowledge: Unearthing the Links between Antimicrobial Properties and Traditional Knowledge in Food and Medicinal Plant Resources of the Secwepemc (Shuswap) Aboriginal Nation.

Unpublished Ph.D. Thesis, Department of Botany, University of British Columbia, Vancouver, 2000.

Battiste, M., and J. Y. Henderson
Protecting Indigenous Knowledge and Heritage: A Global Challenge. Saskatoon: Purich Publishing, 2000.

Beattie, O., B. Apland, E. W. Blake, J. A. Cosgrove, S. Gaunt, S. Greer, A. P. Mackie, K. E. Mackie, D. Straathof, V. Thorp, and P. M. Troffe
The Kwäday Dän Ts'ínchi Discovery from a Glacier in British Columbia. *Canadian Journal of Archaeology*, vol. 24 (2000): 129–148.

Bell, C.
Protection and Repatriation of First Nations Cultural Heritage (Strategic Research Grant Application submitted to the Social Sciences and Humanities Research Council of Canada. 2 October 2001). Online: Project for the Protection and Repatriation of First Nations Cultural Heritage in Canada at:: www.law.ualberta.ca/research/Aboriginalculturalheritage; last accessed on March 20, 2003.

Bicrwcrt, C.
Lushootseed Text: An Introduction to Puget Sound Salish Narrative Aesthetics. Lincoln: University of Nebraska Press, 1996.

Bray, T. L., and T. W. Killion (eds.)
Reckoning with the Dead: The Larsen Bay Repatriation and the Smithsonian Institution. Washington, D.C.: Smithsonian Institution Press, 1994.

Briscoe, D.
Agreement Would Share Profit from AIDS Drug with Samoan Healers. Honolulu: Associated Press, December 13, 2001.

Brown, M.
Can Culture Be Copyrighted? *Current Anthropology*, vol. 39, no. 2 (1998): 193–222.

Brush, S., and D. Stabinsky
Valuing Local Knowledge: Indigenous People and Intellectual Property Rights. Washington, D.C.: Island Press, 1996.

Calloway, C. G., G. Gmunden, and S. Zantop
Germans and Indians: Fantasies, Encounters, Projections. Lincoln: University of Nebraska Press, 2002.

Carlson, C. C.
The (In)Significance of Atlantic Salmon in New England. In *New England's Creatures: 1400–1900*, edited by P. Benes, 1–10. Dublin Seminar for New

England Folklife, Boston University Press, 1995. Reprinted in *Federal Archaeology*, vol. 8, nos. 3/4 (1996): 22–30.

Carroll, R.
It's Green, Prickly and Sour but this Plant Could Cure Obesity and Save an Ancient Way of Life. Johannesburg, *The Guardian*, January 4, 2003. At: www.guardian.co.uk/medicine/story/0,11381,868516,00.html; last accessed January 5, 2003.

Christie, J.
Whose Property, Whose Rights? *Cultural Survival Quarterly* (summer 1996): 34–36.

Coe, M.
The Chinampas of Mexico. *Scientific American*, vol. 211, no. 1 (1964): 90–98.

Cordillera Peoples' Alliance
The Human Genome Diversity Project and Patenting Humans: Genetic Imperialism? *Global Biodiversity*, vol. 4, no. 2 (1994): 24–26.

Council for Scientific and Industrial Research (CSIR)
The San and the CSIR to Formulate Benefit-sharing Model for Anti-obesity Patent. CSIR Media Release, March 2002.

The San and the CSIR Announce a Benefit-sharing Agreement for Potential Anti-Obesity Drug. Joint media release by the South African San Council and the Council for Scientific and Industrial Research (CSIR). March 24, 2003.

Davidson, I., C. Lovell-Jones, and R. Bancroft (eds.)
Archaeologists and Aborigines Working Together. Armidale: University of New England Press, 1995.

Dongoske, K. E., M. Aldenderfer, and K. Doehner (eds.)
Working Together: Native Americans and Archaeologists. Washington, D.C.: Society for American Archaeology, 2000.

Doran, G. H., D. N. Dickel, W. E. Ballinger Jr., O. F. Agee, P. J. Laipis, and W. W. Hauswirth
Anatomical, Cellular and Molecular Analysis of 8,000-yr-old Human Brain Tissue from the Windover Archaeological Site. *Nature*, vol. 323 (1986): 803–806.

Dutfield, G.
Intellectual Property Rights, Trade and Biodiversity. London: Earthscan Publications, 2000.

Erickson, C.
Applied Archaeology and Rural Development: Archaeology's Potential Contribution to the Future. In *Crossing Currents: Continuity and Change in Latin America*, edited by M. Whiteford and S. Whiteford, 34–45. Upper Saddle River, N.J.: Prentice-Hall, 1998.

An Artificial Landscape-Scale Fishery in the Bolivian Amazon. *Nature,* vol. 408 (Nov. 9, 2000): 190–193.

Gibbs, W. W.
Natural Born Guinea Pigs: A start-up discovers genes for tremor and psoriasis in the DNA of inbred Icelanders. Scientific American available online at: www.sciam.com/1998/0298issue/0298techbus3.html; last accessed on February 24, 2003.

Greaves, T.
Intellectual Property Rights for Indigenous Peoples: A Sourcebook. Oklahoma City: Society for Applied Anthropology, 1994.

Harris, H.
Remembering 10,000 Years of History: The Origins and Migrations of the Gitksan. In *At a Crossroads: Archaeology and First Peoples in Canada*, edited by G. P. Nicholas and T. D. Andrews, 190–196. Burnaby, B.C.: Archaeology Press, Simon Fraser University, 1997.

Hollowell-Zimmer, J.
When Archaeological Artifacts are Commodities: Dilemmas Faced by Native Villages of Alaska's Bering Strait. In *Indigenous Peoples and Archaeology, Proceedings of the 32nd Chacmool Conference*, edited by E. Siegfried, T. Peck, and G. Oetlelaar, 298–312. Calgary: University of Calgary, 2003.

Jameson, J. H. Jr. (ed.)
Presenting Archaeology to the Public. Walnut Creek, Calif.: AltaMira Press, 1997.

Janke, T.
Our Culture: Our Future. Report on Australian Indigenous Cultural and Intellectual Property Rights. Surrey Hills, NSW: Australian Institute of Aboriginal and Torres Strait Islander Commission, and Michael Frankel & Company, 1998.

Minding Culture: Case-Studies on Intellectual Property and Traditional Cultural Expressions. World Intellectual Property Organization (WIPO), 2002. Available at: www.wipo.int/globalissues/studies/cultural/minding-culture/index.html#1; last accessed on February 24, 2003.

Johnson, V.
Copyrites: Aboriginal Art in the Age of Reproductive Technologies. Touring Exhibition 1996 Catalogue. Sydney: National Indigenous Arts Advocacy Association and Macquarie University, 1996.

Kahn, P.
Genetic Diversity Project Tries Again. *Science*, vol. 266 (1994): 720–722.

Kamloops Indian Band
Heritage Conservation By-Law. B.C.: Kamloops, 1997.

Laird, S. (ed.)
Biodiversity and Traditional Knowledge: Equitable Partnerships in Practice. London: Earthscan Publications, 2002.

Langbein, W.
Landmark Deal Reached between AIDS Research Group and Samoans on HIV Drug. New York: Reuters Health, December 13, 2001.

Mann R. W., B. E. Anderson, T. D. Holland, D. R. Rankin, and J. E. Webb Jr.
Unusual Crime Scenes: The Role of Forensic Anthropology in Recovering and Identifying American MIAs. In *Case Studies in Forensic Anthropology: A Reader*, edited by D. W. Steadman, 108–116. Upper Saddle River, N.J.: Prentice Hall, 2003.

Markey, N.
Data "Gathering Dust": Traditional Use Studies Conducted in Aboriginal Communities in British Columbia. M.A. Thesis, Department of Sociology and Anthropology, Simon Fraser University, Burnaby, B.C., 2001.

Matsuda, D.
The Ethics of Archaeology, Subsistence Digging, and Artifact Looting in Latin America: Point, Muted Counterpoint. *International Journal of Cultural Property*, vol. 7 (1998): 89–97.

McBryde, I. (ed.)
Who Owns the Past? Melbourne: Oxford University Press, 1985.

McGhee, R.
"Who Owns the Past?" *Canadian Journal of Archaeology*, vol. 13 (1989): 13–20.

Mihesuah, D. A. (ed.)
Repatriation Reader: Who Owns American Indian Remains? Lincoln: University of Nebraska Press, 2000.

National Research Council (NRC).
Study of Human Genetic Diversity Worthwhile, But Ethical Concerns Should Be Addressed First. Press Release, October 21, 1997.

Ndoro, W.
Great Zimbabwe. *Scientific American* (November 1997): 94–99.

Neumann, T. W., and R. M. Sanford
Cultural Resources Archaeology: An Introduction. Walnut Creek, Calif.: AltaMira Press, 2001.

Nicholas, G. P.
The Persistence of Memory, the Politics of Desire: Archaeological Impacts on Aboriginal Peoples and Their Response. In *Indigenous Archaeologies: Decolonising Theory and Practice*, edited by C. Smith and H. M. Wobst. London: Routledge Press, in press.

Nicholas, G. P., and T. D. Andrews
Indigenous Archaeology in the Postmodern World. In *At a Crossroads: Archaeologists and First Peoples in Canada*, edited by G. P. Nicholas and T. D. Andrews, 1–18. Burnaby, B.C.: Archaeology Press, Simon Fraser University, 1997.

Nicholas, G. P., and K. P. Bannister
"Copyrighting the Past?": Emerging Intellectual Property Rights Issues in Archaeology. *Current Anthropology*, vol. 45, no. 3, forthcoming, 2004.

Parks Canada
Unearthing the Law: Archaeological Legislation on Lands in Canada. Ottawa: Parks Canada, 2000.

Parsons, J. P., and W. M. Denevan
Pre-Columbian Ridged Fields. *Scientific American* (July 1967): 92–101.

Phytopharm
Opens New Manufacturing Unit in South Africa. Phytopharm plc Press Release, 2002. At: www.phytopharm.com/News/PressReleases2002/press064-20020411.shtml; last accessed March 20, 2003.

Posey, D. A., and G. Dutfield
Beyond Intellectual Property Rights: Toward Traditional Resource Rights. Ottawa: International Development Research Centre, 1996.

Rathje, W. L.
Once and Future Landfills. *National Geographic* (May 1991): 116–134.

Robbins, A., and M. Becher
Karl May Festival. In *German Indians.* Photographic display at Leslie Tonkonw Artworks and Projects, New York, 1997/98. Available at: robbecher.www4.50megs.com/TonkanowGIimagesframe.html; last accessed on March 20, 2003.

Sheets, P. D.
Dawn of a New Stone Age in Eye Surgery. In *Applying Anthropology: An Introductory Reader*, edited by A. Poloefsky and P. J. Brown, 113–115. Mountain View, Calif.: Mayfield Press, 1989.

Staley, D. P.
St. Lawrence Island's Subsistence Diggers: A New Perspective on Human Effects on Archaeological Sites. *Journal of Field Archaeology*, vol. 20 (1993): 347–355.

Sto:lo Nation
Stolo Heritage Policy. Chilliwack, B.C.: Sto:lo Nation, 1995.

Swanson, T. M.
Intellectual Property Rights and Biodiversity Conservation: An Interdisciplinary Analysis of the Values of Medicinal Plants. Cambridge: Cambridge University Press, 1995.

Taylor, W.
A Study of Archaeology. *American Anthropologist Memoir*, vol. 69, no. 50 (1948): 3 (Part 2).

Thomas, D. H.
Archaeology. 3d ed. New York: Harcourt Brace, 1998.

Skull Wars: Kennewick Man, Archaeology, and the Battle for Native American Identity. New York: Basic Books, 2000.

Trigger, B. G.
A History of Archaeological Thought. Cambridge: Cambridge University Press, 1989.

Turner, N. J.

Food Plants of Interior First Peoples. (Revised and reissued handbook, originally published in 1978 by B.C. Provincial Museum). University of British Columbia Press, Vancouver, and Royal British Columbia Museum, Victoria, 1997.

Plant Technology of British Columbia First Peoples. (Revised and reissued handbook, originally published in 1979 by B.C. Provincial Museum.) University of British Columbia Press, Vancouver, and Royal British Columbia Museum, Victoria, 1998.

Watkins, J.

Indigenous Archaeology: American Indian Values and Scientific Practice. Walnut Creek, Calif.: AltaMira Press, 2000.

Willey, G. R., and P. Phillips

Method and Theory in American Archaeology. Chicago: University of Chicago Press, 1958.

Willey, G. R., and J. A. Sabloff

A History of American Archaeology. 3d ed. New York: W. H. Freeman, 1993.

CHAPTER 12

PRIOR INFORMED CONSENT AND BIOPROSPECTING IN CHIAPAS

Elois Ann Berlin and Brent Berlin

Anthropologists and Prior Informed Consent

In the early 1970s, the U.S. federal government enacted legislation requiring universities to establish review committees whose job was to determine how scientists planning to conduct research with human subjects were to obtain their subjects' "prior and informed consent" (PIC).[1] The initial reaction of anthropologists to these new requirements was surprise and disdain. Field savvy ethnographers, they claimed, "don't do anything to harm our informants." Besides, "There are no words to explain my project in their language." More commonly, "They can't sign informed consent forms since they lack a written language and/or are not literate." Anthropologists would argue that clear verbal permission from community members who agreed to work with them had always been obtained following the time-honored conventions of establishing trust, based on initial short-term interpersonal relations that ultimately led to long-term research commitments. Many times field anthropologists proclaimed in frustration, "Those people on the human subjects committee just don't understand the nature of anthropological fieldwork!"

However, the last forty years have seen a remarkable set of changes in the way anthropologists have come to conduct their work with native peoples. With a growing sense of awareness, anthropologists began to recognize their informants as consultants and later as collaborators, with the entire intellectual and social significance that these terms imply. Our collaborators, in turn, began to appreciate the larger world context in which they lived (access to twenty-four-hour television is the major transformer) and the disparity between the "haves" of that world and themselves, the "have-nots," led to dramatic shifts in expectations about what they should derive from the collaborative fieldwork enterprise. Today, few anthropologists undertake fieldwork without first attempting to make their proposed research understandable and transparent to the peoples with whom they study and to explain what the participating communities will receive in return for their cooperation and support. Some field anthropologists have gone so far as to argue that all good research must yield some direct or indirect value for the study population.

With these new developments in the relationships and responsibilities between anthropologists and their subjects, the need to ensure that individuals and communities are fully informed and able to give consent on the basis of comprehensive understanding of the project's methods, goals, and potential consequences has imbued the notion of PIC with new significance. Unfortunately, presenting one's research goals in ways that are at once transparent, clear, unambiguous, and comprehensive is especially difficult when they are tied to the contentious issues surrounding bioprospecting[2]—issues that were catapulted into world consciousness with the signing of the Convention on Biological Diversity (CBD) in 1993. With the CBD, and its requirements for PIC and just compensation, ethnobotanical fieldwork entered a new era and was changed forever.[3]

The Maya International Cooperative Biodiversity Group (Maya ICBG)

The current chapter presents a much-abbreviated case study of efforts to develop a bioprospecting project in Chiapas, Mexico.[4] We review our efforts to obtain PIC from nearly fifty Mayan communities in the Chiapas highlands before we were required to cease such activities due to political opposition. We show that, ironically, the project ultimately was abandoned not because of our failure to obtain PIC from participating Mayan communities but because of the acrimonious national and international debate that grew up around questions of proprietary versus public knowledge and issues concerning the legal and social legitimacy of local communities' control over their biological resources. Opponents of the project, primarily vocal nongovernmental organizations (NGOs) at the local, national, and international level, often framed their attacks as accusations of biopiracy. It now appears that all of these arguments are best seen as proxies for NGOs' larger political objections to globalization, objections that they frame as efforts by the North to pillage the biological resources of the South as part of the policies on international development led by the United States, the World Trade Organization, the International Monetary Fund, and the World Bank.

The Maya ICBG was a consortium project funded by a U.S. government grant to promote human health, economic development, and biodiversity conservation through sustainable development of medicinal plant resources and associated traditional knowledge of the Maya-speaking populations of the state of Chiapas in southeastern Mexico.[5] The members of this consortium included scientists from a U.S. educational institution (the University of Georgia [UGA]), a Mexican host country research and educational public institution (El Colegio de la Frontera Sur [ECOSUR]), numerous Mayan communities, and a small for-profit company of natural products chemists (Molecular Nature Ltd. [MNL]). Dr. Michael Heinrich of London University and Dr. Jan Wolf of the University of Amsterdam completed the international team.

The Maya ICBG was comprised of three associate programs that focused on drug discovery, pharmaceutical development, medical ethnobiology, floristic inventory, conservation, sustained harvest, and economic growth in the highland Maya region of Chiapas, Mexico.

The aims of the Maya ICBG as originally stated were to

(1) *discover*, *isolate*, and *preclinically evaluate* bioactive agents from pharmacologically important species of vascular plants found in the state of Chiapas, one of the richest and most endangered biodiversity regions on earth;

(2) *discover*, *isolate*, and *evaluate* bioactive species of immediate health significance and potential economic value to the local Maya populations by systematic and comparative study of Maya ethnomedical formulary;

(3) *initiate* ecologically and ethnobotanically sophisticated plant surveys aimed at comprehensive coverage of the vascular flora of the 28 municipalities designated as the study area of the highlands of Chiapas (see figure 12.1, map of study area);

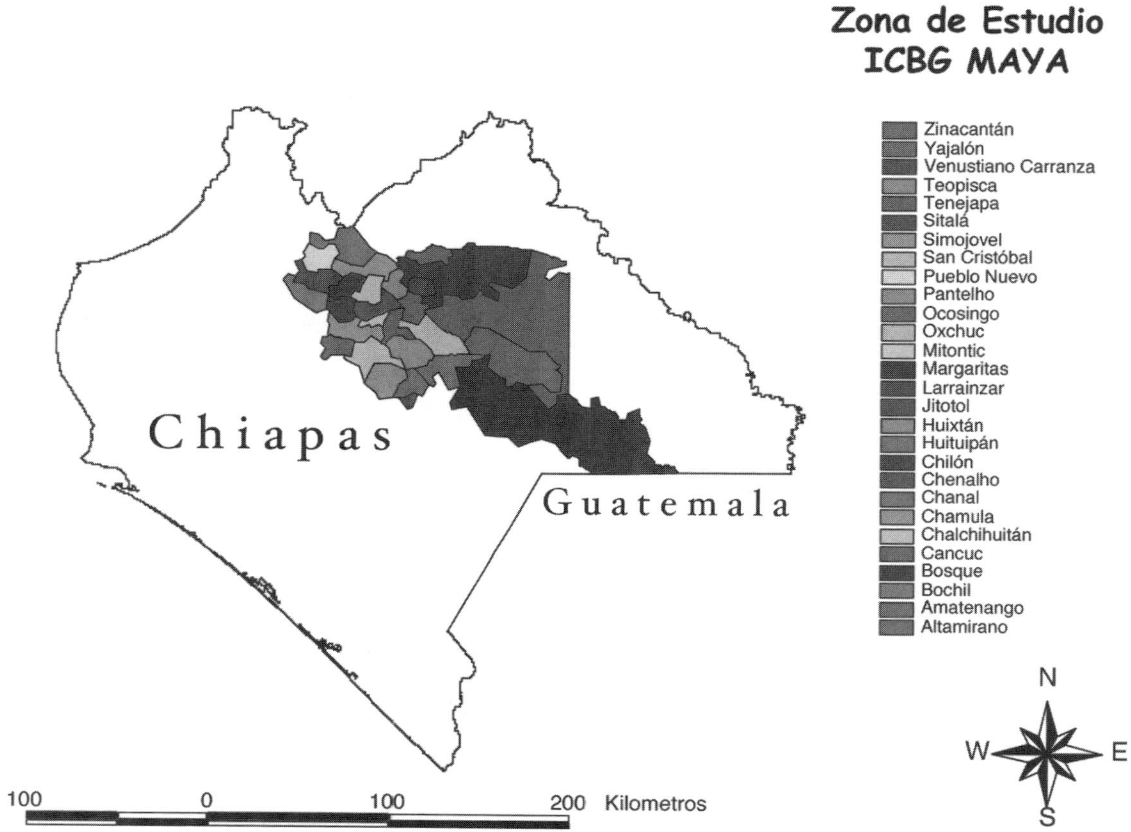

Figure 12.1. Map of the Study Area.

(4) enhance infrastructure and support research and training relevant to the goals of ECOSUR.

The short period that the Maya ICBG functioned produced several important activities that we mention here as illustrative of the complete panorama of the project and that were unfortunately terminated due to the untimely end of the research.

- An ethnobotanical survey of the total vascular flora of highland Chiapas was initiated in four municipalities of the study area, Chenalhó, Oxchuc, Tenejapa, and Las Margaritas, resulting in 6,234 collections.[6] These collections produced an inventory of approximately 1,555 species in about 500 genera in 121 botanical families, two-thirds of the 197 families reported for the state (Breedlove 1996). All collections are accompanied by standard botanical, ethnobotanical, and ecological data which, when complete, were to constitute the data for an illustrated multi-volume ethnoflora of the Chiapas highlands published in Spanish, Tzeltal, Tzotzil, Tojolabal, and English.
- Systematic data collection on natural products formulae were collected as part of a detailed comparative study of Maya ethnopharmacology representing 338 distinct formulae incorporating from one to six ingredients from more than 180 plant species and other nonbotanicals (insects, minerals). Complex descriptions of the curative properties of these herbal remedies included healing (illness), calming (symptoms), stimulating (processes such as appetite, sweating), extruding (substances) bringing out (rash, fever), peeling (tissue), altering (sounds, symptoms), opening (throat, head, ears), giving or resulting in (increased heart rate, dizziness), and many others. This rich ethnopharmacological knowledge was to guide studies of pharmacological activity and physiological target areas for Maya medicinals.
- At the explicit request of Highland Maya communities, we established ten cooperative ethnobotanical community gardens as part of the Maya ICBG's effort at promotion and

maintenance of traditional knowledge of medicinal plants. Composite species inventories of three of the fully established gardens showed at least 324 species in 103 botanical families. While the majority of species are medicinal, other useful plants were also included. These gardens represented one of the most important community development activities of the project as related to its goal of immediate short-term benefits for local communities. Subsequent to the termination of the Maya ICBG, these garden groups have formed two community-based NGOs. Each has acquired outside funding to continue with their gardening efforts.

- Research was also initiated on the floristic composition and structural analysis of the herbaceous plant communities in major habitats under heavy human disturbance. Compilation of quantitative demographic information was compiled on those species targeted as potential semidomesticates for sustained management and those that might show significant biological activity. A preliminary finding of this work indicates strongly that species diversity is significantly greater in areas of heavy human disturbance than in other less anthropogenic habitats. The implications of these findings, if sustained, are considerable for long-term plant management policies in the highlands of Chiapas.

- The project supported continued experimentation with a subset of the most significant medicinal plant species in the Chiapas highlands as biological control agents in local Mayan horticultural systems. Results of the first trials of this research demonstrate that a number of medicinal plant species are highly effective against the cabbage-worm, an insect pest that has significant economic impact on Mayan small-produce farmers.

- At the request of community members, the Mayan women of our team gained the skills necessary to conduct workshops on women's issues including women's rights, family planning, and the life cycle.

- The Maya ICBG provided financial support to a remarkable set of undergraduate, graduate, and postgraduate students at ECOSUR and UGA in ecology, agroecology, systematic botany, ecological anthropology, medical anthropology, biochemistry, ethnobotany, and conservation biology. Recipients completed or are in the process of completing seven doctoral dissertations (five from UGA, two from ECOSUR), two master's theses (ECOSUR), and two BA theses (students from local universities advised by ECOSUR researchers). We also conducted workshops in capacity building of thirteen Mayan collaborators on herbal medicine, laboratory techniques, field botany and ecology, botanical museum curation procedures, computer literacy, geographic information systems technology (GIS), medical ethnobiological, anthropological, and ecological field methods, and Mayan linguistics.

Prior Informed Consent in Bioprospecting

In the early stages of the project, the Maya ICBG developed a specific program for obtaining PIC from prospective Mayan communities in collaboration with our Mayan research assistants. To place our efforts in context, it is important to review the basic regulations underlying PIC as required by the CBD (United Nations Environmental Programme [UNEP] 1992).

Requirements for obtaining PIC for all bioprospecting projects are clearly specified in the CBD and subsequent documents of the Conference of the Parties (COP) of the United Nations. The relevant section of the CBD is Article 15: "Access to genetic resources shall be subject to the prior informed consent of the contracting party providing access to those resources." This requirement has been restated numerous times in subsequent codifications of Article 15 and Article 8 (j) of the CBD, for example, "Access to traditional knowledge innovations and practices of *Indigenous and local communities* should be subject to prior informed consent . . . from the *holders of such knowledge*, innovations, and practices" (UNEP/CBD 1997, emphasis added).[7]

If the CBD's requirement for PIC is unambiguous, answers to basic questions underlying the concept are far from clear. Three basic questions are:

- *What* is PIC?
- *Who* should grant PIC?
- *How* is PIC obtained?

With specific reference to the case of the Maya ICBG, two additional questions are relevant as regards the legitimacy of efforts aimed at attaining PIC. These are:

- *What constitutes evidence* that PIC has been obtained?
- *Who* decides whether PIC has been granted?

What Is PIC?

The notions of "prior" and "consent" in "prior informed consent" in the context of bioprospecting are easily defined. For Ten Kate and Laird "prior" means "before access takes place" (1999: 17) and "consent" indicates explicit approval of the stakeholders that bioprospecting be commenced. *Informed* consent is based on "truthful information about the use that will be made of the genetic resources that is adequate for the [local community] to understand the implications [of such use]" (Ten Kate and Laird 1999: 17).

There is no agreement, however, on how much "truthful information" must be provided or in what form. Must stakeholders for example, understand patent law and intellectual property rights legislation, particularly as it applies to Indigenous knowledge? How much knowledge of conservation biology and historical ecology is necessary to understand the need to assure sustainable harvest of species? What levels of sophistication in modern political ecology constitute an adequate basis for making an informed decision about a project that has biotechnological ends? As importantly, what measures should be used to determine the extent to which members of a community fully understanding the information that has been presented to them about the activities of some particular project? These are not rhetorical questions. They have been presented to us in the context of the Maya ICBG and we have not been able to provide convincing answers, assuming that convincing answers exist.

These questions do, however, lead to one inescapable conclusion: It is unrealistic to assume that truthful information about questions of such complexity as access to genetic resources can be adequately addressed if PIC is considered to be a static, unitary moment in time near the beginning of a project on bioprospecting. We believe, as do others before us (International Society of Ethnobiology 1988; Ten Kate and Laird 1999; Laird 2002; Alexiades and Peluso 2002) that PIC must be considered a ongoing, give-and-take interactive process that begins first by a simple, understandable explanation of the project's activities and intellectual property, then continues to cover issues related to biodiversity conservation, relevant articles of the CBD, and other international agreements on Indigenous knowledge as the project develops over time. From the very outset, individuals and communities should be fully aware that they could freely withdraw from any agreements that are no longer satisfactory to them. In effect, in developing bioprospecting agreements, PIC is a continuing activity, not a single event.

Who Should Grant PIC?

If we can specify what PIC is, the question of "from whom do we obtain PIC?" is more troublesome. Focusing on this question, Ten Kate and Laird provide the following understated observation: "The challenge for the collector [researcher involved in bioprospecting activities] is to identify, at the local level, exactly whose consent is required" (1999: 28).

While there is no universal answer to the question as to who the stakeholders are in the PIC process, there does exist a general international consensus that consent must be obtained from *the local community*.[8] This has become clearer in recent CBD recommendations such as UNEP/CBD 1999, paragraph 161, which that states "PIC is dependent on clear recognition and protection of the rights, knowledge, and innovation and practices of indigenous and local communities."

The Mexican law governing access to biological resources is unambiguous in this regard. The Secretariat for the Environment's Article 87 and 87bis of the country's "General Law on Ecological Equilibrium and Environmental Protection" states "The authorization [of the Secretariat] for biological collections can only be granted when it is supported by the expressed and prior consent of the legitimate owner of the land on which the biological resource is encountered. Furthermore, said legitimate owners have the right to equitable compensation for benefits that might derive from the use of these resources [in the case of Indigenous areas of Mexico, this is by law the community]" (Secretaria de Medio Ambiente, Recursos Naturales, y Pesca 1997).

Furthermore, the 1996 San Andrés accords and the modified version of these accords made by the Committee for Concordance and Peace demand a recognition of the local Indigenous community as "primary in all matters relating to their natural resources." Mexico is called upon to "recognize in national legislation the Indigenous communities as entities of public rights." The nation "must mandate an order of preference that privileges the Indigenous communities in the award of concessions for obtaining the benefits from exploitation and use of [their] natural resources" (Acuerdos de San Andrés, Nuevo marco jurídico 1996).

How Is PIC Obtained?

Of the several countries that have developed legislation for implementing the CBD's Article 15, the Philippine government's regulations provide the most explicit practical guidelines for obtaining PIC. Section 2 of the Philippines' Implement Regulations on Bioprospecting, Executive order 247 (1996) states that PIC has been obtained "from the local community . . . after disclosing fully the intent and scope of the bioprospecting activity, in a language and process understandable to the community and before any bioprospecting activity is undertaken." This includes prior public notification of the intent to conduct bioprospecting with full disclosure of what the activities will involve and where they will be carried out (section 7.1.1). After public notification and a waiting period of two weeks, a detailed description of the proposed activities must be presented at a legitimately convened assembly of the local communities involved (section 7.1.2).

In addition to oral presentations, the Philippine regulations mandate that a brief written summary of the work be prepared *in the local language or dialect* that is understandable to stakeholders. The document must describe the project's proposed activities and include clear statements on benefit-sharing arrangements. In must be clear "that such activity to be conducted [in the areas under the communities' control] will not in any way affect their traditional use of their resources" (section 7.1.2). The Philippine regulations could not be more explicit and should serve as a model for all bioprospecting projects that involve Indigenous communities.

PIC from Local Communities and Access to Biological Resources in the Chiapas Highlands

How might these observations on the first three questions underlying PIC (what is it?, from whom do you get it?, and how do you get it?) be applied in the case study of the Maya ICBG? First it is important to note that highland Chiapas is a region comprised of 8,000 or more Indigenous Mayan communities. While each of these communities is located within the boundaries of politically recognized municipalities (*municipios*), it is commonly the case that municipal government authorities have no ultimate power over decisions of local governance. This is especially true regarding decisions about individual communities' use of their natural resources.

Given well-established guidelines of state, national, and international law, the Maya ICBG's research plan proceeded on the assumption that the Indigenous community was the sociopolitical unit from which PIC must be obtained. We worked to present accurate information about the project's activities "in a manner and language comprehensible to the provider [of the biological resource] (in this case, the indigenous community)" (UNEP/CBD 1999). Based in large part on the suggestions of our Mayan research assistants, we ultimately developed presentations about the project in the form of a theatrical performance. Our "teatro" included a narrator who described, in Tzeltal, Tzotzil, or Tojolabal, a series of mimed skits performed by Mayan project members. After an introduction that described our overall goals, each skit depicted a major component of the project's activities. This included demonstrations of our ethnobotanical collecting procedures (moving from the field collections of plant species in the field to final processing and illustration of specimens in the herbarium), work on Mayan medical anthropology and ethnopharmacology, establishment of ethnobotanical community gardens, and our plans to produce illustrated materials on herbal medicine in Tzeltal, Tzotzil, and Tojolabal.

The theater presentation closed with scenes of laboratory procedures that would be used for evaluating potential bioactivity of medicinal plants. We indicated that this portion of the work might result in the discovery of plant extracts that could ultimately have commercial value. We stated that, if this unlikely event were to occur (we compared its likelihood to that of winning the Mexican lottery), any monetary benefits would be distributed equally among the project's participants—ECOSUR, UGA, MNL, and a trust fund to be established under Mexican law and comprised of representatives of participating Mayan communities.

Our theater presentations did not attempt to explain the notions of patents, material transfer agreements, the legal complexities of joint ownership arrangements, the debates about multinational trade conventions (e.g., TRIPS), or the protests associated with the meetings of the World Trade Organization. It has been our experience that even so-called specialists on these subjects suffer misunderstandings and miscommunication on a regular basis. Expert knowledge does not in any way guarantee that such discussions will be straightforward, unambiguous, and understandable to the professional, let alone the layperson, and in particular, to a nonliterate Mayan farmer and his family.[9] We ultimately concluded that discussions of topics related to biodiversity patent law would be reserved for the moment when such discussions were of practical importance, that is, in the event that a particular bioassay revealed that a plant species merited further laboratory research. At that time, further prior informed consent would be requested and agreements would be negotiated, including up-front payments to participating communities. This decision followed from our understanding of PIC as a process, not a single event.

At the close of the presentation of our Mayan language theater, community members were taken on guided tours of the laboratory and herbarium facilities at El ECOSUR. Topics presented schematically in the previous skits were covered in more detail on these tours and community members were encouraged to ask questions about our planned activities. We described the work carried out in a laboratory and an herbarium. Participants also toured ongoing agroecology projects and the ECOSUR medicinal plants garden. All were asked to offer observations and suggestions for future research on crop and medicinal plant species. The complete informational presentation took the better part of a full day, with a break at midday for lunch.

In addition to the theater presentations and tours, written summaries of the Maya ICBG's goals, activities, and benefit-sharing arrangements were prepared and distributed to community participants. These bilingual materials were produced in Tzeltal, Tzotzil, Tojolabal, and Spanish. The pamphlets repeated the themes covered in the earlier presentations and indicated the benefits (nonmonetary and possibly monetary) that could accrue to the communities as a result of each activity.

If the community members who had participated in the informational sessions agreed to a second meeting in their home communities, arrangements were made and dates were set to present the project's goals once again at a general community assembly. These assembly meetings would generally take place within several weeks to a month of our original presentation. In all cases, the project sent a formal letter of request to visit and received, in return, a formal invitation to come to the community for the specific purpose of presenting an overview of the proposed work. In these community presentations, we again described our proposed benefit-sharing arrangements and emphasized the small likelihood that there would be monetary returns as a result of their participation.[10]

Communities that agreed to participate were asked to indicate their approval by signing a letter of agreement.[11] In most instances, elected community representatives signed the prepared consent agreements (see appendix A). Other communities developed their own statement of agreement (see appendix B). In some communities, individuals who were not elected leaders, but who wished their names to be recorded, also signed. In one community, the heads of households of each family signed. In all instances, the project followed traditional community norms and practices. Of the forty-seven communities that were ultimately approached as potential participants in the brief three-month period that we worked to achieve PIC, forty-six of them signed agreements. The 46 communities that agreed to participate in the Maya ICBG project were distributed widely in 15 municipalities representing $\geq$ 30,000 individuals and 3 Mayan languages—Tzeltal, Tzotzil, and Tojolabal.

What Constitutes Evidence and Who Decides That PIC Has Been Obtained?

Unresolved answers to two remaining questions on PIC and the Maya ICBG contributed significantly to the project's downfall. These are "What constitutes evidence that you've got PIC?" and "Who decides if you've got it?" We believed, as did each of the Mayan communities involved, that our signed agreements were indisputable evidence that PIC had been obtained. However, near the end of the first year of the research, the project began to be attacked, first by a local healers group and then by national and international NGOs.[12] Two broad themes emerge from these attacks. The first concerns *proprietary knowledge*. The second concerns *local communities vs. Indigenous peoples*.

Proprietary knowledge

In 1999 and early 2000, there was a brief period during which it was argued that the knowledge we were studying was secret, proprietary knowledge of specialist healers (Mooney 1999; Picard 2000). We responded that our project did not focus on specialized, secret knowledge of healers but on the ethnomedical plant knowledge of the general populace (B. Berlin and E. Berlin 1999 based in large part on findings reported in Berlin and Berlin 1996).

The healers group (CEOMPITCH) proposed that the state pass laws ceding to them dominion over all knowledge and use of medicinal plants and designating them as beneficiaries of commercialization of any natural resource product of the state of Chiapas.[13]

Little support came forward for this proposition and the debate continued on how best to determine legitimate ownership of biological resources and the traditional knowledge associated with the use of those resources. It was argued that agreements on the use of a medicinal plant species reached in one country or one community ignores the rights of other countries or communities where the same species may be found. By this view, since traditional knowledge of these biological resources often extends beyond the geographic boundaries of any individual local community, PIC must be granted by all relevant communities that hold this knowledge before bioprospecting can proceed.

One non-Indian advisor to the healers group stated that "medicinal plants are not the sole property of Chiapas, they belong to all of Mexico. Furthermore, there are plants in Chiapas that exist in Guatemala. If we [Mexicans] come to an agreement that plants found here can be carried away, patented and sold, this could be the cause of an international controversy with Guatemala because plants that are found in Chiapas are also found in Guatemala" (Alarcón 2000).

RAFI's Pat Mooney declared, "biological resources to be collected [in bioprospecting projects] . . . derive from all [Indigenous] communities. Unless *all* agree, *some* will have their rights violated. Theoretically, the agreement of even one community could legally allow the project to privatize the knowledge/resources of all of the communities" (Mooney 1999, emphasis in the original).

Both of these statements are problematic because each fails to clearly distinguish *biological resources* and *knowledge* of those resources. While it is true that species readily cross regional, state, and international boundaries, in no case do national or international regulations stipulate that a sovereign state must acquire permission of another sovereign state for access to biological resources that exist within its own boundaries. One of the primary aims of the International Convention on Biodiversity was to change the perception that the earth's biological resources were part of the patrimony of all humanity and to shift control to individual sovereign nations who could then exercise rights of ownership for natural resources within their borders.

Mooney later changed his argument to claim that PIC must be obtained from all potential holders of *knowledge* about a particular biological resource. He stated that "Bioprospectors must assume, in the absence of definitive evidence to the contrary, that the same or similar plants and preparations are used by different communities in the same country and very possibly, by communities in other countries. [Since this knowledge is shared] . . . agreement must be reached with each community before bio-prospectors can consider that they have permission to proceed" (Mooney 2000).

Such an argument fails to distinguish between public, widespread knowledge and private, restricted knowledge. Knowledge that extends across many communities, throughout a country, or across national boundaries, by nature of the extent of its distribution, must be deemed to be knowledge in the public domain.

Our own previous research in fourteen Tzeltal- and Tzotzil-speaking municipalities of highland Chiapas shows clearly that the most important medicinal species in the Mayan ethnopharmacopeia occur with the same or similar medicinal uses in many communities of the same municipality, across municipal boundaries, throughout Mexico, and in other areas of Latin America (see Berlin et al. 1996; E. Berlin and B. Berlin 1999; Berlin et al. 2000). *Lantana camara*, for example, is a widespread weedy species in the Verbenaceae, and one of the most important medicinal plants used by the highland Maya and has an almost pantropical distribution. Registered localities found in the Missouri Botanical Gardens' W³Tropicos database show a distribution of this species in the southern United States, Mexico, Belize, Guatemala, El Salvador, Honduras, Nicaragua, Costa Rica, Panama, Puerto Rico, Cuba, Haiti, Dominican Republic, Jamaica, Venezuela, Guyana, Colombia, Ecuador, Peru, Bolivia, Argentina, Paraguay, Madagascar, the Seychelles, Malawi, Tanzania, Comoros, Cameroon, Uganda, Zaire, Zambia, and Vietnam.

Furthermore, a number of the common species used by the highland Maya were introduced from Europe, presumably with the arrival of the Spanish, and most continue to be frequently used both in European and Latin American folk medicine to the present day (e.g., manzanilla *Matricaria chamomilla,* rue *Ruta graveolens,* several species of mint *Mentha* spp., garlic *Allium sativum,* common plantain *Plantago major,* basil *Ocimum basilicum,* oregano *Origanum vulgaris,* valeriana *Valeriana officinalis,* ginger *Zingiber officinale,* anise *Pimpinella anisum,* lemon grass *Cymbopogon citrata,* and a variety of species of citrus *Citrus* spp., to name a few of the most important plants). It is unreasonable to apply the standards for PIC for private knowledge to medicinal plant knowledge that has become so widely distributed that it has entered into the public domain. Furthermore, under no reasonable interpretation of international law could such public knowledge be subject to patent due to considerations of prior art.[14]

On the other hand, if particular knowledge of one of these common species is claimed to be uniquely held by a single individual or group of individuals (say, the discovery of a new use for chamomile, *Matricaria chamomilla,* to treat AIDS and this knowledge were held secretly by some individual or group of individuals) then that knowledge must be assumed to be private knowledge unless proven otherwise and would be subject to all regulations that govern private knowledge.

Local Communities vs. "Indigenous Peoples" Concerning Access to Biological Resources

A second major argument levied against the project, often logically inconsistent with issues just discussed on proprietary knowledge, concerned the CBD's stipulations that control over biological resources rests with the *local Indigenous community* (see earlier). In Chiapas, individuals have recently questioned this fundamental tenet of the convention and national and international NGOs who argue against local communities' control over their biological resources and for vesting this responsibility in larger sociopolitical units referred to in Mexico as *pueblos indios* (Indian peoples).

In the case of the Maya ICBG, the argument assumed two forms. The first was to question the legal status of communities such as those who signed letters of agreement with the project. Ron Nigh, an anthropologist who served at one time as an advisor to the healers group, argued that these communities were actually, "fictions imposed from outside," simply "administrative conveniences that may or may not bear any relationship to local residential patterns or social organization. . . . The representative status, as 'legal decision-making bodies,' of the 46 'communities' that signed agreements with the Maya ICBG is highly variable" (Nigh 2002: 473).[15]

Some Mexican intellectuals, while implicitly accepting the legal status of Indigenous communities, have suggested that their aggregation into recognized municipalities has been a policy of the government specifically aimed to break up historically recognized groupings based on "tribal" ethnicity. Sánchez (1999: 67) argues that the Mexican government attempted to destroy ethnic identity by "deliberately [fomenting] . . . the atomization of Indian peoples [pueblos indios] into fragmented communities." She furthers claims that the Zapatista Rebellion set in motion "changes of great importance, [stimulating] the unification of communities regionally that imply a reconstitution of peoples and ethnic groups" (Sánchez 1999: 68). This movement for Indian autonomy represents a "struggle to transcend the restricted 'geographically bounded' and imposed 'community' and to empower regional social and political formations of *indigenous peoples*" (Nigh 2002: 473, emphasis added).

These new political formations do not correspond to what is commonly referred to as "pueblos indígenas" in Mexico. A review of the literature indicates that the term when used in the sense of Indian peoples refers to groupings of Indigenous populations who are united by virtue of speaking the *same language*. "The name of an Indian people is taken from the name of their language. That is to say, we can suppose that there are as many Indian peoples as there are Indian languages in the country" (Montemayor 2000: 158).[16]

The map produced by the Mexican secretariat of education and the National Council for Arts and Culture, indicating the cultural diversity of Mexico, bears the legend "The Indigenous Peoples of Mexico and Their Languages" (reproduced in Montemayor 2000: 109), and the website for the Indigenous Peoples of Mexico includes a page titled "Indigenous Nations of Mexico," with a list of the names of fifty-seven "nations/ languages" (available at http://www.indians.org/welker/mexman01.htm; last accessed April 19, 2004).

In Chiapas, Article 13 of the state constitution speaks of the Indigenous peoples that reside within its boundaries in terms of their respective languages: "The State of Chiapas sustains a multicultural population in its Indigenous peoples. This constitution recognizes and protects the following Indigenous peoples: Tzeltal, Tzotzil, Chol, Zoque, Tojolabal, Mam, Kachiquel, Lacandón and Mochó"[17] (Gobierno del Estado de Chiapas 2000).

However, while Indigenous language and Indigenous nation may be concordant in some areas of the world, it is generally the case in Latin America that groupings of Indigenous populations who speak the same language (or dialects of that language) do not comprise a single *ethnic group*. One's ethnic identity in the highlands of Chiapas lies not with the groupings of Indigenous peoples who speak Tzeltal or who speak Tzotzil. Here, identity is first and foremost defined by the person's *municipality* membership, followed closely by the person's identity with a particular *community*. Municipalities may be comprised almost exclusively of one or the other major languages or, as is more commonly the case in modern Chiapas, a combination of both. Standards of dress, etiquette, and speech are readily identified by municipality. Within municipalities, individuals' loyalties are to their communities that also exhibit self-identifying features of speech and dress style.

This general lack of correspondence with native language and primary ethnic identity is typical of other areas of Mexico and many parts of Latin America. More significantly, in terms of the environmental policy implications of bioprospecting and PIC, few if any of the so-called native peoples of Mexico (as defined by a common language) have organized themselves into sociopolitical organizations with their own forms of self-government, elected officials, or procedures for the legitimate representation of the local communities that comprise them.

Efforts to establish cohesive ethnic groups as exemplified by those formed by the Zapatista Rebellion are supported by many individuals who speak one or more Indigenous languages, and such groups aim to transcend traditional localized and geographically restricted communities. However, these groupings do not correspond to what are now referred to as Mexico's "pueblos indios."

Ultimately, the Maya ICBG was confronted with an apparent insurmountable obstacle. On the one hand, the legitimacy of permissions received from participating communities was contested in that their legal status to make agreements was denied. Nigh, for example, claims that "Neither current Mexican legislation nor the CBD recognizes the right of such entities [communities] to sign agreements for the disposition of property rights to knowledge or plant genetic material generally acknowledged to be common heritage of all Maya peoples" (2002: 472).

On the other hand, no representative and comprehensive sociopolitical organization (a "pueblo índio") existed in Chiapas to whom PIC requests could be directed nor is one (or more) likely to exist anytime in the near future. As stated by one of the primary supporters of the formation of politically recognized, autonomous "Indian peoples"—"Right now, in Mexico, you cannot get PIC from a pueblo indígena because the definition of what constitutes a pueblo indígena remains undecided" (Neil Harvey, personal communication).

Conclusion

The Maya ICBG project made serious, transparent efforts to obtain PIC, implementing the major recommendations on process called for by the CBD, the Mexican government, and the state of Chiapas. However, the legitimacy of our agreements was denied, first, because the communities that granted these agreements were said to lack legal status, and second, because the rights of communities to exercise control over their biological resources was denied and attributed to larger regional yet-to-be-formed sociopolitical organizations known as "Indian peoples." Mayan communities that had indicated their willingness to participate in the project, lacking any umbrella organization to represent them as a whole, were unable to, or chose not to, become involved in the acrimonious debate that engulfed the project. The negative publicity that besieged the project finally led ECOSUR to withdraw and the project came to an end in October 2001 (see appendix C).

Some future critique of the objections against bioprospecting discussed in this chapter will show them to be proxies for concerns about much larger political questions that include patents, especially patents on compounds derived from natural products, biotechnology in general, and bioengineering in particular, based on the view that all biotechnological advances are under the control of lucrative multinational corporations. Biotechnology and patents, in turn, are viewed as part of the driving forces contributing to globalization and the neoliberalist policies of the developed countries of the North at the expense of developing countries of the South.[18]

Viewed in this light, the issues that faced the Maya ICBG project are in reality just an early glimpse of the social, political, and ethical challenges that bioprospecting and bioscience projects must face in the new century—a century where the rational and equitable uses of biodiversity will be essential to the well-being of the developing world. Unfortunately, even if these challenges are successfully met it will almost certainly be too late for most of world's Indigenous peoples.

Appendix A

Acuerdo Comunitario

Grupo de Cooperación Internacional para la Biodiversidad Maya
ICBG-Maya
Maya International Cooperative Biodiversity Group

Comunidad: [illegible]

Fecha: el 12 de Abril 2000.

PRESENTES

Reunidos en la comunidad mencionada del Municipio de [illegible], Chiapas, y contando con nuestro conocimiento previo, expreso e informado, como propietarios y poseedores de los terrenos en los cuales se realizaran las actividades del proyecto Investigación Farmacéutica y uso Sustentable del Conocimiento Etnobotánico y Biodiversidad en la región Maya de los Altos de Chiapas (ICBG-Maya), MANIFESTAMOS QUE:

Estamos completamente de acuerdo y así mismo damos nuestra autorización para que el proyecto de ICBG-Maya realice las colectas de plantas y hongos para el apoyo a las actividades que el proyecto realizará en nuestra comunidad.

Si por alguna razón la comunidad en algún momento decide no seguir participando con el mencionado proyecto, se deberá hacer llegar por escrito la suspención e inconformidad del mismo, para darle el cumplimiento al documento.

(Firmas y sellos de los autoridades y miembros de la comunidad)

PATRONATO DE MEJORAS MATERIALES BARRIO NUEVO CHANAL, CHIAPAS

[illegible] Gómez López — Patronato de Mejoras materiales

C. Primitivo [illegible] — Srio. del Comité de educación

Appendix B

A C T A   D E   A C U E R D O .

EN LA COMUNIDAD DE [illegible], MUNICIPIO DE [illegible], DEL ESTADO DE-- CHIAPAS, SIENDO LAS 14:00 (CATORCE) HORAS P.M., DEL DIA 04 DEL -- MES DE ABRIL DEL AÑO 2000, (DOS MIL), SE REUNIERON EN LA CANCHA-- DE BASQUET- BOL DE LA ESCUELA PRIMARIA BILINGUE " [illegible] ",- LOS CC. [illegible], AGENTE RURAL MUNICIPAL, [illegible], PRESIDENTE DEL COMITE DE EDUCACION, PATRONATOS Y PRI NCIPALES DE LA MISMA.- -

EL OBJETIVO PRINCIPAL DE LA REUNION ERA PARA INFORMARLES LOS ASAM BLEISTAS SOBRE EL PROYECTO DE ICBG- MAYA, ESTANDO PRESENTE LA MAYO- RIA DEL POBLADO, DONDE SE DISCUTIERON AMPLIAMENTE QUE VENTAJE Y DES VENTAJA TRAE EL PROYECTO, POR FIN TANTO ANALISIS LLEGARON A UNA CON CLUSION QUE SI SE ACEPTA EL DICHO PROYECTO, SE SOMETIO A VOTACION-- POR MAYORIA DE VOTO CONCLUYEN QUE SI.- - - - - - - - - - - - - - -

NO HABIENDO OTRO ASUNTO QUE TRATAR SE LEVANTA LA PRESENTE ACTA-- DE ACUERDO POR TRIPLICADO, SIENDO EXACTAMENTE LAS 17:00 DEL MISMO-- DIA MES Y AÑO, FIRMANDO LOS QUE EN ELLA INTERVINIERON- - - - - - - - - - - - - - - - - - - D A   F E - - - - - - - - - - - - - - - - -

LOS REPRESENTANTES

EL AGENTE RURAL MPAL	EL PRESIDENTE DEL COMITE DE EDUC.
[illegible]	[illegible]
C. [illegible]	C. [illegible]
C. [illegible]	C. [illegible]

AGENTE RURAL MUNICIPAL del Paraje Chalam, Mitontic, Chiapas

Comité de Asociación de Padres de Familia de la Escuela Primaria "LEANDRO VALLE" Clave: 07DPB2453D Chalám, Mitontic, Chiapas

Appendix C

El Colegio de la Frontera Sur
San Cristóbal de Las Casas,
Chiapas, México

October 16, 2001

Dr. Joshua Rosenthal, Director,
International Cooperative Research Groups Program
Fogarty International Center
National Institutes of Health
Bethesda, MD
USA

Dear Josh,

This letter is to inform you that we at ECOSUR have decided to discontinue our participation in the ICBG-Maya project. There are two main reasons why we are taking this difficult decision since I sent my support letter of July 26, 2001. First, presently we have no researchers form ECOSUR willing to participate in the project. Initially, there were three researchers (José Carlos Fernández, Luís García and Mario González), but for different reasons (job change, personal decision, or sabbatical), they are not participating any longer. We have not been able to identify other current faculty who have the background and expertise required to move ahead at this point and who are willing to participate.

The second reason is that despite the developments we have achieved in promoting the active participation of academic institutions on the discussion of controversial issues and in gaining the support of the state government to negotiate with COMPITCH, we believe that these have not moved to a point where we can continue the project without big problems. On the contrary, we believe that in order to advance in these discussions and negotiations, we must unfortunately cancel our participation in it. This might be a wrong decision, but it is the decision we have come to after careful analysis, discussion, and consultation. We regret the effects this might have on other ICBG projects and sincerely hope it will not adversely affect them.

I would like to emphasize that we recognize and sincerely appreciate the highly professional and ethical performances of Drs. Brent and Elois Ann Berlin in their efforts to carry out the Maya ICBG project. As from the initial development of the proposal, we were in total agreement with the goals of the project and we believe that it was the correct approach to conserve knowledge and biodiversity, and to use this knowledge and natural resources on the benefit of the Mayan people of the Chiapas Highlands. Unfortunately, the social conditions have not been favorable or we have not known how to deal with the attacks from COMPITCH and other organizations such as RAFI and Global Exchange. We have learned many important things during the time of this project and we highly appreciate the Berlins' contributions and friendship.

I would like to thank you, very much, for all your support and advice. We are in a position to do whatever needs to be done regarding the cancellation of the project and our commitments. We would like to keep in contact with you and hope that you will feel free to contact us at any time. Our challenge now is to continue the discussions that could lead to the definition of a state and national position regarding bioprospecting and the use of biodiversity. We believe that this is fundamental for the sustainable development of rural areas in Southeastern Mexico and Central America, and we are certain that we will benefit from exchange of ideas and experiences with you.

I would also want to express our gratitude to the ICBG Program, the Fogarty International Center, NIH and all the persons and organizations that have supported the project and have supported us.

Sincerely,

Dr. José Pablo Liedo Fernández,
Director General

Notes

1. From 1932 to 1972, 399 poor African American sharecroppers in Macon County, Alabama, were denied treatment for syphilis. As part of the U.S. Public Health Service Tuskegee Syphilis Study, designed to document the natural history of the disease, these men were told that they were being treated for "bad blood." As reported by the *New York Times* on July 26, 1972, the Tuskegee Syphilis Study was "the longest non-therapeutic experiment on human beings in medical history" (Abstract of the Syphilis Study Legacy Committee Final Report of May 20, 1996). News of this study stimulated public outrage and produced a congressional subcommittee that resulted in the Belmont Report and a complete revision of the Department of Health, Education, and Welfare's regulations for research involving human subjects. These new regulations established the standard for medical research and were gradually expanded to include all federally funded research involving human subjects.

2. Reid et al. first defined bioprospecting in 1993 as "the exploration of biodiversity for commercially valuable genetic resources." While the term may be recent, the search for natural products that may have potential commercial value has been part of the process of discovering new medicines throughout history. Many pharmaceuticals and phytomedicinals on the market today are the result of such long-term exploration of biodiversity.

3. While the United States has not ratified the convention, former President Clinton signed it. Researchers funded by NIH, NSF, and other U.S. agencies are explicitly bound by the relevant CBD regulations if they are involved in research related to bioprospecting. In addition, all such research must satisfy the local, state, and federal regulations on access to genetic resources established by the host country where the bioprospecting project is being conducted.

4. We have aimed to restrict our discussion here to issues relating directly to prior informed consent. A comprehensive ethnographic description of the project is currently in progress (Berlin and Berlin in preparation).

5. This research was generously supported by the U.S. government agencies that included the National Institutes of Health (NIH), the National Science Foundation (NSF), and the U.S. Department of Agriculture. This support is gratefully acknowledged.

6. Botanical collection numbers were made in sets of seven herbarium voucher specimens when possible. A complete set has been labeled and mounted and is available at the Herbarium at ECOSUR. Remaining sets were prepared for distribution to collaborating herbaria in Mexico (the National Autonomous University of Mexico, the Institute of Ecology in Jalapa, Veracruz, and the herbarium of the state of Chiapas). Other sets will ultimately be made available to the Herbaria of the California Academy of Sciences and the University of Georgia.

7. The UN maintains a permanent working group on Article 8 (j) and related provisions of the CBD as they concern Indigenous and local communities. (See UNEP/CBG/COP 2000.) Sarah A. Laird's *Biodiversity and Traditional Knowledge: Equitable Partnerships in Practice* is probably the best introduction available dealing with the complex issues surrounding access to biodiversity and Indigenous knowledge. The bibliographic references in this important monograph provide a good guide to the current literature. Other indispensable references include Reid et al. (1993), Posey and Dutfield (1996), Pan American Health Organization (1996), Svarstad and Dhillion (2000), Zerner (2000), The Crucible II Group (2000), and Ten Kate and Laird (1999). Many of these sources include valuable website addresses for organizations involved in biodiversity issues.

8. As Brosius and others have pointed out (Brosius, Tsing, and Zerner 1998) the terms *local* and *community* refer to concepts that must be contextually defined. We are in agreement with Brosius that it is not "up to the anthropologist to determine who counts as [a] local [community] and who doesn't" (personal communication). We would agree and also add that it is not up to NGOs to determine who counts as a local community. Our discussion of community in this chapter is not something that we determined but represents the consensus views of the Indigenous peoples with whom we have worked, state and federal government authorities, and official government documents that clearly provide legal status to local groupings recognized as *comunidades indígenas*.

9. Formal education for the Indigenous communities in Chiapas is minimal and frequently lacking. The mean level for the state is less than fourth grade (INEI 2000).

10. Our efforts to downplay unrealistic expectations of monetary rewards in return for community cooperation was based in large part on our knowledge of communities' past experience with government projects that promised the world but ultimately provided little or nothing in return. Our Mayan collaborators were perhaps the most adamant on this issue, urging us not to mention "money" be-

cause as soon as we did so, potential collaborators would want to know how much and when it would be received. If we failed to deliver, we would be no better than earlier government programs. Ironically, questions concerning monetary benefits figured prominently in the propaganda campaign against the project. It was assumed, indeed ardently believed, that our research would lead to enormous financial rewards. However, it was also claimed that the project's proposal for benefit sharing was a thinly disguised ploy to deprive Indigenous communities of their equitable share to the millions of dollars that would be earned by participating multinational pharmaceutical companies.

11. We developed an agreement form modeled on guidelines of the U.S. Department of Health and Human Services, NIH, and the University of Georgia Institutional Review Board.

12. The healers group is an aggregation of individuals who produce herbal remedies for sale, both locally and on the Internet. They do not represent local communities. To aid them in their attack on the project, the group contacted Rural Advancement Foundation International (RAFI, who have recently changed their name to the ETC group), a Canadian-based NGO with a long history of opposition to bioprospecting. RAFI's head, Pat Mooney, questioned the validity of our attempting to obtain individual community agreements, arguing instead that the group comprised of traditional healers who opposed the project should be given privileged status in the process of PIC. He asked, "What represents consensus? Are [the objections of] 11 organizations under the Consejo [the healers group known by the acronym CEOMPITCH] not significant enough [to stop the project]?" (Pat Mooney in an email to Darrell Posey, December 9, 1999). RAFI ultimately provided the healers group with a Mexican legal consultant who went to great lengths to sabotage negotiations arbitrated by the government's secretariat for the environment in 2000.

13. In a paper presented at a 1999 workshop of the Center for Advanced Studies in Social Anthropology in San Cristóbal de Las Casas, Rafael Alarcón and Hector Mejias, advisors to the healers group and speaking on their behalf, read a paper titled "Biopiracy of the Resources of Indigenous Traditional Medicine in the State of Chiapas, Mexico." In this paper, they proposed that "[the State of Chiapas] legislate in favor of and with the participation of the state council of Indigenous Healers on the intellectual property related to the knowledge and use of medicinal plants and combinations possessed by these traditional healers. Guaranteeing that everything related to globalization of the management of these natural resources and prospective related commercialization (patents) with research centers and national and international pharmaceutical companies be in benefit of the practitioners of indigenous medicine as well as the producers of natural resources." [Que se legisle, a favor y con la participar:ión (participación) del consejo

Estatal de Médicos Indígenas Tradicionales, sobre la propiedad intellectual relacionada con los sabers y usos que (sic) sobre las plantas medicinales, y combinaciones de éstas, poseen los propios medicos tradicionales. Guarantizando, que todo lo relacionado con la globaiización (sic) en el manejo de estos recursos naturales e interreiación (sic) y empresas farmacéuticas nacionales e internacionales, sea en beneficio para los practicantes de la medicina indigena, asi como de los productores de los recursos naturales.]

14. "The validity of a patent application . . . is considered by examining the prior art base in order to determine whether the invention was known or used by others, or patented or described in a printed publication in this or a foreign country, more than one year prior to the application for patent was filed" (see 35 USC 103, conditions for patentability; nonobvious subject matter). Defensive disclosures, by describing information in a printed publication or other publicly accessible medium, places it in the public domain. This also establishes it as prior art and ensures recognition of its origins, fosters its sharing and use, and potentially impedes patent applications based on this information. In the past, defensive disclosures were limited to traditional publication methods (books, journals, etc.) and were often copyrighted. Recently, the United States Patent and Trademark Office (USPTO) issued a white paper stating that electronic publications, including online databases and other types of Internet publications, are considered to be "printed publications" within the scope of prior art and/or the public domain. Currently, *anything in the public domain is given equal weight by the USPTO in its consideration of prior art.*" Traditional Ecological Knowledge Prior Art Database (T.E.K.* P.A.D.), American Association for the Advancement of Science, website, available at: ip.aaas.org/tekindex.nsf, emphasis added; last accessed on January 15, 2004.

15. In a rebuttal to Nigh (Berlin and Berlin 2002), we challenged him to identify which of the forty-six communities had dubious status as "legal decision-making bodies." We stated that with this information in hand, we would then ask the local community assemblies of these forty-six communities to respond to his assessment of their communities' legal status and then post the results of our inquiry on our website (guallart.dac.uga.edu). Nigh failed to respond to the challenge.

16. "El nombre de los pueblos indios se toma del nombre de sus lenguas. Es decir, debemos suponer que hay tantos pueblos indios cuantas lenguas indígenas existan en el país."

17. "El Estado de Chiapas tiene una población pluricultural sustentada en sus pueblos indígenas. Esta constitución reconoce y protege a los siguientes pueblos indígenas: Tzeltal, tzotsil, chol, zoque, tojolabal, mame, kakchiquel, lacandon y mocho."

18. There is no generally agreed upon definition of this overused term. However, Paul Treanor's definition is probably as good as any:

> Neoliberalism is a philosophy in which the existence and operation of a market are valued in themselves, separately from any previous relationship with the production of goods and services, and without any attempt to justify them in terms of their effect on the production of goods and services; and where the operation of a market or market-like structure is seen as an ethic in itself, capable of acting as a guide for all human action, and substituting for all previously existing ethical beliefs (web.inter.nl.net/users/Paul.Treanor/neoliberalism.html).

References

Acuerdos de San Andrés
Nuevo Marco Jurídico. www.usip.org/library/pa/chiapas/acuerdo_960216.html. [1996]. Last accessed April 19, 2004.

Alarcón, Rafael
Radio interview Radio Station XERA, San Cristobal de Las Casas, Chiapas México, 10 August 2000.

Alarcón, Rafael, and Hector Mejias
La Biopirateria de los Recursos de la Medicina Indígena Tradicional en el Estado de Chiapas, México. Paper presented at the Symposium on Biodiversity, Environment, and Traditional Medicine, Center for Advanced Studies in Social Anthropology, San Cristóbal de Las Casas, Chiapas, Mexico, 1999.

Alexiades, Miguel N., and Daniela M. Peluso
Prior Informed Consent: The Anthropology and Politics of Cross-Cultural Exchange. In *Biodiversity and Traditional Knowledge,* edited by Sarah A. Laird, appendix 7. London: Earthscan Publications, Ltd., 2002.

American Association for the Advancement of Science
Traditional Ecological Knowledge Prior Art Database (T.E.K.* P.A.D.). Available at: http://ip.aaas.org/tekindex.nsf; last accessed January 9, 2004.

Berlin, Brent, and Elois Ann Berlin
Rebuttal to Ronald Nigh. "Maya Medicine in the Biological Gaze." *Current Anthropology,* vol. 43 (2002): 789–791.

Knowledge? Whose Property? Whose Benefits? The case of OMIECH, RAFI, and the Maya ICBG. [1999]. Available at: http://guallart.dac.uga.edu/ICBGreply.html; last accessed January 9, 2004.

The Maya ICBG Project in Chiapas Mexico: Past and Future History. In preparation.

Berlin, Brent, Elois Ann Berlin, Jose Carlos Fernández Ugalde, Luís García Barrios, J. David Puett, and Robert Nash
The Maya ICBG: Drug Discovery, Medical Ethnobiology, and Alternative Forms of Economic Development in the Highland Maya Region of Chiapas, Mexico. In *The International Biodiversity Group Program:* Special Issue of *Journal of Pharmaceutical Biology,* edited by Joshua Rosenthal, 2000.

Berlin, Elois Ann, and Brent Berlin
Medical Ethnobiology of the Highland Maya (with contributions by X. Lozoya, J. R. Ricárdez, D. E. Breedlove, M. Meckes, J. Tortoriello, M. Villarreal, G. Rodríguez, L. Maffi, V. Jara, R. M. Laughlin). Princeton: Princeton University Press, 1996.

General Overview of Maya Ethnomedicine. In *Cultural and Spiritual Values of Biodiversity,* edited by D. A. Posey, 273–275. Nairobi, Kenya: UNEP, Intermediate Technology Publications, 1999.

Breedlove, Dennis E. Listados Floristicos de México
III Flora de Chiapas. Instituto de Biologia, México D. F.: Universidad Nacional Autónoma de México (UNAM), 1996.

Brosius, J. Peter, Anna L. Tsing, and Charles Zerner
Representing Communities: Histories and Politics of Community-based Natural Resource Management. *Society and Natural Resources,* vol. 11, no. 57 (1998): 157–168.

Clark, John, and Michael Blake.
Los Mokayas. In *La Población Indigena de Chiapas*, edited by Victor Manuel Esponda Jimeno, 25–48. Instituto chiapaneco de Cultura, Gobierno del Estado de Chiapas, Soconusco de Chiapas, México: Tuxtla Gutiérrez, 1993.

The Crucible II Group
Seeding Solutions. Volume 1. Policy Options for Genetic Resources: People Plants and Patents Revisited. Rome, Italy: copublished by the International Development Research Centre (IDRC), the International Plant Genetic Resources Institute (IGRI), and the Dag Hammarskjold Foundation, 2000.

Gobierno del Estado de Chiapas
Constitución del Estado. Chiapas, Mexico: Tuxtla Gutierrez, 2000.

Constitución del Estado de Chiapas. Chiapas, Mexico: Tuxtla Gutierrez, 2002. Also available at: http://www.chiapas.gob.mx/; last accessed on December 10, 2003.

Gobierno Federal de México y Ejército Zapatista Liberación Nacional
Acuerdos de San Andrés: Acuerdos sobre derechos y culturas indígenas. [1996]. Available at: http://www.ezlnaldf.org/static/documentos/sanandrs.html; last accessed on September 17, 2003.

Government of the Philippines
Prescribing Guidelines and Establishing a Regulatory Framework for the Prospecting of Biological and Genetic Resources, Their By-Products and Derivatives, For Scientific and Commercial Purposes, and For Other Purposes. Executive Order 247. Manila, The Philippines: 1995.

Heller, Jean
Syphilis Patients Died Untreated. *Washington Evening Star,* 25 July 1972.

Indigenous Peoples of Mexico
Indigenous Nations of Mexico. Available at: http://www.indians.org/welker/mexman01.htm; last accessed on April 19, 2004.

Instituto Nacional de Estadística e Informática (INEI)
National Census. [2000]. IINEGI. Available at: www.inegi.gob.mx.

International Society of Ethnobiology
Declaration of Belem. [1988]. Available at: http://guallart.dac.uga.edu/ISE.

Laird, Sarah A. (Ed.)
Biodiversity and Traditional Knowledge: Equitable Partnerships in Practice (@ p. 361). London: Earthscan Publications, Ltd., 2002.

Lee Whiting, Thomas A.
La Perspectiva Diacrónica y Resistencia Étnica en Chiaps. In *El Arreglo de los Pueblos Indios: La Incansable Tarea de Reconstitución*, edited by Jacinto Arias Perez. Tuxtla Gutiérrez: Secretaria de Educación Pública, Gobierno del Estado de Chiapas, Instituto de Cultura, 1994.

Montemayor, C.
Los Pueblos Indios de México Hoy. D. F., México: Editoriales Planeta Mexicana, 2000.

Mooney, Pat
Call to Dialogue or Call to 911? RAFI Geno-Type, November 2, 2000, Rural Advancement Federation International, www.rafi.org now http://www.etcgroup.org/; last accessed on January 9, 2004.

Messages from the Chiapas Bioprospecting Dispute. RAFI Geno-Type December 22, 1999. Rural Advancement Federation International, www.rafi.org, now http://www.etcgroup.org/; last accessed on January 9, 2004.

Nash, June C.
Mayan Visions: The Quest for Autonomy in an Age of Globalization. New York: Routledge, 2001.

Nigh, Ronald
Maya Medicine in the Biological Gaze: Bioprospecting Research As Herbal Fetishism. *Current Anthropology*, vol. 43 (2002): 451–477.

Pan American Health Organization
Biodiversity, Biotechnology, and Sustainable Development in Health and Agriculture: Emerging Connections. Scientific Publication No. 560. Washington, D.C.: Pan American Health Organization/World Health Organization, 1996.

Picard, Miguel
Los Organismos Genéticamente Modificados: Implicaciones para México y Chiapas. (II/II), Chiapas al Día, No. 175. Centro de Investigaciones Económicas y Políticas de Acción Comunitaria A. C., 2000.

Posey, Darrell A., and Graham Dutfield
Beyond Intellectual Property. Ottawa: International Development Research Centre, 1996.

Reid, W. R., S. A. Laird, C. A. Meyer, R. Gámez, A. Sittenfeld, D. H. Janzen, M. A. Gollin, and C. Juma
Biodiversity Prospecting: Using Genetic Resources for Sustainable Development. Washington, D.C: World Resources Institute, 1993.

Ribeiro, Silvia
"Stop Biopiracy in Mexico!" Indigenous Peoples' Organizations from Chiapas Demand Immediate Moratorium, Mexican Government Says No to Bioprospecting Permits. [October 23, 2000]. Rural Advancement Federation International, www.rafi.org, now http://www.etcgroup.org/; last accessed on January 9, 2004.

Sánchez, Consuelo
Los pueblos Indígenas: Del indigenismo a la autonomía. México, D.F., México: Siglo Veintiuno Editores, 1999.

Secretaria de Medio Ambiente, Recursos Naturales, y Pesca
Ley General de Equilibrio Ecológico y la Protección al Ambiente (LEGEEPA). México, D. F., México, 1997.

Svarstad, Hanne, and Shivcharn S. Dhillion (eds.)
Bioprospecting: From Biodiversity in the South to Medicines in the North. Oslo: Spartacus Forlag, 2000.

Syphilis Study Legacy Committee.
Abstract of the Final Report. http://hsc.virginia.edu/hs-library/historical/apology/report.html. [1996]; last accessed on April 14, 2004.

Ten Kate, Kerry, and Sarah A. Laird
Commercial Uses of Biodiversity. London: Earthscan Publications, Ltd., 1999.

UNEP/CBD
Convention on Biodiversity. Conference of the Parties, May 6, 1997. Available at: www.biodiv.org/decisions/default.aspx; last accessed in April 19, 2004.

UNEP/CBD
Convention on Biodiversity. Conference of the Parties. May 8, 1999. Available at: www.biodiv.org/decisions/default.aspx; last accessed in April 19, 2004.

UNEP
Convention on Biodiversity. Conference of the Parties. June 7, 2000.

United Nations Environmental Programme (UNEP)
Convention on Biodiversity. Nairobi: UNEP, 1992. Available at: http://www.biodiv.org/convention/articles/asp; last accessed on April 19, 2004.

United States Department of Health Education and Welfare
The Belmont Report. Ethical Principles and Guidelines for the Protection of Subjects of Human Biomedical and Behavioral Research. National Commission for the Protection of Human Subjects of Biomedical and Behavioral Research. [1979]. http://ohrp.osophs.dhhs.gov/humansubjects/guidance/belmont.htm#xethical; last accessed on April 14, 2004.

United States Patent and Trademark Office
35 USC 103. Available at: www.uspto.gov/; last accessed January 9, 2004.

Weijer Charles, and Ezekiel J. Emanuel
Ethics: Protecting Communities in Biomedical Research. *Science*, vol. 289 (2000): 1142–1144.

World Trade Organization
Agreements Establishing the World Trade Organization (WTO). Annex 1C Trade-Related Aspects of Intellectual Property Rights (TRIPS). [1994].

Available at: http://www.wto.org/english/docs_e/legal_e/legal_e.htm# TRIPS; last accessed January 9, 2004.

Zerner, Charles (ed.)
People, Plants, and Justice: The Politics of Nature Conservation. New York: Columbia University Press, 2000.

INDEX

Aboriginal Embassy, 7
Aboriginal Indians Protection Ordinance (British Guiana), 101, 104–105
Aboriginal law, Australian, 10; customary rights, 10
Aboriginal Reconciliation (Australia), 7–8
Aboriginal and Torres Strait Islander Commission, 80
"Aboriginality," 8, 10, 18, 314, 316; objects, motifs, symbols of, 10, 12
"Aboriginals" (British Guiana). *See* Guyanese Amerindians
Aborigines, Australian, 6–20, 77, 260, 313, 315; Aboriginal art, 6, 315–316; Aboriginal arts centers, and trademarks, 80; Aboriginal women artists, 15–16, 19; Aboriginal women's knowledge, 15–16; artists' copyright claims, 9, 12; arts and crafts cooperatives, 81; British colonial rule, 8
Aboriginals, Canadian, 311, 322, 325–326, 328, 329. *See also* First Nations
Abuja (Nigeria), 164
academic research. *See* research
access and benefit-sharing arrangements, 115, 154–169
Accord for a Firm and Lasting Peace in Guatemala. *See* Guatemala, Peace Accords
Acre (Brazil), 107
Afinga (NGO), 160
Africa, 155, 161–163
Akabal, Humberto, 205
Alaska, 55–89
Alaska Department of Commerce and Economic Development, 58, 72–73
Alaska Native Arts and Crafts (ANAC), 69–70
Alaska Native Claims Settlement Act (ANCSA), 71–72
Alaska Native Heritage Center, 73–74
Alaska Native Service, 69
Alaska Natives, 55–89, 314; as artists and artisans, 58–89; effects of acculturation, 71; ethnicity determined by blood quantum, 65, 67–68; Native arts market, 55–89; struggles for rights, 83; and

tourism, 57–58, 62, 65, 69–70, 74; trade in walrus ivory, 65
Alaska State Council on the Arts (AKSCA), 74
Alaskan Native arts, 55–89; authenticity, 58–89; counterfeit art, 58–89, 72; "feather law," 63; impact of regulation, 62–63; marketing, 69, 73–74; protection against imports and imitations, 69–70; purposes for creating art, 74
Alberta (Canada), 328
Alhalkere Utopia, Australia, 19
Alta Verapaz (Guatemala), 193
alternative trade organizations. *See* indigenous cooperatives
Alvarado, Pedro de, 176
Amazonia, Peruvian, 32; use of short-wave radio, 38–40
Amazonian peoples, 30; *ayahuasca* patent, 114; link between music and shamanism, 33; traditional music, 32–33
Amazonian Peoples' Resources Initiative (APRI), 36, 38–40
American Indian, 4. *See also* Native Americans
American Indian Arts and Crafts Act, 18, 69, 70, 73
Amerindian Act (Guyana), 99, 101, 105–108, 117n5–n8; legislative reform, 99, 107; regulation of Amerindian life, 105–107
Amerindian Peoples Association (APA) (Guyana), 106, 107, 111, 116
Amerindian Research Unit (Guyana), 114
Amerindian rights movement. *See* Guyanese Amerindian rights movement
Anchorage (Alaska), 77
Anchorage Museum of History and Art, 62
Andean Commission, States of the, 154
Anglo-Australian law, 10; abrogation of indigenous sovereignty, 10; non-recognition of Aboriginal law, 10
anise (*Pimpinella anisum*), 356
antiquities, history of commerce in, 312–314
Aotearoa (New Zealand), 221
appropriation, 6; Aboriginal art, 10; aided by the digital revolution, 30; Alaska Native artistic designs, 77–78; archaeology, 311–323; artistic designs, 8
artistic designs published in books, 77–78; of ceremonial practices and ritual objects, 29; copyright claims, 9; decontextualization of collectively-held knowledge, 30; and globalization, 29, 360; of indigenous iconography, 10; and indigenous sovereignty, 16; lands and private property, 128; of Maori culture, 234; as mechanism of colonization, 10; Russian powwow enthusiasts, 6; repatriation, 6; as stealing, 6
Arawak, 100, 117n1. *See also* Guyanese Amerindians
archaeology, 309–333; control over process and products, 309–312, 325–328; mechanisms for protection, 311, 323–331; repatriation, 310, 328; as shared heritage, 312

Archivo General de Centroamérica (AGCA), 182
Archivo Histórico Arquidiocesano, 182
Arguedas, José María, 37
arogyapacha (*Trichopus zelanicus*), 155, 157–158
art cooperatives, 71
artifact mining, 59, 63
Aryavaidya Pharmacy Coimbatore, Ltd. (India), 156
Association of Indigenous Pharmaceutical Manufacturers (Nigeria), 164
Association of South East Asian Nations (ASEAN), 154
Athabascan artists, 77
Atorads. *See* Wapishana Amerindians
Australia, 5–6, 18, 77, 78; colonial law toward Aboriginals, 8; extra-legal "indigenous copyright, 78; indigenous sovereignty extinguished, 5; new copyright standards, 78; revitalization of cultural traditions, 37
Australian 1968 Copyright Act, 10
Australian Indigenous Art Trade Association, 78

Bali, 59, 63, 86n6
balsamroot (*Balsamorbiza sagittata*), 282, 283–288, 290, 292
basil (*Ocimum basilicum*), 356
Bedrijf Geneesmiddelen Vooriziening Suriname (BGVS), 159
Belize, 176
Belize Indigenous Training Institute, 81
Benjamin, Walter, 28
biocolonialism, 251–273
biodiversity, ix, 157–159, 161–162, 164, 166–168, 252; equitable uses of, 360. *See also* Chapter 10
biopiracy, 113, 114, 251–255, 261, 271, 272, 273n1, 274n13
bioprospecting, 99, 113, 153–169, 252–253, 261, 279–299, 310–311, 341–360, 360n2; compensation of participating individuals, 160–161; equitable uses of, 360 (*see also* Chapter 10, Chapter 12); short and medium-term benefits, 163, 166, 346; use of prior informed consent, 347–353
Bioresources Development and Conservation Programme (BDCP), 162–164, 166, 169
Bismarck (North Dakota), 12
"blood quantum," 257, 273n3
Bolivia, 37, 323
Brazil, 30, 100, 107
Brazilian Makushis, 108
Brazilian Wapishanas, 108, 114
Bristol Myers Squibb Pharmaceutical Research Institute, 159
British Columbia, 282–283, 298, 309, 314, 323–325, 327, 328, 331
British Guiana, 104–106; 117n4; treatment of Amerindians, 102–106
Brown, Michael F., 11, 294, 299, 330
Bureau of Indian Affairs (BIA), 69

Canada, 5, 64, 71, 79
Canadian Bacterial Diseases Network (CBDN), 288
Canadian Broadcasting Corporation Radio Network, 288

Canadian Intellectual Property Office, 327
Cardinal-Schubert, Joane, 6
Carib, 100–102, 188n1. *See also* Guyanese Amerindians
Cavelli-Sforza, Luca, 262, 264, 266–268, 274n17–18, 274n21–24
Center for Andean Ethnomusicology (CAE), 36–37; research activities, 37
Center for the Documentation of Bolivian Music, 37
Central America, 129
Centre for Amerindian Rights and Environmental Law (Guyana), 116
CEOMPITCH, 354, 362n12
Charter of the Indigenous-Tribal Peoples of the Tropical Forests, 130
Chávez, Don Adrián Inéz, 194
Chenalhó (Chiapas), 345
The Cheyenne, 13
Chiapas (Mexico), 342–360, *344*; ethnic identity in, 358. *See also* The Maya, Maya ICBG
Chief Crazy Horse (Rosebud Sioux), 17
Chukchi Sea Trading Company, 81; endorsement of Silver Hand, 81; use of Internet for marketing, 81
Chup, Chivley, 59
Clinton, Bill, 234
Cochabanmba (Bolivia), 37
COICA-UNDP Regional Meeting on Intellectual Property Rights and Biodiversity, 131
Cojti' Cuxil, Dr. Demetrio, 186, 201
Cologne Karnival, 318
Colop, Enrique Sam, 205
Comox Indian Band (Canada), 327
concessions: bioprospecting, 99, 113; lack of control over, 100, 101, 105, 113, 115; land, 99, 103, 109, 112, 115; mineral and mining, 99, 103, 109, 111, 115; negative impact upon Amerindians, 103–104, 109–114; timber, 99, 103, 109, 115
Conference of the Parties (COP), 244–245, 249
Conservation Act (New Zealand) 1987, 232–233
Conservation International (CI), 159, 160, 161, 169
Convention on Biological Diversity (CBD), xi; 153, 157–158, 222, 243–249, 253, 342, 347–351, 356, 359, 360n3, 361n7; Article 8(j), 222, 243–246, 249, 347; guidelines for protecting indigenous intellectual property, xi; sovereignty of nations over natural and genetic resources, xi
Convention on International Trade in Endangered Species (CITES), 62
copyright, 9, 56; Australian Aboriginal artists' claims, 9, 12–13; "collective" copyright law in Panama, 78; contractual agreements, 77; inability to protect collective ownership, 76–77; infringements upon, 77–78; joint copyright agreements, 297, 326–327; protections over creative works, 9
Council for Indigenous Arts and Crafts, 74
Council for Indigenous Arts and Culture, 80, 83
Council of Trent (1545–1546), 176, 191, 200

Covenant Chain (international treaty), 3–4
Cowichan Band Council, 327
cultural activism, 35–40, 82–83; impact of new technologies, 36–40; impact of radio broadcasts, 36, 38–40
"cultural copyright," 13
cultural patrimony. *See* repatriation
cultural property laws, 13, 82
cultural rights, 17; as human rights, 17
cunani bush (*Clibadium sylvestre*), 114

Danza de los Turcos, 37
Declaration of Indigenous Peoples of the Western Hemisphere, 254, 271
Declaration of Principles of the World Council of Indigenous Peoples, 130–131
Department of Indian and Northern Affairs (Canada), 79
DNA (deoxyribo-nucleic acid): bioethics, 254, 256–257, 262–263, 272; controversy over patenting, 253, 256–257, 265, 269, 327–328; controversy over using human DNA in research, 251–253, 256, 269; and Indigenous Peoples, 251–253, 260, 264–265, 272
The Dreaming, Aboriginal, 12; and gender, 13; proprietary rights and relationships bestowed by, 12–13; use rights bestowed by, 12–13
Dreamings, Aboriginal, 9–10; ownership of specific Dreamings, 10
Dreamtime, Aboriginal, 7–8
Durie, Eddie (Chief Judge), 229–230, 243

ecocide, 251, 253–254, 257, 272–273
economic theory, neoclassical, 132
Ecuador, 37, 323
El Colegio de la Frontera Sur (ECOSUR), 343, 345, 347, 352, 359, 361n6
Environmental Genome Project (EGP), 267–268
Esquit, Kaji' Kawoq Alberto, 208
Essequibo River (Guyana), 102, 110
ethnobotany, 280–299; and commercial exploitation, 279–280; conflict between promotion and protection, 287–299; and cultural appropriation, 279–280; and potential for drug discovery, 279–299; reciprocal relationships between plants and humans, 280
ethnocide, 253–254, 257, 272–273
eugenics, 251, 254, 256–257, 268
European Union, 153
expressive traditions, indigenous, 6; and authorship, 6; commercial art production, 55–85; and cultural survival, 30, 37; efforts to conserve and revalorize, 35–40; and global tourism, 55; as indigenous identity, 6; and intellectual property protection, 55; market expansion, 55; misappropriation, 55; as property, 11, 18; suppression of, 32

fair trade legislation. *See* intellectual property law, Western
Federal Trade Commission (FTC), 60, 72, 74
Fimo^{TM}, 77
First Nations, 309, 311, 327–329
Forest Peoples Fund (FPF), 159–160

France, 3
Fulani (Peul), 162
Fund for Integrated Rural Development and Traditional Medicine (FIRD-TM), 164

Gambell (Alaska), 67
Garífuna, 134; land loss, 134
garlic (*Allium sativum*), 356
Gene Giants, 269
genocide, 251–254, 257, 261, 265, 271, 273
Genset, 270
ginger (*Zingiber officinale*), 356
globalization: commodification of culture, 27–29; cultural homogenization, 29; indigenous peoples, 27–28; and marginalization of local and regional music, 31; popular music industry, 31; resistance against, 42; risk to cultural survival, 28; and traditional knowledge, 145; and "traditional" music, 31
González, Gaspar Pedro, 205
Gorinsky, Conrad, 113–114, 117n12; lawsuit filed against, 114
Great Britain, 3–4
greenheart tree (*Ocotea rodiaei*), 113
Guatemala, 173–209; Academy of Mayan Languages of Guatemala (ALMG), 195–198, 204–206; Centro de Estudios de la Cultura Maya (CECMA), 183, 202; Dirección General de Educación Bilingüe-Bicultural (DIGEBI), 186, 197, 202–203, 207; Governmental Accord 1046–87, 181–183, 195; Instituto Indigenista Nacional, 194–195; K'amol B'ey, 208; Lenca speakers, 175; Order of the Society of the Benedictines, 192; Organic Education Law, 190; Peace Accords, 185, 187–188, 206; Pipil speakers, 175, 177; Proyecto Lingüístico Francisco Marroquín (PLFM), 180, 193–195, 198–199, 204–205, 207; Universidad del Valle, 207; Universidad Mariano Gálvez, 207; Universidad Rafael Landívar, 182, 204; Universidad San Carlos, 177, 183, 207; Xinca speakers, 175. *See also* The Maya, Mayan Languages
Guatemala City, 182, 196, 205
Guiana. *See* British Guiana
Guyana, 99–116. *See also* British Guiana
Guyana Geology and Mines Commission, 112
Guyanese Amerindian rights movement, 100–101, 115; influence of global indigenous rights movements, 108
Guyanese Amerindians, 99–116; attitudes toward bioprospecting, 113; Christian evangelization of, 104; discrimination against, 100; impact of "civilization" upon, 104; lack of control over traditional resources and knowledge, 100, 101, 105, 113–115; legal rights reform, 100–101, 115; living conditions, 100; marginalization of, 99–100, 102; perceptions of national government, 108–114; protection and regulation of, 104–107; under British colonial rule, 100–106;

under Dutch colonial rule, 100–102
Guyanese Environmental Protection Agency (EPA), 113

Haeserijn, Father Esteban, 193
The Hagahai (Papua, New Guinea), 265
Haida, 59
Haines, Alaska, 77
Harry, Debra, 258, 260, 274n13
Hausa, 162. *See* ethnic groups in Nigeria
Healing Forest Conservancy, 164–165; Conservancy Constitution, 165
Hoffman LaRoche (Switzerland), 269
Hofling, Charles, 208
Honduran Corporation for Forestry Development (COHDEFOR), 140, 142
Honduras, 127–146, 176; agrarian reform laws, 133; land-titling programs, 132–134; Spanish colonial rule in (impact on land title), 135–136
Hooper Bay, 64
Huadenosaunee, 3; international treaties with European nations, 3–4
Huehuetenango, 177, 197
Human Genome Diversity Project (HGDP), 251, 252, 254, 256, 261–262, 266–267, 272, 273n1, 274n17, 274n19, 275n26; as biocolonialism, 255; as "Vampire Project," 260
Human Genome Project (HGP), 251, 259, 262, 269, 272, 273n11, 274n14
Igbo, 162
India, 155–158; case study for bioprospecting, 155–158; Jeevani, 156; Kani, 155–158; Kerala, 155–156; Tropical Botanic Garden and Research Institute (TBGRI), 155–158
Indian Arts and Crafts Board, 57, 69, 71, 72, 74
"Indianness," 12, 18; symbols of, 12. *See also* indigenousness
Indians. *See* Native Americans
indigenism, 12, 18, 252
indigenous archaeology, 310
indigenous cooperatives, 80–82; global market, 80–81
Indigenous Environmental Network (IEN), 254, 271
indigenous knowledge, x; and art, 9, 12, 55; and biodiversity protection, 127; conflict between promotion and protection, 287–299; as cultural property, 9, 242–243; and development, xii, 287; and drug discovery, 127, 153–169, 251–252, 279–299; and environmental conservation, 127; and gender, 15; land-use systems as a form of, 127, 145–146; protection, non-legal solutions, xiv, 19–20, 292–297; protection under national law, xi–xii, 18; and registry systems, 78; silence or secrecy as means of control over, 15, 18; valuation by developing nations, xii; and Western intellectual property systems, x. *See also* traditional knowledge
indigenous knowledge systems, xii, 281; cultural survival, 28, 30;

equitable sharing, 41; and history of devaluation, xii; and intellectual property rights, 40; loss of control over, 28
indigenous music, 27–44; collective nature of production and performance, 30; commodification for global market, 28–36; global access, 28; misappropriation on the Internet, 31; ownership of, 40–41
indigenous peoples, ix; 27, 41, 145–146; and access to biological resources, 356–359; archaeology, cultural heritage rights in, 309–333; art forms, for global consumption, 55–85; art forms, laws governing, 8–9, 62; collaboration with cultural activists, 35–40; collective rights, 12; cultural products for global consumption, 27–28; 80–81; cultural survival, 35; impact of new technologies, 27–28, 36; land-based claims, 9; language ownership and rights, 173–209; political sovereignty, 9; religion, freedom to practice, 10; rights-based claims, 27; rights to digital cultural property, 31, 41; self-determination, xii, 9, 27, 145; self-representation, 5; special status, 27; traditional knowledge, ix
Indigenous People's Coalition on Biodiversity, 260
Indigenous Peoples' Earth Charter, 130
indigenous rights movement, ix; use of the Internet, ix
Indigenous Women's Network (IWN), 254, 271
indigenousness, 31
indios, 107
Indonesia, 63
informed consent, 41, 251. *See also* prior informed consent (PIC)
Institute of Alaska Native Arts (IANA), 72–73
Inter-American Commission on Human Rights, 174
Interior Salish Peoples, 282–284. *See also* Secwepemc
International Monetary Fund (IMF), 343
Inuit, 59, 64; art cooperatives in Canada, 71; international marketing, 71; use of "igloo trademark," 79; women, 78
Inuit Circumpolar Conference, 81, 83
intellectual property law, Western, x; and biotechnology, 19; in cyberspace, 19; and fair trade legislation, 76–82; inability to protect collective interests, 55–56, 76–77; as "indigenous resistance," 75; non-communal nature of, xi; and non-Western intellectual property systems, xi, 224–226; use of contracts, 289–290, 326–327. *See also* copyright; patent; trademark; royalties
intellectual property rights, 11, 13; and archaeology, 309–333; copyright law, 76–77; as economic rights, 11; for indigenous artists, 76, 82; and local systems of knowledge, 40
intellectual property rights, Indigenous, 127
intellectual property systems, Indigenous: communal nature of,

xi; and land-titling programs, 132–134, 141–143; non-recognition by Western legal systems, xi; protection, 18; as system of rights and relationships, xi, 221–250; and use of registries, 78
intellectual property systems, Western, x, 246; based on individual rights, 30; conflict with non-Western IP systems, 248–249; corporate music industry, 35; legislation to protect indigenous designs, 78; as protection against misrepresentation, 56, 74; as protection against unfair competition, 56; and traditional knowledge, x, 41
Inter-Governmental Committee (IGC), 247–248
International Cooperative Biodiversity Group (ICBG), 158; benefit-sharing agreements, 159–161; in Chiapas, Mexico (Maya ICBG), 342–360; in Nigeria, 158, 164; in Suriname, 158–160; training and technology transfer, 168, 345; use of trust funds, 168–169, 352
international intellectual property law, 19, 56, 99; efficacy in solving local problems, 41; to protect indigenous designs, 56
International Labor Organization Convention 169 (ILO) (Organizacíon Internacional del Trabajo), 131–132
Iroquois Confederacy, 3
Iwokrama Rain Forest Programme, 115, 116

Jackson, Andrew, 4
Jagan, Cheddi, 109
Janki, Melinda, 116
Jeevani, 156. *See also* India
Johnson, Sir William, 4
Juneau (Alaska), 59, 66

Kamloops Indian Band (Secwepemc Nation), 326
Kani, 155–158; traditional healers, 156. *See also* India
Karl May Festival, 318–322
Katsinas (Hopi), 12
Kayapó Indians, 107
Kelly, Ned, 8
Kngwarreye, Emily, 19
Komok, Ron, 60
Kuna, 82; *mola* production, 82. *See also* Panama
Kwäday Dän Ts'ínchi, 328
Kwakiutl, 16

La Campa (Honduras), 134–135, 139–140
Lakota, 6; Standing Rock reservation, 6
land-tenure rights, 127; joint-use rights, 127
land-tenure systems, 127–146; colonialism, 129; private ownership, 129; underpinning IPR and TRR, 129
land-titling programs, 132–134; gender, 133
"language death," 30, 208
Lanham Act, 17
land rights, 5, 7; communally-held nature, 128; expressive culture, 5; linkages to art rights and indigenous identity, 8; sovereignty, 5

Lara, Don Antonio de, 179, 182, 184, 187, 189
Lenca (Honduras), 128, 135; changes in agriculture, 140, 144–145; changes in traditional land tenure system, 139–140; de facto use rights, 135, 143; IIPR/TRR, 128, 137–139, 143–145; identity in land, 137; land and natural resource rights, 137, 139–140; municipal governments, 137; pottery production, 135, 138–139; traditional land-tenure system, 136–139
licensing agreements, 291–292
Loreto, State of (Peru), 38–40; Cocama-Cocamilla peoples of, 40
Ly, Ngoc, 60

MacKay, Fergus, 106, 116n2, 117n5
Makushi Amerindians, 108. *See also* Brazilian Makushis; Guyanese Amerindians
Makusepe Komanto Iseru, 115
Makushi Research Unit, 115
Manybunharrawuy, Daisy, 15
manzanilla (*Matricaria chamomilla*), 356
The Maori, 221–250; and customary law, 228; *Nga Tama Toa*, 229; policies of assimilation and integration, 229; and relationships with Paheka, 225–226, 228–230, 233–234, 239, 250n2; rights and responsibilities, 221–222, 224–226, 240–243; *tikanga* (customary values), 231, 240–242; traditional healing practices, 225–226; worldview, 222–223
Maori Arts Board, 80; Toi Iho™ trademark, 80
Las Margaritas (Chiapas), 345
Marine Mammal Protection Act (MMPA) (United States), 63; exemptions for Alaska Natives, 63
Maroons. *See* Saramaka Maroons
Marx, Karl, 316–317
May, Karl, 318, 321. *See also* Karl May Festival
The Maya: in Chiapas, Mexico, 341–360; Chol, 358; consuetudinal law, 174, 183–184; daykeepers, 206; in Guatemala, 173–209; Kachiquel, 358; *k'utunik*, 184, 208; Lacandón, 358; Mam, 358; Mochó, 358; Tojolabal, 358; *traje*, 188, 209n8; Tzeltal, 358; Tzotzil, 358; Zoque, 358
Mayan Languages: Academia de las Lenguas Mayas de Guatemala, 187–188; Achí, 197, 203, 210n15; Awakateko, 193, 203, 210n15; and bilingual education, 199–204; Ch'olan, 175; Ch'orti', 193, 203, 210n15; Chuj, 180, 193, 196; and goals of publication, 204–206; and history of Spanish suppression, 175–190; Itzaj, 208; Ixil, 193, 201, 203, 210n15; Kaqchikel, 175–179, 181–183, 185–188, 192–193, 196–200, 202, 204–209, 210n15; *Kaqchi' Wuj*, 198, 206, 208; K'iche', 175–176, 178, 182, 185, 191, 193–194, 196–200, 202; Mam, 182, 193, 197, 199–200, 203, 205, 210n15; Mopan, 208; Popti', 193, 197, 203, 205, 210n15; and proselytization, 176–177;

Q'anjob'al, 193, 197, 201, 203, 205, 210n15; Q'eqchi', 182, 185–186, 193, 200, 203, 210n15; resistance against Spanish, 175–176, 188; and Spanish naming practices, 179–182; standardization, 190–199; Tojolabal, 345, 351, 353; Tz'utujiil, 193, 199, 201, 203, 210n15; Tzeltal, 175, 178, 345, 351, 353; Tzotzil, 345, 351, 353; Yucatec, 175, 191
Memoranda of Understanding (MOUs), 114
Menchú, Rigoberta, 208
Mendez, Chico, 107
Mexican law, 349–350
Mexico, 166, 176, 342–360
Migrate Mining, Ltd., 112
Migratory Bird Treaty Act (United States), 62
Milingimbi, 15
Minga-Perú, 36, 38–40
Mining Act of 1989 (Guyana), 112
Ministry for Amerindian Affairs (Guyana), 106, 107
Ministry of Sustainable Resources (Canada), 325–326
Miskito, 134; land loss, 134
Moctezuma, 176
Molecular Nature, Ltd. (MNL), 343, 352
Mooney, Patrick, 260, 273n8, 355, 362n12
Mulpurrurru et al. v. Indofurn Pty. Ltd. et al. (Carpets case), 10, 12, 13, 17, 20n4, 88n18
Murray, Haana, 237–239
music, indigenous. *See* indigenous music
music industry, global, 29; cultural homogenization, 29; technological innovations, 29

Nahuatl, 176–179, 197–198, 200
National Agrarian Institute (INA), (Honduras), 142
National Conference for Amerindian Representatives (AMIRANG) (Guyana), 101, 113
National Congress of American Indians (NCAI), 271
National Council for Arts and Culture (Mexico), 357
National Gallery of Australia, 10
National Indigenous Arts Advocacy Association (NIAAA) (Australia), 78, 80; creation of "Mark of Authenticity," 80
National Institutes of Health (NIH), 257, 266, 360n3, 361n5, 362n11
National Museum of Ethnology and Anthropology (Guatemala), 198
National Organization of Indigenous Lenca People of Honduras (Organizacíon Nacional Indigena Lenca de Honduras) (ONILH), 142
Native American Graves Protection and Repatriation Act of 1990 (NAPGRA), 12, 14, 18–19
Native Americans, 6; Artisans (*see* Alaska Natives); and "German Indian" clubs, 318, *319–322*; and Russian powwow enthusiasts, 6; testimony expunged from the historical record, 14; and United States federal Indian law, 11–12; women's knowledge, 15016. *See*

also Alaska Natives; Cheyenne; First Nations (Canada); Rosebud Sioux; Sioux,
NAtural PRoduct ALERT database (NAPRALERT), 280
The Navajo, 13
New Mexico, State of, 74, 83
Nigeria, 161–167; deforestation in, 161–162; ethnic groups, 162; health care, 162
Nigerian Trust Fund Pilot Project Committee, 169. *See also* ICBG trust funds
Nigh, Ron, 357, 359
Nireaha Tamaki v. Baker, 228
Nome (Alaska), 60, 81
Non-governmental organizations (NGOs), 154
Norango-Morse, Nora, 15
North America, 108
North Dakota, 12
North–South relations, xix, 157, 343

Olympics, 2000 International, 6
Omai Gold Mines Limited, 110; Omai disaster, 109–112; lawsuits filed against, 110
oregano (*Origanum vulgaris*), 356
Organization of African Unity (OAU), 154
Organization of American States, 174
Orange Drug Company of Nigeria, 164
Orinoco River, 33
Oxchuc (Chiapas), 345
Oxlajuuj Keej Mayab' Ajtz'iib' (OKMA), 196, 199, 204, 207. *See also* Mayan languages, standardization

Panama, 78, 84; collective copyright laws, 78; intellectual property law, 82; Kuna, 82; regulation of imports, 82
Paraguay, 166
Parra, Father, 191
patents, 56, 290–291, 327–328, 359; and DNA, 327–328
Peñalosa, Fernando, 205
Pennsylvania State University, 267
Peru, 32–44, 114; African musical influences in, 32; Amazonian musical influences in, 32–33; Andean musical influences in, 32–33; *bombo baile*, 33; *cajón*, 33; *charangos*, 32; *chicha*, 33; *chimaychi*, 33; *conjuntos*, 32; *cumbia*, 33; history of radio and recorded music, 33–35; *huayno*, 33; intellectual property rights debates, 35; music and modernity, 33; *mulizas*, 33; *qarawi*, 32; Spanish colonial encounter in, 32–33; Spanish musical influences in, 32; suppression of indigenous expressive forms, 32; *tanguiño*, 33
Plantain (*Plantago major*), 356
Pomo Indians, 63
Posey, Darrell, 80, 232
potlatch, Kwakiutl, 16; as system of redistribution of goods, 16; women's central involvement in, 16
precautionary approach to publication, 294–297
Prendergast, Chief Justice, 228
prior informed consent, 41, 158, 327, 341–360; Philippine government's regulations, 350–351

property systems, 9; cultural property, 9; embedded in relationships to art, land, and indigenous knowledge systems, 9; indigenous theories, 9; treatment of indigenous motifs, symbols, objects, 11
property law: as "bundles of power," 11; as "bundles of rights," 11, 18
property regimes, Western, 19, 127; national emphasis on private property, 127
property rights, 11; collective rights, 12, 84; as economic rights, 11; "in use" rights, 12; as privacy rights, 13
protestors, indigenous, 7
public domain, 11–12, 18, 77; conflicts with intellectual property protection, 41; reconceptualized, 41
Pueblos Cultures, 270
pueblo indígena, 357, 359, 363n17
pueblo índio, 357–358, 363n16
Pushpangadan, Dr. P., 156–157

Queensland, 7
Quetzaltenango, 177, 182, 188, 194

Radebeul (Germany), 321
radio broadcasts: as enveloping experience, 38; importance of local programming, 38–40; as means for social and political transformation, 40, 186–187; national and international programming, 38; three-dimensional presence, 38
The Rainforest Foundation, 116
red de Archivos Sonoros Andinos, 37
repatriation: cultural knowledge as evidence supporting, 14; of cultural property, 6, 11, 13–16, 83; legislation, 9; redistribution of knowledge and power, 16; relationships and transfer of title, 16
research, 83; control over results, 83; ownership of results, 83
Resource Management Act (New Zealand) 1991, 232–233
Rivkin, Jeremy, 272
Rodrigues, Carolyn, 107
Rodríguez, Q'uq'ulkan Guaján, 188
Roraima, State of (Brazil), 108, 113, 117n11
Rue (*Ruta graveolens*), 356
Rupununi savannas (Guyana), 108, 112, 113
Rural Advancement Foundation International (RAFI), 259–260, 269–271, 355, 362n12

Salvador, 176
San Pedro Sula, 139
Sand Creek (Guyana), 113–114
Sangra de Drago (*Croton lechleri*), 165–166
Santa Clara Pueblo, 15
Saramaka Maroons (Suriname), 159–161; benefit-sharing arrangements with, 160–161; traditional healers, 160–161
scientific research. *See* research
Seattle, Washington (U.S.A.), 69, 271
The Secwepemc Nation, 281–299; Secwepemc Cultural Education Society, 282, 289, 296–297, 299; Secwepemc Ethnobotany Project, 282, 285–289, 291, 296–297
Shaman Pharmaceuticals, Inc., 163–166, 169, 265, 272
Shismaref (Alaska), 67, 81

The Shuswap. *See* The Secwepemc Nation
Shuswap Nation Tribal Council, 282, 297, 299
Silver Hand, 55–89; ability to strengthen IPRs, 75–76; authenticating Alaska Native art, 59–60, 67–69, 72, 75; expansion to protect Alaska Native interests, 75; history of the Silver Hand trademark, 70–75; multiple meanings of, 68; other marks imitating, 66–68; to protect consumer and state interests, 72, 75; as registry program, 65–67; as retailer marketing strategy, 82; as trademark, 65, 70–75; and unethical dealers, 66; use and lack of use, 65, 67
The Sioux, 13
Sioux, Rosebud, 17
Six Nations, 3
Skagway, 66
Snuneymuxw First Nation, 314, 327, 322n4, 333n9
South Pacific Regional Environment Programme (SPREP), 154
sui generis system, 13; approach to indigenous intellectual property rights, 13, 19, 115
Summer Institute of Linguistics International (SIL), 185, 192–195, 198, 204
Suriname, 158–161; Department of Interior, 159. *See also* ICBG in Suriname
Suriname River, 160
The Suyá, 30; indigenous system of control over songs, 30
Tegucigalpa, 139
Tenejapa (Chiapas), 345
Thiophene E, 285–286, 288, 290
Thomas, Dr. Mary, 285, 299
title, 5, 9; communal, 135; ejidal, 135; and indigenous claims, 5; village title systems, 143
title, Native, 9; and cultural property claims, 9, 16, 19; and dispossession, 9; extended to art forms, 9, 16; and land claims, 9; and sovereignty, 10
Toi Iho™ trademark. *See* Maori Arts Board
Torres Strait Islander Society, 78
Torres Strait Islanders, 10; restoration of land title, 10. *See also* Aboriginal and Torres Strait Islander Commission
toshaos, 112; joint lawsuit against Guyanese government, 112
Townsend, William Cameron, 191–192
Trade Marks Act (New Zealand), 233
Trade-Related Aspects of Intellectual Property Rights, Agreement on (TRIPS Agreement), 352
trade secrets, 291
trademark, 56, 72, 324, 327; changing use of protection, 79–80; "collective" trademarks, 78–79; as marker of authenticity, 80; scope of commercial protection, 79; time-span of, 79. *See also* Inuit "igloo trademark"; Silver Hand; Toi Iho™ trademark
traditional knowledge, ix; arts and expressive traditions, ix; commercial interests, x; commodification by outsiders, x;

communally held nature of, x; control over use, 84; ethnobotanical, 153–169; medicinal plants, ix, 153–169; natural resources, ix; protection against exploitation or misappropriation, ix; valuation, xi; worldview, ix. *See also* indigenous knowledge; indigenous peoples
traditional resource rights (TRRs), 84, 127
Treaty of Waitangi. *See* Waitangi Treaty
tribal rights, 5; to self-governance, 5;
Tripp, Kurt, 60
TRIPS Agreement. *See* Trade-Related Aspects of Intellectual Property Rights, Agreement on
Tropical Botanic Garden and Research Institute (TBGRI), 155–158. *See also* India
tset'selq. *See* Balsamroot

Ubico, Jorge, 189–190, 200
United Nations Commission on Human Rights, 203
United Nations Committee on Economic, Social and Cultural Rights (UNCSCR), 107
United Nations Committee on Elimination of Racial Discrimination, 174
United Nations Convention of the Rights of the Child (1960), 173, 185
United Nations Decade of the Indigenous Peoples, 206
United Nations Draft Declaration on the Rights of Indigenous Peoples, 131
United Nations Economic, Scientific, and Cultural Organization (UNESCO), 190
United Nations Economic, Scientific, and Cultural Organization (UNESCO) 1999 Global Assessment on the Safeguarding of Traditional Culture, 18, 78
United Nations Economic, Scientific, and Cultural Organization (UNESCO) 1989 Recommendation on the Protection and Safeguarding of Folklore and Traditional Knowledge, xi, 78
United Nations Environmental Programme, 347. *See also* Convention on Biological Diversity
United Nations International Covenant on Civil and Political Rights (1966), 174
United Nations Universal Declaration of Human Rights (1948), 173
United Nations Universal Declaration of Linguistic Rights (1996), 174
United Nations Working Group on Indigenous Populations, 271
United States, 5, 8; federal Indian policy, 8; federal wildlife laws, 62; indigenous sovereignty limited, 5; repatriation cases, 14–16; repatriation legislation, 9, 14; revitalization of cultural traditions, 37; trade in endangered species, 62; treaty rights, abrogation, 8
United States Agency for International Development (US-AID), 158, 200, 204
United States Customs, 63

United States Department of Energy, 266
United States Fish and Wildlife Service, 86n9
United States National Institutes of Health (NIH), 266
United States National Science Foundation, 266
United States Patent and Trademark Office, 270, 322
University of Amsterdam, 343
University of Georgia, 343
use rights, 13; medicine people, 13; in objects, 13; tribal sovereignty, 13

valeriana (*Valeriana officinalis*), 356
Venus Marx Figurine, *317*
The Virgin of Carmen, 37

Waitangi Treaty, 225–229; violations of treaty, 227–228
Waitangi Tribunal, 221–222, 230–232; testimony concerning intellectual property rights, 231–232; Wai262 Claim, 235–237
Wai Wai Amerindians, 112, 116n1. *See also* Guyanese Amerindians
Wapishana Amerindians, 108, 113–114; attitudes towards bioprospecting, 113–114. *See also* Guyanese Amerindians; Brazilian Wapishanas
Warao Amerindians, 33; function of music in society, 33
Washington, D.C., 257, 271, 273n8
Weiss, Kenn, 267
West Virginia Guild of Artists and Craftsmen, 79
Western law, 11; access to, 11
Wi Parata v. The Bishop of Wellington, 228
women, indigenous: cultural knowledge, 15; customary rights, 15; keepers of rights in cultural property, 15–16; property rights, 15–16; repatriation, 15–16
World Bank, 343
World Health Organization (WHO), 204
World Intellectual Property Organization (WIPO), xi, 78, 115, 245–248
World Trade Organization (WTO), 261, 271, 343, 352
Worldbeat music, 33
Worcester v. Georgia, 5

Yanomami, 265
Yaqui, 258
Yaxte' Press, 205
Yekuana (Venezuela), 43n7
Yoruba, 162. *See* ethnic groups in Nigeria
Yup'ik, 64, 77
Yuchi, 265

Zapatista Rebellion, 357, 358
Zuni Cultural Arts Council, 80

ABOUT THE AUTHORS

Mary Riley is currently a research associate in the Program for Collaborative Research in the Pharmaceutical Sciences at the University of Illinois at Chicago, as well as a law student enrolled in the College of Law at Northern Illinois University. At Northern, she is specializing in international, environmental, intellectual property, indigenous and tribal law. In addition to working with the Vietnam/Laos ICBG, she guest edited (with Katy Moran) a special issue of *Cultural Survival Quarterly* (Winter 2001), which was dedicated to the subject of intellectual property rights and indigenous peoples. She received her Ph.D. in cultural anthropology from Tulane University. Her dissertation research focused on the ethnomedicine of the Makushi Amerindians of the North Rupununi savannas in Guyana.

****

Kelly P. Bannister is assistant professor in the School of Environmental Studies and a research associate with the POLIS Project on Ecological Governance in the Faculty of Law, University of Victoria (British Columbia, Canada). Her doctorate in ethnobotany/medicinal plant chemistry is from the University of British Columbia. She works with local First Nations and internationally on research-related issues of protecting cultural knowledge, with emphasis on nonlegal mechanisms such as community research protocols. Her current research examines ethical and legal issues in collaborative research between communities and universities, She founded the Community-University Connections initiative in 2000 to explore these issues.

Brent Berlin is Graham Perdue Professor of Anthropology at the University of Georgia. He began research in the Highlands of Chiapas in 1960. After a decade of comparative research in Amazonian Peru, he returned to Chiapas where he continued the study of indigenous knowledge systems, focusing specifically on medical ethnobiology. Since the late 1980s, he has been an advocate for indigenous intellectual property rights and just compensation. These combined interests led to his role as principal investigator on the Maya International Cooperative Biodiversity Group that forms the basis for the discussion in chapter 12.

Elois Ann Berlin, associate professor of anthropology, University of Georgia, has been involved in interdisciplinary research first with the Aguaruan Jivaro of Peru and then the Maya of highland Chiapas. Her work focuses on indigenous health and medicine. She is committed to understanding and promoting indigenous medical knowledge as a complex and comprehensive system and validating its efficacy to the broader public. She developed an interest in intellectual property rights (IPR) and just benefits sharing in the late 1980s and drafted the framework that formed the basis the Maya ICBG agreements discussed in chapter 12.

Tressa Berman is research associate of anthropology at the California Academy of Sciences and executive director of *BorderZone Arts, Inc.* She is past president of the Anthropology and Intellectual Property Rights Group of the Society for Applied Anthropology.

Bartholomew Dean is assistant professor of anthropology as well as anthropology coordinator for the Museum Studies Program at the University of Kansas. He is currently in Peru on a Fulbright Scholar grant awarded to support his work with the Amazonian Studies Program at Peru's National University, San Marcos (Lima). In 1995, Dean and his wife Michelle McKinley co-founded the Amazonian Peoples Resources Initiative, a human rights and community development NGO. Dean is also a founding member of the graduate program in Amazonian Studies at the Universidad Nacional Mayor de San Marcos, and currently serves as the contributing editor for Lowland Ethnology for the United States Library of Congress Handbook of Latin American Studies. Dean serves on the editorial board of Amazonia Peruana, the flagship journal devoted to the scholarly study of the Peruvian Amazon.

Julie Hollowell is research associate with Indiana University's Department of Anthropology. Her recent research has focused on the commodification of Native arts and archaeological goods from Alaska's Bering Strait, and her interests include global marketing of cultural property, multiple claims on the material and intellectual past, and the repatriation of knowledge, materials, and research directives to indigenous communities. She received he Ph.D. in 2004 from Indiana University in cultural anthropology.

Marie Annette Jaimes Guerrero is a Native woman and Mestiza author, scholar, activist, novelist, and poet. Born in Arizona, she is a BIA-certified American Indian, among the San Capistrano California Mission Indians (Juaneno/Acjachemen), as well as an unenrolled Yaqui/Opata raised with Mexican American ancestry and culture. Since 1995, she has been in her faculty position as a tenured associate professor in the College of Humanities, Women's Studies, at San Francisco State University, California. She also has taught American Indian Studies for the College of Ethnic Studies there. Her best known work is as the editor and contributor to the award-winning seminal text, titled *The State of Native America*.

Judith M. Maxwell received her Ph.D. in linguistics and in anthropology at the University of Chicago. Since 1982, Dr. Maxwell has been a faculty member of the Department of Anthropology of Tulane University, and head of the interdisciplinary program in Linguistics, also teaching adjunct courses at the Universidad Centroamericana in San Salvador, Universidad Mariano Gálvez, Universidad Rafael Landívar, and Universidad del Valle in Guatemala. She has served as a technical advisor and associate of the Proyecto Lingüístico Francisco Marroquín and collaborates with the Academia de las Lenguas Mayas de Guatemala and with the Dirección General de Educación Bilingüe-Intercultural (the Ministry of Education's bilingual program), giving short courses and in-service training to practicing Mayan linguists.

Katy Moran, an applied anthropologist, has directed the Healing Forest Conservancy since 1992. The Conservancy is an independent nonprofit organization founded by Shaman Pharmaceuticals, Inc., and its division ShamanBotanicals.com. The Conservancy's mission is to develop and implement a process to return benefits to countries and culture groups that have collaborated in Shaman's drug discovery process, after a product is commercialized. Previously, Moran held positions at the Smithsonian Institution and the U.S. House of Representatives. She has conducted field research, lectured and published widely on ethnobiology and policy issues.

George P. Nicholas is associate professor of Archaeology at Simon Fraser University in British Columbia. An American living and working in Canada the past thirteen years, he directs the Simon Fraser University–Secwepemc Education Institute Archaeology Program, located on the Kamloops Indian Reserve, which is the only postsecondary archaeology program explicitly for First Nations in Canada. He has published extensively on Indigenous peoples and archaeology, prehistoric human ecology, early postglacial land use, wetlands archaeology, and other topics. His books include *Holocene Human Ecology in Northeastern North America* and (with Tom Andrews) *At a Crossroads: Archaeology and First Peoples in Canada*. He is editor-in-chief of the *Canadian Journal of Archaeology*.

Maui Solomon is a barrister with eighteen years legal experience specializing in commercial law, resource management, intellectual property and treaty/indigenous peoples' rights issues. He has also been a key legal and political advocate for the recognition of the customary and treaty rights and identity of his own Moriori people of Rekohu (Chatham Islands). Maui has been actively involved in Maori fisheries issues for the past fifteen years and is currently commissioner on the Treaty of Waitangi Fisheries Commission, the largest Maori commercial entity in New Zealand. He represents three of the six tribes in the Wai 262 claim concerning indigenous flora and fauna and cultural/ intellectual heritage rights of Maori which seeks, among other things, to develop a unique system for protection and use of Maori traditional knowledge.

Catherine M. Tucker received her doctoral degree in Anthropology at the University of Arizona in 1996. She is currently an assistant professor of anthropology, and a research associate at the Center for the Study of Institutions, Population and Environmental Change (CIPEC) at Indiana University, Bloomington. Her work focuses on indigenous institutional arrangements, especially land tenure and property rights, and the implications for intellectual property and policies. In related research, she has studied common property forest institutions among indigenous groups, and linkages among local, regional, and national institutions as they relate to social change and processes of globalization. At CIPEC, she works with an international, interdisciplinary team to address multilevel institutional dimensions of forest cover change, with particular reference to the experiences of indigenous and rural populations. She has conducted fieldwork in Honduras, Mexico, Peru, and Guatemala.